COMMERCE BEFORE CAPITALISM IN EUROPE, 1300–1600

In *Commerce before Capitalism in Europe, 1300–1600*, Martha C. Howell challenges dominant interpretations of the relationship between the so-called commercial revolution of late medieval Europe and the capitalist age that followed. Howell argues that the merchants, shopkeepers, artisans, and consumers in cities and courts throughout Western Europe, even in the densely urbanized Low Countries that are the main focus of this study, cannot be best understood as proto-capitalist. Unlike the capitalists described by modern theory, these people did not consider their property a fungible asset. Even though they bought and sold property for a living and developed sophisticated financial techniques to do so, they preserved its capacity to secure social bonds by intensifying market regulations and by assigning new meaning to marriage, gift-giving, and consumption. Later generations have sometimes found such actions perplexing, often dismissing them as evidence that businesspeople of the late medieval and early modern world did not fully understand market rules. By contrast, Howell shows that the practices often considered primitive were governed by a logic specific to their age and that these practices, in fact, laid essential groundwork for the capitalist centuries to come.

Martha C. Howell is Miriam Champion Professor of History at Columbia University. The recipient of awards and fellowships from the Guggenheim Foundation, the Fulbright Commission, and the American Council of Learned Societies, among others, she is the author and editor of many books, including *Women, Production and Patriarchy in Late Medieval Cities* and *The Marriage Exchange: Property, Social Place and Gender in Cities of the Low Countries, 1300–1550*. In 2005, she was named Doctor of Humane Letters, honoris causa, by the University of Ghent.

COMMERCE BEFORE CAPITALISM IN EUROPE, 1300–1600

Martha C. Howell

Columbia University

CAMBRIDGE
UNIVERSITY PRESS

CAMBRIDGE UNIVERSITY PRESS
Cambridge, New York, Melbourne, Madrid, Cape Town, Singapore,
São Paulo, Delhi, Dubai, Tokyo

Cambridge University Press
32 Avenue of the Americas, New York, NY 10013-2473, USA

www.cambridge.org
Information on this title: www.cambridge.org/9780521148504

First published 2010

Printed in the United States of America

A catalog record for this publication is available from the British Library.

Library of Congress Cataloging in Publication data

Howell, Martha C.
Commerce before capitalism in Europe, 1300–1600 / Martha C. Howell.
    p.   cm.
Includes bibliographical references and index.
ISBN 978-0-521-76046-1 (hardback) – ISBN 978-0-521-14850-4 (pbk.)
1. Commerce – History – Medieval, 500–1500.   2. Commerce – History –
16th century.   3. Europe – Commerce.   I. Title.
HF395.H69   2010
381.094 – dc22   2009038067

ISBN 978-0-521-76046-1 Hardback
ISBN 978-0-521-14850-4 Paperback

This book is dedicated to my sisters Jean and Kathy.

Contents

List of Illustrations

MAPS

TABLE

FIGURES

Acknowledgments

This book began many years ago in the municipal archives of Douai, in northern France, but the research for various chapters took me to many other archives, libraries, and countries. Along the way, I was guided by generous colleagues, given material support by several institutions, and offered criticism by a great many colleagues and friends. It is a pleasure to thank them.

Columbia University granted me several leaves that allowed prolonged stays in Europe. There I was supported by the Guggenheim Foundation, the Flemish Royal Academy in Brussels, Reid Hall's Institute for Scholars in Paris, and the Francqui Foundation under the auspices of its Chaire Francqui Internationale. During my time in Belgium I was given additional support by the Université libre de Bruxelles, the Universiteit Gent, and the Universiteit Antwerpen.

Scholars in Europe not only generously welcomed me but also provided essential advice about my research and introduced to me many specialists without whose expertise I could not have finished this project. It is impossible to name all the individuals, but I particularly want to record my thanks to Claire Billen, Marc Boone, Walter Prevenier, Thérèse de Hemptinne, and Peter Stabel. Colleagues in the United States and Europe read my manuscript in whole or in part or gave me opportunities to present portions of my work-in-progress to specialists who provided useful criticism. Included among them were members of reading groups at Columbia University and in New York City and members of seminars, workshops, and conferences at the University of Leeds, Brown University, Harvard University, Dartmouth College, University of Minnesota, Cambridge University, University of Toronto,

Universiteit Gent, Universiteit Antwerpen, Université libre de Bruxelles, Universiteit Utrecht, Université Paris IV (Sorbonne), and Université Charles de Gaulle, Lille III. Peter Arnade, Joel Kaye, Adam Kosto,
and Carl Wennerlind, along with Claire Billen, Marc Boone, and Walter
Prevenier, read chapters as I was working on them and gave me essential advice. Victoria DeGrazia, Jean Howard, Sheryl Kroen, and Judith
Walkowitz read the entire manuscript at various stages of its completion
and made excellent suggestions for revision. My research assistant, David
Horowitz, did a wonderful job editing the manuscript and preparing it
for final production. Annelies Nevelans expertly assisted with research
in Ghent's archives. My editor at Cambridge, Beatrice Rehl, expressed
early enthusiasm for the manuscript and skillfully guided it through
the process of revision and production. Throughout the entire process,
my husband, Edward Whitney, drew on his knowledge of contemporary
finance to help me with technical matters concerning medieval currency
and financial instruments.

Introduction

Between 1300 and 1600, commerce left the margins of the European economy where it had been confined for centuries. Although merchants had long before established trade routes along the subcontinent's coasts and river systems, the European landscape was now littered with densely urbanized regions devoted both to trade and to production for the market.[1] From southern England through the northern coastal areas of the continent, into regions bordering the Scheldt, the Meuse, the Seine, and their tributaries, down the Rhine and the Rhone, and then into the busy fringes of the Mediterranean, commercial cities flourished as never before.

The following chapters examine how the people who populated these cities or who regularly dealt in their marketplaces understood and used property. I argue that commerce was changing their sociocultural practices, giving birth to an economic culture unlike that which had come before and that which would follow. By paying close attention to these practices, we stand not only to grasp the distinctive character of this period in European history but also to appreciate the ways that this age

---

[1] For the early history of European commerce, which provides important corrective evidence about the extent of exchange in Carolingian Europe, see Michael McCormick, *Origins of European Economy* (Cambridge, UK, 2001); also Stéphane Lebecq, *Marchands et navigateurs frisons du haut Moyen Age* (Lille, 1983). For more on the later so-called commercial revolution itself, see Robert Lopez, *The Commercial Revolution of the Middle Ages, 950–1350* (Englewood Cliffs, NJ, 1971); Peter Spufford, *Power and Profit: The Merchant in Medieval Europe* (New York, 2003); Quentin Van Doosselaere, *Commercial Agreements and Social Dynamics in Medieval Genoa* (Cambridge, UK, 2009); and Paul H. Freedman, *Out of the East: Spices and the Medieval Imagination* (New Haven, CT, 2008).

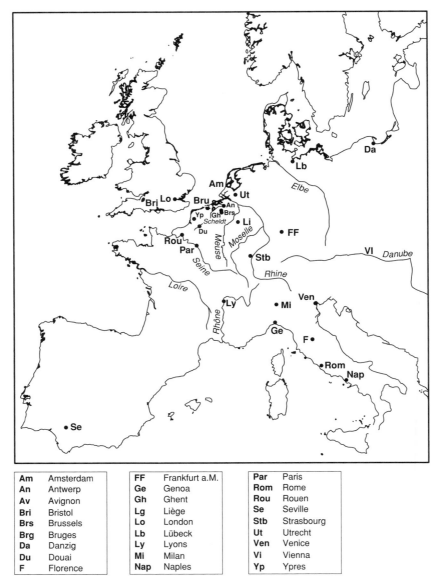

Am	Amsterdam	**FF**	Frankfurt a.M.	**Par**	Paris
An	Antwerp	**Ge**	Genoa	**Rom**	Rome
Av	Avignon	**Gh**	Ghent	**Rou**	Rouen
Bri	Bristol	**Lg**	Liège	**Se**	Seville
Brs	Brussels	**Lo**	London	**Stb**	Strasbourg
Brg	Bruges	**Lb**	Lübeck	**Ut**	Utrecht
Da	Danzig	**Ly**	Lyons	**Ven**	Venice
Du	Douai	**Mi**	Milan	**Vi**	Vienna
F	Florence	**Nap**	Naples	**Yp**	Ypres

Map 1. Major European Commercial Cities, c. 1400.

did – and did not – lay groundwork for the modern western market society.

In Chapters 1 through 3, I begin with three case studies focusing on property law, marriage, and gift-giving, respectively. In each realm

Map 2. Cities and Rivers of the Late Medieval Low Countries.

commerce disturbed received norms, altered practices, and created new meanings. These chapters are based principally on legal, administrative, and financial records produced in cities and courts of northern Europe, particularly in the greater Low Countries, the epicenter of my entire study. This region is not only the one I know best and where I have done almost all my archival work; it was also late medieval Europe's most urbanized area and, along with northern Italy, its most commercialized.

The home of renowned mercantile and industrial centers like Ghent, Bruges, and Antwerp, and then Leiden and Amsterdam, the entire region was precociously saturated by trade. It was in these cities that monetization and commercialization had their earliest and most visible effects in northern Europe and that a social class born of commerce left records that permit me to tell a story about commercialization that goes beyond the strictly economic.

Although the geographic focus of these chapters is by some standards narrow and although at times I have drawn my evidence from just one or two urban archives, my claim is that what happened in this region is representative of what had happened, was happening, or would happen elsewhere in Europe. This does not mean that property law was rewritten in the same way everywhere or that people began to rethink marriage or reorganize inheritance at the same pace or in the same way in other parts of Europe; nor did people exchange gifts in Florence or Lyons just as they did in Ghent or Bruges. It means only that, wherever commerce took hold, it affected ideas about property, marriage, and exchange, and it forced alterations in associated social practices. Often, as I will occasionally comment, the changes elsewhere occurred in precisely the same way as they did in the Low Countries, but that depended a lot on whether traditional practices in those places had resembled those in the Low Countries. In any case, the alterations in distant places came in response to the same forces at work in the cities and courts I have studied.

Historians have by no means ignored these topics; indeed, scholars have regularly observed that property law, marriage practices, and the norms surrounding exchange were in flux during this period, and most have understood that commercialization was the context for these changes. However, I do not treat these issues as incidentally connected episodes in this larger economic history, but as necessarily related aspects of the sociocultural upheaval that came as property changed form under commercialization. Indeed, anthropologists consider property itself, marriage and inheritance, and exchange as main pillars of social order everywhere, so it is no wonder that commerce's impact would have been so clearly registered in these three arenas.

The fourth chapter, which examines the Europe-wide explosion of sumptuary legislation in this age, treats a no less fundamental support of the social edifice: display. Medieval Europe was what anthropologists call a display culture, where luxury goods such as dress, jewels, and arms not only signaled but also actually constituted political power, social bonds, and hierarchy itself; inevitably, the proliferation of such goods changed the meaning of these displays. The fifth chapter turns from the display of material objects to talk about their effects on social and moral order. It describes how, in response to commerce's increasing power from the central Middle Ages forward, moralists, cultural critics, and lawmakers rewrote a centuries-old critique of greed and luxury. Although once again treating Europe as a whole, the chapter ends in the greater Low Countries where, like my study, the northern version of the commercial revolution was rooted.

Commercialization certainly predated 1300. Indeed, medievalists argue that significant sociocultural effects of commerce had been registered much earlier, when Venice and Genoa first opened the subcontinent to regions to the east and south and when northern traders gave new life to commerce in the Baltic and North Sea region. Rather than situating my study in those earlier years, however, I began my research when the sources available in the greater Low Countries became rich enough to reveal how commercial wealth disturbed the traditional practices of both ordinary people and the elite – implicit proof, I have concluded, that changes of the kind I investigated did not occur until this period. Just as the story of commerce and European economic culture did not begin in 1300, it did not end in 1600. In fact, scholars tracing the history of modern western capitalism usually concentrate on the seventeenth and eighteenth centuries, when its institutional and sociocultural infrastructure was in visible formation, not on the years between 1300 and 1600. However, in ending when I did, I am proposing that if it were not for the kinds of changes that took place in these three centuries, the seventeenth or eighteenth century would not have emerged as the turning point in the history of capitalism.

Yet, if the new practices I describe did set the terms for future socio-economic developments, they were not themselves embryonic forms of what we call capitalism. The merchants, artisans, and shopkeepers who lived in places like Ghent, Antwerp, Paris, or Leiden had no words for that concept; they never imagined the market as an "invisible hand," and they used the term *bourgeois* or *burger* only to mean urban citizen. Links between these centuries and the next ones certainly existed, but the most fundamental connections cannot be identified by mining the evidence from this age for early signs of that future. They can be found only by approaching this economic culture on its own terms: by examining how people who lived from commerce managed their wealth, how their practices differed from those of earlier generations, and how their choices reflected the impact of commerce.

COMMERCE AND CAPITALISM

By 1300, Europe's commercial revolution had reached its height. Florence, along with other Italian industrial and banking centers, had joined Venice and Genoa to make the Italian peninsula the engine of European commerce. The southern Low Countries, where Bruges, Ghent, and Ypres dominated the commercial landscape, had become the most urbanized area of Europe. The Rhine, where Cologne had established staple rights, served as a major artery of trade linking the south of Europe to the cities of the Low Countries, England, and northern France and, above all, to the Hanseatic cities that were taking control of the Baltic and North Sea trade. Paris had become a center of luxury consumption, spawning vigorous local industries and nurturing the same crafts elsewhere. Rome and then Avignon, where the papacy single-handedly generated local economies, governed a financial network that stretched out in all directions across the continent. London had begun its ascent, presaging the demographic, economic, and cultural explosion that would begin in the sixteenth century.

Europe was thus no longer an economic backwater of the known world. Its crisscrossing trade routes carried imported spices, gold, and silks; European-made cloth, metalwork, and armor; and timber, coal, and other raw materials to and from ports, inland entrepôts, financial centers, and industrial producers such as Bruges, London, Cologne, and Florence. It was dotted with fairgrounds where merchants and producers from all over Europe met to exchange goods, negotiate credit agreements, settle accounts, and share information.[2] By 1300, Europeans

---

[2] See John H. Munro, "The 'New Institutional Economics' and the Changing Fortunes of Fairs in Medieval and Early Modern Europe: The Textile Trades,

were in the Sudan in search of gold and in the East in search of spices and silks; by 1500, they were poised to traverse the globe in search of even greater commercial profits. Indeed, by 1500 huge swaths of the rural economy, isolated parts of which had long been affected by commerce, were being visibly transformed. In some places a free peasantry had already emerged; in others entrepreneurial landlords were making wage laborers of their dependent peasants; in still others peasants had themselves become market farmers. Industry was moving to the countryside, turning agricultural workers into industrial laborers.[3] Even the plagues and famines that ravaged Europe in the post-1300 period, the wars that all but destroyed some commercial networks, and the class conflicts that broke out sporadically in the late medieval centuries did not halt the march of commerce. They only slowed its progress and diverted it into new channels.

As commerce secured its hold, the men and women who lived from trade established independent sociopolitical status. This was the age of the urban commune and of guild revolutions, the time when words like the German *Bürger*, the French *bourgeois*, and the Dutch *burger* or *poorter* acquired permanent places in northern European vocabulary. It was then that the riches accumulated in trade threatened to dwarf those garnered elsewhere, when the possessors of that new wealth challenged traditional powers, and when both moral codes and law began to change to accommodate commerce. Names like Coeur, Peruzzi, Medici, Boinebroke, and Fugger came to signify power itself. As many scholars have

Warfare, and Transaction Costs," *Vierteljahrsschrift für Sozial – und Wirtschaftsgeschichte* 88/1 (2001), pp. 1–47, for a recent discussion of the literature on the medieval and early modern fair and an excellent guide to the literature. Also S. R. Epstein, "Regional Fairs, Institutional Innovation, and Economic Growth in Late Medieval Europe," *Economic History Review* 47, no. 3 (1994), pp. 459–82; and Evelyn Welch, "The Fairs of Early Modern Italy," in *Buyers & Sellers: Retail Circuits and Practices in Medieval and Early Modern Europe*, eds. Bruno Blondé et al. (Turnhout, 2006), pp. 31–51.

[3] Basic studies include Immanuel M. Wallerstein, *The Modern World System*, 2 vols. (New York, 1974 and 1980) and Peter Kriedte, Hans Medick, and Jürgen Schlumbohm, *Industrialization before Industrialization: Rural Industry in the Genesis of Capitalism* (Cambridge, 1981). Philip Hoffman's more recent *Growth in a Traditional Society: The French Countryside 1450–1815* (Princeton, 1996) is also useful.

told it, by 1600 Europe was poised to give birth to the age of capital, and commerce would be its midwife.[4]

However, the commercial economy of those days was not a capitalist market economy, if by that term we mean the modern western economic system. Prices did not converge over broad regions as a result of negotiations between buyers and sellers, as they are considered to do in a modern capitalist economy.[5] In fact, most agricultural prices in

[4] An essential starting point for the story of European commercialization is the work of Henri Pirenne. See in particular his *Mohammed and Charlemagne* (London, 1939), *Histoire économique de l'occident médiéval*, ed. Emile Coornaert (Bruges, 1951), and *Medieval Cities* (Princeton, 1952). For a critique and an appreciation, see Georges Despy and Adriaan Verhulst, *La fortune historiographique des thèses d'Henri Pirenne* (Brussels, 1986).

For recent interpretations of the process of commercialization that provide a good synthesis of mainstream scholarship, see Jean Favier, *Gold and Spices: The Rise of Commerce in the Middle Ages* (New York, 1998) [Original edition: *De l'or et des épices: Naissance de l'homme d'affaires au moyen âge* (Paris, 1987)] and R. H. Britnell, *The Commercialization of English Society, 1000–1500* (Cambridge, 1993). Also useful are the older studies by Harry Miskimin, such as *The Economy of Early Renaissance Europe, 1300–1460* (Cambridge, 1975); idem, *The Economy of Later Renaissance Europe, 1460–1600* (Cambridge, 1977), as are M. M. Postan et al., eds., *The Cambridge Economic History of Europe*, Vol. 2: *Trade and Industry in the Middle Ages* (Cambridge, UK, 1987) and Vol. 3: *Economic Organization and Policies in the Middle Ages* (Cambridge, UK, 1965). For a general overview of the preindustrial economy, see Carlo Cipolla, *Before the Industrial Revolution* (New York, 1976).

For the Marxist tradition, see in particular Maurice Dobb, *Studies in the Development of Capitalism* (New York, 1946); Paul Sweezy et al., *The Transition from Feudalism to Capitalism* (London, 1978); T. H. Aston and C. H. E. Philpin, eds., *The Brenner Debate: Agrarian Class Structure and Economic Development in Pre-Industrial Europe* (Cambridge, 1985); Peter Kriedte, *Peasants, Landlords and Merchant Capitalists* (Cambridge, 1983); and Robert S. DuPlessis, *Transitions to Capitalism in Early Modern Europe* (Cambridge, 1997).

[5] This was true even in the Low Countries. There, according to Richard W. Unger, "Thresholds for Market Integration in the Low Countries and England in the Fifteenth Century," in *Money, Markets and Trade*, eds. Lawrin Armstrong et al. (Boston, 2007), pp. 349–80, grain prices *within* the urban market itself were highly integrated, particularly for wheat, but *between* cities (even neighboring cities) there was surprisingly little price convergence. Unger thus modestly corrects earlier studies by Marie-Jeanne Tits-Dieuaide and Herman Van der Wee, who had argued that within the Low Countries in the fifteenth century

Europe were not market outcomes in that sense; rather, they were fixed by custom, law, or political exigency and often remained unchanged for decades.[6] Trade was by no means open to all; even in cities in which commerce found its most secure home, it was often only those privileged by birth, citizenship, or corporate membership who were permitted to offer their goods for sale, and some marketplaces were themselves confined to fixed sites and allowed to function only at specified times. For example, a 1407 ruling of the Parisian Parlement reserved the "hale des Blanc Manteaulx" for local artisans and required that they sell only their own goods in that site, and none made by "foreign" craftsmen in other cities.[7] Fairs were one response to these restrictions, for one of their functions was to provide moments of open trade, times when even

there was a high and increasing degree of market integration. See Marie-Jeanne Tits-Dieuaide, *La formation des prix céréaliers en Brabant et en Flandre au XVe siècle* Brussels, 1975) and Herman Van der Wee, *The Growth of the Antwerp Market and the European Economy* (The Hague, 1963), Vol. 1, especially pp. 23–4 and 41). As Unger shows, however, integration was local and at most regional for most of the fourteenth and fifteenth centuries, noting that "levels of transactions costs, warfare, and government regulations worked to prevent exchange" and that "at many points in the fifteenth century and for many parts of the region . . . the level of integration with other urban markets was scant" (pp. 351–2).

Even cloth prices seem to have sometimes been relatively impervious to traditional pressures of supply and demand, even to production costs themselves. See Simonne Abraham-Thisse, "La valeur des draps au moyen âge: de l'économique au symbolique," in *In but not of the Market: Movable Goods in the Late Medieval and Early Modern Economy*, eds. Marc Boone and Martha Howell (Brussels, 2007), pp. 17–53.

[6] A recent study by Mark Aliosio shows that, even in Sicily (a key supplier of grain to urban markets in the south of Europe) prices did not respond to the usual market forces, principally as a result of interference by elites and governing bodies that were "often more concerned with protecting their particular fiscal and commercial privilege than in reducing the cost of regional trade" (p. 308): Mark A. Aliosio, "A Test Case for Regional Market Integration? The Grain Trade between Malta and Sicily in the Late Middle Ages," in *Money, Markets, and Trade*, pp. 297–309. On market integration in England in this period, see John Hatcher and Mark Baily, *Modelling the Middle Ages: The History and Theory of England's Economic Development* (Oxford, 2001).

[7] *Les métiers et corporations de la ville de Paris III. XIVe–XVIIIe siècle*, ed. René Lespinasse (Paris, 1897): Sixième Partie: Tissus, Étoffes, Vêtement, III (Arrêt de Parlement), #11, p. 157.

"foreigners" could buy and sell freely. As Pope Leo's 1519 license to the city of Senigallia put it, "the city of Senigallia is permitted to celebrate a fair, safely and securely, to which all type of merchandise can be brought and removed."[8]

This was emphatically not the "self-equilibrating, self-regulating, hegemonic market economy out from under the constraints of the larger society" imagined by neoclassical theorists. Nor did it resemble the capitalist economy that Polanyi described in almost identical terms: "an economic system controlled by markets alone . . . [where] the production and distribution of goods is entrusted to this self-regulating mechanism . . . [and] there are markets for all elements of industry, not only for goods (always including services) but also for labor, land, and money."[9] In those days, few decisions about production, distribution,

[8] Cited in Welch, "Fairs of Early Modern Italy," p. 34.

[9] The first quotation is from Winifred Barre Rothenberg, *From Market-Places to a Market Society: The Transformation of Rural Massachusetts, 1750–1850* (Chicago, 1992), p. 4; the second is from Karl Polanyi, *The Great Transformation: The Political and Economic Origins of Our Time* (Boston, 1957), pp. 68–9. There, Polanyi continued, "the supply of goods (including services) available at a definite price will equal the demand at that price. . . . Production will then be controlled by prices . . . the distribution of the goods will also depend upon prices."

C. B. Macpherson, in *The Political Theory of Possessive Individualism: Hobbes to Locke* (London, 1962), pp. 51–54, offers a similar definition of what he called the "possessive market society," but unlike Polanyi, who dated its emergence to the mid-nineteenth century, Macpherson thought that in England the principal elements were in place by the seventeenth century.

Also see Y. Ben-Porath, "The F-Connection: Families, Friends and Firms and the Organization of Exchange," *Population and Development Review* 6 (1980), pp. 1–30, who describes capitalism as a system in which "faceless buyers and sellers, households and firms that grind out decision rules from their objective functions (utility, profit) meet . . . for an instant to exchange standardized goods at equilibrium prices": cited in Avner Greif, "On the Interrelations and Economic Implications of Economic, Social, Political, and Normative Factors: Reflections from Two Late Medieval Societies," in *The Frontiers of the New Institutional Economics*, eds. John N. Drobak and John V. C. Nye (San Diego, 1997), p. 60.

Nor does the late medieval economy resemble the system Marx described in *Capital*, where the focus is on the prolongation of the working day to produce surplus value that is automatically appropriated by capital. "This," Marx said,

and consumption were imagined to be the sole province of individuals who were responding to market opportunities; rather, the needs of past and present collectivities played a huge, often decisive, role in decisions about how property was used, transferred during life, and passed on after death. Indeed, Europeans of the late medieval and early modern centuries would have been astonished by the idea, central to modern capitalism, that the public good is best served by allowing individuals to pursue their material self-interests. Augustine's centuries-old attack on lust, whether for pleasure, riches, or glory, still dominated a vitriolic narrative about the evils of commerce that circulated not just among monkish moralists but also throughout the very cities where commerce was a way of life. Even aristocrats had to justify the quest for fame so central to their honor code on the grounds that it served the common good. Avarice, which was now dethroning pride as the greatest of medieval Europe's sins, found no such apologists; raw greed remained unredeemed.[10] It was not until the eighteenth century that even the English, who are generally regarded as the forerunners in the race towards capitalism, could speak of materialist self-interest in positive terms.[11]

"...forms the general groundwork of the capitalist system.": from chapter 16, "Absolute and Relative Surplus Value," of Karl Marx, *Capital: A Critique of Political Economy*, trans. Ben Fowkes. 3 vols. Vol. 1 (New York, 1976), pp. 645–6.

For a useful introduction to the literature on the history of the western market economy, see Thomas L. Haskell and Richard F. Teichgraeber III, "Introduction," in *The Culture of the Market: Historical Essays*, eds. Thomas L. Haskell and Richard F. Teichgraeber III (Cambridge, 1993), pp. 1–17. Neither they nor their authors are committed to a single definition of a "market economy," but are seeking to understand the ideologies that grounded market behaviors in the past. See in particular p. 3

[10] For the reference to greed as the greatest of sins, see Jacques Le Goff, *La bourse et la vie: économie et religion au Moyen Age* (Hachette, 1986), p. 10. The classic work on this theme is Albert O. Hirschman, *The Passions and the Interests: Political Arguments for Capitalism before Its Triumph* (Princeton, 1977).

[11] For this discussion, see Craig Muldrew, *The Economy of Obligation: The Culture of Credit and Social Relations in Early Modern England* (New York, 1998), p. 127. Also see Istvan Hunt and Michael Ignatieff, eds., *Wealth and Virtue: The Shaping of Political Economy in the Scottish Enlightenment* (Cambridge, 1983) and J. G. A.

Nor was commercial wealth then considered capable of infinitely reproducing and augmenting itself as capital, in the modern sense, is thought to do. In fact, Europeans of that era had no ready term for assets of this kind. English speakers generally used words like "treasure," "stock," or "wealth" when they spoke of what we would think of as fixed and working capital. Similarly, Latin writers referred to *bona* or *substantia*, the French to *biens*, German speakers to *Güter*, and Dutch speakers to *goede*. As such words imply, for these men and women commercial property was a store of riches, not an engine of growth.[12] Consumption – of luxuries in the form of silks or jewels, prerogatives in the form of honorific offices, material manifestations of piety in the form of reliquaries, or displays of learning in the form of libraries stocked with elegant editions – was the goal of commerce, not accumulation and reinvestment as described by capitalist theory.[13] In this age, even money itself had not yet developed what an economist today might call full "money functions"; that is, money was not simultaneously a store of value, a measure of value, and a means of exchange. Priced transfers of goods were often bilateral and simultaneous so that money did not serve as a store of value, but simply as a measure of the relationship between the goods being exchanged; money signified price alone, and the price had often not been negotiated in market-like situations. In fact, many priced transfers did not even involve currency, for rents, tithes, and dues were often paid in kind, not in coin.[14]

Pocock, *Virtue, Commerce, and History: Essays on Political Thought and History, Chiefly in the Eighteenth Century* (Cambridge, 1985).

[12] Robert S. DuPlessis, following earlier scholars like Braudel, argues that the term "capital," understood as wealth capable of reproducing and incrementing itself, took shape only in the eighteenth and nineteenth centuries: Robert S. DuPlessis, "Capital Formations," in *The Culture of Capital: Property, Cities, and Knowledge in Early Modern England*, ed. Henry S. Turner (New York, 2002). For Braudel's summary of the history of these words, see Fernand Braudel, *The Wheels of Commerce*, trans. Siân Reynolds, Vol. 2, *Civilization and Capitalism* (London, 1982), pp. 232–7.

[13] See, for example, Chandra Murkerji, *From Graven Images: Patterns of Modern Materialism* (New York, 1983).

[14] The recent *Priceless Markets: The Political Economy of Credit in Paris, 1660–1870*, by Philip T. Hoffman, Filles Postel-Vinay, and Jean-Laurent Rosenthal (Chicago, 2000), emphasizes that this was still the case in later centuries,

Thus, although when seen from the point of view of the eighteenth or nineteenth centur, late medieval Europe would seem to have been heading toward its capitalist future, people in that age thought themselves embarked on no such journey. Instead, they were busily fashioning strategies for accommodating commerce in a world where few people thought of property as capital, where few goods were easily commodified, where many goods that were commodified seldom held that status for long, and where nonmarket modes of exchange – gifts, tribute, and inheritance – were the essential sutures of social relations.[15] This was true not just for people on the margins of the commercial economy but also for those at its center – people who lived in cities like Antwerp or Paris, Florence or London. Even those urbanites were not certain that commercial wealth could secure social hierarchies and establish personal identity, as property had long been thought able to do. Although they lived from commerce, they did not live entirely comfortably in it. During the centuries I concentrate on, they were searching for and finding new ways to use property and producing new discourses about its meaning. Even if their innovations laid groundwork for the capitalist age to follow, we will not understand them or even understand their significance for the future unless we study them as expressions of a distinctive economic culture, one peculiar to their age rather than predictive of one to come.

CIRCULATING GOODS

To do so, we need to appreciate what it meant that commerce made wealth *movable*. To be sure, the phrase "movable wealth" had long been

---

even in Paris; see in particular Chapter 1. For a general discussion of the uncertain relationship among money, priced exchange, and market transactions, see Jonathan Parry and Maurice Bloch, *Money and the Morality of Exchange* (Cambridge, 1989). For more on the relationship among money, price, and market exchange, see pp. 16–19 following.

[15] For the classic discussion of the "commodity situation" of a good (the idea that goods can function as commodities for only part of their "social lives"), see Arjun Appadurai, "Introduction: The Social Life of Things," in idem, ed. *The Social Life of Things* (Cambridge, UK, 1986).

used in common speech to refer to goods that were quite literally movable – the plate and jewels owned by the rich, along with the stores of food, clothing and furnishings, tools and equipment held by all propertied classes. However, the expansion of commerce utterly changed the meaning of such "movables."

It did so most visibly by radically increasing the quantity of luxury goods, such as the silks and spices that had come from distant lands or the elegant cloths and valuable metalwares produced by artisans in places like Ghent or Nuremberg. These goods were the most apparent and symbolically rich evidence of commercialization, but they were only the tip of the iceberg. More prosaic goods circulated in the same marketplaces, accounting for an even larger portion of the assets bought and sold during these centuries.[16] Even pots and linens, eggs and cheese,

[16] Although relatively small part of the entire European economy, such goods dominated the urban markets. For example, the personal effects alone of Jan van Melle, chief tax collector of Ghent, were sold at auction in 1477 for more than 37,000 *groten* (about fifteen years' work by a well-paid artisan). This sale excluded all other forms of van Melle's movable wealth (food stores, equipment, animals, wagons, etc.), as well as urban real estate, which in Ghent was considered movable property: see Walter Prevenier and Wim Blockmans, *The Burgundian Netherlands* (Cambridge, UK, 1986), p. 177. Ordinary householders were relatively even more dependent on movables. A typical householder in fifteenth-century Douai, for example, would have had more than half of his or her wealth in furnishings, food stores, equipment, tools, inventories, clothing and jewelry; counting the residence and attached shop, all the property he owned would have been considered movable under the city's law and thus freely available to the market. The same was true for all but the richest merchants in that city. Gille Blocquel, who married Pierre Du Pond, a Douisien cloth merchant, in 1495, for example, brought only cash and a cash rent to the new household: Archives Municipales de Douai (hereafter, AMD), FF 639/4288.

For a review of the English evidence for a "consumer revolution" during the late Middle Ages, see Maryanne Kowaleski, "A Consumer Economy," in *A Social History of England 1200–1500*, eds. Rosemary Horrox and W. Mark Ormrod (Cambridge, 2006), pp. 238–59. For rich detail about consumer markets in thirteenth-century Paris and London, see Martha Carlin, "Shops and Shopping," in *Money, Markets and Trade*, eds. Blondé et al., pp. 491–537. A recent study of product innovation in early modern London provides useful detail about the variety and extent of trade in movables and a good guide to the literature on that aspect of commercialization in England: John Styles, "Product Innovation in Early Modern London," *Past and Present* 168 (2000), pp. 124–69. Joan

sacks of seed corn and plows, household furnishings and clothing – all once essentially the means for rendering the land productive and providing basic subsistence – now were potential commodities. They could be sold, and their marketability increasingly determined both their value and the reason for their existence. Animals, the harvest of orchards, and grain – all products of the land that were sometimes called chattels in law and once had been so easily assimilated to land in the cultural imagination – were drawn into this realm as well. Now, more than ever, animals were raised for sale, a good portion of the harvest went to nearby cities, and much of the grain was shipped to long-distance markets.[17] Now these goods were truly movable, separable from the land as never before. Eventually, and still more unsettling for contemporaries, land, which in law and common speech alike was characterized as "immovable," would be freed from its moorings.[18] Even by the fourteenth

> Thirsk's *Economic Policy and Projects: The Development of a Consumer Society in Early Modern England* (Oxford, 1978) remains the classic text on the so-called consumer revolution in early modern England. Also see, more generally, Jan de Vries, "The Industrial Revolution and the Industrious Revolution," *Journal of Economic History* 54, no. 2 (June 1994), pp. 249–70 and idem, Jan de Vries, *The Industrious Revolution: Consumer Behavior and the Household Economy, 1650 to the Present* (Cambridge, UK, 2008). For examples from the early modern Low Countries, see Bruno Blondé, "Botsende consumptiemodellen? De symbolische betekenis van goederenbezit en verbruik bij de Antwerpse adel (ca. 1780)," in *Adel en macht: Politiek, cultuur, economie*, eds. Guido Marnef et al. (Maastricht, 2004), pp. 123–39.

[17] On rural commercialization before 1300, see Adriaan Verhulst, "La genèse du régime domanial classique en France au haut moyen âge," in *Agricoltura e mondo rurale in Occidente mell' alto medioevo* (Settimano 13, Spoleto, 1966): pp. 135–60; idem, "Der Handel im Mereowingerreich: Gesamtdarstelling nach schriftlichen Quellen," *Early Medieval Studies* 2 (= *Antikvariskt Arkiv* 39) (1970), pp. 2–54. For overviews of the later period, see in particular William N. Parker and Eric L. Jones, eds., *European Peasants and their Markets: Essays in Agrarian Economic History* (Princeton, 1975) and DuPlessis, *Transitions*.

[18] In law, the category of immovables was capacious, but land was its fundament. Jean Brissaud, in *A History of French Private Law*, trans. Rapelje Howell (Boston, 1912), provides a summary of the types of property treated as immovable in the Middle Ages: the land and everything that is an integral part of the soil, buildings, crops growing on branches or roots; the movables that adhere to the immovables in the quality of accessories or appendages of the latter; rights over the land that are like the ownership because of their duration (servitude,

century (and much earlier in a few areas) peasants and lords alike were often buying and selling land and land rights in parts of Europe, and city dwellers everywhere were beginning to acquire rural properties, whether as investments, as sources of food supplies for their urban households, or as secondary residences.[19]

To render property economically movable was to render it fungible, and this alteration to the character of property gradually gave birth to new practices and new ideas about wealth and commerce. By definition, economically movable goods could easily be turned into other kinds of wealth – produce into jewels, jewels into clothing, clothing into rents, rents into tapestries, tapestries into land, all into coin. Fungibility meant abstraction – the expression of property as immaterial value – for if one good was to be equated with another, it had to be abstracted. Then, as now, price was the means of abstraction. However, when a good's value was expressed simply as price and when it circulated on that basis, it lost material identity. Whether a dwelling or a dress, a jewel or a barrel of wine, the good was in some sense ephemeral, no longer what it had been, no longer identifiable except by means of what it had become or might become. As they passed from hand to hand, goods so dematerialized could be lost from memory, even the traces of their existence erased.

Money itself made abstraction and the resulting fungibility of material wealth especially disturbing: to take Marx's famous example, how can a money value – a price – make twenty yards of linen the same thing as a coat?[20] Although by the thirteenth century there was a sophisticated scholarly literature explaining how price could create equivalences among unequal or dissimilar things, the process was difficult to understand and harder still to accept as "normal."[21] Indeed, as an early

quit-rent, and rents) and rights that, according to the feudal conception, were connected with the land itself (the right to administer justice or tolls, for example); rights like established rents and salable offices that had movables as their object but which were immovable or feudal in their origin (pp. 270–2).

[19] For a fuller discussion of the land market in these centuries, see pp. 34–42 in this chapter.

[20] Marx, *Capital*, Vol. 1, pp. 139–42.

[21] For a discussion of the scholastic (principally Franciscan) literature on price, money, and commerce, which in some respects anticipated modern neoclassical theory, see Giacomo Todeschini, *Richesse franciscaine: De la pauvreté volontaire à la*

fourteenth-century bishop put it, money was a *cose moult obscure* – "a very mysterious thing."[22] Even as late as the sixteenth century, according to Jean-Christophe Agnew, English people thought "the very liquidity of the money form – its apparent capacity to commute specific obligations, utilities, and meanings into generic, fungible equivalents – bespoke the same boundless autonomy that Aristotle had once condemned as an unnatural, 'chrematistic' form of exchange."[23]

There was even more to the problem, for the complexities of the contemporary monetary systems made it very hard to be sure how price would be translated into currency and currency back into goods. In medieval and early modern Europe, prices were typically expressed in monies of account.[24] A money of account was only a label; it stood as the middle term between coins and things, as a way of relating one to the other. A price quoted as "10 pennies sterling" meant only that a buyer was expected to render a coin that was considered "worth" 10 pennies sterling. In such a case, payment might indeed be rendered in an actual penny sterling, but the relationship between the price (expressed by the money of account) and the bullion value of the penny was uncertain. Most commonly, coins lost purchasing power because they were deliberately debased as issuers (cities and princes) re-minted them at a lower rate or fineness.[25] A coin's purchasing power might also change

---

société de marché (Paris, 2008). For additional discussion of contemporary ideas about commerce and guides to the literature, including more on the Franciscan scholars, see Chapter 5 of this book.

[22] Cited in John H. Munro, "Money and Coinage: Western Europe," in *Europe 1450 to 1789: Encyclopedia of the Early Modern World*, ed. Jonathan Dewald (New York, 2004), p. 176.

[23] Jean-Christophe Agnew, *Worlds Apart: The Market and the Theater in Anglo-American Thought, 1550–1750* (Cambridge, 1986), p. 42.

[24] For lucid discussions of money of account, see Peter Spufford, "Money of Account," in *Money and Its Uses in Medieval Europe* (Cambridge, 1988), Appendix II, pp. 411–14, and John H. Munro, "Money and Coinage in Late-Medieval and Early Modern Europe," *História e Economia: Revista Interdisciplinar* 4, no. 1 (2008), pp. 13–71.

[25] The weight of the English penny, for example, fell from 1.446 grams in 1257 and 1.315 grams in 1344 to 0.691 grams in 1526; for these figures see Table 7 in John H. Munro, "The Economic History of Later-Medieval and Early-Modern Europe: Lecture Topic No. 3," http://www.economics.utoronto.ca/munro5/

as a result of independent market forces. For example, if new sources of bullion were found, a coin would lose value because the bullion it contained was less scarce. Still worse, the value of a silver coin, for example, might rise or fall in relationship to a gold coin as the price ratio between the two bullions changed, producing the same kind of instabilities.[26] To add to the confusion, there were countless varieties of monies of account, many of them called pounds, and most of the pounds – but not all – were made up of 240 pennies.[27]

Having no necessarily fixed relationship to the money of account, coins themselves were not stamped to indicate any numerical exchange value; in effect, they had no fixed price. Rather, they were identifiable only by the emblems pressed into them, their size, and their shape. The confusion born of their unstable exchange value was thus compounded

03MONEY.pdf. Coins could be "cried up" (i.e., called in and re-minted at a heavier weight or greater fineness). They could also circulate at rates above their bullion content, their value a reflection of their usefulness in trade and the population's confidence in the government. Thus, the holder of the English penny might find that the coin was exchangeable for less or more than something priced in terms of a penny with exactly the same name.

[26] These changes could often be observed over these centuries, as silver became scarce when European mines were exhausted in the late fourteenth century, as gold supplies increased with early discoveries in the New World, or as silver flowed into late-sixteenth-century Europe from what are now Bolivia and Peru. For example, the gold–silver ratio rose from 9.308 in 1257 to 12.390 in 1344, fell to 10.332 in 1411, and had risen again to 11.158 in 1464: see Munro, "Money and Coinage," Table 3.

[27] The monies of account that will appear most often in these pages were the *livre tournois* and *livre parisis* of the French crown, each simply the sum of 240 silver *deniers*; and the *pond groot* of Flanders with 240 silver *groten* (*gros* in French), along with several other pounds based on the same *groot*, including the *livre parisis monnaie de Flandre* (see Appendix I). There was also the pound sterling of the English realm, with 240 silver pennies. A price expressed as 5 *livres parisis*, for example, would cost some other amount of *livres tournois*, and still another amount in the *pond groot* or the pound sterling. Other systems were tied to gold coins of relatively stable value, like the Venetian gold ducat or the Florentine gold florin. A few monies of account had, however, no particular material referent. They referred to a fictitious coin of fixed bullion content, usually gold, and they were used by merchants to ensure that payments received for goods came in coin with bullion values equal to those used in providing the goods. The German *Kaufmansgulden* was one such money of account, its name ("merchant's florin") conveying exactly its use.

by the fact that they were hard to identify, easily clipped, often counterfeited, and regularly copied by competing sovereigns. Because only skilled moneychangers were able to distinguish the "true" coin from the "false," they were not readily accepted outside the areas where they had been minted.

In combination, the instabilities of coin values, the lack of direct correspondence between prices and the bullion content of coins to which they referred, the variety of coins in circulation, and the difficulties of authenticating their identities created massive opportunities for confusion, fraud, and unearned gain. A scene in the fourteenth-century *Livre des Métiers*, a French-Flemish language manual produced in Bruges that offered to teach the protocols and vocabulary of trade in foreign places, dramatized the possibilities for confusion and fraud with particular charm. There, a woman cloth retailer argues with her potential customer about the "good" money and "bad" he offers in exchange for the cloth; in the end, she agrees to take his coin, but it is not clear whether she believes the money to be "good" or whether she is pricing her wares to adjust for the weakness of the currency proffered.[28] Although the text may well have been intended to inform its audience about the multiple currencies in circulation in fourteenth-century Bruges, not merely to entertain, both seller and buyer appear to be playing with money's mysteries.

> Sire, quell monnnoie me donnés vous?
> *Sir, what money are you giving me?*
>
> Demiselle, bonne monnoye : che sont gros tournois
> tell y ha de Flandres;
> il autre du tans saint Loys
> que on appielle vies gros.

---

[28] This Flemish-Picard conversation book is published with some of its imitations in J. Gessler, *Het Brugsche Livre des Mestiers en zijn navolgingen*, 6 vols. (Bruges, 1931). The text quoted is from pp. 16–17 of the original *Livres des Mestiers*. The manual can probably be dated between 1367 and 1377 (Raymond van Uytven, "De datering van het Brugse Livre des Mestiers," *Archief en bibliotheekwezen van België* 48 [1977], pp. 649–53, which also revises the early dating of the other manuals in Gessler's edition). For a recent analysis, see P. Jeannin, "Der Livre des Métiers: Das älteste vielsprachige Kaufmannslexikon," in *Brügge-Colloquium des hansischen Geschichtsvereins 26–29 Mai 1988: Referate und Diskussionen*, ed. K. Friedland (Vienna, 1990), pp. 121–30.

My lady, good money: these are gros tounois
such as those of Flanders;
the others are from the time of St. Louis
which one calls old gros.

Sire, que valent il?
Sir, what are they worth?

Dame, le vies XVIII denier,
et le flamenc XII:
vous le devés bien savoir
qui tan d'argent rechevés.

My lady, the old {are worth} 18 deniers,
and the Flemish, 12:
you should know that
given that you take in so much money.

Vous dites voir, sire,
mais nous ameriemes meius
escus du roy,
angles d'or et lyons d'or
courrones d'or ou neumes,
frans ou cayeres,
mailles et vies esterlines:
de telle mononoye
nous paieroit on bien.

You are right, sir,
but we would rather have
ecus de roy,
gold angels and gold lions,
gold crowns and gold helmets,
francs *or* cayeres
mailles *or old sterlings:*
with such money
we will be well paid.

Dame, aussi feroit o:
de deniers de douse mites.

My lady, so should you be
with deniers of 12 mites.

Vous dites voir, sire:
tout est bonne monnoye.
Biaus sire, je me loch de vous;
si que, s'il vous faloit
aucunes denrees
dont je me melle,
vous les porriés emporter
sans maille et sans denier:
si bien m'avés vous payet.

You are right, sir:
all is good money.
Good sir, I take your promise
so that, if you need
any goods
which I have,
you can take them
without {paying} maille or denier:
so well have you paid me.

Whether written to amuse or to teach, the text reveals just how complex market exchange could be in cities like late medieval Bruges. The three known later editions of the bilingual text – in Flemish-German, French-English, and in French-Flemish as was the original Bruges edition – preserve a version of this scene, although none of them is an exact replica of the Bruges text. Rather, the later editions altered the terms in play to reflect current monetary systems, certain evidence that the authors were each addressing a specific audience. For example, the French-German translation of around 1420 speaks not of "old" *gros tournois* and "*ecus de royals*, gold angels and gold lions, gold crowns and gold helmets, *francs* or *cayeres mailles* or old sterlings" as did the Bruges version. Instead the negotiation starts with an "ask" of 2 shillings "*grote tournoyse*" per yard of cloth, thus 24 shillings for the 12 yards at issue, but an offer of only 20. The buyer and seller settle at 22 shillings a yard, but the scene closes with a laborious calculation of how to convert those shillings into "pont parasise," apparently no simple matter.[29] The same text includes as well an apology by the supposed narrator that he is "not so smart about coinage that he can perfectly name [the coins] because every day there are new ones in a country or city."[30] Caxton's French-English version of 1483 introduces different currencies: "grotes of England/such ether be of Flaundres"; "plackes and half flackes/the olde grotes of English/which be worth v pens"; "Rynyssh guldrens/scutes of the kyng/tyallis nobles of England/salews of gold lyons/olde sterlingis pens."[31] The French-Flemish version of 1501 reflects still different local realities. Its opening passages promise to teach all that is necessary about pounds, shillings, and pennies, and in the closing pages the text names the various currencies of concern: "pont grote, pont parisijs (along with their shillings and pennies), the "mijte and half mite, the marc and the marc destrelin."[32]

The risks associated with trade in those days compounded the problems presented by money itself. It was not unheard of for a good to lose half its value almost overnight or for supply to tighten so dramatically that its price doubled just as quickly. Changes more likely came in smaller increments, but unless prices had been fixed in advance, a producer or merchant could not know what changes had actually occurred until the goods were offered to prospective buyers. Structural conditions of the day made it very hard to make these judgments: information networks – the essence of efficient markets – were fragile, transportation systems unreliable, politicians untrustworthy, laws inconsistent and unevenly applied, raw materials scarce, and consumers unpredictable.

[29] Gessler, *Het Brugsche Livre des Mestiers, Gesprächsbüchlein*, pp. 15–16. The closing scene reads: "Here, die twalef ellen/te tswensich groten de elle,/dat ware/twelef pont/parasise,/under dar is over/ in elke elle/ twie scilling;/das sint/vier unde twwensich scillinge;/das in der sommen/dritsien pont/unde vier schilling." The buyer replies, "Nemt,vrouwe,/ich waen wael dat ich haen wael ghetelt." ("Sir, the twelve yards at 20 groten each made twelve pounds parasis, of which 2 shillings per yard remains or 24 shillings, or in all 13 pounds and 4 shillings.... Take [my money] madame, I know that I have reckoned accurately.")

[30] Gessler, *Het Brugsche Livre des Mestiers, Gesprächsbüchlein*, p. 21.

[31] Gessler, *Het Brugsche Livre des Mestiers, Right Good Lernyng*, p. 20.

[32] Gessler, *Het Brugsche Livre des Mestiers, Vocabulaer*, pp. 67–8.

To some extent, this combination of elements is always present in commerce, perhaps no less today than in the late Middle Ages. Then, as now, the risks inherent in trade were unevenly distributed, a problem for which people sought and sometimes found solutions. In those days hansas, family firms, Florence's famous dowry fund, primitive forms of "venture" insurance, and the assistance that guilds and confraternities provided in old age, illness, or marriage went some way to shield individuals and their dependents from the ravages of unstable markets.[33] But the archives of the time give concrete evidence of how hard it was to protect buyers and sellers alike. Stories of bankruptcies, of entire shipments and even fleets lost to storms or pirates at sea and the fortunes that financed them lost with them, of trade embargoes that ruined an entire urban industry almost overnight – all these tales remind us how vulnerable people then were. Less directly, the same archives record how such risks threatened, even shattered marriages and family relations – widows left destitute, sons set adrift, daughters bereft of marriage portions, brothers squabbling over the tattered remains of a business.[34] As

[33] For a still reliable overview of these techniques, see Postan et al., eds., *Cambridge Economic History of Europe*, Vol. 3.

[34] For recent studies of these risks, see Van Doosselaere, *Commercial Agreements*, Chapter 4 and passim; Thomas Max Safley, "Bankruptcy: Family and Misfortune in Early Modern Augsburg," *Journal of European Economic History* 1 (2000), pp. 53–73 and Muldrew, *Economy of Obligation*. The story of Zambin Ziliol's loss of his ship, a catastrophe that would haunt family memory for generations, is illustrative: described in Anna Bellavitis, *Identité, marriage, mobilité sociale: Citoyennes et citoyens à Venise au XVIe siècle* (Rome, 2001), p. 286. The Florentine householders' notebooks (*ricordanze*) of the period are full of similar stories. The texts, which were kept by Italian professionals and businessmen from the late thirteenth century forward, include accounts of land purchases and marriage settlements, but also served as personal diaries of a casual kind. Buonaccorso Pitti's (written 1412–22) contains, for example, a lively narrative of fortunes won and lost through trading and gambling; see *Two Memoirs of Renaissance Florence: The Diaries of Buonaccorso Pitti and Gregorio Dati*. ed. Gene Brucker (Prospect Heights, IL, 1991). Additional examples from Italy are provided in Gerald W. Day, *Genoa's Response to Byzantium, 1155–1204: Commercial Expansion and Factionalism in a Medieval City* (Urbana, IL, 1988).

Even as measures to protect investors, merchants, and producers were put in place, however, they were often overtaken by rampant commercialization. Some scholars have argued that the sense of market dangers peaked in the

scholars have emphasized, such misfortunes were not locally contained. The collapse of one family's fortune brought other families down; their private disaster also reverberated through the finances of their city, to which these people were alternately creditors and obligors; the bankruptcies in one city in turn implicated families elsewhere in domino effects that could stretch across the continent.[35]

The techniques of regional and long-distance trade compounded the mysteries attending commerce. Bills of exchange, international fairs, moneychangers, and third-party dealings meant that trade was being conducted by faceless people, unknown and unknowable except by way of the goods delivered, the pieces of paper passed around, and the money exchanged. As Fernand Braudel argued, to trade via letters and bills of exchange was, even in the closing years of the Middle Ages, "a constant source of amazement. If money itself was 'a difficult cabbala to understand,' this type of money that was not money at all, and this juggling of money and book-keeping to a point where the two became confused, seemed not only complicated but diabolical."[36] Even the greatest financiers worried. As Braudel tells us, the Fuggers complained that

sixteenth and seventeenth centuries, but that assessment probably reflects the quality and abundance of the available evidence, which varied from region to region depending on the pace of commercialization and local institutional histories. In England, the sixteenth and seventeenth centuries seem to have witnessed especially intense anxiety about commerce and its dangers; for that interpretation, see Agnew, *Worlds Apart*.

[35] Thomas Max Safley, *Bankruptcy: Economics and Ethics in a Capitalistic Age* (forthcoming) provides detailed case studies illustrating exactly these points.

[36] Braudel, *Capitalism and Material Life: 1400–1800*, Vol. 1 (London, 1973), p. 471; Braudel's quote, "a difficult cabbala to understand," is from M. de Malestroit, "Memoires sur le faict des monnoyes..." in *Paradoxes inédits du seigneur de Malestroit*, ed. Luigi Einaudi (Paris, 1937), p. 105. As Herman Van der Wee has noted, it was not until the seventeenth century that negotiable sight notes became fully autonomous and credible commercial instruments – another measure of this culture's difficulty with abstracted trade: Herman Van der Wee, "Monetary Credit and Banking Systems," in *The Cambridge Economic History of Europe*, Vol. 5: *The Economic Organization of Early Modern Europe*, E. E. Rich and C. H. Wilson, eds. (Cambridge, UK, 1977), p. 329; also see John Munro, "The Medieval Origins of the Financial Revolution: Usury, *Rentes*, and Negotiability," *International History Review* 25, no. 3 (September 2003), pp. 505–62.

"doing business with the Genoese [preeminent bankers of the later six-teenth century] meant playing with pieces of paper, *mit Papier*, whereas they themselves operated with real money, *Baargeld* – the typical reaction," Braudel commented, "of traditional financiers failing to understand a new technique."[37]

Although paper was indeed, as the Fuggers recognized, a sign that the credit market was changing, credit itself was not new. For centuries, ordinary people had bought and sold using credit at weekly markets, in boutiques, on the streets, and in their homes, seldom paying at the point of sale and often not paying in coin.[38] The "black money" (coins of copper and mixed metals) that circulated in their world had little intrinsic value and could serve only as a token, not as a reliable store of value. In any case, it was in short supply. Everyone was in debt, virtually all the time, whether to neighbors, employers, servants, superiors, fathers, brothers, mothers, or even children. The records kept were rudimentary; many transactions were recorded by tally or, most often, simply committed to memory.[39] Hence, people often paid by giving their word and frequently settled by performing a service or providing another good that was similarly valued.

Such credit arrangements were personal, made between people who could trust one another, and even the rich shared in this culture. A letter writer's manual apparently compiled at Oxford between 1220 and 1240 illustrates the typical practice. All but one of the ten model letters and responses in the manual presupposed that loans were secured simply by the word of the borrower, whom the merchant knew personally; significantly, however, eight of the ten anticipated difficulty in collecting. One sample letter, from an earl to his vintner, closes with the assurance that "we shall pay your money on the day named without any argument

---

[37] Braudel, *Wheels*, p. 394.

[38] On the importance of credit in the ordinary medieval marketplace, see J. Day, *The Medieval Market Economy* (Oxford, 1987); J. Kermode, "Money and Credit in the Fifteenth-Century," *Business History Review* 65 (1991), pp. 475–501; P. Nightengale, "Monetary Circulation and Mercantile Credit in later Medieval England," *Economic History Review* 43 (1990), pp. 560–75.

[39] Muldrew, *Economy of Obligation* provides rich detail about these practices. See, for example, p. 96.

or delay." The vintner was given two model replies. One expresses confidence "that on the day named, according to your custom, you will pay your debt to me in full." However, a second reply agrees to the sale but beseeches "anxiously that you pay me in full your old debt, which is in arrears, equally with this new debt." Another has the earl pleading with his skinner to send furs for Easter even though he does "not have the money to pay for them [now]." Another letter has one person refusing a loan to another on the grounds that he himself had previously been denied aid by the man now pleading for help. And still another has an earl asking a client to trust him for 100 shillings so he could replace his dead palfrey because "we do not have a horse in which we can trust." One letter describes a case where trust had run out: an earl offers his draper a pledge of ten gold rings and ten silver cups as the guarantee his person could no longer supply, so past due were his debts.[40]

The personal trust that sustained this system also depended, at least implicitly, on communal acknowledgment of the relationship between borrower and lender.[41] Tradesmen often expressed their verbal agreement concretely, in effect displaying it to the community: a glass of wine shared, an exchange of "God's penny," and even a meal taken together – all part of the typical business negotiation in this age – were lively efforts to give buyers and sellers specific identities and to make their relationship visible, as a signature of their mutual trust.

Without such credit arrangements, whether the short-term agreements among neighbors or the long-term deals that linked suppliers with consumers who were hundreds, even thousands, of miles distant, commerce would not have been possible.[42] "Unstinting credit," as

---

[40] All these examples are taken from Carlin, "Shops and Shopping," pp. 531–6.

[41] On the importance of personal relationships among merchants in those days, see Oscar Gelderblom, "The Governance of Early Modern Trade: The Case of Hans Thijs, 1556–1611," *Enterprise and Society* 4, no. 4 (2003), pp. 606–39. For a more theoretical discussion of the issue, see Avner Greif, "The Fundamental Problem of Exchange: A Research Agenda in Historical Institutional Analysis," *European Review of Economic History* 4 (December 2000), pp. 251–84.

[42] See Day, *Medieval Market Economy*; Kermode, "Money and Credit"; Nightengale, "Monetary Circulation." David Nicholas, "Commercial Credit and Central Place Function in Thirteenth-Century Ypres," in *Money, Markets, and Trade*, pp. 310–48, provides fascinating detail about the mutual indebtedness of the Yprois at the end of the thirteenth century. As a series of recent studies on

Robert Lopez put it, "was the great lubricant of the Commercial Revolution."[43] However, as the commercial economy expanded, it gave rise to professional lenders, including pawnbrokers, moneychangers, and bankers in cities, towns, and even villages, whose activities strained this rather informal system.[44] Credit arrangements, no longer bilateral and short-term agreements among neighbors or buyers well-known to their suppliers, expanded in size, number, and complexity. Even for merchants the system became more opaque as credit networks stretched farther and farther and became loaded with interdependent obligations; people unknown to one another were joined to the chain of debt, and the chain itself spread across distant landscapes, even into foreign parts. Goods and the obligations attached to them circulated more rapidly and in greater quantities; money, paper representations of debt, and instruments for transferring financial obligations became ever more mysterious. This age thus came to suffer what economists typically refer to as a "crisis of information," a time when participants had lost intellectual control – knowledge – of the system to which they were bound because institutions did not exist that could make risk quantifiable and thus capable of being offset.[45] Hence, as Peter Mathias has explained in

the early modern French aristocracy has shown, the rich also lived from debt, spectacularly so and often at the pleasure of their social inferiors: see Denis Richet, "Les liens de clientèle: L'exemple de la 'robe' en France aux XVI et XVII siècles," in *Klientelsysteme im Europa*, ed. A. Maczak, pp. 147–52, and Denis Crouzet, "Recherche sur la crise de l'aristocratie en France au XVIe siècle," *Annales: Histoire économies et sociétés* 1 (1982); also see Muldrew, *Culture of Obligation.*

[43] Lopez, *Commercial Revolution*, p. 72.

[44] For a recent discussion of these financial specialists and their roles in urban commerce of the Low Countries, see Marc Boone, "Le crédit financier dans les villes de Flandre (xive – xv siècles): Typologies des crédirentiers, des créditeurs et des techniques de financement," *Barcelona Quaderns d'Història* 13 (2007), pp. 59–78.

[45] For one such statement, see Joseph Stiglitz and Andrew Weiss, "Credit Rationing in Markets with Imperfect Information," *American Economic Review* 71 (1981), pp. 393–410.

According to Muldrew, *Economy of Obligation*, p. 3, the number of bankruptcy suits rose exponentially in England during this period, reaching a peak between 1580 and 1640. In a somewhat later age, when worries about credit had reached another crisis, Daniel Defoe would describe the domino effect that followed

speaking of the early modern period, an extraordinarily high premium was put on what *was* knowable, which meant "individual dealings with known individuals, personal trust, and the kinship nexus." In fact, he argued, this might constitute a general law of economic culture: personal relationships, attested to in some way by public acknowledgment, must substitute when precise measures of economic capacity and institutions capable of guaranteeing that capacity do not exist.[46]

The cultural response was the emergence of "credit" as what Raymond Williams called a keyword – a "strong, difficult and persuasive word" used in everyday speech, which, although "beginning in particular specialized contexts, become[s] quite common in descriptions of wider areas of thought and experience."[47] Derived from the Latin *credere* (to believe or to trust) and originally a reference to the quality of the person who could be trusted, the word now served to endow the untrustworthy thing – the loan – with the qualities of the person who could be trusted. Buttressed by the personal word of an individual and public acknowledgment of that bond, credit acquired substance, and only when trust failed would a borrower be obliged to pledge his plate or jewels, as the hypothetical earl of the Oxford manual was forced to do. As a recent scholar put it, "credit-based honesty . . . [cast] two incongruent textualities (personal reputation, impersonal paper) into discursive reciprocity," making the borrower's honesty give substance to what was epistemologically insubstantial.[48] Daniel Defoe would later eloquently express that insubstantiality: "[Credit] gives Motion, yet it self cannot be said to Exist; it creates Forms, yet has it self no Form; it is neither

one break in the chain: "A is a great Merchant . . . he loses 20 or 30 thousand pound; and the Consequence is he breaks; his Breaking falls heavy on B, C, D, E and others; perhaps 5 or 6 Tradesmen in London." Daniel Defoe, *Review* 3:7 (January 15, 1706): p. 26; quoted in Sandra Sherman, "Promises, Promises: Credit as Contested Metaphor in Early Capitalist Discourse," *Modern Philology* 94, no. 3 (February 1997), p. 329.

[46] Peter Mathias, "Risk, Credit and Kinship in Early Modern Enterprise," in *The Early Modern Atlantic Economy*, eds. John J. McCusker and Kenneth Morgan (Cambridge, UK, 2000), p. 17.

[47] Raymond Williams, *Keywords: A Vocabulary of Culture and Society* (New York, 1976), p. 14.

[48] Sherman, "Promises, Promises," p. 330; on the semantic link between credit and reputation in this age, also see J. G. A. Pocock, *The Machivellian Moment* (Princeton, 1975).

Quantity or Quality; it has no Whereness, or Whenness, Scite, or Habit. I should say it is the essential Shadow of Something that is Not."[49] A man of credit was thus more than a reliable business associate. Because his personal "credit" alone could guarantee the smooth functioning of a society in which, as Craig Muldrew has pointed out, the market had become the site where social status was communicated, he embodied the premier social virtue.[50] A man of credit had become a man of honor.

In Fernand Braudel's interpretation, the emergence of credit as what I have labeled a keyword was one aspect of a general disruption of what he alternately (and somewhat confusingly) called "economic life," "the market economy," "the normal economy," or "the transparent economy" of traditional European society.[51] These "normal" and familiar transactions had occurred in face-to-face encounters in a world in which production was typically managed in small artisanal shops, there were few intermediaries between producer and consumer, and credit arrangements were highly personal and short term. In Braudel's words, this was "a world of transparence and regularity, in which everyone could be sure in advance, with the benefit of common experience, how the process of exchange would operate."[52] Early modern commerce, he thought, began violating all these norms because it was increasingly controlled by anonymous others – essentially long-distance merchants who once had operated in a more or less separate sphere.[53]

The normal market, to use Braudel's term, was imagined as – and often was – a physical space. As Jean-Christophe Agnew explained,

Early markets did not so much control space as they were controlled by spatial arrangements growing out of the organization of other kinds of social exchange,

---

[49] Daniel Defoe, *An Essay upon Publick Credit* (London, 1710), p. 6; quoted in Sherman, "Promises, Promises," p. 327.

[50] Muldrew, *Culture of Obligation*, pp. 148 and passim. On the sociocultural meaning of credit in early modern England, also see Alexandra Shepard, "Manhood, Credit, and Patriarchy in Early Modern England, c. 1580–1640," *Past and Present* 167 (2000), pp. 75–106.

[51] Braudel, *Wheels*, pp. 21, 22, 25, and 456; also see Fernand Braudel, *Afterthoughts on Materialism and Capitalism*, trans. Patricia Ranum (Baltimore, 1977).

[52] Braudel, *Wheels*, p. 455.

[53] See James Murray, *Bruges: Cradle of Capitalism* (Cambridge, 2005), for evidence about the degree to which long-distance traders in this age were connected to (and dependent) on the operations of local traders, money traders, and producers.

including gift and tributary practices. These markets were, in every possible sense of the term, *situated* [emphasis in original] phenomena; that is to say, they were assigned to precise sites – in space and time – in societies where the particularities of place and season were intricately linked to the dominant patterns of meaning and feeling and where the configuration of the landscape was itself used as a mnemonic repository of collective myth, memory, and practical wisdom.[54]

The marketplaces Agnew and Braudel had in mind were often situated in churchyards or adorned with market crosses, which were, as Agnew put it, "intended to preserve the transparency of exchange and the accountability of its participants in a setting where personal identity was formally framed or 'subsumed' with a structure of familial or household relations."[55] Even though much local trade was not confined to these public sites, the "private" trade that took place in boutiques, homes, taverns, or on the street did not supersede these more formal modes of market exchange and, in fact, could not have existed without them. This is one reason why civic and royal authorities so strenuously sought to protect public markets.[56] Although their regulations were explicitly intended to ensure quality, guarantee supply, and feed their

[54] Agnew, *Worlds Apart*, pp. 18 and 30.

[55] Agnew, *Worlds Apart*, p. 30. Marketplaces were as much social and political spaces as economic; for that discussion, see in particular James Masschaele, "The Public Space of the Marketplace in Medieval England," *Speculum* 77 (2002), pp. 383–421.

[56] On shopkeeping and shops in late medieval and early modern Europe, see Peter Stabel, "Markets in the Cities of the Late Medieval Low Countries: Retail, Commercial Exchange and Socio-cultural display," in *Fiere e mercati*, ed. Simonetta Cavaciocchi (Florence, 2001); Peter Stabel, "From the Market to the Shop: Retail and Urban Space in Late Medieval Bruges," in *Buyers and Sellers*, pp. 79–109; for priced exchange outside of shops and formal marketplaces, see, for example, Richard Britnell, "Markets, Shops, Inns, Taverns and Private Houses in Medieval English Trade," in *Buyers and Sellers*, eds. Blondé et al., pp. 109–25; Fabrizio Nevola, "'Piu honorati et suntuosi ala Republica': Botteghe and Luxury Retail along Siena's Strada Romana," in *Buyers and Sellers*, eds. Blondé et al., pp. 65–78; Derek Keene, "Sites of Desire: Shops, Selds and Wardrobes in London and Other English Cities, 1100–1550," in *Buyers and Sellers*, eds. Blondé et al., pp. 125–53; Vanessa Harding, "Shops, Markets and Retailers in London's Cheapside, c. 1500–1700," in *Buyers and Sellers*, eds. Blondé et al., pp. 155–70.

Figure 1. *The Market as Place.*
Dutch School, *Cloth Market in 's-Hertogenbosch*, Netherlands, 1530.
's-Hertogenbosch, Noordbrabants Museum. Photo Credit: Erich Lessing / Art
Resource, NY.

own coffers, the laws simultaneously established the norms for the trade being conducted in less public settings. For example, the prices at which householders sold their surplus ale in homes or taverns would implicitly be governed by the public price of grain. Similarly, merchants who met in inns to negotiate sales of cloth, dyes, or metalwares would have relied on the controls enforced in public marketplaces or by official supervisors of the crafts to ensure the quality of goods not yet seen and maybe not yet even produced. In short, public markets or public scrutiny of market production "forced a market" in the economist's abstract sense of the term by providing sellers and buyers the information on which all market exchange depended.[57]

Nevertheless, unplaced exchange could and did threaten these market norms because buyers and sellers operating out of public view were able to benefit unfairly by subverting the rules. Private could mean secret, and secret too often meant lawless. Even the exchanges that took place in boutiques rather in the public marketplaces could be a worry. Although this sort of trade was conducted face to face, and thus in accord with the ethic of Braudel's normal market, the shopkeepers often had not produced the goods they sold and were not obligated to verify their origin; they were just one of many intermediaries between an unknown producer and his or her unknowable consumer. They were thus not as firmly bound by the rules of "fair trade" as were those who did business in full public view.[58] Once commerce completely exited the public space, often to be conducted anonymously through third and fourth parties and by means of obscure legal instruments, Braudel argued, it verged toward what he called early modern "capitalism" – an alien sphere of accumulation, speculation, high risk, and monopoly that was

---

[57] Derek Keene points out that in London's Cheapside markets, shops and selds (stalls) that were privately owned were nevertheless subject to public supervision in some sense; trade in wardrobes, however, where the rich tended to do business, and in private houses was free of such oversight: Keene, "Sites of Desire," p. 127.

[58] As Derrick Keene has commented, the trade that took place in inns, taverns, and other "secret places . . . sometimes at night by candlelight . . . was regarded [as] contrary to the rules of the market and as potentially a cover for dealing in fraudulent goods, since it was not open to public view." Keene, "Sites of Desire," pp. 127–8.

as far removed from the practices and norms of the traditional market economy as it was from the industrial capitalist world to follow. Braudel insisted that there was a "crucial difference" between the "normal market of economic life" and this alien being, and early modern Europeans recognized the difference. These were "two economic worlds, two ways of living and working": one was "economic life," the right one; the other was corrupt, the new "capitalist" one.[59]

Critics have often complained that Braudel's categories are murky and his argument about their intersections confused. Indeed, Braudel often admitted the difficulty of drawing clear boundaries between them.[60] As he told it, "capitalists" always lurked at the borders of the normal market, ready to grab control, and the normal economy was sometimes described as belonging to that almost ahistorical world of the *longue-durée*, the home of subsistence production and limited market exchange. Whatever the leakiness of Braudel's categories, however, they help us see what worried lawmakers, commentators, theorists, and ordinary people during the late medieval and early modern centuries. As commerce abstracted ever more goods and ever more easily obscured the identity of people who traded in markets, as it made property seem infinitely fungible, and as it destabilized exchange values, trade itself was loosened from a set of sociocultural norms, many inscribed in law, that had long seemed able to contain it. If we are going to understand the economic practices of this age, we must place them in this context.

This is not, however, a story about panic, crisis, or ineptitude, as though in the fourteenth through sixteenth centuries people saw themselves in constant danger or were not yet skilled in the ways of commerce. Nor is it a story about the baby steps they were taking on their way to becoming the economic people of modernity. Rather, the story that interests me is about how they responded to the loosening of trade from the sociocultural norms that Braudel described, for this loosening motivated their decisions about how to use property and how to adjust social relations that were founded on a property relationship. That tale is the

---

[59] Braudel, *Wheels*, p. 456.

[60] For examples of such complaints, see Maarten Prak, "Introduction," in *Early Modern Capitalism*, ed. Maarten Prak, pp. 7–8, and Haskell and Teichgraeber, "Introduction," pp. 14–17.

key to understanding both their practices and the relationship between this period and the capitalist age to come.

THE GROUNDS OF SOCIAL ORDER

The clearest sign of the loosening that Braudel had in mind was an erosion of the idea that land was immovable property. Of course, land is immovable in a literal sense; unlike a dress, a chest, a plow, a cow, or a wagonload of grain, land cannot be transported, hidden, or misplaced. Nor does it depreciate or "waste" in the normal sense of the term; rather, in the medieval centuries land was imagined to produce year after year, generation after generation, even century after century, and for all practical purposes it did so. Together, these two qualities made it "immovable" in law, an issue I take up more specifically in Chapter 1. Here, however, I want to emphasize how its immovability was thought to stabilize social ties and how its increasing marketability eroded that capacity.

As understood in those centuries, land was not just a piece of earth. Land implied rights in the form, for example, of tenancies, leases, and perpetual (and heritable) rents, as well the appurtenances of land such as mills and orchards, barns and granaries; land could even include the animals and grains that grew on it as well as the people who worked it. In this sense, land was the bedrock of the medieval economy, the direct source of most subsistence and the font of riches. Even in the very latest years of the Middle Ages, some 85 percent of what we would call the gross national product was composed of agricultural goods. More than an asset that contained appurtenances, dependents, and products, land was also a livelihood, a permanent revenue stream that simultaneously supported users of different classes – lords who lived from it, rentiers who took its profit, peasants who worked it to bring forth its fruits. A source of subsistence today, land also guaranteed income for tomorrow, an implicit pledge that old age would be cared for, that social standing would be preserved, and that the next generation would enjoy the same rank, the same security, the same future. This was as true for peasants as for aristocrats and as true for royalty as for commoners. No wonder, then, that people clung so fiercely to their land and so ardently sought it when they did not have it.[61]

As the cement of a social order that was expected to remain unchanged from generation to generation, land could not be fully possessed by a single individual. Instead, individuals had only temporary rights in land, and the rights were divided among several categories of possessors. In addition to lords who collected its surplus, dependent peasants or tenants who worked it, and creditors who had purchased rights to its earnings, there were the heirs of those possessors whose residual claims to the property made alienation hard, if not impossible. Law inscribed these meanings, for even in the late decades of the Middle Ages and the centuries that began the modern era, statute, contract, and custom alike joined to restrict land's alienability and preserve its power for the generations to come.

This did not mean that land was never transferred in ways that resembled sales. Even before the turn of the first millennium, we have documents that record *venditiones, pretia*, and the like. It is hard to know how extensive these transfers were, but it is clear that they became more

[61] For a general discussion of land's status in premodern Europe and the meaning of a "land market" in the Middle Ages, see *Le marché de la terre au moyen âge*, eds. Laurent Feller and Chris Wickham (Rome, 2005). Also see Christopher Dyer's "The Peasant Land Market in Medieval England," in *Le marché de la terre*, eds. Feller and Wickham, pp. 65–76, who emphasizes the difficulty of measuring the extent of sales or, more seriously, of interpreting their meaning. For a thoughtful essay on the meaning of a "land market" among the medieval English peasantry, see L. R. Poos and Lloyd Bonfield, "Law and Individualism in Medieval England," *Social History* 11, no. 3 (October 1986), pp. 287–301. Also see, for a recent comparative study of land markets in western Europe, eastern Europe, and China during the late medieval to early modern period, the articles gathered in a special issue of *Continuity and Change* 23 (1), 2008, pp. 3–200, as "The Institutional Organization of Land Markets."
Land would retain its importance in the French economic imagination (and elsewhere in Europe) for centuries to come, even as movables, especially manufacturing wealth, acquired a larger share of the economic whole. As Judith Miller recently pointed out, the Physiocrats considered agriculture the only source of incremental wealth: Judith Miller, "Economic Ideologies, 1750–1800: The Creation of the Modern Political Economy?" *French Historical Studies* 23, no. 3 (2000), p. 500.

frequent as the Middle Ages drew to a close.[62] But even in commercialized regions, the transfers were not necessarily market transactions in a robust sense of the term. Instead, they were so embedded in social logics that, whatever the purely economic imperatives that may have helped motivate them, they belonged to a market only in the most impoverished sense.[63] Land and land rights that were exchanged on the basis of price – whether allodial land, leases, free or customary tenures – had often not been negotiated in arm's-length transactions as a normative market transaction is thought to be. Sometimes the property was being transferred to kin or close neighbors in fulfillment of a social obligation or a desire to knit a social bond, and other than that the exchange was priced, the transfer more closely resembled an inheritance or a gift than a sale in the classic sense. The prices themselves might have been set low to enable a relative to acquire the land or set high because the buyer was outside the kin group or local community; alternatively, they might have been set by custom or by seigneurial order.[64] This was true

[62] Jonathan Dewald, *Pont-St.-Pierre, 1398–1789: Lordship, Community, and Capitalism in Early Modern France* (Berkeley, 1987), pp. 51–2 presents evidence indicating that by the fifteenth century land sales were as common as they would be in the eighteenth and that in any case transfers by price then exceeded transfers by inheritance. Just whether those prices were market outcomes, however, is not clear.

[63] In addition to the sources cited in n. 61 above, see B. J. P. van Bavel, "Land and Lease Markets in Northwestern Europe and Italy, c. 1000–1800," *Continuity and Change* 23, no. 1 (2008), pp. 13–54 for a review of the long process of commercialization, with particular emphasis on how slowly and unevenly immovables (land and land rights) were commercialized in comparison to manufactured goods, products of the land, and personal property.

[64] The essays in *Le marché de la terre*, eds. Feller and Wickham, offer examples of these patterns, as do examples provided by Poos and Bonfield, "Law and Individualism in Medieval England." Also see, for a concrete example, data presented by Chris Briggs, "Credit and the Freehold Market in England, c. 1200 – c. 1320: Possibilities and Problems for Research," *in Credit and Rural Economy in North-Western Europe, c. 1200–1850*, eds. T. Lambrecht and P. Schofield (Turnhout, forthcoming), p. 17. Briggs reports that in 1295 in Barton, England, one-half acre of arable was sold for 11 shillings (132 p.); the entire six-acre holding from which that one-half acre came paid an annual rent of 2s5d (29 p.), implying an annual rent of 2.4 p. per half-acre. At market rates (assuming a

even in northern France and the southern Low Countries where commerce had early begun to erode traditional ideas about the immobility of land and where urbanites were active investors in rural properties.[65] For example, to preserve seigneurial rights, a 1280 Charter of Elesmes in Hainaut forbade unfree peasants to sell land to knights, the church, or a foreign *bourgeois*. "In this way," Ghislain Brunel has commented, "personal liberty was countered by freezing of assets."[66] Even in eastern England, where all evidence suggests that from the twelfth to fourteenth centuries (and surely thereafter) peasants actively transferred land *inter vivos* and that supply and demand affected the rate of transfer, there were visible constraints. There, too, inheritance and succession laws, as well as family interests more generally, seigneurial controls, or communal pressures could restrict a transfer, affect the price of a transfer (of

5% discount rate), however, a half-acre that sold for 132 p. would have rented for 6.6 p. annually, not 2.4 p. Conversely, the half-acre would have sold for 48 p. – not 132 p. Obviously, either the rent or the sales price or both were not "market" prices in any meaningful sense of the term.

A recent study of upper Swabia from the fifteenth to the eighteenth century provides another instructive example precisely because it comes from a later period when the land market is thought to have been even better developed. Although, as expected, peasant properties there were slowly being subjected to a regime of accounting and commodification during the period, land was almost never sold under "free market" conditions, but was transferred among the kin group on the basis of prices that do not seem to have been market driven: Govind P. Sreenvasan, *The Peasants of Ottobeuren, 1487–1726: A Rural Society in Early Modern Europe* (Cambridge, 2004).

[65] For the Low Countries and northern France in particular, see L. Génicot, "Aspects de la vie rurale aux environs de Gand dans la première moitié du XIIIe siècle," *Etudes rurales* 21 (April–June 1966), pp. 122–4; Ghislain Brunel, "Le marché de la terre en France septentrionale et en Belgique: Esquisse historiographique," in *Le marché de la terre*, eds. Feller and Wickham, pp. 99–111; and B. J. P. van Bavel, "Agrarian Change and Economic Development in the Late Medieval Netherlands," in *Agrarian Change and Economic Development in Europe before the Industrial Revolution*, eds. R. Brenner, J. de Vries, and E. Thoen (forthcoming).

[66] Brunel, "Le marché de la terre en France septentrionale et en Belgique: Esquisse historiographique," in *Le marché de la terre*, eds. Feller and Wickham, pp. 99–111, p. 109.

those that were transferred according to price), or channel the transfer in certain directions.[67]

The land market's thinness in these centuries was part and parcel of the greater market's underdevelopment. Without efficient information networks, good systems of transportation, reliable monetary systems, and transparent rules of exchange, there could have been no "real" market in land. However, my point here is different: in this society people had trouble thinking of land as a commodity. As Laurent Feller put it in speaking of the central Middle Ages, "by treating the land as though it were a commodity, we deprive it of its particular character and we seem to misunderstand the collection of features that show exactly that land was not an object like others and that it could not be easily considered a normal element of commercial exchange."[68] Chris Wickham has similarly remarked that

---

[67] See Phillipp R. Schofield, "Manorial Courts and the Land Market in Eastern England," in *Le marché de la terre*, eds. Feller and Wickham, pp. 237–71, for a discussion of this issue.

Paul Freeman has pointed out that North American medievalists have tended to cast the question about the peasant land market in terms of a tension between "individualism" and "community," in which land sales stand for the former and their relative absence for the latter (and the Black Death as the caesura that led to the disintegration of community and the rise of individualism, aka the market economy): Paul Freeman, "North American Historiography of the Peasant Land Market," in "Axe 2: Le marché de la terre au Moyen Age," http://lamop.univ-paris 1.fr/W3/Treilles (accessed September 19, 2008). My claim that collectivities had a major role in determining land sales well beyond the mid-fourteenth century is not, however, an assertion that the community trumped individualism. I am arguing that even then, and for a few centuries to come, a decision to sell land and the terms of sale itself were so embedded in a matrix of nonmarket calculations and imperatives – family strategies, inheritance customs, seigneurial pressure, and social ambitions more generally – that neither the sale itself nor, especially, the sales price can be taken as a transparent index of the market's vigor. For similar reasoning, see Monique Bourin, "Introduction," http://lamop.univ-paris1.fr/W3/Treilles/introduction.html (accessed September 19, 2008).

[68] Feller, "Enrichissement, accumulation et circulation des biens: quelques problèmes liés au marché de la terre," in *Le marché de la terre*, eds. Feller and Wickham, p. 8.

selling one's holding in the middle ages was not like selling fruit or cloth, products of the land but relatively isolable ones; nor was it like selling one's house today, which . . . is at least clearly part of a set of market relationships with known rules. It was more like, in the modern world, selling one's [privately owned] company or one's factory . . . which means ceding to others the whole basis of one's wealth or a large part of it, a momentous act and one with great recognizable, social and political implications.[69]

Thus, even in a city like late medieval Ghent where commerce reigned, as we see in Chapter 1, land's access to the market was limited by inheritance and marital property law even well into the early modern period. In short, land was not simply a productive asset; because its sociopolitical power did not derive from its value in exchange, it could not easily be transferred according to the rules of a market society.

As a result, the history of land law everywhere in premodern Europe is a story of struggle over when, how, to whom, and by whom land could be alienated. For example, in England, even land subject to common law (in medieval England this meant land held in fee simple, later called freeholds), although fully alienable in principle during the life of the possessor, could be (and was) entailed or subjected to other restrictions that kept the property in designated lines of descent (usually male).[70] Land held according to the rules of customary tenure (copyhold land) was subject to manorial custom, not common law, and although the rules governing its alienability varied from manor to manor, nowhere did peasants holding customary tenures have unrestricted access to markets

---

[69] Chris Wickham, "Conclusions," in *Le marché de la terre*, eds. Feller and Wickham, p. 638.

[70] By the close of the thirteenth century, land at common law and held in fee simple was alienable and could be bequeathed by testament (although heirs had automatic claims to land of which the deceased was seized at death), but the statute of *De donis* (1285) protected the interest in the male heir by restricting alienation by parents; entails were generally upheld, and it was only at the end of the fifteenth century that robust mechanisms were available for barring them. Entails were even accepted in customary law of the period. For these and other details of medieval and early modern property law, see J. H. Baker, *An Introduction to English Legal History*, 3rd ed. (London, 1990).

for their holdings.[71] Although the distinction between freehold and copyhold land gradually eroded in the late medieval centuries, it was not until the sixteenth and seventeenth centuries that it was effectively obliterated. But even then people found new ways to restrict land's alienability via, for example, the strict settlement.[72]

The situation was similar on the northern continent, despite the difference in the legal systems there. Typically, the interests of heirs and successors (surviving spouses) were put above those of the present holder of the property, and, as in England, customary tenancies were usually reserved for kin (or the lord) at the death of the tenant.[73] As we shall see in Chapter 1, such constraints operated even in the major commercial centers of the late medieval North. In the south of Europe, where Roman law traditions theoretically provided present holders wide latitude on how to dispose of their land (and all their property), local custom frequently intervened to produce results not unlike those in the North. In early modern Béarn (southwestern France), for example, family members were given one year to buy back land that had been sold by a household's head. As Allan Tulchin commented in reviewing the literature on such practices in southern France, "because people in

---

[71] For representative studies of sales of customary tenures in late medieval England, see C. Dyer, "The Peasant Land Market in Medieval England," in *Le marché de la terre*, eds. Feller and Wickham, pp. 65–76; P. D. A. Harvey, *The Peasant Land Market in Medieval England* (Oxford, 1984); P. D. A. Harvey, "The Peasant Land Market in Medieval England – and Beyond," in *Medieval Society and the Manor Court*, eds. Z. Razi and R. Smith (Oxford, 1996), pp. 392–407; P. Hyam, "The Origins of a Peasant Land Market in England," *Economic History Review* 23, no. 1 (1970), pp. 18–31.

[72] On the strict settlement, see L. Bonfield, *Marriage Settlements, 1601–1740: The Adoption of the Strict Settlement* (Cambridge, 1983); H. J. Habakkuk, "Marriage Settlements in the Eighteenth Century," *Transactions of the Royal Historical Society*, 4th series, 32 (1950), 15–30. Also see R. W. Hoyle, "The Land and Family Bond in England," *Past and Present* 146 (1995), pp. 151–73, and the sources he cites.

[73] For a discussion of these rules, see Robert Fossier, *La terre et les homes en Picardie, jusqu'à la fin du xiii siècle*, 2 vols. (Paris, 1968); Robert Fossier, *Peasant Life in the Medieval West* (New York, 1988). Fossier argues, however, that after 1300 the market economy steadily eroded these rules. I do not dispute his general claim but argue instead that the erosion was slow, uneven, and sometimes so fiercely resisted that it was temporarily halted.

the region had firm ideas about how the family should be organized that were not well served by Roman law principles, they developed a set of local customs that were."[74]

Even leases and rents, which proliferated as the Middle Ages gave way to the early modern period, were slow to disrupt social expectations about land's immobility.[75] For example, it was not until late in the early modern period in England that long-term lessees acquired rights in real property. For their part, land rents were carefully distinguished from other kinds of credit instruments (in fact, in most northern legal systems they were not recognized as credit instruments at all) and, like land itself, were considered immovable in customary law.[76]

The legal scholars L. R. Poos and Lloyd Bonfield have recently cautioned that, even when the law seemed to permit land's alienability, practice did not necessarily follow. They remarked that positive law (which they defined as "a set of strictures, prohibitions and coercions which can be sought in definitive statements and applied to particular circumstances") "must not be understood as *directing* behavior, not just because law is malleable but also because normative standards not captured by recorded law significantly governed practices." Hence, they concluded, "the approach to understanding the relationship between law and society is to observe *actual practice*."[77] Historians who base a claim that there was a land market in late medieval Europe on legal judgments or even statutes thus risk misunderstanding economic culture itself. Records of practice can also be deceptive, for even if they more closely reflect what people actually thought possible, they are sometimes easy to misinterpret. With particular regard to the land market,

[74] Allan Tulchin, "Same-Sex Couples Creating Households in Old Regime France: The Uses of the Affrèrement." *Journal of Modern History* 79 (September 2007), p. 622. His source for the Béarn evidence is Anen Zink, *L'héritier de la maison: Géographie coutumière du Sud-Ouest de la France sous l'ancien régime* (Paris, 1993). See his references for additional literature on the same theme.

[75] For the development of leasing during the late medieval and early modern period and a general discussion of land markets themselves, see B. J. P. van Bavel, "The Organization and Rise of Land and Lease Markets in Northwestern Europe and Italy, c. 1000–1800," pp. 13–54, in a special issue of *Continuity and Change* 28 (1), 2008, "The Institutional Organization of Land Markets."

[76] See Chapter 1 for an explanation of this system.

[77] Poos and Bonfield, "Law and Individualism in Medieval England," p. 289.

as I emphasized earlier, the mention of a "sale" in a document from the Middle Ages does not necessarily mean "sale" in the modern economist's sense, and one sale does not imply a "market."

Thus, although land and land rights were indeed bought and sold in late medieval and early modern Europe, law could be fashioned or manipulated to limit their circulation, even as the opportunities for sale increased with the expansion of commerce more generally. As Chapters 1 and 2 will investigate, this process was registered most clearly in marital property law and in the associated laws of inheritance and succession, for these were the premier mechanisms by which property secured the social order. Throughout the entire premodern period, indeed until well into the contemporary era, marriages in western Europe were explicitly constructed by the transfer of property, whatever the social class of the couple – whether aristocrat or peasant, noble or commoner, merchant or artisan.[78] And inheritance, in most of the North at least, followed from marital property law.

Property exchange was essential to marriage for the obvious reason that the new couple could not set up a household or support their children without these assets, but it served other purposes as well. Marriages formed in this way solidified ties of kinship by giving them firm material bases, linking families and individuals in long-lasting social bonds. The terms of the marriage exchange itself also structured gender relationships by defining each spouse's ownership, management, and succession rights over marital assets. Inheritance rules, which in most of the North were formally or informally linked to marital property law, did similar work. They assured social place to subsequent generations, for material assets were the supreme, if hardly the only, basis of class in late medieval culture. Like marital property arrangements, inheritance practices also helped determine the meaning of male and female gender identities in society at large, for in most legal regimes inheritance was

[78] Although the exchange of vows was central to the ecclesiastical definition of marriage, even the vow was popularly understood to be a promise to render property at some future date. "No marriage without dower," went a widely quoted medieval aphorism, a sentiment frequently elevated to the status of law, even appearing in twelfth-century canon law texts (the very texts that otherwise claimed that mutual consent alone constituted a valid marriage). For more on the ecclesiastical laws of marriage, see Chapter 2.

also gendered. Women were typically given different amounts or different kinds of goods, whether by custom or by means of a will or marriage contract, and among women, it was usually only widows – and only some widows – who could independently manage their wealth.

Only immovable wealth seemed capable of securing social relations in this way; movables, by nature a wasting asset, were too short-lived to provide the stability required. Hence, land and land rights were the preferred coin of the marriage exchange, and they were the substance of the patrimony intended for the next generation. Whatever the particular terms of the marriage bargain, it was land that sealed the marriage and secured the future of its offspring. This did not mean that other kinds of property were excluded from the marriage exchange or from inheritances, for animals and equipment, household goods and food stores were always part of the mix. But it is no exaggeration to say that these goods, like the buildings that attached to land, had traditionally derived their meaning from their association with land to such an extent that the marriage and inheritance were based on the economy of land. Luxury goods like jewels, arms, coin, and expensive garments could also be part of the marriage exchange, but few in medieval Europe owned significant amounts of such goods. Those who did were very rich in land as well and gave land and land rights overwhelming pride of place in making their marriages and settling their estates.[79]

Such was the stabilizing power of this asset that all forms of the typical medieval marriage agreement and the inheritance practices that flowed from the marital arrangement itself possessed a social rationality that derived from land's permanence and its immobility. Because marriages were sealed by an exchange of rights in land, it was possible to imagine

---

[79] Although historians acknowledge the importance of land in the medieval social order, they have seldom emphasized its role in the marriage exchange. Amy Louise Erickson, *Women and Property in Early Modern England* (London, 1993), is more attentive to this issue, even though the distinction between movable goods and land had more fully been eroded in the period (seventeenth century) she studied. For other general remarks on land's importance in the marriage bargain, see Sandra Cavallo and Lyndan Warner, *Widowhood in Medieval and Early Modern Europe* (Essex, UK, 1999), and Nancy E. Wright and Margaret W. Ferguson, eds., *Women, Property, and the Letters of the Law in Early Modern England* (Toronto, 2004).

that structural connections, not just between the spouses but also among their respective kin and between their future offspring and those same kin, could be maintained by fixing their individual relationships to shared property. Depending on the terms of the marital property law governing a particular union and setting succession rules in place, land could, for example, tie a widow to her late husband's kin or forge a permanent link between father and son. It could even grant patriarchal authority to a married woman if her dowry would return to her as a childless widow or to the men of her line, as it did in many marital property arrangements.

The stability of the social bonds sealed by land did not, however, ensure untroubled social relations. People so joined through life (and even beyond) inevitably disagreed at times; they might well have felt trapped by their bondage to the land and to its rules of transmission and use, and borne long enmity toward those whose competing rights to the asset overrode their own needs and desires. A daughter who carried land from her father to the children she would bear, for example, was normally positioned only as the land's trustee, not as its owner, and her obligations to maintain the asset in the interests of others would often have weighed heavily. A woman made dowager widow, to mention another often tense situation, would have been utterly dependent on the land to which she had use rights, and many such women were regarded as impediments to their own sons' adulthood and resented for the claims they had on the dower.[80] Nevertheless, as painfully as these ties sometimes bound and as long as some of the resulting disputes lasted, the bonds also promised stability of social status for the generations to follow, stability of the

---

[80] For studies illustrating some of these difficulties in the medieval and early modern periods, see Rowena Archer, "Rich Old Ladies: The Problem of Late Medieval Dowagers," in *Property and Politics: Essays in Later Medieval English History*, ed. T. Pollard (Gloucester, UK, 1984), pp. 15–35; J. Senderowitz Loengard, "'Of the gift of her husband': English Dower and Its Consequences in the Year 1200," in *Women of the Medieval World*, eds. Julius Kirshner and Suzanne Wemple (Oxford, UK, 1985); L. E. Mitchell, "The Lady Is a Lord: Noble Widows and Land in Thirteenth-Century Britain," *Historical Reflections* 18 (1992), pp. 71–87; Maura Palazzi, "Female Solitude and Patrilineage: Unmarried Women and Widows during the Eighteenth and Nineteenth Centuries," *Journal of Family History* 15 (1990), pp. 443–59.

conjugal bond, and stability of the gender hierarchy inscribed by the marital property exchange. No wonder marriages made by exchanging such assets seemed firmly grounded, capable of making close allies of distant neighbors, of founding dynasties that would endure through time, and of creating between woman and man a life bond so strong that they needed scarcely to have been introduced to be declared "well matched."

As commerce expanded, however, land could no longer serve as the sole ground of the social order. Urban people, except for the very rich, had few of their assets in rural properties. As merchants, artisans, and shopkeepers they lived almost entirely from movables and urban real estate (which in many customs of the North was considered movable in law). Even people with landed estates could not assume their property's immobility because these holdings were also gradually acquiring the status of a commodity, especially for rich urbanites who had bought the property as an investment, as a source of revenue, or as a supplier of foodstuffs for their households. People were learning that economically movable goods were inherently ephemeral, always susceptible to transformation, and thus no one could be sure just what their future might be. How, then, were people who lived entirely from such wealth to make the marriage bargain? How were even the landholding classes – whether peasants, yeomen farmers, or rentier elites – simultaneously to profit from the market and keep their land immobile? Which goods should be given to support the new household and provide for the next generation? What value should be assigned to a bride's marriage gift or dowry if it was to be used in a business as risky as medieval businesses often were? What restrictions should be placed on her husband's use of her wealth?

Even upside potential brought risk. Movable wealth could multiply in value just as it could disappear, sometimes reproducing at unimaginable rates in a way land rarely did. Money invested in sea voyages could earn fortunes; wool bought cheap could be sold dear; grain could be stored for times of famine and then sold for triple or quadruple its present value; a skilled artisan could produce a good that sold for many times the value of its raw materials or the labor invested in it. But how then to structure the marriage agreement? Should a contract be written with an eye to that possible future to assure the bride (and her family) some share of the possible gain? And if so, at what risk of possible losses? Should a child get his or her share of the expected parental estate at marriage, as was the custom in many places, or would it be wiser to wait in hope of further gain during the remaining years of the parents' lives?

Europeans' responses to commercialization were most profoundly registered as people sought to make movable goods do the work of securing social and gender hierarchy and establishing personal identity. In the chapters to come, I follow them in their search. Because the process did not play out chronologically, however, like a chain reaction set off by the fall of one domino, I organized the chapters conceptually, beginning with property itself and then moving to other arenas of sociocultural life in which the changes in property's meaning were as clearly registered. As my sources demanded, I occasionally exceeded the temporal boundaries of my study, using a particularly illustrative record from the 1200s or 1600s, and at times, especially in Chapters 4 and 5, I shifted my gaze from the Low Countries to Europe as a whole. Because I ranged so widely – chronologically, thematically, and geographically – I necessarily deployed a variety of sources and diverse reading strategies. A few words about methodology are therefore in order.

The three case studies are principally based on legal, administrative, and financial documents from the greater Low Countries, although I also rely on similar material taken from secondary literature and draw upon other scholars' interpretations to situate my own evidence. Chapter 1, "Movable/Immovable: What's in a Name?" traces three centuries of change in the customary law of Ghent, in Flemish Flanders, arguing that commerce eroded the distinction between movable and immovable wealth that the people of Ghent, along with many other northerners, had used to separate fully alienable wealth from property reserved for kin. In effect, I have read this legal history as sociocultural history. Nevertheless, the chapter necessarily depends on a close study of law itself and although by a legal historian's standards my touch is very light, this is recognizably legal history and at times considerably more technical than subsequent chapters. It comes first in the book because the record of how property was legally "ungrounded" during these centuries is more than a story about law. It is also a story about the gradual reconceptualization of property itself and its role in securing social order; the effects of that reconceptualization reverberated, as we shall see, far beyond the chambers where law was written and adjudicated.

The next chapter, which examines the conjugal bond in nuclear households that lived from commercial wealth, builds directly on Chapter 1 to make a more forthrightly sociocultural argument. As property changed meaning, so necessarily did marriage, for in those days marriage was explicitly based on a property relationship, and the kinship nexus formed by marriage was similarly founded on the devolution or sharing of property. The result was not only a modification of marital property and inheritance law but also a cultural change in marriage itself. The third chapter logically follows, moving from property to its exchange and once again deploying sources from the North, principally from cities and courts in the Low Countries. Here I draw extensively from anthropological literature, proposing that as commerce released more property to the market and created new goods for that realm, it changed the form and significance of what scholars have often labeled the gift economy. However, commerce did not erode the power of the gift, as many scholars have thought; rather, gifts took on new significance in these commercial economies.

The next chapter on sumptuary legislation takes a pan-European perspective, and it depends on published sources and literature rather than close archival work. Its claim is thus of a different order. Whereas my case studies were used to illustrate specific instances of change in property law, marriage, and gift-giving under the pressure of commerce, Chapter 4 pays attention to the particular and the local only as a means for discovering what all such legislation had in common. This approach allowed me to see what more focused studies might have obscured – that sumptuary laws everywhere were the record of a Europe-wide cultural crisis unleashed by commerce. Whatever else they were – and they were other things as well – the laws were part of a larger struggle to reimagine the relationship between a person's appearance and his or her identity – or between outward self-presentation and "that which lay beneath," to deploy Hamlet's famous phrase.

In the last chapter, which interrogates contemporary discourses about commerce's dangers, my focus is also pan-European. Although acknowledging that a centuries-old critique of luxury and greed acquired new force as commerce expanded in these centuries, I argue that cultural commentators, moralists, and lawmakers alike did not rely solely on well-worn arguments about its necessity in responding to commerce's many critics. They also offered to cure it by suppressing its capacity for deceit and by channeling the desires that fueled consumption. With its heavy reliance on literary texts, moralist tracts, images, and economic theory of the day, this chapter often roams far outside the usual method-ological boundaries of the social historian. Whether here or in other chapters, however, my forays into such material are intended only to illustrate the convergences between these sources and the legal, finan-cial, and administrative texts grounding my research. The frequency of the intersections between the language of regulatory acts and literature, for example, or between economic practices portrayed by visual artists and the descriptions retrievable from wills or financial records suggests, as a single genre of evidence could not, how thoroughly the economic culture of the period was being transformed by commerce.

I Movable/Immovable: What's in a Name?

PEOPLE WHO LIVED FROM COMMERCE NECESSARILY LIVED FROM wealth that was alienable, "movable" in the fullest sense of the word. They provisioned their households in local markets, either in whole or in part. As merchants and artisans, they acquired raw materials in markets, stocked their warehouses with goods to be sold, and delivered their merchandise to markets. They regularly borrowed and lent money; they used complex credit instruments to purchase their houses and tenures; and they let real estate to others; the richest among them bought and sold land as investment properties. At the same time, however, they had to protect a significant amount of their wealth from the vagaries of the marketplace because it was their principal means of preserving hierarchies of class, age, and gender. Commercial people were thus faced with the seemingly contradictory tasks of managing their property as though it was fully alienable and, at the same time, treating it as fixed patrimony.

In much of northern Europe during the latter half of the Middle Ages, the difference between the goods available to the market and those reserved as patrimony was inscribed in customary law as a difference between "movables" and "immovables." It was not always clear, however, whether a particular good was movable or immovable in law, and as commerce steadily drew more property into its vortex, it was even harder to preserve the presumed equation between immovables and patrimonial wealth. By the end of the early modern period, that equation had been broken, but the route to that end was by no means smooth. This chapter explores the sociocultural implications of that history, arguing that the story of how people dissolved the equation between patrimonial wealth and immovable property is at its heart a story about how commerce changed the way property was used to secure social hierarchies and thus changed the meaning of property itself.

The legal terms "movables" and "immovables" (in Latin, *mobilia* and *immobilia*) came from Roman law, but during the Middle Ages northerners used the words in common speech to distinguish goods that were literally movable from those that could not be transported from place to place. By the later Middle Ages, however, the Latin terms, along with their equivalents in French (*meubles/immeubles*), Dutch (*meublen/immeublen*), or German (some form of *bewegliche Güter/unbewegliche Güter*), had also been inscribed into most customary legal regimes of the region. There they were mapped onto concepts deeply rooted in these legal cultures and expressed in a vocabulary that had long predated the Latin imports. In these regions, French speakers had traditionally spoken of *cateux* and *heritages* (*héritages* in modern French), not *meubles* or *immeubles*. Dutch speakers had used the words *cateylen* and *erve* for the identical concepts, whereas German speakers typically had written *Fahrnis* and *Erbgüter*.[1]

The distinction among these vernacular renditions of what in modern English are generally called chattels and patrimony was not, however, precisely the same as the commonsense notion of the difference between movable goods and immovables; nor was it the same distinction that prevailed in Roman law. Chattels (*cateux*, *cateylen*, or *Fahrnis*) *were* income. As we shall see, chattel could be a crop still in the ground or even a house. In the commonsense notion of the term "movable," however, only a harvested crop would qualify as movable and a house could not. For their part, patrimonial goods (*heritages*, *erve*, or *Erbgüter*) *produced* income. They had perpetual lives, yielding fruit or income from one generation to the next. Hence an *heritage*, *erf*, or *Erbgut* could be a perpetual rent or an income from a toll. In his famous customal of the late thirteenth century, Beaumanoir perfectly expressed this logic: *"heritages"* produced

---

[1] For a fuller discussion of these concepts, see in particular Philippe Godding, *Le droit privé dans les Pays-Bas méridionaux du 12e au 18e siècle*. Mémoires de la Classe des Lettres series 2, 14/1 (Brussels: Académie Royale de Belgique, 1987), esp. p. 142, and Dirk Heirbaut, *Over lenen en families: Een studie over the vroegste geschiedenis van het zakelijk leenrecht in het graafschap Vlaanderen, ca. 1000–1350* (Brussels, 2000).

revenues that "held value for years" and were perpetual because an "*heritage* cannot falter."[2] In contrast, the commonsense notion of an immovable and its meaning in Roman law were one and the same: a property that was not transportable from place to place. In that conception, immovable meant land and the things tied to land.[3]

Yet, even though an *heritage* (or its equivalents in other vernaculars) as understood in the customary law of the North was a considerably broader term than immovable, in the North, as in the South, land was considered the modal *heritage* because the other principal forms of perpetual income – rents and tolls – were originally produced by land rights. Hence, in customary law of the North, not only was "immovable" readily conflated with land but both the term and the thing were also thought of as equivalent to patrimony or, in the vernaculars, as *heritages*, *erve*, or *Erbgüter*. Accordingly, "throughout the Middle Ages," as Anne-Marie Patault commented, thereby assigning to an immovable the essential quality of an *heritage*, "productivity [was the defining feature] of the immovable: the basis of its social utility."[4]

According to the logic that had produced the terms *heritages*, *erve*, and *Erbgüter*, and according to the customary law that inscribed this patrimonial logic, goods with perpetual productive capacity were not owned in the sense we understand that concept today. Because their productive life far exceeded that of any individual, they were not fully available to a single person during his or her lifetime; they were intended to serve generations of a family. Any possessor of such a property, even

---

[2] Philippe de Remi Beaumanoir, *Coutumes de Beauvaisis* 2 vols., ed. Amédée Salmon (Paris, 1899), nos. 672–8; cited in Paul Ourliac and Jean-Louis Gazzaniga, *Histoire du droit privé français de l'an mil au code civil* (Paris, 1985), p. 233.

[3] Heirbaut explains that "the movable-immovable distinction in Roman law has relevance only with respect to tangible (corporeal or material [*lichamelijke*]) property. For customary law it makes no difference whether a good is tangible or not. So long as a good has permanent existence and is productive, it is *erve* and thus usually immovable. The terms movable and immovable in the acts of practices of the thirteenth century thus have no sense in Roman law. They are only substitutes for the concepts of *cateyl* and *erve*." Heirbaut, *Over lenen en families*, pp. 22–3.

[4] Anne-Marie Patault, *Introduction historique au droit des biens* (Paris, 1989), p. 283.

someone holding the property in allodium (that is, independently of a lord or lessor), was nothing more than a possessor and, as such, always had to take account of the interests of relatives by blood or marriage, whether born or not-yet-born. As a recent historian of French law put it, "the idea of patrimony, today considered as an extension of the person, is foreign to old law."[5] Patault more fully explained that in the North, the term "proprietor" did not imply "ownership" in the modern sense; moreover, it had nothing to do with the sense implied by Roman law:

The word ["proprietor"] does not designate the control of the physical property but only the use of its fruits. It no more evokes the proud, powerful individual of Roman law, who does not take into account human relations. He [the possessor of property in the conception of northern custom] is only the partial master, embedded in the network of relationships with others and legitimated by the group. "Property" is not sovereignty, it is only, and quite practically, the legitimization of rights to take the profit from land. It does not encompass the physical property itself, it is nothing but the exploitation of the physical property.[6]

Although the equation between immovables and patrimony in the North (*heritages, erve, Erbgüter*) was rough and – as we shall see – unstable, the equation between movables and chattels was considerably less messy. Movables *were* chattels (*cateux, cateylen, Fahrnis*). Hence, movables were usually thought to be "owned" in the way we might understand the term today and in the way Roman law conceived it. Typically such goods followed no necessary route of transmission at the death of their owner and in fact were thought to change ownership simply with physical transfer. According to most customs they could be bequeathed by

---

[5] Ourliac and Gazzaniga, *Histoire du droit privé français*, p. 254.

[6] Patault, *Introduction historique au droit des biens*, p. 19; she further explained that "during the central Middle Ages the words *proprietas, dominium* were always used by the scribes who were mechanically reproducing a desiccated vocabulary from Roman law; there are many texts that refer to 'property' but from the thirteenth century the Roman-law jurists . . . generalized the Roman-law terms *proprietas, dominium*, to designate a polymorphous technique of [wealth-] appropriation that has nothing in common with the Roman-law sense of 'property' except the name itself," p. 19. Also see Heirbaut, *Over lenen en families*, p. 23, and Godding, *Le droit privé*, esp. sections 190–2 on pp. 141–3.

testament with comparative ease, although testamentary laws frequently limited the total value of such goods that could exit the family line. Hence, as Patault put it, circulation – the right to buy and sell, alienate, or encumber a good – was understood in northern customary law as "the defining characteristic of the movable. . . . From the Middle Ages until the [French] Revolution, the movable was the only valid basis for the freedom to alienate."[7]

Given the awkward fit between the term "immovable" either in Roman law or in common speech and the northern concepts of patrimony, given that a northerner subject to customary law could not "own" patrimony (no matter whether it was called immovables, *heritages*, *erve*, or *Erbgüter*), and given that it was not exactly clear what was movable and what was not, there was bound to be trouble. The confusion showed up in litigation records, statute law, and written custom of the age, especially in commercial settings.[8] Commerce separated the products of land such as crops and animals from the land itself, rendering them potential commodities, movables in the fullest sense of the word; it also gave valuable movables like jewels and furs quasi-patrimonial powers; and it even threatened to make land, medieval Europe's preeminent immovable, economically – if not physically – movable. "Movable" no longer necessarily meant physically movable, but only economically movable; still worse, physically immovable no longer meant economically immovable. These instabilities fueled both a gradual, if uneven and uncertain, reconceptualization of the terms "movable" and "immovable" themselves and a radical readjustment of property law.

THE RECORD OF CHANGE IN GHENT

These instabilities and the reconceptualization that followed are clearly recorded in the Flemish city of Ghent, one of northern Europe's most important commercial and industrial centers of the late Middle Ages.

---

[7] Patault, *Introduction historique au droit des biens*, p. 291.

[8] Legal historians have documented the technical changes in law in various regions, but only rarely have they called attention to the larger implications of this story. See, for one exception, the comment by Godding in *Le droit privé*, pp. 142–3.

As in most customary legal regimes of the North, in Ghent the struggles over the meaning of movables and immovables or chattels and patrimony (known to the Dutch-speaking people of Ghent, the Gentenaren, as *meublen* and *immeublen* or *catelyn* and *erve*, respectively) took place surrounding marriage. Marital property law, along with laws of succession and inheritance that were tied to it, was the principal vehicle for managing property transfers between families and between generations; it was thus the primary arena in which Gentenaren used property to do patrimonial work.

Under Ghent's custom, as under most northern customs of the period, when couples married they automatically created a conjugal fund, which was made up of two categories of property. One comprised jointly owned goods, and the other was made up of goods reserved for the individual spouses and what was often referred to as their "line," meaning children from the marriage or, in their absence, collateral or ascendant lineal kin.[9] The first kinds of goods, those jointly owned, were called "partible" (*deelbar*) because they were divisible among the heirs of the deceased spouse and the surviving spouse (or the heirs of that spouse if both wife and husband were dead). Ghent's partible account was thus what legal scholars usually call (as did many contemporaries) the community property fund or common account, its name evoking the fact that such property was shared by husband and wife (and eventually their children and other heirs). Although the fund was technically co-owned, during the marriage it was in most regimes entirely managed – and effectively owned – by the husband. As the head of household he could buy, sell, exchange, alienate, or encumber the assets however he wished, without asking permission of his wife, their children, or any potential heir of either spouse.[10]

---

[9] According to some regional customs *all* property brought to a marriage or acquired thereafter was considered joint; "universal" community property accounts, as they were called, were customary in, for example, Douai and Orchies.

[10] Article XXI-7 of the draft custom written in 1546 explained, "During the marriage he may alienate or transport all houses, leases, gold, silver, whether minted or not, secured and unsecured redeemable rents, peat or peat ground, wherever it is or whence it came, on land, fief, or heritable property, without her consent, wish, or knowledge." The clause was repeated, almost verbatim,

The second kind of goods, those reserved for the line of the deceased spouse and thus assigned the patrimonial task, were called "impartible" (not *deelbar*). At death, the impartibles of the deceased spouse passed to lineal heirs (and were divided among them according to rules particular to each legal regime); in Ghent and in many other places with similar customs, the surviving spouse had lifetime rights to half the *income* produced by the assets that went to the deceased spouse's heirs, but his or her heirs did not assume those rights at the surviving spouse's death. During marriage the husband typically could manage his wife's impartibles, but sometimes only under the direct supervision of her natal kin, and he could not alienate them without her express permission.

In Ghent, just as in many other places, the distinction between community (or partible) and lineal (or impartible) goods roughly paralleled the distinction between movable property (*meublen*) and immovable property (*immeublen*) and the approximately equivalent division between *cateylen* and *erve*, but the parallelism was very rough indeed. The result was instability, and the equations' instabilities were the source of constant legal trouble in Ghent. It was here that Gentenaren conducted and registered their struggle to decide just how freely the "market" should operate.

In one respect, things seemed relatively simple: all goods defined as movable in law were considered *cateylen*, and no matter whether they were referred to as *meubles* or as *cateylen* they were partible.[11] As we shall

in the Homologized Custom of 1563, article XX-23. See note 15, this chapter for a full description of these sources.

It was only when her husband died that the woman acquired her rights, but even then she assumed ownership of only half the assets; the other half passed to the deceased husband's lineal heirs. Even if those heirs were minor children born of the marriage and the widow managed the assets on their behalf, she did so only as a trustee and under the supervision of adult relatives of the deceased husband. The reverse was also true; if the wife died first, the 50% of the community account that ultimately belonged to her passed to her lineal heirs, preferentially to her children; the survivor of her marriage, even if he was the father of those children, did not have full authority over that portion of the community account.

[11] Sometimes movable goods were referred to as *meublen*, echoing the Latin; more often they were referred to with the indigenous term *cateylen*. André Castaldo has argued that, in some places, the term *cateux* did acquire a distinct meaning as

see, however, it was no simple matter to decide whether a good was movable or not. The greatest problem came as immovables entered the market, for once available to the market they lost or threatened to lose their capacity to do patrimonial work. In effect, they were no longer what Gentenaren called *erve*. Some of these immovables came to be judged partible (movable in an economic sense), creating the somewhat odd term "partible [i.e., movable] immovables." As we shall see, other immovables, although also made movable in an economic sense, did *not* lose their quality as impartible *erve*; that is, as wealth that had somehow to be reserved for the family line from which these immovables came. They were thus effectively "movable" in one sense but they were not partible; in effect, they were movable impartibles, although no one actually coined that phrase. The story of these developments is complicated, and some of its elements are lost to us. But the broad outlines are clear, and in the following pages I sketch just how it was that Gentenaren managed not only to make some immovables economically movable and also partible, thus depriving them of patrimonial capacity, but also to make other immovables economically movable but *not* partible, thus preserving their status as *erve*; that is, as patrimonial property or what Gentenaren often referred to as property "of the line."

Although this story was particular to Ghent, because customary law was by definition local and particular, the tensions registered in Ghent's sources were felt everywhere commercial people confronted a legal system that similarly distinguished movable from immovable goods and elided those terms with chattels and patrimony, and wherever marital property law was the vehicle for establishing and preserving the patrimonial status of property.[12] In its general structure, the

goods that were, strictly speaking, not movable but that were not being treated as heritable: "Beaumanoir, les cateux et les meubles par anticipation," *Tijdschrift voor Rechtsgeschiedenis* 68:1 (2000), pp. 1–46. In one scholar's description, these were "the less important goods, the less durable, the consumables or those which did not actually produce revenues." Marcel Fréjaville has, however, noted [*Des meubles par anticipation* (Paris, 1927)] that in Ghent *meublen* and *cateylen* were, in effect, equated even though there too the texts often took the trouble to use both terms.

[12] Local custom reigned in the Low Countries and northern France as it did nowhere else, not even in German-speaking lands, England, or the Scandinavian territories. In both regions, private law (law governing relations between

Ghent system was like those throughout the Low Countries, although each place had its peculiarities and there were some exceptions to the general rule. Ghent's custom also resembled those of northeastern France, northwestern Germany, and England in that most of those regimes combined a community property account with a lineal account, just as Gentenaren did, in effect making the first account "partible" and the second "impartible" (although few others used these precise terms).

Ghent was not only generally representative of regional custom but was also an important city. The second largest northern city of the fourteenth and much of the fifteenth centuries, Ghent was also the region's leading center of commercially oriented industry until the end of the Middle Ages when Antwerp and then Amsterdam displaced it.[13] With a base in both production and commerce, it stood at the center of the commercial revolution – an even purer creature of movable property than Bruges, its more glamorous but smaller neighbor, or Paris, the political, cultural, and demographic giant of the urban North. The city's influence thus extended beyond its walls, and as customary law was gradually homologized in the region during the sixteenth century, decisions taken in Ghent would have been reflected elsewhere.

The city has left rich sources for tracing the long history of its customary law. Most of the accessible documents are normative in character, ranging from occasional proclamations to rulings to formal statements of customary practices; most date from the late thirteenth century to

---

individuals rather than between public authorities and individuals) was consequently highly nonuniform, varying from region to region, even from city to city. The situation in the Low Countries was, however, particularly unsettled, in part because in that highly urbanized region movable wealth played a much larger economic role than it did in the French realm.

[13] Ghent is estimated to have had a fourteenth-century population of sixty thousand and Paris had about one hundred thousand to one hundred and fifty thousand residents. Some scholars put London apparently ahead of Ghent, and many have argued that before the Black Death London was larger still, but most agree that London's population did not pass fifty thousand until the sixteenth century. See Derek Keene, "Sites of Desire: Shops, Selds and Wardrobes in London and Other English Cities, 1100–1550," in eds. Bruno Blondé, Peter Stabel, Jon Stobart, and Ilja Van Damme, *Buyers & Sellers: Retail Circuits and Practices in Medieval and Early Modern Europe* (Tournhout, Belg., 2006), p. 125.

the first formally Homologized Custom of 1563. Similar records survive
from later years, of course, but after 1563 the records belong to a larger
story of legal change driven by the ducal court and by legal theory
drawn more systematically from Roman law, so that we can never be
certain who or what was driving change. Alongside these normative
texts stand two principal forms of "records of practice": (1) a selection
of judgments (*vonnissen*) rendered by the aldermen of Ghent's *Gedele*, the
committee of the aldermen who dealt with matters of inheritance and
who thus adjudicated many disputes about rights to property,[14] and
(2) a selection of binding legal opinions (*turben*) delivered to the aldermen at the request of one of the parties to a suit and issued by a board
of experts.[15]

[14] The other board of alderman, called the *Keure*, was largely responsible for
witnessing and sealing documents concerning property transfers, judging disputes, deciding criminal cases, and drafting and issuing ordinances. For a fuller
description of these judicial bodies and their functions see note 50.

[15] Four principal normative texts, supplemented by occasional proclamations,
charters, and similar texts, are one basis of this study. Most have been published:

1. The *Grande Charte* of 1297, a privilege granted by the Count of Flanders to
   what was already his most important industrial center: "Grande Charte des
   Gantois" (8 April 1297, n.s.) in *Coutumes des pays et comté de Flandre: Coutumes
   de la ville de Gand* I, ed. A. E. Gheldolf (Brussels, 1868), pp. 426–95:
   abbreviated hereafter as GC.

2. A text prepared by Ghent's aldermen (*scepenen*), which exists in three
   manuscript versions, summarizing the customary rules of succession in
   Ghent and dating from the early sixteenth century: "Costumen gheusseert
   ende onderhauden binnen der stede von Ghendt in materie van successien
   ende verdeelen" (approx. mid-sixteenth century), in Eduard M. Meijers, *Het
   Oost-Vlaamsche Erfrecht* [abbreviated hereafter as OVE] (The Hague, 1936),
   Bijlage III, pp. 104–13: abbreviated hereafter as SC.

3. A draft of the city's entire custom, prepared by the aldermen in 1546: "Cahier
   primitive de la coutume de Gand" (1546), in. ed. Gheldolf, pp. 169–383:
   abbreviated hereafter as DC.

4. The 1563 Homologized Custom, a revision of the 1546 custom that finally
   earned ducal approval: "Coutume homologuée de la ville de Gand," in ed.
   Gheldolf, pp. 1–167: abbreviated hereafter as HC.

A selection of the huge archive of records of practice has also been edited.
However, most lie – unindexed and largely unexamined – in Ghent's municipal
archive and are realistically accessible only in small samples. Still, enough

The terms "movables" and "immovables" appeared in the earliest records of this sort, almost always in phrases that equated them with chattels (*cateylen*), on the one hand, or patrimony (*erve*), on the other. Certain goods posed few problems. Clothing and stored provisions; domesticated animals; and household or commercial goods such as furniture, utensils, inventories, raw materials, and hand tools were all indisputably movable and chattel-like.[16] They were thus partible. All extant summaries of custom from this period listed the goods considered *cateylen*

> material concerning actual practice is available to test the applicability of formal statements of law and to trace change and contest in a way that the normative documents can only suggest:
>
> 1. *Registers van Gedele* (aka *Weezenboeken*): beginning in 1349, running continuously (selectively published in *Coutumes* I and in Meijers, *OVE*, Bijlage I, pp. 3–77).
> 2. *Turben* (opinions having the status of law) (published in Meijers, *OVE*, Bijlage II, pp. 77–104).
>
> These texts are supplemented by other documents edited in *Coutumes* I (and cited here separately). Three secondary studies using the same sources constitute another basis of this study: Meijers, *OVE*, which provides a useful guide to archival material concerning inheritance and a discussion of selected texts from that archive; Mariane Danneel, *Weduwen en Wezen in het laat-middeleeuwse Gent* (Leuven-Apeldoorn, 1995), and Godding, *Le droit privé*.

[16] Various clauses of the Homologized Custom of 1563 laboriously detailed the items in the category: article XXV-4, for example, listed "trees grown to the width of a man's hand span and chest high, logs, chattels, leases and mortgages, minted and unminted coin, jewels and baubles, household furnishings, weapons, bows, stocks of munitions, horses and harnesses, peat and stone that has been mined . . . excepting the shade trees and best residence on a fief that are expected to follow the fief"; article XXV-6 listed houses or parts of houses in addition to all movables acquired during marriage; article XXV-22 listed annuities (*lijfrenten*); article XXV-24 listed income due from leases but not yet paid; XXV-27 included the income from repurchasable rents (*losrenten*); XXV-28 specified nonhypothecated (*onbesette*) rents, even if they had been purchased with impartibles that "held side"; article XXV-30 included windmills on fiefs, excepting the parts that were not physically movable; windmills on simple *erve*, however, were movable in their entirety; XXV-31 provided that watermills were movable just like houses and trees, even if on a fief, but in that case the *stoel metten legghere* ("chair with mill-stone") went with the fief; subsequent articles XXV-32–XXV-38 provided detailed instructions about trees and fish, whereas XXV-39 declared all "personal debts arising from expenses" partible.

or movables. Because the lists were usually embedded in the sections of the customs or rulings that treated marital property law, the goods were often simply called partible, without further designation. The *vonnissen* and *turben* I consulted were almost always generated in disputes about marital property law, so here too the question was simply whether a good was partible. Despite the care with which aldermen made their lists, however, there were many areas of uncertainty and many kinds of goods that were hard to classify or whose classification was changed as a result of challenges or further reflection. The following four sections illustrate not only how hard it could be to decide what was movable in law but also how much was at stake in that decision.

Products of the Land

Products of the land posed special problems because, being quintessentially "of" the land, they were in some sense immovable *erve* and hence impartible according to the logic of custom. Nevertheless, they were physically separable from the land and, moreover, easily marketable. However, law could not easily imagine such goods as commodities, things to be bought and sold like cloth or beer, used up, converted into cash, or perhaps lost in market speculation.

In 1399, the status of unsown seed corn was in dispute. Although apparently unsown seed corn was usually considered movable and thus partible, the aldermen were called upon to confirm a widow's claim that it was in fact movable and thus 50 percent hers.[17] Almost two hundred years later, when the Homologized Custom was issued, the status of seed corn still remained unsettled. That document explained that seed corn

---

One of the few cases appearing to question this norm concerned a bed (*bedde*) that was deemed partible because it was "feathered" (*een bedde daer plumen inne waren*). See Meijers, *OVE*, Bijlage I, *Vonnis* of 28 August 1358, #12, p. 12. Tools for a trade were also usually considered movables, but, to give just one example, in the small city of Uccle near Brussels, cauldrons used in enameling were immovable. Mills in the southern Low Countries were also variously categorized, depending on whether they could be transported and whether they were built on land held in fief, and so on. For these examples, see Godding, *Le droit privé*, p. 145.

[17] *Coutumes* I, pp. 564ff.

could be divided 50/50 between the surviving spouse and heirs, as chattels were supposed to be, but only if the surviving spouse provided the aldermen with proof of its value (and presumably proof that it had been purchased out of the community account).[18] The court seemed to say that seed corn might well be partible, but any widow or widower making that claim had to prove it.

In contrast, a seeded crop, one already in the ground but not yet ready for harvest, was usually considered part of the land and thus securely immovable. But, according to a *vonnis* of 1350, the surviving spouse of a marriage was to be compensated for the costs of sowing the seed, presumably because the couple had borne those costs together, out of their joint property. The reasoning must have been that, having paid 50 percent of the planting costs, the surviving spouse had to be repaid for his or her expenses.[19] That 1350 ruling assumed, however, that the crops were not ready for harvest. When the crop was closer to harvest, the decision was reversed on the theory that by then the seed had become a marketable crop and hence it was movable.[20] According to the same ruling, summer crops became movable after mid-May, a position reiterated in a *vonnis* of 1415.[21]

[18] HC, article XXIV-51.

[19] Meijers, *OVE*, Bijlage I, *vonnis* of 26 July 1350, #2, pp. 3–4. Also see idem, *vonnis* of 13 February 1370 (ns?), #14, p. 72.

[20] A *vonnis* of 1371 decreed that "winter" crops in the ground were immovable, but only if the death of the landowner had occurred before mid-March: Meijers, *OVE*, Bijlage I, #24, pp. 21–3, *vonnis* of 10 December 1371. Winter crops or "winter fruit" were those planted in fall for spring harvest.

[21] *Coutumes* I, pp. 588–90. These are crops sown in early spring for summer harvest. One document from that period that listed customary norms regarding inheritance and marital property arrangements made no distinction between summer and winter crops, assigning the mid-March cut-off date to both; SC, article 23. Meijers, *OVE*, p. 37, n. 6, however, argues that this is a textual error.

Other goods considered products of the land were subject to the same uncertainty. According to a 1363 judgment, for example, peat, a major source of heating fuel in the region, was partible once harvested (or when the harvest was "underway"), but peat land itself was patrimony (although leased peat land was chattel): *vonnis* of 29 June 1363, in Meijers, *OVE*, Bijlage I, #17, p. 16. However, the early-sixteenth-century statement of customary rules extended peat's movability much further, counting it (along with the stone in the ground) as movable, apparently without consideration of its relationship to the expected

Trees caused even more confusion, so much more that we have an extraordinarily rich record of these disputes. Apple trees (*appelboomen*) more than "knee high" were specifically labeled movable in the early-sixteenth-century listing of customary rules (the aldermen's drafts), a statement seeming to confirm a *vonnis* from 1367 (though there the term is *bogarde* or orchard).[22] However, a *turbe* of 1525 seems to have revised this norm, for it deemed all "fruit trees" (*fruutboomen*) movables, without qualification regarding height.[23] The Homologized Custom of 1563 repeated the same blanket convention, adding that if the trees were located on a fief (which was *impartible*), along with its principal dwelling and major "shade" trees, they were nevertheless divisible as movables (here they were called *fruytboomen*).[24] Although clear at one level – apple or fruit trees are movables – these texts are ambiguous at another, for it is not clear whether the trees had to have reached a certain stage of growth. It is not even clear whether "apple trees," "fruit trees," and "orchards" were the same things in the eyes of litigants and the court alike. Nothing in the available sources directly tells us, but it is reasonable to suspect that the instability of terminology and the frequency with which fruit-bearing trees appear in our sources are the traces of ongoing debate over their legal status.

When we turn from fruit trees to trees without edible fruits, we confront an even more dizzying record. Some texts flatly labeled all trees movable, but others implied that only certain trees, of certain heights or age or in certain locations, were movable. A 1371 *vonnis*, for example, flatly labeled trees (*boemen*) movable, as did others of 1399 and 1415; both the draft custom of 1546 and the Homologized Custom of 1563

harvest date. Fish also showed up in court. To judge from a ruling rendered in 1367, all fish were movable, but the early-sixteenth-century customal extended movability only to pond fish, a ruling reiterated in a *turbe* of 1525, and the customal of 1563 elaborated the clause to include fish in the ramparts, along with nets and fishing equipment: see *vonnis* of 12 May 1367, in Meijers, *OVE*, Bijlage I, #22, pp. 20–1; and Meijers, *OVE*, Bijlage II, *turbe* of September 1525, #1, p. 79.

[22] *Vonnis* of 16 June 1367, in Meijers, *OVE*, Bijlage I, #23, p. 21.

[23] *Turbe* of September 1525, in Meijers, *OVE*, Bilage II, #1, p. 79.

[24] Articles XXV-4 and XXV-34.

used the same term in many clauses.[25] But other litigation records (and even certain sections of the same normative texts otherwise referring simply to "trees") complicated matters to the point of apparent chaos. A *vonnis* of 1363 decreed bushes (*bosch*) movable if "one customarily cut them," and another of 1367 confirmed that willows (*wulghen*) were movable, with both texts suggesting that litigants had contested the principle and were seeking exceptions.[26] The early-sixteenth-century aldermen's drafts introduced still more vocabulary. Article 17 flatly declared "grown trees, dry or green" (*upgaende boomen, drooghe often groene*) movable, whether on fief or free land, whether inside the city or outside it. Article 20 declared oaken stumps (*tronckycken*) movable if the branches or twigs (*trijshoudt*) were older than seven years (the branches themselves were also movable, the authors of the document took pains to remark). Pine hedges (*dornehagen*), however, were movable only after three years (article 21), and alder hedges (*elshaghen*) had to wait five years (article 22). However, a *turbe* of 1531 seemed to overturn the earlier statement regarding oaken stumps; it declared them movable even if located on a fief, and no age limit was indicated.[27] A slightly earlier *turbe* of 1525 provided the same ruling but also introduced entirely new terms: wood (*hauten*) was movable, even if on a fief, but the shade trees (*schauboomen*) were not, and cut wood (*slachoudt*) was movable so long as the shoots or limbs (*schueten*) were at least three years old.[28]

---

[25] *Vonnis* of 12 October 1367, in Meijers, *OVE*, Bijlage I, #24, p. 21; *Vonnissen* of 1399 and 1415 in *Coutumes* I, pp. 564–9 and 588–90; DC of 1546, article V-3; HC of 1563, XX-3 and passim.

[26] *Vonnis* of 29 June 1363, in Meijers, *OVE*, Bijlage I, #17, p. 16; *vonnis* of 12 May 1367, in ibid, #22, pp. 20–1.

[27] *Turbe* of 17 May 1531, in Meijers, *OVE*, Bijlage II, #37, pp. 99–100.

[28] *Turbe* of September 1525, in Meijers, *OVE*, Bilage II, #1, p. 79. The DC of 1546 compounded the confusion. It simply declared that *boomen* ("trees") were movable, excepting only the *schauboomen* ("shade trees") on a fief. The HC of 1563 seemed to revert to the kinds of distinctions elaborated in earlier texts. The movable account, it explained, was to include only those "shade trees" whose trunks were wider than two hands and higher than the chest, along with *troncken*, again excluding the shade trees on fiefs: articles XXI-14 and XXI-31 of the 1546 DC; articles XXV-4 and XXV-18 of the 1563 HC. Article XXV-32 of that text again named *slachoudt* ("cut wood") movable, confirming

Contemporaries had good reason for their concern about such seemingly minute technicalities, for products of the land were extremely
valuable assets. Seed yields then were only about 4:1 or 5:1, and crop
yields seldom exceeded five bushels per acre (today in Western countries they are easily ten to twenty times that amount). These low yields
made foodstuffs so expensive that a family's subsistence diet took up a
significant portion of the daily wage of an adult male unskilled worker,
and in some years took all of it.[29] Under those conditions, any surviving
spouse, no matter how rich, would have taken care to ensure a crop's
partibility (in which case he or she walked away with half the asset),
whereas the heirs of the land would have been as eager to have a decision
counting it impartible (in which case they got it all and had to share only
half of any income it produced during the life of the surviving spouse).
Whether used for their fruit, as fuel, or for furniture and construction,
trees were even more valuable than a crop in the ground. Ghent was in
the part of Europe where most woodland had long ago been decimated,
where lords valued their privileged access to forests above most other
rights, where Baltic lumber was not yet a regular import, and where
peat was the sole readily available fuel substitute. Even the rich hoarded
wood carefully and used it sparingly; so cherished was this item that
some people made special bequests of it in their wills.

Ghent's *Weezenboeken* (Orphans' Books), in which most disputes concerning succession and inheritance were recorded, contain many cases
that demonstrate my point. In 1367, for example, the aldermen were

---

the minimum age of three years, and the next article (XXV-33) reiterated that
doornehagen were movable if three years old but was more specific, adding that
the *rys, haer of waey* ("twigs, sprigs, or branches") were included in that ruling.

[29] For measures of subsistence wages in the fourteenth and fifteenth centuries, see
Jean-Pierre Sosson, *Les Travaux publics de la ville de Bruges, XIVe–XVe siècles: Les
Materiaux, les hommes* (Brussels, 1977), pp. 230–1 and 308–9. For the sixteenth
century, see Johan Dambruyne, *Corporatieve middengroepen: Aspiraties, relaties en
transformaties in de 16 de-eeuwse Gentse ambachtswereld* (Ghent, 2002) and the
sources he cites. Also see Raymond van Uytven, "Splendor or Wealth: Arts
and Economy in the Burgundian Netherlands," in *Production and Consumption
in the Low Countries, 13th–16th Centuries* (Aldershot, UK, 2001), pp. 103–4;
originally published in *Bijdragen en Mededelingen betreffende de Geschiedenis der
Nederlanden* LXXXVII (The Hague, 1972), pp. 60–93.

called upon to decide a case involving a few of the city's richest merchant families who were at odds over the division of property between the husband's heirs and his widow (who was herself a second wife). Several landed estates, including property held in fief, were at issue, and the case generated at least three separate *vonnissen*.[30] Many of the items under contention were ordinary household goods, movables that might seem to us of such little value that wealthy people would not bother to bring them to court. For example, one of the ten points covered in the first of these documents treated the provisions that remained in the pantry or cellar of the widow. Another item concerned the movables on the various properties that were to be divided between the widow and the heirs.[31] The subsequent *vonnis*, delivered less than one month later, settled an argument regarding the status of fences (*hekken*) that were located on land otherwise classified as *erve*. Although the widow strenuously argued that the fences belonged to the *erve* she had brought to the marriage and should thus remain hers, the court ruled otherwise, confirming the heirs' claim that they were truly movables and thus eligible for partition between them and the widow. The last ruling published in this series provided a detailed scheme for dividing the trees and willows (*wulghen*) on three separate land holdings.[32]

Similar disputes clogged other European courtrooms wherever law created the partible/impartible divide, basing it on whether property was movable or immovable and assigning different privileges to each. According to Amy Erickson, in early modern English law,

[certain] moveables . . . were classified by arcane legal reasoning as adjuncts to a freehold – and therefore belonging to the heir [in Ghent's terminology, these

---

[30] *Vonnissen* 1367, in Meijers, *OVE*, Bijlage I, #s 20–2, pp. 18–21.

[31] The settlement required that the *vinders* (experts called in to represent each side and reach agreement) select a "handbickere" (wood carver) and a "temmerman" (carpenter) to represent their side and that each of these experts appraise the movables in question. The precise nature of the movables in question is unknown, but we can assume that trees, lumber, and wooden structures were the most important of them, because both specialists came from the woodworking crafts.

[32] *Vonnix* of 12 May 1367, in Meijers, *OVE*, Bijlage I, #22, pp. 20–1.

would be labeled impartibles] . . . : grass or trees on the ground; glass windows, window shutters, wainscots, coppers, leads, ovens or anything (including tables and chairs) affixed to a freehold; any object designated in a will as an 'heirloom' which 'customarily' goes with the freehold; vats in the brewhouse; anvils, millstones and mangers; keys in a box or chest with the owners 'evidences'; hawks, hounds, doves in the dove-house and fish in the pond.[33]

In England, it seems, the line between partible and impartible was sometimes even more difficult to draw than it was in Ghent.

Houses and Buildings

Ghent's troubles with crops, trees, or fish would not have surprised English people, but the Flemings' decision about houses might well have, for in Ghent houses were considered movable. A *vonnis* of 1350, another of 1359, a third in 1399, and a fourth in 1415 all routinely included houses (*huusen*) as movables or chattels, usually by simply announcing that they were partible.[34] A *turbe* of 1529 repeated the principle, whereas the aldermen's drafts of the early sixteenth century elaborated further: article 16 intoned that "all houses or parts of houses" were movable, a ruling repeated in a subsequent article as well.[35] The draft custom of 1546 made the point more strongly: "houses in Ghent are, according to the custom, partible and considered chattels and movable property."[36] The Homologized Custom of 1563 repeated that clause almost verbatim. The only issue that appeared unsettled

---

[33] Amy Louise Erickson, *Women and Property in Early Modern England* (London: Routledge, 1993), pp. 33–4. On this issue, also see Albert Rigaudière, "Connaissance, composition et estimation du 'moble' à travers quelque livres d'estimes du Midi français (XIVe–XVe siècles)," in *Gouverner la ville au Moyen Âge* (Paris, 1993), esp. p. 338.

[34] *Vonnis* of 18 February 1350 (ns), in Meijers, *OVE*, Bijlage I #4, p. 3; *vonnis* of 8 April 1359, in ibid, #14, p. 14; *vonnis* of 1399, in *Coutumes* I, p. 564; *vonnis* of 1415, in *Coutumes*, pp. 588–90.

[35] *Turbe* of 5 June 1529, in Meijers, *OVE*, Bijlage II, #17, pp. 87–8; SC, article 17.

[36] Article X-25; repeated in VI-19 of the HC of 1563; also see article XXI-31 of DC 1546, where houses in the city are once again specifically labeled partible.

concerned houses located on land held in fief, for some texts provided that they passed with the fief as patrimonial property (impartible *erve*).[37]

If a social logic informed Ghent's decision to treat houses as movables, it was the logic of commerce. Urban citizens found it convenient to be able to divide and subdivide, buy and sell, lease and sublease houses without restriction, without asking permission, and without worrying about the rights of the next generation to that specific piece of real estate. They were confident that houses were movable and partible. The same logic seems to have governed similar legal decisions in Lille, Antwerp, several cities in West Flanders, and some outside the Low Countries where houses were also ruled movable. In all those places, however, that practice came late, so late that we have a record of the time when houses were all considered immovable and effectively impartible. Not so in Ghent.[38] There houses were, "from time out of mind," movable.

---

[37] Although many of the available texts labeled residences on land held in fief movable, as did article 17 of the early-sixteenth-century aldermen's drafts cited earlier, others introduced qualifications. For example, a *vonnis* of 1411–12 exempted houses on fiefs held by the Duke of Burgundy, ruling that their status was determined by the feudal court with specific jurisdiction: *Vonnis* of 1411–12, in *Coutumes* I, pp. 582–4. A *turbe* of 1525 exempted the "beste vuurst" (best residence) on a fief, and the DC of 1546 provided that a house in the countryside, although movable, could be kept whole by the landowner if he or she compensated the half-owner(s) for their share of its value: *Turbe* of September 1525, in Meijers, *OVE*, Bijlage II, #1, p. 79; DC of 1546, article XXI-36; repeated in HC of 1563, article XXV-35.

[38] For West Flanders, see Meijers, *OVE*, p. 33, n. 4, and more generally for the Low Countries, Godding, *Le droit privé*, pp. 143–4. For Germany, see Ashaver von Brandt, "Mittelalterliche Bürgertestamente: Neuerschlossene Quellen zur Geschichte der materiellen und geistigen Kultur," *Sitzungsberichte der Heidelberger Akademie der Wissenschaft, philosophisch-historische Klasse* 5–32 (Heidelberg, 1973).

Some scholars have argued that such rules were relics of the days when buildings were shabby constructions unlikely to last more than a few years and for that reason unworthy to be designated immovable. Although it may be true that rural customs had evolved as they did in such circumstances, that explanation will not do for cities like Lille, Ghent, or Antwerp. Although there were surely ramshackle sheds and collapsing shacks in all of these cities, the preponderance of buildings – and most of those owned by Ghent's prosperous merchants and artisans, who were, after all, the effective arbiters of custom – were

Land

Although Ghent was not the only place to label houses as movables, the city seems to have been alone in modifying custom so that most land was also deemed partible and thus movable. This story of how this came to be the city's custom is complicated, but it clearly originated from the citizens' insistence that houses were movable. As a result of that provision of custom, when a house and its tenure were being transferred at the end of a marriage, the house would be divided between the survivor of the marriage and the deceased's lineal heirs as a movable, whereas the land on which it sat, being considered patrimonial and thus impartible, would pass directly to heirs or be entirely kept by the survivor, depending on whose "line" could claim it. Consequently, the possessor of the land would never be the full owner of the house that stood on it, and the occupant of the house would possess the land only if he or she could claim it as lineal property.[39] At some point during the fourteenth century, Ghent's aldermen decided to simplify matters by treating both the house and the land as movable property but *only* if the land was encumbered by rental payments, presumably on the theory that the rental payments had been assumed in order to acquire land for building the house.[40] Later even that condition was dropped, and

> built to last, and they, along with the tenure on which they sat, were worth a lot of money.
>
> [39] When a loan (a rent) had been arranged to build or buy a house (or when the property was simply used as collateral for a loan), the odd situation became even odder, for the land was effectively encumbered to finance a house that would have been only half-owned by the obligor on the rent. The GC of 1297 acknowledged the possibility of such a loan in article 122, titled "Regarding encumbering houses located on another man's heritable property (*herve*)." The charter required that the obligation be witnessed (and implicitly authorized) by the landowner and one or more officials (*vor eenen hervachteghen men ofte meer*), a rule reappearing in the HC almost three hundred years later; for the HC, see VII-1 and VII-8.
>
> [40] One of the earliest studies of private law in this region, Meijers's *Het Oost-Vlaamsche erfrecht*, has carefully traced this history. The transition is documented as early as the fourteenth century, when a *vonnis* of 1353 declared that *erve* within Ghent on which rent (*landcijns* or simply *cijns* in the vocabulary of Ghent) was being paid were partible; others from 1371 and 1450 repeated the judgment.

all land in the jurisdiction of Ghent, whether or not it paid rent and whether or not it was built, was considered partible.[41] Thereafter, only land outside Ghent or land held in fief was impartible *erve* or, as we shall see, potentially so.[42]

Meijers understood these judgments to refer to land on which a house had been built and that was paying *landcijns*, for it was exactly the building of the house that had occasioned the *landcijns* itself: *vonnis* of 22 June 1353, in Meijers, *OVE*, Bijlage I, #4, pp. 4–7; *vonnis* of 10 December 1371, in idem, #24, pp. 21–3; *vonnis* of 1450 in *Coutumes* I, p. 628.

Vonnis of 1 April 1359, in Meijers, *OVE*, Bijlage I, #13, p. 12, confirms that land with a house on it is an heritable immovable *unless* the land is paying *landcijns*. Although presumably referring to land on which a house had been constructed and debt had been incurred (hence the *landcijns* or rent), the article does not specifically say that built land is intended. Article 25 of the SC confirms that land in Ghent (that is not in the domain of St. Pieter's or St. Bavon's) that pays rent is partible. It is possible to read article 25 as including unbuilt land paying *landcijns*, but that is not Meijers' reading.

Also *vonnis* of 22 November 1363, in idem, #19, pp. 17–8, which argued that *landcijns* received on land was common (movable) property even if the land producing the income was immovable *erve* and not part of the common account. Note, however, that the issue here was that the husband had used *cateylen* in the marriage's common account to improve the land and thus increase its value as a rented property. Although the *vije eerve* was his, the movables that went with the land were joint, and it was on those grounds that the widow had an equal (or proportionate) claim to the income.

[41] The ruling is first visible in a *turbe* of 1529 in which "all land within the jurisdiction of Ghent" was deemed *cateyl*: *Turbe* of 1529, in Meijers #22, pp. 91–2 of Bijlage. Section XXI-27 of the 1546 DC was equally precise: "Land 'holds side' (i.e., is impartible) *except* [emphasis added] land that is within the city, which is movable." The 1563 HC extended the reach to the suburbs of Ghent: "land holds the side from which it came, along with the usufruct attaching to it, *except* [emphasis added] the land inside the city and outer fortifications of the city [which] is partible": HC, article XXV-29. The clause further deems land outside the fortifications but within Ghent's jurisdiction to be partible unless it is held of a lord secular or ecclesiastical.

[42] Danneel, *Weduwen en wezen*, cites two cases (p. 268, note 81) appearing to indicate that, if a house with land paying rent had been acquired before marriage or had come to one of the spouses as a gift or inheritance during marriage, the land portion was treated as heritable and only the house entered the community of goods. (See pp. 79–82 following for the significance of the rule concerning patrimonial goods brought to a marriage.) I have been able to check only one

Debts, Credits, and the Associated Encumbered Property

Debt obligations were an even more complex matter. In principle, debts were unsecured, so creditors had to make their decision to extend a loan based not on the worth of any particular asset but on the personal credit of the borrower. Hence, only movables, the sole property "personal" to the borrower, could be used to service debts. A French adage of the day expressed the concept succinctly: "movables are the seat of debts" (*meubles sont sièges des dettes*).[43] Although a particular loan might be understood as having been generated, for example, by the purchase of horses, beer, or cloth, it was not the horses, beer, or cloth that was pledged to the lender as security for the loan. Instead, it was the borrower's word alone, his or her own personal pledge to pay. If he or she defaulted, the creditor could begin a legal process to seize the movables of the debtor, not just the horses, beer, or cloth.[44]

This basic rule was preserved in all the normative statements issued by the aldermen and in all the rulings issued by municipal courts. For example, a *vonnis* of 1350 flatly declared that debts were to be charged against the movable account of a marriage.[45] Another of 1371 was similar: all "payments or receipts on debts, income and expenses" (*huutsculden, insculden, baten ende comer*) were movable.[46] Article 2 of the early-sixteenth-century aldermen's drafts confirmed the rule, specifically naming all "obligations arising from income and expenses" (*schulden van baten ende van commerce*), whereas article 32 of the same text mentioned

of Danneel's cases: *Gedele* 330, #39, fols. 133–4, 13 April 1491. There we indeed find an *eervachticheden* ("patrimonial property") consisting of land and a house, and the aldermen did indeed determine that the land "held side" (was impartible), whereas the house itself was partible. However, this land was not in the jurisdiction of Ghent, but in Deestinghem, and according to Ghent's custom as then expressed such land would indeed have "held side."

[43] Patault, *Introduction historique au droit des biens*, p. 282.

[44] The notion that debts were personal and thus payable out of personal – movable – property alone had important implications for economic life. Debts "owned" by lenders (what we might call "collectibles, "accounts receivable," "debt payments due," and the like) could easily be bought and sold, allowing lenders to trade future income for present cash.

[45] *Vonnis* of 15 August 1350, in Meijers, *OVE*, Bijlage I, #3, p. 4.

[46] *Vonnis* of 10 December 1371, in Meijers, *OVE*, Bijlage II, #24, pp. 21–3.

"all debts" and article 26 broadly included all "encumbered revenue" (*besproken blat*). A *turbe* of 1531 listed all contracts and obligations (*contracten* and *obligatien*).[47] The draft custom of 1546 continued the litany, and the Homologized Custom of 1563 repeated it.[48] Other texts specifically mentioned the income received by creditors when borrowers made payments. These payments too, the texts insisted, were movable, as were lease payments made or received, on the grounds that they were personal obligations of the lessee, not secured by the property itself (which remained the possession of the lessor).[49]

The *Jaarregisters* (literally, Annual Registers) of Ghent's aldermen of the *Keure* testify to the ubiquity of such unsecured debts.[50] In December

[47] *Turbe* of 12 July 1531, in Meijers, *OVE*, Bijlage II, #38, p. 100.

[48] In DC of 1546, articles XXI-39 and 44. In HC of 1563, articles XXV-39 and 44.

[49] See, for example, a *vonnis* of 1415 in *Coutumes* I, pp. 588–90; another of April 15 1357, in Meijers, *OVE*, Bijlage I, #10, pp. 11–12 and idem, *vonnis* of 12 May 1357, #11, p. 12; a *vonnis* of April 1359 in idem, #13, pp. 12–14, and another of 10 December 1371 in idem, #24, pp. 21–3. These rules were repeated, intact, in the 1546 DC (articles XXI-22 and 26).

[50] From the fourteenth century forward, civil (private) matters were dealt with by two separate groups of aldermen (*scepenen*): the *Keure* and the *Gedele*. The former dealt with matters of property transactions, debts, etc., and the latter largely with inheritance and what were called *zoenen* or compensation payments for personal (and physical) injury. The annual registers of the *Keure* (the *Jaarregisters van de Keure*, series 301) were transcriptions of financial agreements voluntarily brought to the aldermen for registration. They cover the period 1339 to 1679 (with some interruptions); there are sixty-six folio volumes for the fourteenth and fifteenth centuries combined. Although registration was voluntary and originally did not serve as legal evidence of a transaction or agreement, by the late fourteenth century, the record was coming to serve as evidence.

Most registrations in the early *Jaarregisters* concern movables, not real property. Before the fourteenth century, most transactions of real property were registered with what were called *viri hereditarii* or *erfachtige lieden*, which by the early fourteenth century had come to mean those who owned real property. Most of these transactions involved ecclesiastical institutions. Nevertheless, some of the entries in the early *Jaarregisters* are transcriptions of agreements that had previously been made with the *erfachtige lieden* and thereafter registered with the aldermen, presumably as an added protection. By the late fourteenth century, the institution of the *erfachtige lieden* had lost importance, at least for lay people in Ghent, and the aldermen had all but replaced them as registrars. For a fuller

1400 alone, for example, Gentenaren registered 114 debt agreements with the aldermen. Fifty-nine of the entries – more than half – recorded obligations of unspecified origin and without specific security, just as custom imagined.[51] For example, Willem Raetveld simply acknowledged that he owed Jacop Santewaghen Doudins 2 pounds, 8 shillings *gros tournois*.[52] Hughe van Graumes, a knight (*ridder*), acknowledged that Jan Baron had loaned him 11 French crowns.[53] Another 15 of the 114 did casually mention how the debt had originated. Jan Kriekersteen, for example, acknowledged owing Jan van den Heede 10 nobles for "Easter beer."[54] Jacob Zoeteman admitted he owed the "Kartuizers bij Gent" 22 shillings, 6 pennies *gros tournois* for horses.[55] The mention of beer or horses was simply descriptive, however, and played no formal role as security for the loan; in any case, the beer would have been sold or drunk before it could have been seized for nonpayment of the debt.

Both church law and secular custom were responsible for people's apparent insistence that "movables were the security for debts," as the French adage put it. The problem of concern for the church was usury, for payments on a secured loan looked suspiciously like interest charges unless they totaled no more than the precise amount of the loan – a deal

study of this source, see Philippe Lardinois, "Diplomatische studie van de akten van vrijwillige rechtspraak te Gent van de XIIIe tot de XVe eeuw," Licenciaat, U. Ghent, 1975–6. A summary was published in *Handelingen der maatschappij voor Geschiedenis en Oudheidkunde te Gent* 31 (1977), pp. 65–75.

[51] This material is all taken from the inventories and case summaries of the *Jaarregisters* published by the municipal archive of Ghent: J. Boon, ed., *Regesten op de jaarregisters van de schepenen van de Keure te Gent 1339–40, 1343–44, 1345–46, 1349–50* (Ghent, Belg., 1968); Boon, ed., *Regesten op de jaarregisters van de schepenen van de Keure te Gent 1353–54 en 1357–58* (Ghent, Belg., 1969); Boon, ed., *Regesten op de jaarregisters van de keure: Schepenjaar 1400–1401* (Ghent, Belg., 1967–72) [hereafter *RJR*]. Also see David Nicholas, "Commercial Credit and Central Place Function in Thirteenth-Century Ypres," in *Money, Markets and Trade in Late Medieval Europe: Essays in Honour of John H. A. Munro*, eds. Lawrin D. Armstrong, Martin Elbl, Ivana Elbl, and John H. A. Munro (Boston, 2007), pp. 310–48, for a description of recorded debt transactions in thirteenth-century Ypres, where patterns appear to be similar.

[52] *RJR*, #485, fol. 22/10.

[53] *RJR*, #495, fol. 23/6.

[54] *RJR*, #487, fol. 22v/8.

[55] *RJR*, #563, fol. 27v/5.

no long-term lender could accept.[56] The problem in secular custom involved patrimonial rights. Because only an *heritage* could properly secure a long-term loan – it alone holding and producing value over time – people had to pledge assets that were considered patrimonial in order to borrow long term. However, such assets were the source of wealth due to heirs, and in the medieval imagination those heirs were due their property free of debt. No individual, it was thought, could encumber his or her heirs. Accordingly, the only obligations that could attach to or pass with patrimonial assets were those integral to their use, and such obligations were generally understood to be permanent and of a tenurial nature. The old medieval *cens* (*census* in Latin, *cijns* in Dutch) and *aides*, the dues or honorific payments that lords traditionally exacted, typified such arrangements.

However, it was precisely the *cens* that provided the necessary structure for secured debt because it was early and easily conflated with what was called a *rente foncière* or *bail à rente*.[57] Originally considered a kind

---

[56] John H. Munro, "The Medieval Origins of the Financial Revolution: Usury, *Rentes*, and Negotiability," *International History Review* 25, no. 3 (September 2003), pp. 505–62, provides a full discussion of usury laws and their effects on financial markets. For additional material on usury laws in the period, see Chapter 5.

[57] The fullest study of rents, as they had evolved by the end of the Middle Ages and developed in sixteenth-century France (Paris above all), is Bernard Schnapper, *Les rentes au XVIe siècle: Histoire d'un instrument de crédit* (Paris, 1957). Also see Godding, *Le droit privé*; Munro, "Medieval Origins"; James D. Tracy, *A Financial Revolution in the Habsburg Netherlands: Renten and Renteniers in the County of Holland, 1515–1565* (Berkeley, 1985); and James D. Tracy, "On the Dual Origin of Long-Term Urban Debt in Medieval Europe," in *Urban Public Debts: Urban Government and the Market for Annuities in Western Europe, 14th–18th Centuries*, eds. M. Boone, K. Davids, and P. Janssens (Turnhout, Belg., 2003).

Before approximately the thirteenth century, the only possibility for raising money by securing assets was by literally (legally) transferring the property securing the loan to the creditor. This produced what was called the "mort-gage," whereby the debtor ceded the property interest to the creditor who collected its fruits against the debt but later returned the property interest; see in particular Hans Van Werveke, "Le mort-gage et son role économique en Flandre et en Lotharingie (aux XIIe et XIIIe s.)," *Revue belge philologie et histoire* 8 (1929), pp. 53–91, and F. Vercauteren, "Note sur l'origine et l'évolution du contrat de mort-gage en Lotharingie du XIe au XIIe siècle," in *Miscellanea L.*

of perpetual lease of land in exchange for a perpetual rent (thus, *bail à rente*), this instrument could also be seen as a sale of land in exchange for a perpetual rent (*rente foncière*). In either case, no loan was involved – thus, no usury. The church was satisfied, and so were the heirs.

The critical shift, however, was to what were called *rentes à prix d'argent* or *rentes constituées*. In this case, a creditor provided cash in exchange for rent payments in perpetuity, and the debtor (the person paying the rent) used the money either to purchase the asset securing the debt or, more commonly as time went on, to invest elsewhere. In the latter case, the rental payments were generated by an asset (originally understood to be land) that the debtor already possessed. Although this device had all the earmarks of a secured debt, Gentenaren managed to conceptualize it as the creditor's sale (of money) in return for a perpetual rent (and the debtor's purchase of money against the promise to pay rent), thus aligning it with the *rente foncière* or old *census* and avoiding both usury prohibitions and disgruntled heirs.[58]

A series of church rulings in the fifteenth century confirmed the ecclesiastical position: so long as the rent contract was secured by an immovable, the interest rate did not exceed 10 percent, and the payer

Van der Essen (Brussels, 1948), pp. 217–27. After the thirteenth century, the *obligation général* was developed, whereby a debtor issued what we might describe as a pledge of all his or her assets. Creditors thereby acquired a right to pursue immovables, but only under highly restrictive and unfavorable conditions. Somewhat later, these disabilities were lessened when it became possible to issue *obligations spéciales*, which provided creditors claims to specific assets. On this, see Godding, *Le droit privé*, sections 364–8 on pp. 216–9, and Schnapper, *Les rentes au XVIe siècle*, pp. 50–60 and passim.

The issue of the heritability of debts was especially fraught, and it was only in the thirteenth and then the fourteenth century that, in the southern Low Countries at least, the practice was fully accepted. Even then, uncertainties abounded. How were debts to be apportioned among creditors? Who decided how pursuit was to be organized? See, once more, Godding, *Le droit privé*, section 722, pp. 406–8.

[58] The market in rents had developed in the closing years of the Middle Ages in this region, especially as cities learned to use them to raise money for their own purposes (including paying increasingly burdensome taxes to overlords). Recent studies, including those citied in note 57 above, include Jaco Zuijder-duijn, "Assessing a Late Medieval Capital Market: The Capacity of the Market for *Renten* in Edam and De Zeevang (1462–1563)," *Jaarboek voor middeleeuwse Geschiedenis* 11 (2008), pp. 138–65.

of the rent (the borrower) could, at will, redeem his or her obligation by returning the amount borrowed, these contracts were not usurious. By the late Middle Ages, such contracts were ubiquitous. Gentenaren called them *erfrenten* and labeled the rental payments *landcijns*, a term that directly recalls the medieval *cens* (*cijns* in Dutch). About one-third of the entries in the indexed volumes of the *Jaarregisters* concern such debts. For example, in exchange for an unnamed amount of money, Jan Sersanders issued a rent (*erfelijke rente*) to Jan van Maelgavere of 2 shillings *gros tournois* per year, secured by a house and tenure.[59] Simoen Specht acknowledged owing Willem van der Hage 8 pounds *gros tournois* for "land," an implicit acknowledgment that a rent would pay for the land's acquisition.[60]

According to Ghent's custom, all such rents were treated as patrimony and were thus impartible. For example, a *vonnis* of 1352–3 clearly declared "eerve, eerveliike rente" [sic] impartible, and again in 1372 the same language appears.[61] The rule is invariable and is repeated with casual assurance throughout the period studied. Such obligations passed, with the patrimonial property itself, to the heirs. In November 1400, for example, Heinric Seranents [sic] bought half an *erfrent*, paying 20 shillings per year (he paid 7 pounds 10 shillings *gros tournois*, suggesting an interest rate of about 13 percent). The rent itself had been inherited by the seller's wife, Lysbette Boens, from a relative, Lysbette van Maelte (who may have been her mother).[62]

If the perpetual rent could be redeemed by the borrower (as was required by usury laws), however, the aldermen then had trouble deciding whether the rent was movable or immovable. These *losrenten*, as they were called in Ghent, were structured just like *erfrenten* except

---

[59] *RJR*, #510, fol. 24v/1. The property was already encumbered with a rent of 2 shillings *gros tournois*, payable to a third party, so Sersander's ability to borrow against it a second time indicates that the property produced at least 4 shillings of income a year.

[60] *RJR*, #492, fol. 22v/10.

[61] *Vonnis* of 22 June 1353, in both *Coutume* I, pp. 529–40, and Meijers, *OVE*, Bijlage I, #4, pp. 4–7; *vonnis* of 12 November 1372, in idem, #25, pp. 23–9.

[62] *RJR*, #454, fol. 25v/4. However, the general principle deeming perpetual rents patrimonial could be disturbed in small ways. See *Vonnis* of 29 June 1363, in Meijers, *OVE*, Bijlage I, #17, p. 16; *Vonnis* of 22 November 1363, in Meijers, *OVE*, Bijlage I, #19, pp. 17–18; *Vonnis* of 1421, in *Coutumes* I, pp. 598–602.

that the borrower could repay the obligation, whenever desired, at some amount that had been fixed in the original loan agreement, usually between sixteen and twenty times the annual rent.[63] Because these loans were detachable from the asset when redeemed, the rents could logically be considered movable, as indeed several early-sixteenth-century texts provided.[64] However, later texts differed. A *turbe* of 1528 declared all secured rents immovable (except annuities), thereby implying that because *losrenten* were secured they were immovable (or specifying that only secured *losrenten* were immovable).[65] The draft custom of 1546 and the Homologized Custom of 1563 were clearer still: all "realized" *losrenten* (by definition, "realized" rents were secured) were treated as patrimonial immovables, even if the security was a "movable" house, for under such conditions the rent attached to the real property and followed it.[66]

---

[63] A rent paying 2 shillings a year and redeemed at sixteen times implied a loan of 1 lb., 12 s. and an interest rate of 6.2%; one paying 2 shillings and redeemed at twenty times implied a loan of 2 lbs. and an interest rate of 5%.

[64] A *turbe* of 5 June 1529, in Meijers, *OVE*, Bijlage II, #17, pp. 87–8, specified that they were partible unless purchased with the proceeds of the sale of an immovable *erve*. Another of 10 December 1529, in idem, #23, p. 92, treated *losrenten* as movables in that they were part of a common account.

[65] *Turbe* of 9 September 1528, in Meijers, *OVE*, Bijlage II, #9, pp. 83–4, where secured (*besette*) *losrenten* were treated as immovables.

[66] By then, the term *besette* (secured) had come to imply *gherealizeerd* or "realized." The term "realized" rents first appears in sixteenth-century texts, as an explicit reference to a process of formal registration (which could have been oral) of a secured obligation. Once "realized," a debt was pursuable in court and the security underlying it attachable. I am grateful to Prof. Philippe Godding for this explanation. The clause is found in DC XXI-18 and in HC XXV-8 (the term appears elsewhere in these texts as well; see, for example, XXV-40 of the HC). Article 27 of the early-sixteenth-century SC repeated the same rule, as did a *turbe* of 10 October 1530, in Meijers, *OVE*, Bijlage II, #31, p. 96.

The income received by the lender of the funds was treated as a movable (HC, article XXV-27). The logic is, however, clear. *Losrenten*, being secured by immovables, had to stay attached to that immovable if the creditor was to be properly secured. Although the income from the rent could float free of the property and be considered "personal" to the lender, the capital tied up in debt had to be attached specifically to the asset generating the debt; in that way the creditor was still secured, even if the property was sold to a third party or passed on to heirs. Similar confusion plagued the French, although in Paris, as

Clearly, Genetenaren conceptualized perpetual rents not as "debt" but as a quasi-tenurial arrangement. As such, these assets ultimately lodged with the family line and were not freely available to the market. The individuals paying the rents (the borrowers) also treated their payments as patrimonial in that they passed to heirs along with the property securing the rent, as what Gentenaren called *besetten* rents. Thus, a perpetual rent followed the property and could be divided as many times as the property was being divided so that, for example, a rent secured by a house and building lot was divided between heirs and the successor to a portion of the house.

By the late Middle Ages, a new form of the *rente constituée* was at least as common, and its appearance further disturbed traditional norms. This was the annuity or, in the better-known French term, a *rente viagère* (*lijfrent* in Dutch). Although structured exactly like the *rente constituée* in that it was in effect created by a loan, the annuity payment was due only for the life of the creditor; after the creditor's death, the borrower would own the pledged property free and clear, and the obligation to pay rent ceased entirely.[67] In this case, the connection between the financial instrument and its security was temporary, and the annuity payments themselves had a limited term. They were thus treated as partible property, and the annuity payments were similarly treated as an obligation of the community account.[68] Like any such debt, annuities could be

---

in Ghent, it was ultimately determined that such rents were immovable. See Schnapper, *Les rentes au XVIe siècle*, pp. 250–8.

[67] Or the group of creditors, because such annuities were typically written on several lives – husband and wife, or the entire nuclear family. In November 1400, for example, Peter Weylin and his wife Mergriete Karimans sold a life rent to Paesschine van der Leene. In exchange for the loan he made (the amount of which is not specified in the document), van der Leene would receive 2 pounds *gros tournois* per year, which would be provided by the income from two of the borrowers' properties, both of which were rented rooms with their tenement (perhaps a kind of boardinghouse or workshop): *RJR*, #398, fol. 21/3.

[68] *Vonnis* of 14 August 1355, in Meijers, *OVE*, Bijlage I, #6, p. 8 (here it was explained that the rent had been purchased with common property during the marriage, so the income was, naturally, common as well). A *vonnis* of 1 April 1359, in idem, #13, pp. 12–14, specified that, even if the rental payment was secured by immovables that belonged to one spouse alone, the obligation to service the annuity was movable. A *turbe* of 9 September 1528, in idem, Bijlage II, #9, pp. 83–4, went on to specify that they were partible even if secured

bought and sold, and Ghent's custom easily assigned them to the partible account.[69] Rates on these instruments regularly exceeded 10 percent, and when issued by cities, which were the major borrowers in this market, they were not secured by immovables but by excise tax receipts.[70]

The long and complicated history of Ghent's struggles to decide the status of debt instruments was, in short, an effort to make a distinction between short-term and long-term debt and to align that distinction with the partible/impartible divide. The former were, as Ghent's legal texts regularly and casually insisted, movables; hence creditors assigned the sum due to them to the common (partible) account of their marital estate, and debtors treated their obligation to pay as a charge against their own common account. Rents were a different matter. Because they were conceived of as a form of the old tenurial dues, they did not count as "debts" but as obligations that attached to property that produced income over time and in perpetuity. They were thus immovable and impartible. Only life rents, what we call annuities, could not be assigned to that account, because they would become detached from the asset securing the rent payment at the death of the creditor, and the property in question would pass to the rent payer, whose obligation to pay rents would cease. All other rents, including secured redeemable rents (*besette losrenten*), were treated as impartible *erve* even if they were secured by assets considered movable, such as a house. In that case, the house was divided between the heirs and surviving spouse; so too was the rent divided, but unlike the house the rent counted as an immovable in the old sense – an impartible. It was, just as Gentenaren repeatedly said, an *erfrent*.

by *erve* (*besetten*). These rules were repeated in the SC of the early sixteenth century (article 26) and in the DC of 1546 (XXI-20), as well as the HC of 1563 (XXV-22).

[69] In December 1400, for example, Gillis de Jaghere sold the portion of the life rent he had inherited from Pieter van Kets to a certain Mergriete van der Linden (presumably the annuity had been written on his life as well): *RJR*, #506, fol. 27v/3.

[70] On Ghent's issuance of such annuities and their rates, see Marc Boone, "'Plus dueil que joie': Les ventes de rentes par la ville de Gand pendant la période bourguignonne; Entre intérêts privés et finances publiques," *Crédit Communal* 176 (1991–2), pp. 3–25.

THE UNCERTAIN PROGRESS TOWARD
ECONOMIC MOVABILITY

Taken together, all the disputes about the status of particular goods – from seed corn to trees, from houses to land and financial instruments – enlarged the category of movable wealth, in effect leaving a small, if precious, group of goods that could be considered impartible: most rents and all land outside the city's jurisdiction. Every other kind of property that a Gentenaren might own was now judged movable: houses, all land in the city's jurisdiction, annuities, and a great many products of the land itself had joined the furniture, cash, raw materials, inventories, clothing, jewelry, arms, kitchenware, household provisions, domesticated animals, and accounts receivable that had traditionally counted as movables. All such goods were partible, and thus they were available for sale, they could be seized by creditors, and they could be given away while the owner lived. As heads of household, husbands – the *maîtres* or *barons* of their wives in French texts from the region – had a free hand in managing them, and when the husband died his widow was free to manage her half of the movables as she saw fit.

From this evidence alone, we might conclude that Gentenaren were well on their way toward the capitalist future of modernity. That is certainly where they wound up, but during the centuries I studied and even during the two or three to follow, their steps took a more crooked path than it might first appear. In fact, even as they increased the category of movable wealth during the centuries of concern here, Gentenaren not only preserved the term "immovable," but they also made sure that what were becoming their most important immovables could be sequestered as impartibles. There was only one route to that status, however: marriage. The goods eligible for impartibility – land outside the jurisdiction of Ghent and rents on property anywhere – became impartible only when they were funding a marriage (and, implicitly, the future of children to be born of the marriage). Thus, if they came with either the bride or groom to the new household or if they were received by either as inheritance or predesignated gift, they were impartible.[71]

---

[71] Article XXV-29: "Land [*gronden van erfven*] 'holds side' from which it comes *except the land within {the city's jurisdiction}*, which is partible [unless it is held

If, however, they were acquired by a single person or if acquired by a married person with "common money" (i.e., funds from the community account), they were partible.[72]

Marital property law was so mighty an instrument that it not only provided the sole means for creating impartibles; it also trumped other ordinances and rulings. Consider, for example, a twelfth-century text (a comptal privilege) that declared anyone free to sell or alienate patrimonial property (*erve*) in Ghent's jurisdiction, even over the objections of relatives (thus seeming to allow land in the city, which was in those days still considered impartible under customary law, to be bought and sold at will). On the face of it, this privilege granted extraordinary property rights; in reality, however, it did not affect property that had been brought to a marriage.[73] Indeed, the later Charter of 1297

of another lord or is subject to ecclesiastical rules of inheritance]" (emphasis added).

[72] However, should a single person later marry, those properties would enter the impartible account and thus be reserved for "the line" As explained in HC, articles XXV-12: "Land, perpetual and heritable rents and realized redeemable rents [*gonden van erfven, eeuwelicke ende erffelicke renten ende gherealiscered losrenten*]" that were acquired during marriage were partible, as were fiefs acquired with "common money" (article XXV-22) and annuities (article XXV-22). In contrast, land and rents were impartible ("held side") if they came with the marriage, as did any such assets that were received during marriage by gift or testament (articles XXV-1, 29, 40 55). Also article XX-5: "The husband may not alienate, encumber, sell or otherwise dispose of the heritable property of the deceased [wife], whether fief, land [*erfve*], or non-redeemable rents coming from her side without her express consent."

[73] The Latin reads: "Est autem tanta libertas oppidi Gandensis quòd, si quis hereditatem suam infrà justitiam oppidi contentam vendere vel invadiare voluerit, licet ei tam extraneis quam proximis, nec aliquis ratione consanguinitatis vel proximitatis poterit contradicere." ("The liberty of the city of Ghent is such that, if anyone wishes to sell or pledge patrimony belonging to him and subject to the jurisdiction of the city, whether it be to outsiders or relatives, no one shall be able to contest [the act] on the grounds of consanguinity or close kinship."): *Coutumes* I, p. 394. The text is dated 1192 in this edition, but see Walter Prevenier, *De Oorkonden der graven van Vlaanderen (1191–aanvang 1206)*, vol. 2 (Brussels, 1964), pp. 1–16, who corrects the date of the originally edited version to September/October 1191.

explained that heirs could challenge any sale of land (*erve*) during the first year after a transfer, thus suggesting that it was up to the seller to prove the right of alienation: if the property was "of the line," a status created by marriage, it belonged to the heirs.[74] Even legal judgments from the sixteenth century would have been voided by marital property and inheritance law. For example, a *turbe* of 1528, which promised that "either a man or a woman is authorized to dispose of his or her property while still living without requiring permission from anyone," could *not* have been understood as permission to alienate lineal goods without *any* regard for the successor or heirs: as article XX-27 of the Homologized Custom explained, neither spouse could dispose of goods, by testament or otherwise, that would undermine contractual or customary survival rights of the other.[75] Another *turbe* of 1530, which insisted that "according to the custom of this city, which has so long been honored that no one remembers otherwise, any person free and of sound mind can dispose of his property during his life as he wants, whether by sale, gift or otherwise, and outside the kin network," would have had a similarly restricted impact, for marital property law firmly prohibited gifts to "anyone." Specifically, spouses did not have the right to make gifts to one another during marriage or to write wills that "advantaged" the surviving spouse more than he or she would have been "advantaged" by custom.[76] Martial property law also forbade any

---

[74] For the thirteenth-century statement, see GC, article 116. We can see these principles in action in a sale registered with the aldermen in 1400. There, Lisbette Clercs sold 3 measures (*gemeten*) of land to Willem Wenemaere and Pieter den Brunen, who were acting on behalf of a hospital. Should, however, Clerc's heirs object to the sale, she promised to pay the hospital 7 *gros tournois* (presumably the selling price of the parcel or a fine): RJR #569, fol. 29/3.

Schnapper, *Les rentes au XVIe siècle*, pp. 50–5, explains that in French custom, only *rentes constituées* could be contested by kin because they alone represented a transfer of (i.e., a diminution of) the perpetual revenues earned by the land.

[75] See also article XX-18.

[76] For the judgments confirming freedom of alienation, see *turbe* of 27 August 1528, in Meijers, *OVE*, Bijlage II, #8, p. 83: *turbe* of 9 December 1530, in idem, #34, pp. 97–8. Even in the highly commercialized region of the southern Low

testator to make bequests that would impugn the interests of the surviving spouse without first obtaining that spouse's permission.[77] With
respect to testaments in particular, other provisions of law required that
two-thirds of *all* the testator's goods go to the heirs.[78]

There is no question that the rules about marital impartibles were
upheld, and the best evidence we have about that matter is the consistently reiterated and apparently strictly enforced rule that Gentenaren
could not write marriage contracts overruling custom. Only in 1563
did the Homologized Custom permit Gentenaren to do what people in
some parts of the North were already doing – issuing marriage contracts

Countries, where market exchange would so erode the traditional idea that
property should not be freely transferred, very few places granted such liberty.
To judge from these rulings alone, the market had triumphed. On this issue,
see Philippe Godding, "Le droit au service du patrimonie familial: Les Pays-Bas
méridionaux (12e–18e siècles)," in *Marriage, Property, and Succession*, ed. Lloyd
Bonfield (Berlin, 1992), pp. 15–36.

For examples of the specific restrictions imposed by marital property law,
however, see SC, articles 6 and 7, and DC, article XXI-2, where it is remarked
that "people are forbidden to make marital property agreements that would
advantage either spouse or successor or heir after death or annulment or separation of bed and board more than the custom would have done." For example,
a husband would have been forbidden to pass any of his impartibles on to his
wife or to any of her heirs who were not also his descendants; also see article
XXI-11 of the DC. Articles XX-21 of the HC denied spouses the right to make
gifts to one another during marriage unless the gift would not advantage the
spouse more than custom would have; article 22 denied one spouse the right
to make a gift to the other by testament except to the extent of one jewel or
one *catheyl* according to the condition of the recipient and donor. Also article
XX-27 of the HC.

[77] For the restriction, see HC, article XX-27; also see article XX-18.

[78] SC, articles 9 and 10; DC, article XXIV-3; HC, article XXXVIII-2 and 3.
Ghent's testamentary law was markedly liberal in allowing a Gentenaren to
bequeath a full third of all assets, of any kind, to whomever he or she wished
by means of a will. This seems to have been the custom throughout the county
of Flanders, but elsewhere in the Low Countries it was different. In some
places, in fact, testators had no freedom at all with respect to patrimonial
property, the southern county of Hainault and Luxembourg being particularly
strict in this regard: Godding, "Dans quelle mesure pouvait-on disposer de ses
biens par testament dans les anciens Pays-Bas méridionaux?" *Tijdschrift voor
rechtsgeschiedenis* 50 (1982), pp. 279–96.

that altered the principles of custom.[79] Gentenaren thus rarely wrote such contracts before the early modern period, and when they did they almost never violated even the smallest provision of custom.[80] However, it is close to impossible to know precisely how many of these instances there were, for the only records we have of such contracts are buried in the hundreds of manuscript volumes of *Jaarregisters van de Keure* housed in Ghent's municipal archive, the registers in which private agreements of sales, loans, debt settlements, and the like were recorded.[81] A search

[79] In areas governed heavily by Roman law, marriage contracts were the rule, but even there people adhered to local custom in matters concerning the size and composition of the dowry, the amount of the "increase" typically promised to the widow, any counter-gifts given by the husband, and so on. For discussions of these systems and their contrast even with northern practices that seemed to resemble the dotal systems of the South, see Robert Jacob, *Les époux, le seigneur et la cité: Coutume et pratiques matrimoniales des bourgeois et paysans de France du Nord au Moyen Age* (Brussels, 1990). In contrast to the South, community property law in most northern regions was slow to permit marriage contracts, or people in those regions were slow to use them. We thus have very few such documents before the late fifteenth century, except for the nobility (and not that many for them). Douai, in French Flanders, is one of the few exceptions to that rule. For the Douaisien story, see Jacob, *Les époux*, and Martha C. Howell, *The Marriage Exchange: Property, Social Place, and Gender in Cities of the Low Countries, 1300–1550* (Chicago, 1998).

[80] *Vonnis* of 1352–3, pp. 529–40. Also see *vonnis* of 22 June 1353, in Meijers, *OVE*, Bijlage I, #4, pp 4–7: "According to the law of Ghent . . . all dowries, deals, promises and gifts have no force, power, virtue or worth, but each must remain in the community [of goods] in order to divide according to the law and honor of the city of Ghent"; also SC, article 6 and DC, article XXI-2: "Because people are forbidden to make marital property agreements that would advantage either spouse or successor or heir after death or annulment or separation of bed and board more than the custom would have done." Also see XXI-11.

Article XX-20 of the HC flatly overruled these proscriptions: "From now on people may make marital property agreements so long as they do not disadvantage creditors."

[81] See n. 51 for an explanation of the *Keure*. Indices have been published for only seven years of the medieval centuries, and these provide our only systematic guide to the frequency and nature of such contracts. Of the 1,427 entries in the *Jaarregisters* indexed for the six years 1339–40, 1343–4, 1345–6, 1349–50, 1353–4, and 1357–8, only ten marriage contracts are mentioned, two of which the aldermen later crossed out as inoperative. Among the 1,580 entries for the single year 1400–01, there are only two. Thanks to David Nicholas's *The*

of some sixty years of these registers, between 1339 and 1400, yielded only twenty-six marriage contracts, fewer than one per year, in a city where there may have been four hundred to five hundred marriages annually, with perhaps one-third to one-half of them between people with enough property to care about these matters.

Of these twenty-six marriage contracts, eleven do not appear to have violated custom at all.[82] Fifteen contracts did, but only in small ways.[83] Nine of those fifteen provided some kind of dower to the widow, but six of these laboriously specified that prospective heirs who might be injured by the contracts had explicitly given their consent.[84] A contract from 1361, for example, allowed each of the spouses full dower rights to the couple's residence, but not without justifying the breach of custom:

So that the longer living of Heinric [the husband] and Jongvrouw Mergriete, his aforementioned wife, may peacefully possess it as explained, consent has been given by Jan van Hoese, Heinric van Hoese, Jongvrouw Aneese van Hoese, Jan vanden Berghe, her husband and guardian [vocht], and Jonvrouw Isabelle von Hoese, all four Heinrics children van Hoese as heir of the said Heinric. Further consent has

Domestic Life of a Medieval City: Women, Children, and the Family in 14th-Century Ghent (Lincoln, NE, 1985), we know, in addition, of some sixteen additional marriage contracts issued between 1345 and 1390 and also registered in the *Jaarregisters van de Keure.*

[82] See, for example, SAG, serie 301, nr. 77 (1343/44), fol. 13/4 (2 March 1344); nr. 73 (1353/54), fol. 110v/4 (5 November 1353); nr. 91 (1353/54), fol. 112v/4 (27 November 1353); SAG, serie 301, nr. 142 (1345/46), fol. 21/2 (26 January 1346); similarly, see SAG, serie 301, nr. 6/2 (1377/78), fol. 57v/2 (9 August 1378); nr. 4/1 (1372/73), fol. 33v/1 (26 July 1373); nr. 4/1 (1372/73)I, fol. 29v/1 (18 May 1373); nr. 11/1 (1387/88), fol. 108v (16 June 1387); SAG, serie 301, nr. 3/2 (1371/72), fol. 3v/3 (15 September 1370); SAG, serie 301, nr. 12 (1389/90), fol. 83/2 (14 August 1390); nr. 2/2 (1365/66), fol. 29v/2 (4 May 1366).

[83] SAG, serie 301, nr. 993 (1400–01), fol. 59/7 (March 24, 1401); nr. 1479 (1401–02), fol. 85v/3 (21 July 1401); nr. 8 (1353/54), fol. 106v/5 (10 August 1353); Also see, similarly, SAG, serie 301, nr. 1 (1352/53), fol. 104/2 (7 August 1353) and SAG, serie 301, nr. 86 (1343/44), fol. 14/1 (5 April 1344); serie 301, nr. 44 (1339/40), fol. 7/2 (25 July 1340).

[84] SAG, serie 301, nr. 1 (1360/61), fol. 232/3 (1360), nr. 514 (1349/50), fol. 80v/2 (25 June 1350); serie 301, nr. 187 (1353/54), fol. 127v–128 (18 April 1354).

also been given by Jan vaden Hamme, Jongvrouw Mergriete, his sister, and Jan Peister, her husand and guardian, both of them children of the said Mergriete[s] children, as heirs of the said Mergriete. And all the aforesaid heirs on both sides and individually have promised to make no claim for a part or a right to the said house and property as long as the longer living of Heinric and Jongvrouw Mergriete his wife shall live.[85]

Another contract, which made each spouse the heir of an annuity on their joint lives, was similarly approved by the "heirs on both sides" – all seventeen of them.[86]

It is not hard to understand why Gentenaren chose to designate rents and land outside Ghent as impartible, for that kind of property could best guarantee stable social relations and had therefore become the most important assets in the portfolios of prosperous Gentenaren. If carefully sequestered from the risks of the marketplace, they could do the necessary patrimonial work – they could continually generate income, assure the surviving spouse's comfort, and guarantee the future of heirs.

But even if Gentenaren restricted the use and alienation of goods considered impartible in the ways just described, they did not ignore the imperatives of the market. Indeed, in that age and in a society like Ghent's, it would have been unwise and in fact almost impossible to deny these assets any access to the market. Thus, in partial accord with statements in law about people's right to buy and sell "at will," Gentenaren allowed such impartibles to be sold *but only if* proceeds of the sale were reinvested in assets that would automatically acquire impartible status. This rule appeared even as early as the late thirteenth century, in the Grand Charter. Its article 114 implied that impartible goods could be alienated *if and only if* goods of the same value (though not necessarily of the same kind) replaced them; they too would be considered impartible. The same rule was written into the sixteenth-century Homologized Custom, and it is fair to assume that it had

---

[85] SAG serie 301, nr.1 (1360/61), fol. 229v/2 (12 January 1361).

[86] SAG, serie 301, nr. 2/2 (1365/66), fol. 44/2 (21 July 1366). Also see SAG, serie 301, nr. 4/2 (1373/74), fol. 23/2 (8 March 1374); SAG, serie 330, nr. 4/5 (1369/70), fol. 40/7; and SAG, serie 301, nr. 2/2 (1373/74), fol. 43/2 (18 July 1374).

operated during the centuries that separated the Charter of 1297 and the Homologized Custom of 1563.[87] To judge from this normative evidence, it seems that Gentenaren were as eager to maneuver in markets as they were to deny market imperatives. After all, one country estate might be traded for another, better one; one plot of rural land might best be sold and another bought that lay next to a field already owned; a rental income from a house in Ghent might be sold and replaced by a rent secured by other assets. However, at the same time, social order had to be guaranteed, and to do so Gentenaren had to preserve the impartibility of certain assets. Gentenaren accomplished both goals by restricting the sale or alienation of particularly cherished goods that produced income indefinitely, while at the same time allowing their alienation if they were replaced with property that could do the same social work.

Thus, the legal record summarized here – statements of custom, court disputes, and even the few marriage contracts and wills issued to modify custom – speaks eloquently not only about the dilemma Genentaren faced as they confronted commerce but more particularly about the tensions embedded in the property relations constructed by marriage. As several scholars have pointed out, these tensions were in part the result of exogamous marriage, for such marriages pitted the nuclear family or conjugal pair (*le ménage*) against the "line" (*le lignage*) or kin network.[88] But that structural condition alone cannot

---

[87] GC, article 114 is titled: *Van herven te wisselne: ende so wie die wisselt herve omme herve, dat herve dat ghewisselt weert, blyft in alsulken pointe alse often het niet ghewisselt ne ware [concerning heritable property that is exchanged and the ruling that whoever exchanges a heritable property for another (is obligated to) to treat the new property in every respect as though it were the original unexchanged property]*. The DC (a text never enacted), however, had proposed treating the new properties as after-acquired properties if the originals had been sold with the wife's consent (article V-13). But the HC, article XX-13, returned to the older rule, explaining that it was necessary to "prevent fraud." Note too that *onbesetten* rents were partible *even if* acquired by selling impartibles: HC XVV-28.

[88] Georges Chevrier has explicitly argued, for example, that in the county of Burgundy late medieval customary law expressed exactly this structural tension: Georges Chevrier, "Sur quelques caractères de l'histoire du régime matrimonial dans la Bourgogne ducale aux diverse phases de son développement," in *Mémoires*

explain the struggles in Ghent, for exogamous marriage had been the European tradition for centuries.[89] Here the problem was not so much the competing interests of the conjugal unit and the lineage, although those surely existed, but the competing needs of the market and the "family" tout court. The force that drove this legal transformation in Ghent (and, I would venture, everywhere else in commercialized Europe during the age) was the change in the nature of wealth as economically movable goods exploded in quantity and kind. With this explosion, the traditional axes along which property relations had been organized – the distinction between patrimony and chattels, between family or kin interests on the one hand and individual interests on the other – was disturbed. The competing interests of the *ménage* and the *lignage* could no longer be neatly contained by assigning one kind of property to one party and another kind to the other; everything was becoming economically movable, so the problem was how to make this huge category of movable goods do patrimonial work.

WEALTH AS CAPITAL, CAPITAL AS PATRIMONY

Gentenaren solved their problem by releasing all wealth to the market, but at the same time securing the *value* of secured rents and rural land-holdings – if not the specific assets themselves – for the family that had provided them to a marriage. Their strategy expressed a specific vision of their property interests, for it was not "property" they sequestered but specific kinds of property: rural land and rents. These assets had special

---

de la Société pour l'Histoire du Droit et des Institutions des anciens pays bourguignons, comtois et romands (Dijon, 1966). Also see Godding's more general discussion of the argument in Le droit privé, pp. 280–314, esp. pp. 284–6, and for an examination of the legal history of this tension in Douai, see Jacob, Les époux.

[89] For a structural analysis of these exogamous marriages and the social tensions they produced, see Jack Goody, *Production and Reproduction: A Comparative Study of the Domestic Domain* (New York, 1976) and his *Development of the Family and Marriage in Europe* (New York, 1983). The basic text for this approach is Claude Lévi-Strauss, *The Elementary Structures of Kinship*, trans. J. H. Bell et al. (Boston, 1969).

characteristics, powers beyond those inherent in their market value. In the contemporary sociocultural imagination, a landowner was directly linked to the traditional medieval source of prestige, and a *rentier* (even if the rents came from urban property) was an aristocrat.[90] But not all secured rents and rural land could grant such power. Only those that had been brought to the marriage (or acquired in exchange for such properties, received as inheritance, or obtained as a predesignated gift) were impartible. And if bought with "common funds" during marriage, they became impartible only in the second generation, after they were passed to sons, daughters, or other relatives at marriage, by inheritance, or by gift. Once "in the family," however, such property could be repeatedly transferred from generation to generation, endlessly guaranteeing social standing. Over time, such patrimonial holdings could even enhance class status, for the older the property the more powerfully it established social rank. Any Gentenar seeking to preserve or create a stable social lineage was thus well advised, indeed compelled, to collect rents and rural properties and to pass them on as gifts or inheritances.

Gentenaren were hardly the only Europeans of the period to make these choices. As a seventeenth-century observer in France remarked, "The majority of the property [of the bourgeoisie] consists today of

[90] Many rental payments on rural land that were held by urbanites were in fact paid in kind, which reinforced the association between rents and land. See Schnapper, *Les rentes*, esp. pp. 80–3, for evidence from the Parisian region. The *Jaarregisters van de Keure* in Ghent provide scattered information confirming the same pattern. Although it seems that most rents in Ghent were *expressed* (if not paid) in monies of account (the pound *groot*, the pound *parisis*, or the *gros tournois*), they were actually paid either in coin or kind. A few entries suggest the mix: for example, *RJR*, #576, fol. 28/6 ("tot het betalen van 2 last torven [turf] op 4 schilden"); 36, fol. 25v/5; *RJR*, #606, fol. 30v/5 ("een erfrente van 4 lb. 15s. par. + 4 6/8 kapoenen"); *RJR*, #620, fol. 91v/2 ("tot het betalen van 7 zakken en 7 mud tiendekoren [Aalsterse maat]").

The "Orphans' Books" (*Weezenboeken*) from Ghent provide concrete evidence of Gentenaren's commitment to land and rents. Any so-called orphan standing to inherit any significant amount of property would have been registered here, and the properties to which he or she was heir would be listed, at least in summary form. For the four years from 1349/50 to 1352/53, about one-third of the listings contained rural properties of some kind; almost all contained rents.

constituted rents."[91] Propertied urbanites in Germany, Italy, England, and the rest of the Low Countries made the same choices.[92] Almost next door to Ghent, in Douai, the pattern is especially clear, thanks to the rich trove of marriage contracts left by its citizenry.[93] As in Ghent, law elsewhere was adjusted to enable these choices. Ralph Giesey demonstrated, for example, that early modern Parisian elites adapted testamentary, marital property, and inheritance law so that they could protect rents and bureaucratic offices for heirs by labeling them *propres*.[94] This was their term for lineal goods, analogous to Ghent's impartible account.

The rewards from such holdings, whether in Ghent, Paris, Douai, or elsewhere, came mostly in the form of social advancement, for they

[91] In Pierre de L'Hommeau, *Maximes générales du Droit Francais divisées en trios livres par M. P . . . de L . . . Sieur du Verger* (Paris, 1665), cited in Schnapper, *Les rentes au XVIe siècle*, p. 244. Jonathan Dewald, "The Ruling Class in the Marketplace: Nobles and Money in Early Modern France," in *Culture of the Market*, eds. Haskell and Teichgraeber, pp. 43–66, concluded that by the seventeenth century many French nobles were entirely invested in rents, not land.

[92] Case studies such as Michel Mollat's *Jacques Coeur ou l'esprit d'entreprise au XVe siècle* (Paris, 1988) or Robert Forster's *Merchants, Landlords, Magistrates: The Depont Family in Eighteenth-Century France* (Baltimore, 1980) give particularly rich texture to this social history, and sociologically inspired research confirms the patterns. See, for illustrative evidence, Robert S. Duplessis, *Lille and the Dutch Revolt* (New York, 1991); Barbara Diefendorf, *Paris City Councillors* (Princeton, NJ, 1983); Sylvia Thrupp, *The Merchant Class of Medieval London* (Chicago, 1948); Albert Rigaudière, *L'assiette de l'impôt à la fin du XIVe siècle: Le livre d'estimes des consuls de Saint-Flour les années 1380–1385* (Paris, 1977); Ph. Wolff, *Commerce et marchands de Toulouse (vers 1350–vers 1450)* (Paris, 1954); R. Fédou, *Les hommes de loi lyonnais à la fin du Moyen Age* (Paris, 1964). George Huppert, *Les Bourgeois Gentilshommes: An Essay on the Definition of Elites in Renaissance France* (Chicago, 1977) surveys and summarizes the literature on France, with references to other countries.

[93] For the Douaisien history, see Jacob, *Les époux* and Howell, *Marriage Exchange*.

[94] Ralph E. Giesey, "Rules of Inheritance and Strategies of Mobility in Prerevolutionary France," *American Historical Review* 82:2 (April 1977), pp. 271–89. He is building on previous work by French scholars, especially Charles Lefebvre, *Les fortunes anciennes au point de vue juridique* (Paris, 1912). See Giesey, note 2, p. 272, for further references. Godding, *Le droit privé*, p. 143 and passim and Jacob, *Les époux*, are among the scholars of the Low Countries who have also called attention to this tendency.

yielded little current income. Because such investment strategies seemed to favor social position over immediate financial returns, turning merchants into aspiring gentry and office holders in state bureaucracies, they reflected what some historians have termed the "future-oriented" attitudes typical of the so-called noncommercial bourgeoisie of early modern Europe. Braudel even rejected the term "noncommercial bourgeoisie" for these people, preferring instead either *honorables hommes* or even gentry, because these investors were distinguished not by their entrepreneurial use of capital but by a way of life derived from their investment and inheritance practices. As Braudel described the early modern French version of this class, these people

were more than comfortably off, possessing solid fortunes drawn from three chief sources: land, methodically farmed; usury, practiced primarily at the expense of peasants and gentlemen [i.e., rents]; and lastly offices in the judiciary or in the royal finances. . . . But most of these fortunes were inherited rather than constructed: they consolidated and extended them, it is true, for money begat money and made social breakthrough and triumphs possible. But the launching of the dynasty was invariably the same: the gentry had sprung from trade, something it sought to hide from prying eyes and kept as dark as possible.[95]

Some historians have concluded that because this wealth was relatively "immobilized," meaning that it was denied access to the market and rendered economically inert, it "stifled" capitalistic development.[96] That is certainly correct if measured on strictly financial grounds, but as Ralph Giesey pointed out in describing the early modern Parisians who made these choices, the investment decisions were neither economically illogical nor without significance for the future of capitalism. Investments in land, rents, and offices may have "restricted the freedom of successive heads of the family in favor of the perpetual corporate integrity of the lineage," but they also expressed a strong commitment to what Giesey called "family possessiveness." If this was not yet what Macpherson has characterized as the "possessive individualism" that distinguishes capitalism, Giesey argued that it was a step toward

[95] F. Braudel *Wheels*, p. 485.

[96] The quotations ("immobilized" and "stifled") are from Giesey, who is quoting others: "Rules of Inheritance," p. 278.

that future.[97] Braudel also credited these people with a role in the capitalist future, even if he refused to consider them a proto-capitalist bourgeoisie. He held that the changes in investment and inheritance patterns such as those investigated here provided a vehicle for the social promotion of the newly rich, thus unsettling the traditional aristocracy's hold on power.

The history of property law in Ghent, I would argue, constituted an ever more fundamental step toward a capitalist future because it evidenced a reconceptualization of property itself. Crops, trees, houses, buildings of all kinds, urban real estate of all kinds, leases and rents, even rural land – *all* were positioned to be put to work so that they could replace themselves economically and produce new wealth. In that sense, all were capital assets. But Gentenaren, like Giesey's Parisians and the people whom Braudel had in mind, were not capitalists manqués. Although they had found a way to let all property freely circulate, they also ensured that rents and rural land – economically stable property that was considered the most culturally significant – would be replaced by similar assets if alienated and that they would then descend to lineal heirs as impartibles. In this way, the market could flourish but hierarchy would be shored up, risks of social derogation minimized, and newcomers more easily kept out.

The confusion about the terms movable and immovable, chattel and patrimony, and partible and impartible that plagues the city's legal sources was not just about words; it was not even fundamentally about

[97] Giesey, p. 286; also see René Filhol, "Propriété absolue et démembrement de la propriété dans l'ancien droit francais," in *Travaux et recherches de l'Institut de droit comparé de l'université de Paris* 22 (1963), whom Giesey cites in note 51, p. 286. Since Giesey's article appeared others have returned to the subject. Barbara Diefendorf, for example, has examined marriage contracts and customary law in sixteenth-century Paris, showing how both were manipulated to further protect lineage assets, with significant (negative) consequences for women's property rights: Barbara B. Diefendorf, *Paris City Councillors in the Sixteenth Century: The Politics of Patrimony* (Princeton, 1983). Both Giesey and Diefendorf depend directly on Francois Olivier-Martin's *Histoire de la coutume de la prévoté et vicomté de Paris*, 2 vols. (Paris, 1922–6). For Macpherson's argument, see C. B. Macpherson, *The Political Theory of Possessive Individualism: Hobbes to Locke* (London, 1962).

law. It was the record of a sociocultural revolution that emptied the term "immovable" of economic meaning, broke the venerable equation between land and patrimony, and reconceptualized what Gentenaren usually called "goods" (*goeden*) as capital even as they found a way to secure patrimonial status for a special category of these "goods."

2   "Pour l'amour et affection conjugale"

TOWARD THE END OF THE MIDDLE AGES, WESTERN EUROPEANS
began to put new emphasis on conjugal love, describing it not simply as
an ingredient of a good marriage, but as its motivation and principal seal.
The best evidence of this development comes from the nuclear households
of northern European cities and market towns, and historians have often
reasoned that the rhetoric was a natural expression of such couples'
experiences as joint managers of their small household economies.
Husbands and wives in these settings were positioned as partners, even if,
as most scholars have acknowledged, the partnership was unequal. For
such people, religious teaching and law readily combined with social
experience to deepen the discourse of love and mutuality by making the
consent of both spouses the only basis for a valid marriage and thus giving
women a new voice in marriage. Poets and storytellers joined in, providing
a language of romance that celebrated heterosexual passion and eternal
commitment between lovers. Thus was born, many scholars have thought,
an early version of modern Europe's "companionate" marriage, a union
based on a mix of sustained desire, partnership, and easy companionability.

   This chapter interrogates that history. I argue that the irenic
"companionate" marriage would have been hard to imagine in households
that were as demographically unstable and as sternly patriarchal as nuclear
households of this period usually were. For their part, the ecclesiastical
rules about marriage, especially about individual consent, were not easily
adopted in these settings, for they conflicted with long-standing social
practices, and the stories about romance that then circulated provided
little in the way of a usable cultural text for these people. Changes in the
nature of property described in the Introduction and Chapter 1 added to

the tensions. People who lived principally from movable wealth, as many of these couples did, could not rely on property to define the relations between husband and wife, assure the future of children, and secure the kinship network. Seen from this point of view, their talk of conjugal love was not a "natural" expression of social circumstances and cultural understandings, but an ideological tool that helped seal a marital bond in need of strong cement.

In 1558, Jean Vallain the elder, described as a bourgeois of Douai, and Marie de Paradis, his wife, wrote what was called a *ravestissement par lettre*, a kind of mutual donation in which each spouse left all his or her worldly goods to the survivor of the marriage:

Jean Vallain the elder, bourgeois of Douai, and Marie de Paradis, his wife, who live in Douai, Marie being sufficiently empowered by her husband, which empower-ment she has received happily, as she has stated, declared, and warranted, *because most other goods, debts, rents and héritages consist of properties acquired in the course of their marriage through their labor, industry and common property, for this reason and for the conjugal love and affection they hold for one another* [emphasis added] . . . these partners, the said woman being empowered as above, wanted and want that, at the death of the first, the survivor has the entire and total enjoyment and use of all the goods, both patrimonial and after-acquired, which belong to them and of which they are the possessors on the day of the said death.[1]

Sentiment (*pour l'amour et affection conjugale*) joins labor and common property (*par la labeur industrie et biens communs*) as rationale for the mutual donation. The document seems to say that husband and wife share their wealth in life and after death and do so both because they have produced it together and because they love each other.

Such language seems to have first arrived in Douaisien *ravestissements* during the sixteenth century. Although Europeans had long spoken of conjugal affection, even "love," in other contexts, none of the hundreds of *ravestissements* from the late thirteenth through the fifteenth century that I have read – the earliest we have – used such terms; they were solely concerned with the property agreement itself. However, by the 1550s, such talk of love had become the rule in Douaisien *ravestissements*, which

[1] Archives municipals de Douai (hereafter AMD) FF 655/5564, 8 November 1558.

all implicitly or explicitly, as in the de Paradis–Vallain donation, linked love with the promised property exchange. In Douai at least, people now thought it appropriate, or necessary, to explain that love motivated a couple to share their wealth or, conversely, that their shared labor and property engendered love. One document offered a "proper mutual love" (*bon amour mutuel*) as the explanation for the mutual donation; another spoke of "a proper love and a natural conjugal affection" (*la bonne amour et affection naturelle et conjugalle*). A third referred indirectly to custom's rule that only childless couples needed to write a *ravestissement* because fertile couples automatically produced the same effect.[2] Their text explained that they had chosen this agreement "for the good love that they have for each other, also because they have no children of their own and for many other reasons."[3]

The understanding of conjugality expressed by the equation between *amour* on the one hand and *labeur*, *industrie*, or *biens communs* on the other was born, I argue, of the particular circumstances of people like these Douaisiens. They lived from movable wealth that required attentive management if it was to secure their family's future as immovable wealth was thought able to do. In the language of modern finance, they lived to a significant extent from working capital, not from fixed capital – thus

[2] For the Douaisien customary laws of inheritance, succession, and marital property relations, see Robert Jacob, *Les époux, le seigneur et la cité: Coutume et pratiques matrimoniales des bourgeois et paysans de France du Nord au Moyen Age* (Brussels, 1990); idem, "Les structures patrimoniales de la conjugalité au moyen âge dans la France du Nord. Essai d'histoire comparée des époux nobles et roturiers dans les pays du groupe de coutumes 'picard – wallon'" (Ph.D. diss., Université de Droit, d'Economie et de Science Sociales de Paris, 1984); and Howell, *Marriage Exchange*. According to Douaisien customary law, couples to whom a child had been born ("whose cry had been heard") automatically created a mutual donation (*ravestissement*) of all conjugal property, movable and immovable. It was thus for the most part childless couples who would have written *ravestissements*. Jacob has reasoned, however, that some of the *ravestissements* were written as supplements to marriage contracts that had reserved lineal property for kin rather than allowing it to enter the conjugal fund that would be subject to a *ravestissement*; the *ravestissement* thus served to guarantee that the property not covered by contract would pass to the surviving spouse. However, my own search of the archive of marriage contracts and *ravestissements* has uncovered only one or two such cases, although there may be more.

[3] AMD, FF 655/5551, 5 March 1555; FF 655/5582, 1 February 1567; and FF 655/5584, 25 August 1570.

from assets that turned over regularly. Although they had a lot to gain if they succeeded in business, their assets were always at some risk, and if they did not succeed they were in serious trouble, for guilds, charities, and similar organizations offered only temporary help and their families were rarely able to provide adequate aid in the event of a business catastrophe. Without extensive communal or familial support and faced with the uncertainties of a life in commerce, the couple was under pressure: if they worked together effectively they could jointly prosper; if not they could jointly fail. The language of *amour et affection conjugale* that de Paradis and Vallain called upon provided ideological cement for their union, doing the work, as it were, that property alone no longer could. The love of which they spoke thus had a particular meaning. It could not have been the wild passion that drove the lovers of romance fiction or troubadour poetry. Nor was it a simple expression of the mutual commitment that preachers and theologians considered the obligation of the spouses. Although their love may have acquired a spiritual cast and although the word evoked something of the desire described in romances of the day, for them *amour* was embedded in a resolutely materialist, or practical, conception of marriage, exactly like that implied by de Paradis and Vallain's *ravestissement.*

THE NUCLEAR HOUSEHOLD, THE FAMILY ECONOMY, AND THE CONJUGAL BOND

De Paradis and Vallain's claim that they had jointly provided their marital estate was surely accurate, and the same could have been said for most couples in cities like Douai, one of the period's leading textile producers and commercial centers. In the southern Low Countries where Douai was located, as in much of northwestern Europe, families were indeed nuclear in structure, and their residences were populated only by the couple, their minor children, a few servants or apprentices, and the occasional dependent relative.[4] Although such couples retained ties to their

---

[4] For this demographic history, see in particular John Hajnal, "European Marriage Patterns," in *Population in History*, eds. D. V. Glass and D. E. C. Eversley (London, 1965), pp. 101–46; Peter Laslett and Richard Wall, eds., *Household*

natal families – ties, as we have seen in the previous chapter, that had to be honored – they did not live with kin, and they typically shared property with them only through inheritance. Despite having received marriage gifts that initially funded their household, the husband and wife were independently responsible for their family enterprise; their well-being and that of their offspring, as well as their ability to honor their obligations to kin in their wills or through the customary routes of inheritance, depended on their effective management.[5] In places like Douai, where the family enterprise was by definition a commercial enterprise, the couple's responsibilities were especially great; shops had to be run, raw materials purchased, production well executed, credit arranged

and Family in Past Time (Cambridge, UK, 1972); Richard Michael Smith, "Some Reflections on the Evidence for the Origins of the 'European Marriage Pattern' in England," in The Sociology of the Family: New Directions for Britain, eds. Chris Harris and Michael Anderson (Keele, UK, 1979), pp. 74–112. In addition, Theo Engelen, "The Hajnal Hynpotheis and Transition Theory," in Marriage and the Family in Eurasia: Perspectives on the Hajnal Hypothesis, eds. Theo Engelen and Arthur P. Wolf (Amsterdam, 2005), pp. 51–71. For the evidence of nuclear families in Douai and its region, see Jacob, Les époux; idem, "Les structures patrimoniales."

Scholars agree that the nuclear household had become dominant in northwestern Europe only toward the end of the Middle Ages and that even in the early modern period it was by no means hegemonic outside that region. Flandrin estimated that as late as the late seventeenth and early eighteenth century, between 32% and 43% of households were extended or multi-nuclear, whereas only about half were nuclear: Jean-Louis Flandrin, Families in Former Times: Kinship, Household and Sexuality (Cambridge, 1979, new ed., 1984), esp. pp. 65–92; cited in Allan A. Tulchin, "Same-Sex Couples Creating Households in Old Regime France: The Uses of the Affrèrement," Journal of Modern History 79 (September 2007), pp. 613–47. That figure includes France south of the Loire; in contrast, in England (and in the Low Countries), the nuclear household was the norm.

[5] For discussions and guides to the literature on the family economy of this society, see Martha C. Howell, Women, Production and Patriarchy (Chicago, 1986); idem, The Marriage Exchange: Property, Social Place, and Gender in Cities of the Low Countries, 1300–1550 (Chicago, 1998); Myriam Carlier and Tim Soens, eds., The Household in Late Medieval Cities: Italy and Northwestern Europe Compared (Leuven, 2001); and Shennan Hutton, "'On Herself and All Her Property': Women's Economic Activities in Late Medieval Ghent," Continuity and Change 20, no. 3 (2005), pp. 325–49.

and given, the household provisioned in sometimes uncertain market-places, and – if all went well – accumulated wealth wisely invested in luxuries, rents, and land.

As an example of such a family economy, consider Jean Le Libert's story. A resident of Douai like de Paradis and Vallain, Le Libert was a butcher, and when he first married in 1389, all he was able to contribute to the marriage was a group of "biens" and "meubles" worth only 80 *livres parisis*, which would have been enough to buy a very small house, plus 40 *biestes a laine* (sheep in fleece). His bride had little more: only some cloth, clothing, and some *biens*, all valued at 160 *livres*, the price of only a slightly less unprepossessing dwelling.[6] In 1402, Le Libert, now widowed, remarried. His contribution to this marriage is not listed in the surviving marriage contract, but we know that at this time he now had at least two houses and 100 *francs* (165 *livres*) to divide among the five children his first wife had borne him, and we know that Françoise Rohard, his second wife, was considerably better endowed at her marriage than his first bride had been at hers.[7]

To judge from these two contracts, separated by just thirteen years, Le Libert had evidently prospered since his first marriage, and his children would prosper as well. One of his sons, born of his first marriage, Nicaise Le Libert, wrote a will in 1443.[8] Apparently a butcher like his father, he left his widow the property he had promised to her in the marriage contract written seven years previously, and he stipulated that his *heritages* (property considered patrimonial) were to be divided between his two children (apparently of a prior marriage). However, he went on to make elaborate individual bequests to the church, to his

---

[6] AMD, FF 594/780 (11 October 1389). According to the document, the marriage had actually occurred during the previous August. I tell a fuller version of this story in *Marriage Exchange*.

[7] AMD, FF 600/1258 (29 May 1402). Rohard brought 200 *francs royaulx* (330 *livres*) in coin, furnishings, cloth, and jewels, plus 5 *rasières* of land to her marriage – the *francs* alone were worth twice the first wife's entire contribution to her marriage. Rohard was also much better provided for in her widowhood, another measure of her relatively higher economic status: the value of the property Le Libert promised her as his widow was about 650 *livres*, almost triple the 240 *livres* that the first wife would have received as Le Libert's widow.

[8] AMD, FF 875 (28 April 1443).

eldest son (who was, it seems, also his business partner), and to various kin and friends. In addition, selected members of his parish received 57 *sous*; candles, votives, and lamps went to his church; 4 *sous* were offered for each of an unlimited number of masses; 12 *rasières* of grain were set aside for bread for the poor on each day his *obseques* were said; money was designated for the poor who attended his funeral; and 48 *sous* were left for the members of his craft who accompanied his bier. Hanotin, the eldest son mentioned above, also received two new houses plus his father's chief residence, another building lot in Douai, a half-interest in another house, 30 *sous* due on an outstanding bill, numerous rents in kind and money owed Nicaise and Hanotin jointly, several small land holdings, some luxury cloaks and outerwear, household furnishings, arms, and jewelry.

The Le Libert family's story of upward mobility is surely happier than many others from fifteenth-century Douai, but there is something typical about their tale. Like all propertied Douaisiens of the day, the Le Liberts were traders: they regularly exchanged houses for cash, cash for clothing, clothing for arms, arms for land. The marriage contracts and wills that we have to trace these exchanges tell only a small part of the story, but they are eloquent witnesses to the ease with which property and people changed place in Douai. Le Libert himself rose several notches in economic status during his life, and his son Nicaise died a truly rich man. We also know that at some point in the course of assembling these lands, rents, houses, arms, clothing, jewels, furnishings, and coin mentioned in his will, Nicaise had traded away his share in two houses and 100 *francs* he had gotten from his mother's estate (Le Libert's first wife). For their part, the sheep with which his father and mother had begun married life just fifty-three years earlier were long gone, and probably long forgotten.

As many historians have emphasized, nuclear households like Le Libert's were well suited for their managerial task. Their relative inde-pendence from kin rendered them agile, able to act much more quickly and decisively than couples who formally shared their wealth during life, and sometimes even their residences, with relatives who conse-quently had a major say in how property was handled both during mar-riage and after the death of one of the spouses. Nuclear couples could make new investments with greater ease, shed assets of declining worth, and – above all – apply their *industrie* and *labeur*, as de Paradis and Vallain put it (and as Le Libert and his wives had evidently done), to protecting, perhaps increasing, the wealth that would be theirs and their children's alone.

The household's relative independence also demanded close cooperation between husband and wife. Because the men who headed these households had only a small number of apprentices or journeymen, they had to rely on the labor of their wives not just for execution of what we would call domestic responsibilities but also for assistance in producing for and managing the household enterprise. In keeping with this practical imperative, women played a by and large unchallenged role in market production and trade during the early centuries of commercial development.[9] To be sure, a sexual division of labor prevailed; certain tasks were typically female and others male, but that division was not as rigid as scholars once supposed. In any case, the line dividing female work from male did not neatly overlap with the murky boundary between work for subsistence and work for the market. Rather, throughout northern Europe, both men and women produced goods for sale, both worked for wages and as pieceworkers, and both ran shops or other commercial establishments.

Some women entered the market simply by producing and selling the kinds of goods that they had traditionally made for domestic use, such as butter and cheese, beer and ale, cloth and clothing. Many married women also crossed into what was traditionally a male economic space, selling the goods men produced in shops attached to the house or assisting in the workshop itself. Other wives represented husbands who traveled as merchants, keeping their books, storing their merchandise, and handling local sales. Propertied widows regularly succeeded husbands as managers of the family workshops, as sole proprietors of

---

[9] See Heide Wunder, *He is the Sun, She is the Moon: Women in Early Modern Germany* (Cambridge, MA, 1998), which provides a lucid discussion of this social logic. In these households, she explains, "the bride and groom combined their resources to provide the basis for an independent life as a married couple. This life had to be secured by the work of the spouses, usually throughout their lives: through housekeeping in the narrower sense, but at times and in case of need through every conceivable kind of work" (p. 68).

market stalls that were sometimes passed from generation to generation, or occasionally as skilled participants in regional and long-distance
trade of manufactured goods, raw materials, and credit instruments. The
records that survive from cities of the late Middle Ages regularly mention these female artisans, retailers, merchants, peddlers, shopkeepers,
and pieceworkers. Less often women appear in guild records as mis-
tresses, usually as widows of masters but occasionally with independent
rights to the craft.[10]

Scholars have also argued that community property law, which
was the customary form of marital property law in much of northern Europe during these centuries, both expressed and institutionalized
these practices.[11] As explained in Chapter 1, under such systems much –
and in some cases all – property brought to a marriage or acquired during its course was deposited in a communal account. The survivor of
the marriage succeeded to a good portion of it, sometimes all of it. The
ravestissement written by Vallain and de Paradis at the beginning of this
chapter was a formal expression of such a system. Presumably they wrote
it because no child had been born of their marriage, and they wanted
to ensure the mutual donation that custom alone would have provided
had there in fact been a live birth.[12] Even in places where some property
was excluded from the community property fund and reserved for heirs

[10] For representative empirical studies, see Margaret Wensky, *Die Stellung der
Frau in der stadtkölnischen Wirtschaft im Spätmittelalter* (Cologne, 1980); Barbara
Hanawalt, "Women and the Household Economy in the Preindustrial Period:
An Assessment of Women, Work, and Family," *Journal of Women's History* 11,
no. 3 (Autumn 1999), pp. 10–16; idem, ed., *Women and Work in Preindustrial
Europe* (Bloomington, IN, 1986); Howell, *Women, Production and Patriarchy*;
Carlier and Soens, eds., *The Household in Late Medieval Cities*; Monica Chojnacka,
Working Women of Early Modern Venice (Baltimore, 2001); Hutton, "'On Herself
and All Her Property'"; Wunder, *He is the Sun*; Merry Wiesner, *Working Women
in Renaissance Germany* (New Brunswick, NJ, 1986).

[11] See, for example, Tine de Moor and Jan Luiten van Zanden, "Girlpower: The
European Marriage Pattern (EMP) and Labour Markets in the North Sea Region
in the Late Medieval and Early Modern Period," www.iisg.nl/hpw/papers/
demoor-vanzanden.pdf. My thanks to the authors for allowing me to cite this
paper. For a fuller development of their argument, see idem, *Vrouwen en de
geboorte van het kapitalisme in West-Europa* (Amsterdam, 2006).

[12] For an explanation of this feature of custom, see note 2.

of the deceased, as it was in customary regimes such as Ghent's, widows typically had the same succession rights to the communal account and to their own lineal property as did widowers. Thus, in contrast to areas where dotal systems distinguished the wife's property from her husband's, in this region people were obliged to share property, and husbands and wives easily could have thought of one another as the legitimate successor to household wealth.[13] Even when men wrote wills that intervened in the customary systems of succession, they nevertheless regularly named their wives executors of their wills, left them large bequests, and made them guardians of underage children (in preference to or as partners of male relatives of the deceased).[14]

[13] By the late Middle Ages, the rules about control of the dowry both during marriage and widowhood varied from place to place; in some places widows could themselves control the dowry, although that right was usually limited and often challenged. See Isabelle Chabot, "La loi du lignage: Notes sur le système successoral florentin (XIVe/XVe–XVIIe siècle)," *Clio* 7 (1998), pp. 51–72; for evidence from Venice, where the situation seems to have been different (and better) for women, see Linda Gazzetti, *Venezianische Vermächtnisse: Die soziale und wirtschaftliche Situation von Frauen im Spiegel spätmittelalterlicher Testamente* (Stuttgart, 1998) and Stanley Chojnacki, "The Power of Love: Wives and Husbands in Late Medieval Venice," in *Women and Power in the Middle Ages*, eds. Mary Carpenter Erler and Maryanne Kowaleski (Athens, GA, 1988), pp. 126–48. On Italy more generally, see Thomas Kuehn, *Law, Family & Women: Toward a Legal Anthropology of Renaissance Italy* (Chicago, 1991).

Other scholars have pointed out that artisanal families elsewhere in the South frequently formed community property accounts, presumably because that system best facilitated management of the family economy. See Jean Hilaire, *Le régime des biens entre époux dans la région de Montpellier du début du XIII siècle à la fin du XVI siècle* (Paris, 1957); Diane Owen Hughes, "Urban Growth and Family Structure in Medieval Genoa," *Past & Present* 66, no. 1 (1975), pp. 3–28; Jutta Sperling, "Marriage at the Time of the Council of Trent (1560–70): Clandestine Marriages, Kinship Prohibitions, and Dowry Exchange in European Comparison," *Journal of Early Modern History* 8, no. 1–2 (May 2004), pp. 67–108; and Tulchin, "Same-Sex Couples."

[14] According to many customs, wives automatically assumed that role in intestate successions, itself evidence that women's economic abilities were generally acknowledged. For examples, see Ariadne Schmidt, "Touching Inheritance: Mannen, vrouwen en de overdracht van bezit in de zeventiende eeuw," *Historisch Tijdschrift Holland* 33:4 (2002), pp. 175–89; and Danneel, *Weduwen en wezen*.

According to an influential body of scholarship, these circumstances encouraged precisely the kind of affective ties that seemed to be expressed in de Paradis and Vallain's *ravestissement*. Marriages forming nuclear households were necessarily partnerships based on mutual commitment, not only to the enterprise but also to one another; *amour* followed, the reasoning goes.[15] Accordingly, the *amour* invoked in de Paradis and Vallain's *ravestissement* is thought to have been more than the *dilectio, caritas, amicitia, affectio,* or sometimes even *amor* that medieval

Barbara Hanawalt's *The Wealth of Wives: Women, Law and Economy in Late Medieval London* (Oxford, 2007) provides abundant material exposing women's access to and control of property in that city's economy; as on the northern continent English women who lived under forms of communal property law played active roles in commercial economies, whether as producers, managers, or transmitters of wealth.

[15] For scholarship emphasizing how shared management of such households produced an ethic of cooperation and partnership, even love, see in particular Alan MacFarlane, *Marriage and Love in England: Modes of Reproduction, 1300–1840* (Oxford, 1986). For more on the affective bonds of medieval and early modern marriages, see James F. Traer, *Marriage and the Family in French Law and Social Thought* (Ithaca, NY, 1980); Jeffrey R. Watt, *The Making of Modern Marriage: Matrimonial Control and the Rise of Sentiment in Neuchâtel, 1550–1800* (Ithaca, NY, 1992); Hanawalt, *The Ties That Bound;* Ariadne Schmidt, *Overleven na de dood: Weduwen in Leiden in de Gouden Eeuw* (Amsterdam, 2001); Leah Otis-Cour, *Lust und Liebe* (Frankfurt, 2000). Lawrence Stone, *The Family, Sex, and Marriage in England, 1500–1800* (New York, 1977) famously argued that this ideal took firmest root in such nuclear families, but that the discourse of romance that informed this conception was the work of the gentry and professional classes of the seventeenth and eighteenth centuries. He acknowledged that small nuclear families like the de Paradis–Vallain household were sternly patriarchal structures, hardly the perfect site for romance and mutuality, although he believed that the discourse eventually "trickled down" to them. Chojnacki, "The Power of Love," argues that merchant families in late medieval Venice enjoyed the same kind of relationship. See, however, Christiane Klapisch-Zuber, *Women, Family, and Ritual in Renaissance Italy* (Chicago, 1985) and Chabot, "La loi du lignage" for alternative views about elite Italian merchant families.

Recent surveys of marriage and family in this period include Mary S. Hartman, *The Household and the Making of History: A Subversive View of the Western Past* (Cambridge, 2004); Ralph A. Houlbrooke, *English Family, 1450–1700* (London, 1984), largely superseded by Peter Fleming, *Family and Household in Medieval England* (New York, 2001).

moralists had long considered essential to marriage. As David Herlihy
has reminded us, medieval commentators used these words indiscrimi-
nately to refer to bonds with neighbors, kin, lords, and allies, as well as
to those between parents and children or between spouses themselves.
In fact, contemporary theorists sometimes ranked spouses very low in
the affective hierarchy, well below kin, lords, or even children.[16] In
contrast, scholars have argued, commercial people like the Douaisiens
described here developed a more robust, even a more romantic, sense
of conjugal love. As the Puritan writer Daniel Rogers would explain
a century later, couples like these were drawn by a "sympathie" that
caused "the heart of one to incline to the other . . . [and] oftimes a reason
cannot be given by either partie, why they should be so tender each to
other; it being caused not by any profitable or pleasurable meane, but
by mere sympathie, which is far the more and noble cement of union
than what else so ever."[17]

However, we need only look at the demographics of the day to
suspect that something is the matter with this interpretation of de
Paradis and Vallain's document and, by extension, of such expressions
used by similar couples throughout the North. Nuclear households like
theirs were so demographically unstable that such couples would have
found it hard to nurture the intimacy, trust, and sense of partnership
imagined by the *amour* associated with today's ideas about conjugal love
or even as invoked by the Puritan writer a century later. In premodern
Europe only a minority of marriages actually survived into a couple's
old age; in fact, scholars have estimated that death brought an early

---

[16] On the medieval language of "love," see David Herlihy, "Family," *American
Historical Review* 96, no. 1 (Feb. 1991), pp. 1–16; also see Rüdiger Schnell,
"The Discourse on Marriage in the Middle Ages," *Speculum* 73, no. 73 (1998),
pp. 771–86, who argues that *dilectio* was the word most often used to refer to
conjugal love and that it merely connoted dutiful affection.

[17] Daniel Rogers, *Matrimoniall Honour* (London, 1642), pp. 147–8, cited in
Edmund Leites, "The Duty to Desire: Love, Friendship, and Sexuality in Some
Puritan Theories of Marriage," *Journal of Social History* 15 (1982), pp. 383–408.
Also see Roland M. Frye, "The Teachings of Classical Puritanism on Conjugal Love," *Studies in the Renaissance* 2 (1955), pp. 148–59. Leites, "The Duty
to Desire," summarizes this marriage ideal as "the union of erotic, spiritual,
domestic, and ethical bonds" (p. 386).

end to marriages then just as often as divorce does in our time.[18] In the North at least, widowers and widows were stunningly quick to remarry, sometimes within months of their previous spouse's death. For example, in a sample of marriage contracts from fifteenth-century Douai, about 30 percent of the brides were widows, some of them marrying for the third time and some of them just a short time after losing their last husband.[19] It is thus no surprise that the famous *Le Ménagier de Paris* of the fourteenth century casually assumed that the child bride being instructed in the book would remarry when her elderly husband died. Widowed men remarried even more regularly, sometimes outliving three, four, or five different wives and having children with each of them. Alongside the combined households that resulted from frequent remarriage, this region contained a significant number of female heads of household, for not all widows chose to remarry and some could not.[20] It is thus wrong to imagine that men and women spent most of their adult lives living in the same nuclear household with the same spouse.

It ought to come as no surprise that the "sentiment" described by the Puritan writer quoted earlier played only a minor role in making marriage. This is not to deny that first-time brides and grooms courted by exchanging tokens, kisses, and sometimes sex, all suggesting the kind of attraction associated with romantic love in the modern West. However, flirtations and premarital sex were usually supervised, approved, and encouraged by the families of these young people, not to mention the community itself, practices that suggest that a lot more than young

---

[18] For a study that exposes the instability and permeability of the nuclear household, see Miranda Chaytor, "Household and Kinship: Ryton in the Late 16th and Early 17th Centuries," *History Workshop* 10 (1980), pp. 25–60.

[19] AMD, FF 609; AMD, FF 616; there were about fifty marriage contracts in the first sample and about eighty-five in the second. For further discussion and examples, see Howell, *Marriage Exchange.*

[20] In the South there were more unmarried widows, probably because marital property systems there penalized widows who remarried by reducing the income they received as a survivor of the marriage. For studies of Florence that expose these patterns, see David Herlihy and Christiane Klapisch-Zuber, *Les Toscans et leurs familles: Une etude du "catasto" florentin de 1427* (Paris, 1978); Klapisch-Zuber, *Women, Family and Ritual*; and Chabot, "La loi du lignage."

love was at issue.[21] Men and women marrying for the second or third time seem to have been even less sentimental. The pattern of widow remarriage is especially instructive, for their tendency to marry widowers in trades related to their late husbands' suggests that the need for help running a household economy trumped romance. The same seems to have been true for many widowers, at least to judge from the fact that they married widows almost as often as widows themselves married established widowers.[22] Even when old men married women barely out of girlhood, it is hard to know how much carnal desire motivated their choices. Although the contemporary comic literature delighted in telling that story, texts like the *Ménagier de Paris* give no hint of such passion.[23] In any case, whatever the husbands in these December—May matches had in mind, I suspect that few of these child brides would have thought themselves smitten. If they "freely" consented to the match, which all but a small minority surely did, they did so principally for material and social reasons.[24]

The combined and recombined nuclear households that resulted from these frequent remarriages were not the perfect matrix for domestic harmony. Because husbands and wives were regularly being replaced, because the new spouses often brought children with them, and because the new match likely produced more children, nuclear households in

[21] For excellent evidence of this pattern, see Shannon McSheffrey, "Place, Space, and Situation: Public and Private in the Making of Marriage in Late-Medieval London," *Speculum* 79 (2004), pp. 960–90 and idem, *Marriage, Sex, and Civic Culture in Late Medieval London* (Philadelphia, 2006), as well as Hanawalt, *The Wealth of Wives.*

[22] Eight of the twelve widows who wrote contracts for new marriages (in a sample of forty-one contracts) in the early 1420s in Douai, for example, had minor children, which suggests that the women were no longer fresh-faced girls; significantly, many of the contracts specified that the groom was also widowed: AMD, FF 609. Similarly, at least ten of the twenty-six widows who married in 1441–3 had minor children, and many of them were also marrying widowers: AMD, FF 616.

[23] Gina L. Greco and Christine M. Rose, eds. and trans., *The Good Wife's Guide: Le Ménagier de Paris, A Medieval Household Book* (Ithaca, NY, 2009).

[24] For evidence of remarriage by women and men alike in this region, see Howell, *Marriage Exchange*; Danneel, *Weduwen en wezen*; Schmidt, *Overleden naar het dood*; and the sources they cite.

this age were easily beset by rivalries and distrust born of competing family interests. We have only to consult a few of the thousands of court cases that display children squabbling with their half-siblings or stepparents over inheritances to be convinced of these tensions. In addition, countless folktales feature cruel stepmothers, absent mothers, and lost fathers, all giving voice to the cultural tensions that followed from demographic realities. Significantly, even though the French called stepmothers *belles-mères*, they also coined the word *marâtre* to describe the "evil stepmother" so demonized in European folktales.

The radically hierarchal gender system of the period produced additional tension, sometimes pitting men against women in ways that make a mockery of the notion of conjugal tranquility.[25] The community property laws of cities like Douai, Ghent, and Paris expressed this contradiction clearly. Although these systems gave widows about the same succession rights as widowers, they made the husband the sole and absolute manager of the communal fund, which in Douai included all property that his wife brought to the marriage or acquired during its course.[26] The *ravestissement* that began this chapter compellingly articulates the patriarchal logic: we are told that De Paradis had been *"sufficiently empowered by her husband, which empowerment she has received happily, as she has stated, declared, and warranted* [emphasis added]." In other words, she had to have her husband's permission to give him her share of the communal property. As this document makes clear, a woman married under community property law was enclosed in a space ruled by a man, and her property was in the service of his household. Just as her property was her husband's, so too were her labor and her person. Married men

[25] Judith Bennett has provided perhaps the fullest discussions of medieval systems of patriarchy (and their stubborn intractability); see, for example, "Confronting Continuity," *Journal of Women's History* 9 (1997), pp. 73–94, and *History Matters: Patriarchy and the Challenge of Feminism* (Philadelphia, 2007). Patricia Crawford and Laura Gowring, eds., *Women's Worlds in Seventeenth-Century England: A Sourcebook* (London, 2000) describe marriage in early modern England as a mix of "partnership and hierarchy, love and mastery" (p. 170). This is an apt characterization, but I would emphasize the contradictions of the system more than they do.

[26] For these norms, see Jacob, *Les époux*; Philippe Godding, *Le droit privé dans les Pays-Bas meridionaux du 12e au 18e siècle* (Brussels, 1987), and Howell, *Marriage Exchange*.

represented the family in the community. They had explicit authority to "govern" family members, which included the right to beat both wives and children for "disobedience."[27] As the recent translators of *Le Ménagier de Paris* commented, the ideal wife of much of the moralist literature of the age was modeled on the patient Griselda who always submitted to her husband's will. Here we have what they characterized as "the always paradoxical medieval model for marriage, where the wife makes a pact to be dominated, though her role must confusingly also include that of business partner."[28]

For all its rigid patriarchalism, however, community property law was Janus-faced because when the husband died, the law assigned his role to his widow. She acquired control of at least half and sometimes all of the communal property (plus all her lineal goods if any had been reserved), and the archives from late medieval northern cities confirm that widows often readily took charge of the now diminished household, even when there were adult sons.[29] A widow could also serve as guardian of minor children, with no more supervision by her husband's kin than he would have had to endure as widower.[30] In some places widows who headed households even represented the household in civic affairs.[31]

[27] On domestic violence, see Myriam Greilsammer, *L'envers du tableau: Mariage et maternité en Flandre médiévale* (Paris, 1990); Susan Dwyer Amussen, "Being Stirred to Much Uniqueness: Violence and Domestic Violence in Early Modern England," *Journal of Women's History* 6 (1994), pp. 70–89; idem, "Punishment, Disciplines and Power"; Margaret Hunt, "Wife Beating, Domesticity and Women's Independence in Eighteenth-Century London," *Gender & History* 5, no. 1 (1992), pp. 10–33; Manon van der Heijden, "Women as Victims of Sexual and Domestic Violence in 17th Century Holland: Criminal Cases of Rape, Incest, and Maltreatment in Rotterdam and Delft," *Journal of Social History* 33 (2000), pp. 623–44.

[28] Greco and Rose, eds., *The Good Wife's Guide*, p. 31.

[29] For examples, see Wensky, *Stellung der Frau*; Hanawalt, "Women and the Household Economy"; idem, ed. *Women and Work in Preindustrial Europe*; Howell, *Women, Production and Patriarchy*; Danneel, *Weduwen en wezen*.

[30] For a close study of these practices in late medieval Ghent, see Danneel, *Weduwen en wezen*.

[31] In medieval Frankfurt am Main, for example, widows who headed households were required to equip a man for guard duty on the city walls, thus hiring a substitute for the civic duties they were themselves unable to perform (just as

Although the widow technically transferred these capacities to her new husband when she remarried, his effective powers would be reduced if he was her junior (perhaps her deceased husband's apprentice) or if she had written a marriage contract to overwrite custom and to preserve her control of the property she brought to the marriage, an option that was available to women in some cities of the Low Countries and elsewhere.

Commerce heightened these tensions. Although, as other scholars have pointed out, it could position wives as "partners" or "helpmates" to their husbands in shops or workplaces that supported the family, married women had no legal rights to the property and no formal say over how it was used. In such a situation, anxiety over market conditions, disputes about business decisions taken, a wife's failures as salesperson of her husband's wares or a husband's ineptness as craftsman could put enormous pressure on marital harmony. So too could a wife's expenditures for domestic provisions or her activities as an independent entrepreneur, for as legal head of the household, the husband was solely responsible for all debts incurred by family members. Positioned to act in her husband's name, a wife could ruin him.[32] If, in contrast, she was successful, a businesswoman could challenge her husband's rule because her earnings gave her a voice that social, cultural, and legal norms

incapacitated or rich male heads of households did): Karl Bücher and Benno Schmidt, eds., *Veröffentlichungen der historischen Kommission der Stadt Frankfurt a.M.*, VI: *Frankfurter Amts-und Zunfturkunden bis zum Jahre 1612*, I.1 and I.2 (Frankfurt a.M., 1914), I, no. 10, p. 4. In medieval France, women sat as *maîtres jurés* of guilds in which they held masterships (they lost these rights in the early modern period): James Collins, "The Economic Role of Women in Seventeenth-Century France," *French Historical Studies* 16 (1989), pp. 436–70, p. 458.

[32] Hence the logic of the "feme sole" (*kopvrouw, coopwijf,* and various names in Dutch; *femme marchande publique* in standard French; *Kauffrau* in standard German), which allowed a husband to separate himself legally from his wife and her creditors. The same logic informed the German convention of *Schlüsselrecht,* which, by granting the wife a fixed credit line with local retailers and service providers, limited the obligations she could incur in the course of provisioning the household. For a recent study of the practice in England, see Marjorie Keniston McIntosh, "The Benefits and Drawbacks of Femme Sole Status in England, 1300–1630," *Journal of British Studies* 44, no. 3 (2005), pp. 410–38.

denied.[33] James Collins has described how similar conditions in early modern France upset gender order:

When women found more [economic] opportunities as individuals, they began to pose more of a threat to patriarchal order. The independent business woman, although still socially part of a household, was economically distinct from it and from her husband. Young, single women came to possess cash resources, the fruits of their labors as servants and *journalières*, that helped to free them from parental tutelage. As the chief producers of cash for their households, rural women may have become more threatening to their husbands in an economy in which cash was increasingly important.[34]

The expanding wage economy more directly weakened the patriarchal structure of these households, for women who were paid wages had their work schedules, their pay, and sometimes the spaces of their work determined by employers, not by their husbands or fathers.

Even when things went well in the family economy, there could be friction. Because commercial assets changed form regularly, changing value as they did so, it was almost impossible to keep track of how much and what each spouse had brought to the communal account or contributed to it afterward, especially in this age of primitive bookkeeping methods and insecure monetary systems. All the couple could realistically know was the value of their total assets, but even that calculation was not easy to make. Following the logic of community property law, all wealth in the common account was joint property, so that each spouse had a residual claim to at least 50 percent of it, but in many households this principle did not reflect what each spouse thought was rightfully his or hers.

---

[33] See Hans Medick, "Zur strukturellen Funktion von Haushalt und Familie im Übergang von der traditionellen Agrargesellschaft zum industriellen Kapitalismus: Die proto – industrielle Familienwirtschaft," in *Sozialgeschichte der Familie in der Neuzeit Europas: Neue Forschungen*, ed. Werner Conze (Stuttgart, 1976), pp. 254–82 for a study of this tension in villages where wage work was available to women.

[34] Collins, "The Economic Role of Women," pp. 467–8. On the new independence given to wage-earning women, see De Moor and van Zanden, *Vrouwen en de geborte van het kapitalisme*.

There could be more trouble of this kind when the husband died if the marital estate had to be divided between the widow and the heirs of the deceased (children or, in their absence, natal kin). In most regimes, as in Ghent's, community property would be split between the widow and the heirs, but property that was not considered communal would pass to the heirs as lineal property. According to most customs, the lineal account was restricted to all immovables and named movables brought to the marriage, whereas the community account usually contained all remaining movables and all "after-acquired" property, movables and immovable alike. As commerce intensified, however, there ceased to be a real distinction between movable and immovable property or, in effect, between original and after-acquired goods. The assets brought to the marriage as lineal goods, whether immovable or movable, certainly would have produced income in the course of the marriage. A herd of sheep would have been shorn and their fleece sold, a house let for rental income, or a strip of land might have been leased out for pasture.[35] As the previous chapter's study of Ghent's customary law exposed, these instabilities rendered the old equation between immovable property and lineal (patrimonial) property almost meaningless. Multiple uncertainties followed. Would the earnings from lineal property fall into the community account as "after-acquired movables," or would they return to the lineal account? What if the herd, the house, or the tenancy had been sold and replaced with raw materials that had been turned into merchandise and then into revenue? Would the money fall into the community account? How would one keep track?[36]

Just as the changes in Ghent's property law described in Chapter 1 bear witness to these difficulties, so too do the postmortem inventories that proliferated during this period. Such inventories served to identify community assets so that they could be divided between the surviving spouse and the heirs as the law required, and they were often drawn up

[35] For a fuller discussion of this problem, see Howell, "Fixing Movables: Gifts by Testament in Late Medieval Douai," *Past & Present* 150 (February 1996), pp. 3–45.

[36] In most regimes, the widow (and sometimes the widower) could collect a lifetime income from a portion of the lineal property that returned to the heirs of the deceased, but the property itself belonged to the heirs, and the surviving spouse's own heirs had no rights to it or to any income from it.

because there was (or was expected to be) trouble in determining the content of that account. In late-fourteenth-century Paris, for example, the court approved a request for an inventory because the widow (who had remarried) and her son were fighting (the court itself referred to it as *un débat*) about the community account's value.[37] In another inheritance dispute, the same court ordered the heirs to "deliver, declare, name, display, and describe all the deceased's remaining goods that were held in common," clear evidence that the disputants disagreed about the content of the account.[38] In a third case, the court felt compelled to specify that the *biens* in question were *meubles*, which reminds us that in a commercial city like Paris, just what it meant to be "movable" might not be clear (just as in Ghent, as we saw in Chapter 1).[39]

The first of the Parisian court cases mentioned, in which the son and his mother requested an inventory because of a *débat*, exposes another aspect of the problem. The mother's remarriage had put the movables she had taken from the first marriage into the hands of her new husband, who, according to customary law typical of the North, thereby gained full control of the wealth. It is likely that it was this issue, not his mother's claim itself, that had brought the son to court, for the new husband could invest the property as he wanted, keep half as his own if his wife predeceased him, and pass that property on to his own children. Understandably, the son of his mother's prior marriage would have thought the property his, a legacy from his own father and mother. A case before the aldermen of nearby Douai in 1440 documents precisely these possibilities. The aldermen confirmed the right of Jehenne de Hourdain's third husband to collect the income from property one of Hourdain's previous husbands had left to their minor children but that she was to manage it until the children reached the age of majority, as the customary law anticipated. But Hourdain had remarried, and the responsibility for this task – along with the income – was now her new husband's.[40]

---

[37] Archives nationales, Y5221, fol. 60 in Gustave Fagniez, ed., "Fragment d'un répertoire de jurisprudence parisienne au XVe siècle," *Mémoires de la Société de l'histoire de Paris et de l'Ile-de-France* XVII (1890).

[38] Archives nationales, Y5220, fol. 168v, in Fagniez, *Fragment*, no. 81.

[39] Archives nationales, Y5220, fol. 140v, in Fagniez, *Fragment*, no. 80.

[40] AMD, FF 292, fols. 62–4 and 117–8 verso. In return for the income from her deceased husband's property, she was expected "to govern, feed, house and dress the children, to send them to school and teach them a trade." Hourdain's

In effect, community property law passed wealth and children from one man to another.[41] It is no wonder then that the unmarried widow was a stock figure of comic tales of the period; free of male control, she displaced men as heads of household and her unloosed sexuality enabled her, if she married again, to transfer property and parental authority from one man to another. Indeed, Phyllis riding Aristotle or the woman in breeches were favorite images in popular literature of the day.[42]

Things could be much worse in the event of economic disaster because commercial couples had only primitive institutional supports to which they could turn, and few had either private resources sufficient to withstand significant losses or kin rich enough to bail them out. These

marriage contract with her previous husband is found at AMD, FF 613/2069 (1436); the first and third marriages are mentioned in AMD, FF 292, fols. 62–4 and 117–8 verso.

[41] In cases where the widow was the customary successor rather than beneficiary of a marriage contract that set the terms of her succession, the risk to a previous husband's line would have been even greater, for she would have had rights not just to income but also to the property itself, as would her new husband if she remarried. For example, Marie Le Grand, a Douaisien widow who had survived three husbands and, it seems, one son, wrote a will in 1402 distributing all the property she had accumulated in three marriages to twenty different people, none of them apparently related to any of her deceased spouses: AMD, FF 869 (13 April 1402).

A widow who had succeeded to land left by her husband would similarly transfer possession of the property to a new husband if she lived under a custom of "universal" community, as some did. Few communal property regimes allowed this transfer, however, for most kept "immovables" or "patrimonial property" (by which land and land rights were understood) out of the communal account, at best giving the surviving spouse usufruct on them. Further, even if land were part of the widow's succession rights, it would possess a visibility and permanence that, imaginatively at least, would link it to the previous spouse and his kin. In some cases it might be possible to sell it, but land was never as easily bought and sold (or as *necessarily* bought and sold) as cattle, wool, cloth, or other commercial goods.

[42] The "woman on top" trope was famously described by Natalie Zemon Davis in "Women on Top: Symbolic Sexual Inversion and Political Disorder in Early Modern Europe," in *The Reversible World: Symbolic Inversion in Art and Society*, ed. Barbara A. Babcock (Ithaca, NY, 1978). For examples of such images, see Keith Moxey, *Peasants, Warriors, and Wives: Popular Imagery in the Reformation* (Chicago, 1989).

couples were isolated and exposed, as though adrift on treacherous seas – sometimes in leaky boats.[43] A suit from fifteenth-century Douai nicely illustrates these risks. Jehanne Buisson had been married in 1433 under a contract rather than customary law, and the contract had evidently been written to protect her should her husband's business fail, for under customary law she would have been liable for debts attached to the estate (in proportion to the amount of the estate to which she was successor). However, according to the marital property agreement she obtained, she could exit her husband's estate with half "of all the goods, movables, chattels, and patrimonial goods [*heritages*] they had owned" (just as Douaisien custom would have provided), but she apparently had no responsibility for debts commensurate with that portion of the estate. The other half "burdened with expenses . . . and debts" would go to his closest kin.[44] In addition, the contract gave Buisson the right – a right denied by custom – to take her "bed and its furnishings, cloths, clothing, jewels and the 'furnishings for her body' [*aournemens {sic} pour son corps*]," off the top, as it were, of the estate. She also had lifelong use of the couple's residence, and it is clear that no debts were to come with any of this property – not her rights to the house, not her furnishings, and not her personal effects. When the groom died in 1435, less than two years after his wedding, he had incurred debts to wholesalers, and immediately after his death the creditors descended. Buisson simultaneously moved to take the property she had been promised out of the estate, leaving the creditors to fight over the meager remains. Her mother-in-law was the customary heir of half these remains and thus liable for the debts; in an effort to cover the losses, she had sued Buisson to force her (with her property) to stay in the estate. Buisson won the case, as the law required. With her bedroom furnishings, clothing, and use of the residence in hand – debt free – along with her half of the

---

[43] On the fragility of the nuclear household, see Peter Laslett, "Family, Kinship and Collectivity as Systems of Support in Pre-industrial Europe: A Consideration of the 'Nuclear-Hardship' Hypothesis," *Continuity and Change* 3 (1988), pp. 153–75.

[44] AMD, FF 612/1934, 1433. Buisson's parents-in-law owned a dry goods business, and they had contributed the house in which the couple lived, their son's wedding clothes, and 400 *écus* in merchandise to their son's own dry goods business.

remaining assets (which may also have been free of debt), she remarried within the year.[45]

Even in dotal marriages city people suffered many of the same uncertainties as they did in places like Douai. Dowries made up of wealth that had no fixed form, place, or value were managed (if not fully owned) by husbands who were merchants or tradesmen and thus liable to put the assets at risk.[46] When called upon to support a newly widowed woman and to finance a new marriage for her, the dowry might well be gone, lost in some business catastrophe. Even if still intact, the money might have been invested in illiquid assets and its value hard to extract from heirs (quite possibly the widow's own children) who did not have the ready cash, who were reluctant to liquidate a business asset to make the payment, and who often delayed for months and years before finally settling the debt. The archives of Florence, where the best studies of dotal marriages in commercial societies have been done, are full of dramas bearing eloquent witness to the terrible uncertainties that beset dotal marriages made with marketable movables, stories that have been well told by scholars such as Christine Klapisch-Zuber, Julius Kirshner, Isabelle Chabot, and Thomas Kuehn.[47]

---

[45] AMD, FF 290, fols. 164–5; AMD, FF 291, fol. 81 verso (both dated 1436).

[46] As Anna Bellavitis's research on Venetian marriage contracts has shown, most dowries were composed of movables – cash, objects, clothing, jewels, and rents (the last of which were considered movable, in accord with Roman law). In theory, women were not supposed to be dowered with immovables, although in fact some 10%–15% of propertied Venetians did give such assets to their daughters (counting immovables in the countryside, which were deemed movable in Venetian law, the figure approached 25%): Anna Bellavitis, *Identité, mariage, mobilité sociale: Citoyennes et citoyens à Venise au XVIe siècle* (Rome, 2001), p. 185. It was the same throughout northern Italy, according to Jane Fair Bestor, "Marriage Transactions in Renaissance Italy and Mauss's Essay on the Gift," *Past and Present* 164 (August 1999), pp. 6–46.

[47] Few of the families described by these scholars were strictly nuclear in form: men were typically much older than their teenage brides; the social, economic, and political ties between the marital household and the patriline were usually much tighter than is the case in the modal nuclear family; and sometimes the conjugal pair did not establish an independent residence. In these settings, commerce alone seems to have produced the kinds of tensions to which I refer. Klapisch-Zuber, *Women, Family and Ritual*; Chabot, "Le loi du lignage"; Kuehn, *Law, Family, and Women*; and Julius Kirshner, "Wives' Claims against Insolvent

WHAT GOD HAS JOINED TOGETHER

Most historians have emphasized that religious teachings worked with social circumstances to inform contemporary ideas about marriage. Although acknowledging that churchmen had once been ambivalent about marriage and especially about sexual pleasure in marriage, they point out that by the central Middle Ages, marriage's role in the earthly life was consistently praised, even if marital sex was only cautiously endorsed. Preachers now celebrated the union as a potential vehicle of grace, and confessors offered detailed counsel on proper comportment for husband and wife alike. By the thirteenth century, marriage was widely considered a sacrament.[48]

As the church gave spiritual significance to the marital bond, its lawyers also established the legal status of marriage in an attempt to suppress forms of cohabitation and heterosexual relations that did not correspond to their emerging conception of Christian marriage. First, and of supreme importance in the cultural history of marriage, during

Husbands in Late Medieval Italy," in *Women of the Medieval World*, eds. Julius Kirshner and Suzanne F. Wemple (Oxford, 1985), pp. 256–303.

Although it seems that in Italian cities of the period artisan households, unlike those of elites, were organized very much like those in the North, historians have not argued that the rhetoric of conjugal love took hold in these settings; to the extent scholars have credited Italians with the these attitudes, they have located them in elite families. See, for an example, Chojnacki, "The Power of Love." For studies of artisan families' household structure, see Diane Owen Hughes, "Kinsmen and Neighbors in Medieval Genoa," in *The Medieval City*, eds. Harry A. Miskimin, David Herlihy, Abraham L. Udovitch, and Robert Sabatino Lopez (New Haven, 1977), pp. 3–28; and idem, "Urban Growth and Family Structure in Medieval Genoa"; Chojnacka, *Working Women*; and Gazzetti, *Venezianische Vermächtnisse*.

[48] See James A. Brundage, *Law, Sex, and Christian Society in Medieval Europe* (Chicago, 1987); Christopher Nugent Lawrence Brooke, *Medieval Idea of Marriage* (Oxford, 1989); Philip Lyndon Reynolds and John Witte, eds., *To Have and to Hold: Marrying and Its Documentation in Western Christendom, 400–1600* (Cambridge, 2007); Peter Everard Coleman and Michael J. Langford, *Christian Attitudes to Marriage: From Ancient Times to the Third Millennium* (London, 2004); and John Witte, *From Sacrament to Contract: Marriage, Religion, and Law in the Western Tradition* (Louisville, KY, 1997).

the twelfth century canonists ruled that mutual consent alone constituted a valid marriage. A binding union was immediately contracted if
words of "present consent" were used (*per verba de praesenti*, as in "I marry
you"). In contrast, a promise to marry was expressed by words of future
consent (*per verba de futuro*; as in "I will marry you"); if these words were
followed by consummation, the union was also binding. Although there
had to be witnesses to the exchange of vows if the marriage was to stand
up in ecclesiastical court, no particular form of publicity, no formal solemnization, and no parental consent were required. To be sure, as early
as Lateran IV (1215), canonists had declared that marriages should be
announced publicly to allow members of the community to protest the
union if there were impediments (prior marriage, consanguinity, and
the like), and the church thereafter tried to ensure that bans were read
at specified times and places, that witnesses were present, and that a
priest officiated.[49] But marriages performed without the proper publicity and rituals were nevertheless valid, even if they were condemned
as "clandestine" and "illegitimate" unless followed by appropriate solemnization. As one contemporary theologian wrote, consent "is of the
essence of marriage" for it was based on what a recent scholar has called
"the liberty of love."[50]

[49] Canon 51 of the Fourth Lateran Council; for the text, see Paul Halsall, ed.,
"The Canons of the Fourth Lateran Council, 1215," *Internet Medieval Sourcebook*,
http://www.fordham.edu/halsall/basis/lateran4.html (accessed September 15,
2008).

[50] "It is not of the essence of marriage to contract it in the presence of the church
and according to the custom of the country, but a matter of propriety. The fitness
of the parties [and the consent between them] is of the essence of marriage."
Hay, *William Hay's Lectures*, (p. 31) [cited in John Witte, "The Reformation of
Marriage Law in Martin Luther's Germany: Its Significance Then and Now,"
Journal of Law and Religion 4, no. 2 (1986), pp. 293–351, p. 302]. John Thomas
Noonan, "Marriage in the Middle Ages," *Viator* 4 (1973), pp. 419–34 provides
an account of the theoretical basis of the doctrine of consent and an analysis
of its practical and doctrinal importance. Although he acknowledges that the
standard "scarcely maximized free choice, . . . [it] acknowledged rights of the
individual not dependent on family." He concluded that the basis of the consent
doctrine was "the liberty of love," and he quoted a fifteenth-century commentator who intoned that "marriage signifies the conjunction of Christ and the
Church, which is made through the liberty of love" (p. 454).

In addition, canonists sought to render marriage monogamous and indissoluble. Without exception, they condemned extramarital sex as adultery, and it was sporadically prosecuted. The church defended even more vigorously the indissolubility of marriage, so that from about the eleventh century when the church rules were firmly in place, until the sixteenth century when Protestants allowed divorce in certain cases, western Europeans possessed few legitimate means for ending one marriage and entering a new one, and all of them were expensive or clumsy.[51] The church also attacked what was referred to as incest (marriages defined as endogamous) by prohibiting marriages within specified bounds of kinship, both biological and spiritual. By Lateran IV it was

In late medieval England, the usual marriage began with an exchange of vows in the presence of witnesses (a vow in the present tense was a marriage; a vow in the future tense was a betrothal) followed by the calling of bans and a church solemnization: McSheffrey, "Place, Space, and Situation." Roughly the same practices prevailed in fifteenth-century France. Marriage normally took place in two stages: a betrothal (promise of the future) followed by a solemnization, although there, too, valid marriages could be made simply by a vow in the present tense. See the examples provided by Pierre Charbonnier, "Les noces de sang: Le mariage dans les lettres de rémission de la fin du XVe siècle," in *Le mariage au Moyen Âge (XIe–XVe siècle)*, ed. Josiane Teyssot (Clermont-Ferrand, Fr., 1997), pp. 133–54.

[51] On the history of medieval ecclesiastical marriage law in England, see R. H. Helmholz, *Marriage Litigation in Medieval England* (Cambridge, 1974) and Michael M. Sheehan and James K. Farge, *Marriage, Family and Law in Medieval Europe: Collected Studies* (Toronto, 1994). For France and Europe more generally, see Juliette M. Turlan, "Recherches sur le mariage dans la pratique coutumière (XIIe–XIVe s.)," *Revue d'histoire de droit français et étranger* 35 (1957), pp. 477–528; Brundage, *Law, Sex, and Christian Society;* Charles J. Donahue, "'Clandestine' Marriage in the Later Middle Ages: A Reply," *Law and History Review* 10 (1992), pp. 315–22; idem, "The Canon Law and Ecclesiastical Jurisdiction from 597 to the 1640s," Review of R. H. Helmholz, *Law and History Review* 25:1 (2004); A. Esmein, *Études sur l'histoire du droit canonique privé: Le mariage en droit canonique* (Paris, 1891); Beatrice Gottlieb, "Getting Married in Pre-Reformation Europe: The Doctrine of Clandestine Marriage and Court Cases in Fifteenth-Century Champagne," Ph.D. diss., Columbia University, 1974; Brooke, *Medieval Idea of Marriage;* Charles J. Reid, *Power over the Body, Equality in the Family: Rights and Domestic Relations in Medieval Canon Law* (Grand Rapids, MI, 2004).

understood that all descendants of a common great-great-grandparent were ineligible spouses, as were godparents or their children.[52]

The ban on divorce did not, however, secure marriage. Noble men whose wives had not produced an heir, who were no longer of use in securing political alliances, or who stood in the way of a better match had casually divorced them in the early centuries of the Middle Ages, and they clung to these privileges even as the church clarified and began to enforce its rules about indissolubility. When divorce was no longer possible, annulment (and murder) were; although both came with costs, there are many such stories about their use in the late Middle Ages and early modern period. We know less about the practices of ordinary people, but it is clear that they could be equally casual about the status of their unions: the wives of men who had been absent for years often sought and won the right to remarry; men who changed addresses often changed wives as well, in effect becoming bigamists in the eyes of the church.[53]

However, the rule about consent provided the greatest challenge to church authority because it allowed couples not only to defy parents but also to hide a previous liaison, to ignore the permitted degrees of

[52] Jack Goody, in *Development of the Family and Marriage in Europe* (Cambridge, 1983), has famously argued that the church fashioned the rules for its own material benefit. The church's insistence on monogamy and indissolubility served both to distribute property outside closed kin networks and leave it under the control of widows who were not only empowered but also inclined to pass property on to the church at their deaths.

[53] Nor were the church rules about marriage strictly honored. Many people violated laws of incest by marrying closely related kin in order to keep the bride's dowry or marriage portion in the family line, and they managed to do so until well into the early modern period, even if their disobedience sometimes cost them. Ordinary people probably had even more freedom to marry within the prohibited degrees of kinship, because unless they lived in cities of some size it would have been hard to find eligible spouses who were sufficiently distantly related.

By the late Middle Ages, when the data are more abundant, we do have indications that people sought to obey church rules in marrying. Douaisien marriage contracts of the period, for example, formulaically began with a phrase announcing the upcoming wedding "if the holy church assents," an implicit reference to rules about bans and presumably also about the restrictions against intermarriage of families.

kinship, or to avoid the bother and expense of religious rituals. Indeed, it seems that most marriages labeled "clandestine" were not undertaken as challenges to parental authority. And when they were, parents had a powerful weapon to fight back – property. In England and Flanders, to mention just two examples, parents threatened to deny, and actually did so if the children did not concede, customary inheritance rights to children who married against their wishes, a powerful disincentive in an age when marriages were financed and life chances determined by interfamilial transfers of material goods.[54] The evidence we have thus suggests that most people who undertook what were deemed "secret" or "clandestine" weddings did so to avoid the rules of a church that found itself, in effect, hoist by its own petard.[55] With the reforms of Trent, the

[54] For pre-Reformation England, see Eric Josef Carlson, *Marriage and the English Reformation* (Oxford, 1994) and R. B. Outhwaite, *Clandestine Marriage in England, 1500–1850* (London, 1995). For Flanders, see Greilsammer, *L'envers du tableau.* In 1438, the city of Ghent issued an ordinance forbidding clandestine marriages and disinheriting women seduced into such unions (cited in Frans De Potter, *Petit cartulaire du Gand* (Ghent, 1885); my thanks to Walter Prevenier for bringing this document to my attention. For evidence about abduction as a means of social mobility in medieval Flanders, see Walter Prevenier and Thérèse de Hemptinne, "Ehe in der Gesellschaft des Mittelalters," in *Lexikon des Mittelalters*, III, Lief. 52, 1986, kol. 1635–1640; Walter Prevenier, Thérèse de Hemptinne, and Marc Boone, "Gender and Early Emancipation in the Low Countries in the Late Middle Ages and Early Modern Period," in *Gender, Power and Privilege in Early Modern Europe*, eds. Jessica Munns and Penny Richards (London, 2003), pp. 21–39, 176–80; Walter Prevenier, "Violence against Women in a Medieval Metropolis: Paris around 1400," in *Law, Custom, and the Social Fabric in Medieval Europe: Essays in Honor of Bryce Lyon*, eds. B. S. Bachrach and D. Nicholas (Kalamazoo, MI, 1990), pp. 262–84; Walter Prevenier, "La stratégie et le discours politique des ducs de Bourgogne concernant les rapts et les enlèvements de femmes parmi les élites des Pays-Bas au XVe siècle," in *Das Frauenzimmer: Die Frau bei Hofe in Spätmittelalter und früher Neuzeit*, eds. J. Hirschbiegel and W. Paravicini (Stuttgart, 2000), pp. 429–37; Walter Prevenier, "Les multiples vérités dans les discours sur les offenses criminelles envers les femmes dans les Pays-Bas méridionaux (XIVe et Xve siècles)," in *Retour aux sources: Textes, études et documents d'histoire médiévale offerts à Michel Parisse*, eds. S. Gouguenheim et al. (Paris, 2004), pp. 955–64.

[55] Some recently published evidence about technically clandestine marriages that had been contracted in southern Europe (outside Italy) during the sixteenth century underlines this point. All but a few of those that came to court in

church finally abandoned the rule that allowed couples to make their own marriages, and thereafter marriages that had not been performed before witnesses and the presence of a priest were declared invalid.[56] In

Rome had violated no rules except those requiring special religious procedures; although these "clandestine" marriages were unions of choice in some sense, "choice" in no way implied indifference to their family's wishes or to their own material concerns. This data are from 1564, when some 44% of petitioners to Rome from all over Catholic Europe applying for a dispensation from kinship prohibitions were considered to have been married clandestinely. Although some of these marriages may have been undertaken secretly, most were clandestine only in the technical sense that the ceremony had violated the rules about the bans, even in a minor way, or had been performed without the proper rituals: Sperling, "Marriage at the Time of the Council of Trent." The same patterns prevailed in late medieval and early modern England; see Outhwaite, *Clandestine Marriage*; B. J. Sokol and Mary Sokol, *Shakespeare, Law, and Marriage*; and Shannon McSheffrey, *Marriage, Sex, and Civic Culture in Late Medieval London* (Philadelphia, 2006); for Italy, see Céline Perol, "Le mariage et les lois somptuaires en Toscane au XIVe siècle," in *Le mariage au Moyen Âge (XIe–XVe siècle)*, ed. Josiane Teyssot (Clermont-Ferrand, Fr., 1997), pp. 133–54.

As a recent scholar put it, the canonical rules actually produced clandestine marriages because they were both "too simple and too complex. Too simple, because the arranged marriage of noble houses left no essential role for churchmen to play in *effecting* [her emphasis] a marriage; too complex because they suggested that several customary features had to be present at once . . . – the already agreed-upon marriage pact, an exchange of property, and the sexual act itself": Irven M. Resnick, "Marriage in Medieval Culture," *Church History* 69, no. 2 (June 2000), pp. 350–71.

[56] In 1563, with the decree of *Tametsi* issued by the Council of Trent, the Catholic Church ruled that marriages that did not take place in the presence of the parish priest and before appropriate witnesses were invalid, and these rules gave families effective power over choice. The French refused, however, to promulgate the decree and used inheritance law to achieve the same effect. A royal Edict of 1557 went some way toward writing these views into law, and the famous Ordinance of Blois of 1579 finally succeed in wresting control from the church. It required all minors to obtain parental approval before marrying and proof of age from all prospective spouses; to strengthen the effect of that requirement, the ordinance also raised the age of majority for women from 17 to 25 and that for men from 20 to 30. In addition, it defined clandestinity to include *rapt de violence* and *rapt de seduction*, thus allowing the state to prosecute elopements as criminal acts. For this explanation and the evidence, see Sarah Hanley, "The Jurisprudence of the Arrêts: Marital Union, Civil Society, and

the process, families also got what they wanted, for the requirements about publicity effectively reincorporated them into the marriage decision, even if Trent did not explicitly grant them veto power. Protestants followed suit. Although discarding most of the medieval church's doctrine on marriage, they would similarly embed the couple's consent in a social complex, like the Catholics returning marriage to the community and the kin network where medieval people had always thought it should reside.

PASSION

During the same period in which ecclesiastics were taking control of marriage, there also developed a new language about earthly desire. In poems of the troubadours and tales of chivalric romance, human love could be elevating, fidelity to the beloved could be an ennobling virtue, and sexual passion could even be understood as a human version of the divine. In the hands of lay people and churchmen alike, these themes would be taken up in a complex cultural narrative that interpreted the church's ruling regarding mutual consent to mean that individual choice should be the sole basis of marriage. It followed that a man or a woman could ignore family, neighbors, and the church in deciding to marry. In an even more radical interpretation of the canonists' rule, consent was equated with romance so that to marry by consent was often understood to mean to marry for a sexualized and heady definition of "love," the kind celebrated in many courtly love poems and stories.[57]

State Formation in France, 1550–1650," *Law and History Review* 21, no. 1 (Spring 2003), pp. 1–41.

[57] A large body of recent work on the textual traditions treating courtly love, romance, and marriage has gone beyond old debates about whether courtly love was "real," whether it honored women, and whether its texts were widely circulated. Representative literature on the courtly love tradition includes Willy van Hoecke and Andries Welkenhuysen. *Love and Marriage in the Twelfth Century* (Leuven, 1981); Joan Ferrante, *Woman as Image in Medieval Literature, from the Twelfth Century to Dante* (New York, 1975); and Stephen Jaeger, *Ennobling Love: In Search of a Lost Sensibility* (Philadelphia, 1999). For a critique of the genre itself, see E. Jane Burns, "Courtly Love: Who Needs It? Recent Feminist Work

The equation between marital "choice" and "love" even became a minor theme of comic literature during the later Middle Ages. The couple's desire was pitted against the family's material and political concerns, making parents, particularly fathers, seem the enemy of young love. For example, in the *fabliau* known as *Vilain mire*, an impoverished young noblewoman is forced by her father to marry a brutal but prosperous peasant. In *Les trois bossus*, another woman is given to a stingy and jealous hunchback. In *Auburée*, a poor maiden of good family is courted by a young man whose merchant father refuses to allow his son to follow his heart, instead forcing him to marry into a moneyed family; meanwhile, the young woman he was forced to abandon is given over to a rich old man. In all three stories, however, the "bad" marriages fail: the young poor maiden who had been denied to the merchant's son takes a lover, cuckolding the old man she had married; the miserable wife of the hunchback refuses to obey her husband; and the first woman gives the brutal peasant a sound beating.[58]

The same pairing of romance and marriage sometimes appeared in the legal record as well. One court case from late medieval France, for example, describes women who were prosecuted for witchcraft because they had concocted a potion that was supposed to "make a husband fall madly in love and live as a good spouse."[59] Similar tropes appear in

in the Medieval French Tradition." *Signs: The Journal of Women in Culture and Society* 27, no. 1 (2002), pp. 23–57.

On marriage and love more generally during the Middle Ages and early modern period, see Neil Cartlidge, *Medieval Marriage* (Woodbridge, UK, 1997); Jean Hagstrum, *Esteem Enlivened by Desire* (Chicago, 1992); Xenja von Ertzdorff and Marianne Wynn, *Liebe, Ehe, Ehebruch in der Literatur des Mittelalters* (Giessen, 1984); Robert Edwards and Stephen Spector, eds., *The Olde Daunce* (Albany, 1991); Michael Dallapiazza, *Minne, Husere und das ehlich Leben* (Frankfurt, 1981); Ulrike-Marianne Schulz, *Liebe, Ehe und Sexualität im vorreformatorischen Meistersang* (Göppingen, 1995); Henry Ansgar Kelly, *Love and Marriage in the Age of Chaucer* (Ithaca, NY, 1975); and Otis-Cour, *Lust und Liebe*.

58 Marie-Thérèse Lorcin, "Le sot, la fille et le prêtre: Le mariage dans les contes à rire," in *Le mariage au Moyen Âge (XIe–XVe siècle)*, ed. Josiane Teyssot (Clermont-Ferrand, Fr., 1997), pp. 125–32.

59 N. Gonthier, "Les rapports du couple d'après les sources judiciaries à la fin du Moyen Âge," in *Le mariage au Moyen Âge (XIe–XVe siècle)*, ed. Josiane Teyssot (Clermont-Ferrand, Fr., 1997), pp. 155–65.

French pardon tales from the fifteenth century, the texts that supported the official *rémissions* issued to delinquents who had managed to convince the court that they deserved to be let off.[60] Like the *fabliaux*, these tales frequently feature the tensions between property, represented by the family, and free choice, sometimes explicitly described as true love. One pardon tale, for example, describes the elopement of a young noble and his beloved who chose this route to marriage because one or the other of their families was blocking their union. Another less happy but nevertheless satisfyingly resolved tale concerns a young woman who was forced to marry "against her will" and then compelled to live with her husband's parents, although it had been promised that the couple would reside with her family, not his; in retribution, she burned down her in-laws' house.

Although such stories about romantic love and marriage circulated widely in the period, few of the narratives were actually making an easy alliance between the two. In fact, most of the stories about romance, whether in traditional romances or in comic literature, were not about marital love.[61] Courtly love was typically and most "romantically" extramarital, and it entailed secrecy, anguish, and deceit, not sharing and partnership. The best known chivalric romances, particularly the beloved Lancelot tales, featured illicit lovers, with only a few exceptions like *Eric and Enide* or von Eschenbach's version of *Parzival* portraying romantic love within marriage.[62] Andreas Capellanus's *Art of Courtly Love* even asserts that love and marriage were incompatible.[63]

---

[60] Charbonnier, "Les noces de sang." Although fictions of a kind themselves, these texts are a considerably better index of cultural assumptions than the *fabliaux*, because the petition for pardon would not have been accepted (not even for the money that usually accompanied the pleas for leniency) if it had not closely tracked cultural norms. On pardon tales as sources for social history, see in particular Natalie Zemon Davis, *Fiction in the Archives* (Stanford, 1987).

[61] See E. Jane Burns, "Courtly Love," in *Women and Gender in Medieval Europe: An Encyclopedia*, eds. Margaret Schaus, Thomas M. Izbicki, and Susan Mosher Stuard (New York, 2006) pp. 173–7, for an argument that this corpus tells various and sometimes incommensurate stories about love, marriage, and desire. Her bibliography is an excellent guide to the literature and sources.

[62] For this argument, see Brooke, *Medieval Idea of Marriage*.

[63] See Book Three of Capellanus's text.

Comic tales from the period did even more to undo any link between romance and marriage. Although some did feature young love and courtship, most of these texts told of love gone wrong, of sexual desire run amok, of adultery, and of tension and conflict in marriage. Scholars have even labeled much of the comic literature of the age "anti-marriage" because its stories about conjugal relations are so vexed.[64] Chaucer's *Canterbury Tales*, for example, are so heavily infused with the complexities of marital relations that scholars long ago identified a "marriage group" consisting of the Wife of Bath's prologue, the Clerk's Tale, the Merchant's Tale, and the Franklin's Tale, all of which take the difficulties of marriage as their theme. A recent scholar has even extended the list to include the Knights' Tale of two marriages, the Miller's *fabliau* of the foibles of courtly love, the Reeve's *fabliau* of domestic life, the Shipman's Tale of cuckoldry and exchange, Melibee's tale of household governance, and the Nun's Priest's Tale of a literally henpecked husband.[65]

The fifteenth-century *Quinze joies de mariage* (*Fifteen Joys of Marriage*) also takes up the attack on marriage. The husbands in these tales are tormented by flirtatious and vain wives who are more interested in jewels, fashion, and other men than in housekeeping or the serious issues of the day. No happy marriages here. The author of the *Fifteen Joys* is also thought to have penned the hundred stories in the famous *Cent Nouvelles Nouvelles* composed at the Burgundian court, in part after Boccacio and previous *fabliaux*, but also in part after stories told by various members of the court, including the future Louis XI of France. The same themes and tropes pervade these tales: trickery in marriage, cuckoldry, love gone wrong, the social order upended. The first story recounts a tale of adultery, the fourth of cuckoldry, the seventh of a strange (and

---

[64] As Michael Camille, *The Medieval Art of Love: Objects and Subjects of Desire* (New York, 1998) noted, in the medieval literary tradition, marriage was positioned as incompatible with romantic love, even as its antithesis.

[65] Eve Salisbury, "Introduction," in *The Trials and Joys of Marriage* (Kalamazoo, MI, 2002). Others have objected, however, that Chaucer regularly made explicit connections between love and marriage: see D. S. Brewer, "Love and Marriage in Chaucer's Poetry," *Modern Language Review* 49 (1954), pp. 461–4, and Henry Ansgar Kelly, "Clandestine Marriage and Chaucer's 'Troilus,'" *Viator* 4 (1973), pp. 413–501.

very funny) *ménage à trois*, the eighth of an out-of-wedlock pregnancy, and so on. Plenty of sex and romance, little marital bliss.[66]

As the tales from the *Quinze Joies de Mariage* illustrate, the attack on marriage was frequently linked to commerce and embedded in misogynist diatribes. Women, it was charged, were vain, greedy, lustful, and deceitful, willing to do anything for the luxuries that merchants and artisans now laid before their eyes. Although women had been called vain and sexually loose for centuries in a critique of luxury and excess that was as old as western culture itself, the charges acquired new force as commerce intensified, making women's desire for things seem boundless and turning their sex into a commodity as easily available as cloth, beer, or corn.[67] For example, in Chaucer's Shipman's Tale, a merchant's wife trades her body to a cleric claiming to be the husband's relative in exchange for money to pay for elegant finery. The Italian sumptuary laws of the day, which so obsessively focused on women's dress and ornamentation, offer a particularly vicious version of the rhetoric. The priors of Florence's *Officiale della donne*, the body charged with enforcing the laws in the mid-fifteenth century, put it this way:

That these officials . . . have an honest desire . . . to restrain the barbarous and irrepressible bestiality of women who, not mindful of the weakness of their nature, forgetting that they are subject to their husbands, and transforming their perverse sense into a reprobate and diabolical nature, force their husbands with their honeyed poison to submit to them. . . . These women have forgotten that it is their duty to bear the children sired by their husbands and, like little sacks, to hold the natural seed which their husbands implant in them, so that children will be born. They have also forgotten that it is not in conformity with nature for them to decorate themselves with such expensive ornaments.[68]

[66] De Vigneulles, *Les cent nouvelles nouvelles*.

[67] For this argument, see Howard R. Bloch, *Medieval Misogyny and the Invention of Western Romantic Love* (Chicago, 1991).

[68] In Ronald Rainey, "Dressing down the Dressed-Up: Reproving Feminine Attire in Renaissance Florence," in *Renaissance Culture and Society*, eds. John Monfasani and Ronald G. Musto (New York, 1991), pp. 217–37, p. 232. Also see Ronald Rainey, "Sumptuary Legislation in Renaissance Florence" (Ph.D. diss., Columbia University, 1985).
  Giacomo della Marca, a Franciscan polemicist, begged husbands to "have another look when the[ir wives] leave the house. They dress up in anticipation

RETHINKING MARRIAGE

What then are we to make of the *amour* about which de Paradis and Vallain spoke? If not the equivalent of the passion described in romance literature, if not an evident source of spiritual comfort, if not a direct expression of ecclesiastical rules about "free" consent, and if not the "natural" outgrowth of their social circumstances, what was it? For people who lived as de Paradis and Vallain did, it was neither one of these things nor a simple sum of all of them. Rather, it was an ideological construction that drew on these disparate narratives to address the instabilities threatening marriages like theirs. The rhetoric of conjugal love thus developed in households like de Paradis and Vallain's provided the sense of partnership necessary for cooperative work and domestic harmony. By doing so, it positioned the couple as effective managers of their small economies. Commerce, or at least "work," "industry," and "property," as de Paradis and Vallain put it, thus prompted the new emphasis on love expressed in the couple's mutual donation, but commerce did so not as the unambiguously positive force other scholars have imagined but rather as a potentially disruptive power that made "love" essential.

I am thus connecting commerce and love to marriages in nuclear households in a way that others, as far as I know, have not. According to explanations offered by several distinguished predecessors, commerce helped "privatize" the family imaginatively (if not in fact) and made domesticity seem the antithesis of commerce, thus deepening and giving new meaning to the conjugal bond. In his 1990 presidential address to the American Historical Association, for example, David Herlihy reasoned that affection and love between husband and wife, indeed among members of the nuclear family as a whole, intensified during Europe's late medieval centuries in part because commerce had made the arena outside the family unstable, competitive, and insecure. The external world came to be considered "hostile and demanding . . . contractual obligations and cash connections now linked households within the

---

of their own pleasure, but when they come home they take off their jewels and look like bakers' wives": S. Jacobus, *Sermones Dominicales*, vol. 1, p. 112; cited in Diane Owen Hughes, "Distinguishing Signs," *Past & Present* 112, no. 1 (1986), pp. 3–59, p. 25.

larger society . . . the moral seems clear: contract and cash, which govern relationships in the outer world, should not do so within the family."[69] The family thus became what Christopher Lasch has termed a "haven in a heartless world," a place where trust, mutual commitment, permanence, and love were thought to rule.[70] In a similar vein, Lawrence Stone's *Family, Sex, and Marriage* argued that "affective" bonds in the nuclear family – between wife and husband, parents and children – took root after about 1500 as market production moved out of the home, into an abstracted public sphere that operated according to different rules.[71] These scholars were not the first or the only to characterize the

---

[69] Herlihy, "Family," p. 15.

[70] For a well-known critique of this vision of the family, but one that nevertheless treats it as an ideological and a social reality, see Christopher Lasch, *Haven in a Heartless World* (New York, 1977).

[71] Stone, *Family, Sex, and Marriage*; on the link between the companionate marriage and "modernization"; also see Michael Mitterauer and Reinhard Sieder, *The European Family* (Oxford, 1982), and André Burgière et al., *Histoire de la famille*, vol. 1, *Mondes lointains, mondes anciens*, and vol. 2, *Le choc des modernités* (Paris, 1986).

As Stone explained it, the nuclear household of de Paradis and Vallain's age was patriarchal, but it gradually lost that aspect as the household ceded responsibility for what would be considered "public" functions to the emergent state. Because these families thus came to be focused almost exclusively on social and biological reproduction, interpersonal relations among family members were rendered more "intimate" and "affective," no longer patriarchal in his understanding of the term. Mitterauer and Sieder's *European Family* similarly links the development of the ideology of the companionate marriage to the "modernization" of state and society.

For a critique of Stone's argument, see Christopher Hill's review, "Sex, Marriage, and the Family in England," *Economic History Review* 31:3 (August 1978), pp. 450–63. Hill pointed out that Stone's theory could not explain why these small householders so eagerly took up the rhetoric (or how, in fact, the aristocracy later came to adopt the nuclear family form). Others have complained that Stone's history of the family was aggressively progressive, Whigish, and Weberian in its celebration of individualism and modernity. Many have also objected that he misread evidence about medieval attitudes and practices, was blind to feminist critiques of the bourgeois family and the particular system of male dominance it instantiated, and ignored the way the ethic of the companionate marriage delegitimized the social practices of people whose material opportunities were profoundly different. See, for example, John R. Gillis, "Affective

commercial world in these terms and to imply that the emotional lives of the nuclear family changed as the outside world commercialized. In his 1949 *The Idea of Usury*, for example, Benjamin Nelson similarly concluded that friendship and trust could not survive in the "realm of commerce," where principles of self-interest and rational calculation reigned.[72] Those values had to be nurtured in private spaces, outside the unfriendly hurly-burly of self-interested exchange.

In this interpretation, the language of love that de Paradis and Vallain described marked the nuclear family's ideological retreat from commerce. However, De Paradis and Vallain were making no such retreat; in fact, they were asserting a connection. Although prosperous bourgeois of the centuries to come (and even a few in de Paradis and Vallain's day, as we shall see) might well learn to do so, de Paradis and Vallain by no means distinguished the conjugal from the commercial, not in practice and not in the imagination. De Paradis and Vallain's *ravestissement* is a striking example of these ideas about marriage and the clearest articulation of the link that I have come across in legal sources, but it is not the only record we have. Cultural texts of the period that restlessly interrogated the relationship between marriage and love, marriage and property, and marriage and sex often sought to make the same connection. Nowhere were such discussions more highly charged than in the Low Countries where de Paradis and Vallain lived. The region's many artists left particularly compelling evidence of the conversation, sometimes even explicitly situating marriage in trade as though conjugal relations had to be thought about in connection not just to property,

Individualism and the English Poor," *Journal of Interdisciplinary History* 10:1 (1979), pp. 121–8, for its discussion of Stone's neglect of, even disdain for, the culture of the poor; Philippe Ariès, "Review of *The Family, Sex and Marriage in England, 1500–1800* by Lawrence Stone," *American Historical Review* 83:5 (December 1978), pp. 1221–4, for Stone's misunderstanding of early modern child-rearing practices; Alan MacFarlane, "Review of *The Family, Sex and Marriage in England, 1500–1800*," *History and Theory* 18 (1979), pp. 103–26, for Stone's many misreadings of secondary literature and his ignorance of the medieval experience; and for a feminist critique, Lois Schwoerer, "Seventeenth-Century English Women Engraved in Stone?" *Albion* 16, no. 4 (1984), pp. 389–403.

[72] Benjamin Nelson, *The Idea of Usury* (Princeton, 1949).

but more specifically to commercial property.[73] Consider, for example, the famous Arnolfini marriage scene reproduced on the next page.

Painted in 1434 by Jan van Eyck, a Fleming who served in the Duke of Burgundy's court, it depicts a man and woman from prosperous merchant families living in Bruges. The couple is placed in a bourgeois interior, surrounded by objects that evoke an excess of associations regarding marriage – its sacramental status, its carnality, its power to make and unmake political relations, its function as the bedrock of community, and so on.[74] But another layer of meaning adheres as well, a meaning derived from the luxuriousness of the objects on view, their evident commercial value, and their role in the couple's lives. Arnolfini wears velvet and furs, probably sable; his wife is adorned in rich woolens and ermine; their chamber is decorated with gold, bronze, brass, silver, and carved objects, with draperies and rugs worth small fortunes. Oranges, an unimaginably precious commodity in the fifteenth century, lie about. The bed itself is an object of "estate." Although certainly a reference to conjugal sex and procreation and a reminder of the woman's material contribution to the marriage, for in the North at least it was traditionally the bride who provided the marriage bed, the bed also eloquently testifies to the couple's identification with movable wealth.

[73] On the art market in the region during the period, see Filip Vermeylen, *Painting for the Market: Commercialization of Art in Antwerp's Golden Age* (Turnhout, 2003). For more on art and commerce in the region, see Bret Rothstein, "The Problem with Looking at Pieter Bruegel's *Elck*," *Art History* 26, no. 2 (April 2003), pp. 143–73; Ethan Matt Kavaler, *Pieter Bruegel: Parables of Order and Enterprise* (Cambridge, UK, 1999); P. F. Moxey, "The Criticism of Avarice in Sixteenth-Century Netherlandish Painting," in *Netherlandish Mannerism*, ed. Görel Cavalli-Björkman (Stockholm, 1985), pp. 21–3; and Elizabeth Alice Honig, *Painting and the Market in Early Modern Antwerp* (New Haven, 1998).

[74] The literature on this painting is huge. The basic text is Erwin Panofsky, "Jan van Eyck's 'Arnolfini Portrait,'" *Burlington Magazine* 64 (1934), pp. 117–27; also see Edwin Hall, *The Arnolfini Betrothal: Medieval Marriage and the Enigma of Van Eyck's Double Portrait* (Berkeley, 1994); Linda Seidel, "Jan van Eyck's 'Arnolfini Portrait': Business as Usual?", *Critical Inquiry* 16 (1989), pp. 54–86; Craig Harbison, "Sexuality and Social Standing in Jan van Eyck's Arnolfini Double Portrait," *Renaissance Quarterly* 43 (1990), pp. 249–91; Margaret D. Carroll, "In the Name of God and Profit: Jan van Eyck's *Arnolfini Portrait*," *Representations* 44 (1993), pp. 96–132. Also see Lorne Campbell, *The Fifteenth-Century Netherlandish School* (London, 1998).

Figure 2. *Marriage and Mercantile Wealth.*
Jan van Eyck, *The Arnolfini Marriage* (1434). Oil on oak panel, 82.2 × 60 cm, 32.4 × 23.6 in. National Gallery, London, England. © National Gallery. Photo credit: London / Art Resource, NY.

This handsome bedstead, dressed with down coverlets and hung with precious fabrics colored with medieval Europe's costliest dye – red – would have easily cost the equivalent of today's luxury automobile or even a private jet. Contemporaries viewing this painting would have known that.

Although the portrait's many meanings derive in part from these commodities, it displays little anxiety about such goods; instead, it seems to express contentment, satisfaction, quiet acceptance. But perhaps van Eyck's talent was precisely his ability to render the scene so serenely, to deny, as it were, the ways that a couple dependent on such wealth might have interpreted and experienced their situation. To be sure, Arnolfini and his bride were rich, and abundant wealth provided its own assurance. The records also show that Arnolfini himself (and, we can be certain, she as well) owned land and land rights so that he was not dependent solely on the kinds of objects displayed in this portrait. But the portrait captures the essential feature of their social lives – they were both from commercial families, and their wealth was derived from trade and the skills required for commercial success. As a magnificently rich merchant, Arnolfini ultimately owed his status, as did his bride, not to his land holdings, but to his immersion in trade and his achievements in the commercial world, which this elegantly appointed interior displays. In that respect, this couple was like most urban couples in this region – and in Italy where Arnolfini and his bride's family had originated – although only a few were as rich as he.

Most of Arnolfini's neighbors, even those who were well propertied, had no rural property at all and relied instead entirely on movables and urban real estate. They were thus without assets of the kind that could perpetually produce wealth or be imagined to do so; they were funded by and responsible for wealth that would change form and value over the course of the marriage, wealth that had only current income value, wealth that in all likelihood they would themselves outlast. Quentin Metsys's "Money Changer and His Wife," on the next page painted about a century later, seems to give visual form to a marriage in exactly that social setting, where people lived from movable wealth.

Although appearing to be simply another version of a scene commonly painted in those days – a banker's workplace, where he assembles his merchandise, assays his coinage, weighs his bullion, and tallies

Figure 3. *Marriage and Business.*
Quentin Metsys, *The Moneylender and His Wife* (1514). Oil on panel, 71 × 68 cm. Paris, Musée du Louvre. Photo credit: Erich Lessing / Art Resource, NY.

up his earnings – Metsys's version hauntingly breaks with the genre's conventions.[75] Rather than giving us the customary rude commentary

[75] Van Reymerswaele's "Moneychanger and his Wife," painted in 1539, follows Metsys, not quite duplicating but clearly quoting the earlier painting. Many scholars have seen such portraits, especially the Reymerswael versions (there were several), as critiques of commerce and banking, but for a claim that the artists intended no such venom, see Manuel Santos Redondo, "The Moneychanger and His Wife: From Scholastics to Accounting," http://www.ucm.es/BUCM/cee/doc/00–23/0023.htm (accessed September 08, 2008) and the sources he cites. Classic studies of Metsys and the period's genre paintings include Lorne Campbell, "Quentin Massys, Desiderius Erasmus,

on merchant greed and untrustworthiness, Metsys's study is contemplative, subtle – and ambiguous. Surrounded by the implements of the husband's craft, the couple, each of whom is modestly dressed in old-fashioned costume, is firmly placed in a world of trade and coin, nestled among objects of luxury and value, alone except for a strange figure reflected in a small mirror. Although the husband is at work, serious work that the portrait seems to respect, the wife is no longer at her presumptive task. Instead, she is drawn from her prayer book and studies her husband's busyness, perhaps in longing, perhaps in regret that for him commerce trumps prayer. Perhaps she gazes merely in reflection, perhaps in idle boredom.

Looked at this way, this marriage seems to be disturbed by commerce – the nature of the couple's relationship called into question, the connection between their marriage and commerce foregrounded, the respective duties of husband and wife somehow problematized, an uncertainty about the meaning of married life in commerce powerfully, if mysteriously, rendered. At the same time, however, the painting hints at an intimacy born of commitment to the husband's trade, and I think our fascination with this painting owes much to that possibility. Each of the spouses focuses on the glittery objects in his shop, and they lean toward one another, as though business both absorbed and united them, giving them common purpose. Thus, whereas trade appears to pull the wife from her devotions in a way that disturbs, it also seems to draw the couple together in a way that evokes companionship and partnership.

Lucas van Leyden's "Engagement" or "Betrothal" on the next page, painted at about the same time as the Metsys painting, seems to point to a different conception of marriage, suggesting that it could or should be a matter of romance alone.

In this portrait, no family, community, or priests attend; it depicts no workshop or neighborhood. Although the couple does not appear to be in the throes of wild passion, but seems fully cognizant of the

Pieter Gillis and Thomas More," *Burlington Magazine* 120, no. 908 (1978), pp. 716–24; Max J. Friedländer, *Early Netherlandish Painting* (London, 1956); Erwin Panofsky, *Early Netherlandish Painting* (Cambridge, MA, 1953); Paul Philippot, *La peinture dans les anciens Pays-Bas* (Paris, 1994); Leo van Puyvelde, "Un portrait de marchand par Quentin Metsys" *Revue belge d'Archéologie et d'Histoire de l'Art* 26, (1957), pp. 3–23; Jean C. Wilson, *Painting in Bruges at the Close of the Middle Ages* (University Park, PA, 1998).

Figure 4. *Love and Marriage.*
Lucas van Leyden, *The Betrothal* (1527). Oil on panel, 30 × 32 cm. Antwerp, Koninklijk Museum voor Schone Kunsten. Photo credit: Scala / Art Resource, NY.

seriousness of their choice, it is clear that their love alone is the seal of their union – they gaze into one another's eyes; their hands touch. To some scholars, this painting has seemed a celebration of marriage by consent alone and an implicit criticism of church rules, parents' interference, and community pressures – perhaps even a representation of a clandestine marriage.[76]

[76] See Larry Silver, "Love and Marriage in the Art of Lucas van Leyden," in *In Detail: New Studies of Northern Renaissance Art in Honor of Walter S. Gibson*, ed. Laurinda S. Dixon (Turnhout, 1998), pp. 97–111, where he concludes that "Lucas's Strasbourg painting [i.e., "The Betrothal"] anticipates this general cultural shift in affective marital emotion and consensual behavior normally ascribed to the following century. . . . What Lucas has given us in his Strasbourg *Betrothal*

We cannot know whether van Leyden himself intended a celebration of marriage based on romance alone, but one of his later commentators offered a biting critique of such foolishness. A copy of the painting, done a few years later by another hand, bears a banderole (a banner apparently added still later) that sternly warns: "Marry in haste and you repent at leisure" (*het es haest ghetrowt das langge rowt*).[77]

Unknown or ambiguous as Metsys's or van Leyden's intended message may be, the paintings reveal how unsettled the discourse about marriage was in the sixteenth-century Low Countries. Was a pure love match possible? A good thing? Just what was the relationship between the property exchange and the marriage vow? Metsys's portrait seems to depict one answer to those questions, an answer that I think was also implied by Vallain and de Paradis's *amour et affection conjugale*. They felt "conjugal love and affection" precisely because, as they put it, they shared "labor, industry and common assets." Their love was not the passion that van Leyden's copyist seemed to criticize when he added the banderole warning against hasty marriages. What they meant by love was sober and well considered. Desire, however essential, was to be harnessed for the serious work of cementing the conjugal bond, not unleashed to cause anguish, social upset, and rash action, as the comic literature of the day so often cautioned.

Heidi Wunder has argued that this was exactly what the sixteenth-century German burghers she studied meant when they spoke of conjugal love.[78] Protestants of the day preached a similar message. Luther, Calvin, and their followers taught that marriage was a gift to humankind, given by God for the benefit of human souls, an indispensable site of spiritual growth for men, women, and children. Because it existed to fulfill the needs of human beings who were embodied – fleshy – Puritans would even insist not only that husbands and wives honor the

is an exceptional work, especially for its time, of two lovers in sympathy. The painting shows a strikingly non-judgmental and tender rendering of mutual attraction leading to a pledge of marriage," p. 107. Also see Elise Lawton Smith, *The Paintings of Lucas van Leyden* (Columbia, MS, 1992); Jacques Lavalleye, *Pieter Bruegel the Elder and Lucas van Leyden* (London, 1967); and Max J. Friedländer, *Lucas von Leyden* (Leipzig, 1924).

[77] Reproduced in Smith, *Lucas van Leyden*.

[78] Wunder, *He is the Sun*.

institution by honoring each other but also, somewhat surprisingly and entirely oxymoronically, that they had what one scholar has termed "the *duty* to desire" each other [emphasis added]. For Puritans, "sexual and sensual delight" was "essential" to the comfort that marriage provided in earthly life.[79] Although this was not the "divine madness admired in the cult of romantic love," as Edmund Morgan has cautioned us, it was nevertheless a sexualized love.[80] By the seventeenth century, Catholics had also adopted much of this rhetoric, with the result that all Christians in the West were being similarly instructed not only about the moral status of marriage but also about the importance of putting sexual desire in the service of conjugality, solidifying the conjugal bond and at the same time domesticating sex.[81]

As the van Leyden portrait reminds us, however, it was possible for people in the sixteenth-century Low Countries to imagine marriage differently, to studiously bracket *amour* from *labeur* and *industrie* in a way that seemed to make the partnership innocent of work and property. This was true even in sixteenth-century Douai, where de Paradis and Vallain wrote their *ravestissement* and where the principles of community property had been respected most carefully. Although the old *ravestissement* would long remain the "official" custom in Douai, so that any couple without a marriage contract or another document overriding custom would automatically create a mutual donation of all their property if a child was born of the marriage, and although some couples still wrote *ravestissements par lettre* as de Paradis and Vallain did, the city's most prosperous families were gradually abandoning the mutual donation. By that time, the city's premodern archive of marriage agreements

[79] Leites, "Duty to Desire," p. 395.

[80] Morgan, *The Puritan Family* (Boston, 1944), p. 53.

[81] Anthropologists studying the ideal of the companionate marriage in contemporary nonwestern societies have made a similar argument about the role of desire in such unions. As the editors of a recent collection of articles summarized it, "While romantic love may be something that companionately married couples strive to maintain during married life . . . privileging romantic attraction and individual choice when selecting a spouse is, in fact, quite different from being able (and wanting) to prioritize the ongoing affective primacy of the conjugal unit": Jennifer S. Hirsch and Holly Wardlow, eds., *Modern Loves* (Ann Arbor, MI, 2006), p. 3.

(misleadingly labeled *contrats de marriage* in the archive) was dominated, not by *ravestissements* as it had once been, but by formal contracts crafted precisely to overturn what both the customary and the written *ravestisse-ment* guaranteed – the mutual donation.[82] To judge from these documents, the conjugal bond existed independently of a property bond, for husband and wife each kept a major portion of their wealth – inevitably the most secure forms of wealth – in separate accounts designated for their own heirs, not for their spouse. Such contracts also ensured patrilineal power by preventing the widow from transferring wealth from her deceased husband's family into the hands of another man, as both the Parisian widow mentioned earlier or as Jehenne de Hourdain of Douai had done. They also guaranteed that property was reserved for children born of the particular marriage at issue, and therefore not available to children fathered by men the bride might have previously married or might marry in later years.[83] This guarantee established women as

[82] Of 133 marriage documents sampled from the fourteenth century, 80 were *ravestissements*; more than one-third of the 53 contracts in that sample were written by simple artisans and shopkeepers. Of the 300 marriage documents sampled from the fifteenth century, only 40 were *ravestissements*; even then, however, about 40% of the contracts were written by simple artisans and shopkeepers, and of the 18 *ravestissements* whose authors' social status could be identified, 20% were merchants or drapers. In contrast, of the 105 marriage documents sampled from the first half of the sixteenth century, only 6 were *ravestissements*, and among them was just one authored by a member of the city's economic elite – a draper. Simple artisans and merchants still wrote almost a third of the contracts, but now people who were clearly *rentiers* constituted 20% of the contract writers, compared to less than 10% in the fourteenth-century sample and just 10% in the fifteenth-century sample; for further details, see Howell, *Marriage Exchange*, Tables 1–3.

[83] A marriage contract written for Isabel Le Dent, for example, was explicitly designed to replace the communal system decreed by local custom with something more dotal-like in structure and more considerate of lineal interests. The document provided that, as a widow, Le Dent have what she brought to the marriage along with dower rights to some land contributed by her husband to the marriage. The contract further stipulated, however, that if the husband were to sell his land during the marriage or reduce the rents it earned (presumably by selling them), he must replace the lost property with another (or others) of precisely the same value, as approved by men appointed by Le Dent's father as her trustees: AMD, FF 616/2321 (23 April 1441). Another granted the widower only usufruct on his wife's real property (denying him the ownership that

carriers of property from father to husband and onto children, rather than as active producers and managers of wealth, and widows were given no managerial rights to the assets from which they lived. It was the same in Ghent, as we have seen, and in early modern Paris as well, where legal standards for much of the French realm were then being set. As Chapter 1 explained, in Paris the bourgeoisie learned to use testamentary, marital property, and inheritance law to reserve rents and bureaucratic offices for their heirs by assigning them to the lineal account (what they called *propres*), in effect ensuring that they were not distributed outside the patrilineal family or dissipated in unsuccessful market transactions.[84]

In areas where no community property fund was created by customary law governing marriage, but where Roman legal traditions prevailed and wives brought dowries that were sequestered during the marriage, the marital property regime itself did, and had long been doing, similar work. But even in these places people seemed to have thought it necessary to find additional ways to protect commercial wealth for the "line." For example, marriage contracts or wills could be written in ways that denied the widow any of the usual "increase" on her dowry or bequests from her husband's will should she remarry. As the medieval centuries slid into the early modern, these arrangements became more common, particularly among the rising class of urban entrepreneurs and merchants, even in the North where customary law had rarely known such dotal-like provisions.[85] By the seventeenth century it was usual for merchant families and the most prosperous artisans in northern

custom would have granted) and reserved devolutionary rights for any children to be born or, in their absence, for her kin: AMD, FF 616/2366 (21 September 1442). Another required that the widow pass her dower on to the children of the first marriage or to her deceased husband's nearest kin if she remarried: AMD, FF 875 (28 April 1443). Such provisions took many forms. For example, another from the same period secured for children of a first marriage rights to the property of their deceased father (which their mother presently controlled and was taking into a new marriage): AMD, FF 616/2347 (26 November 1441). For additional examples and statistics about the frequency of such practices, see Howell, *Marriage Exchange*.

[84] Ralph E. Giesey, "Rules of Inheritance and Strategies of Mobility in Prerevolutionary France." *American Historical Review* 82, no. 2 (1977), pp. 271–89; also Godding, *Le droit privé*; Jacob, *Les époux*; and Barbara B. Diefendorf, *Paris City Councillors in the Sixteenth Century: The Politics of Patrimony* (Princeton, 1983).

[85] In general, see Jacob, *Les époux* and Howell, *Marriage Exchange*.

cities to arrange their marriages in ways that resembled the southern dotal systems and sometimes to impose further restrictions on widows.[86] Everywhere, it seems, Europe's bourgeoisie was abandoning the idea that husband and wife were "one" in property. Now it was "love" alone or at least a version of "partnership" that did not involve shared ownership of property that sealed a marriage.

The sexual division of labor during this period was also changing, seeming to reflect this new vision of partnership. Among the same class of people who were abandoning the old mutual donation and the common property fund (or limiting the fund to small amounts of personal goods), men were taking more exclusive control of market production and women were being confined to (or taking over) the increasingly "domesticated" and newly privatized space of the home. In industrial cities, guilds sometimes literally documented the shift by legislating that women would no longer be admitted to certain trades or, more commonly, simply by letting regulations lapse that had as a matter of course included widows, wives, and daughters among the membership.[87] Government records and merchant accounts sometimes reflected the same process, either by describing a more limited role for wives and widows or, more often as time went on, simply by omitting any mention of women. Significantly (and unsurprisingly), the sexual division of labor did not change for all classes of women, for only the more prosperous merchants, shopkeepers, and artisans had property that could be set aside, held as "immovable" patrimony. The wives and widows of small retailers and less prosperous artisans who were dependent on property that had short lives and required constant management (with all the risks that involved) continued to participate in their husband's businesses, by helping with sales, keeping books, or even unofficially assisting in the workshop itself. Poor women went on working for wages, peddling used goods on the street, or setting up boutiques where they sold their hats or ribbons. But the women who would come to define proper bourgeois womanhood were quietly and tentatively submerging

---

[86] On this development, see in particular Jacob, *Les époux.*

[87] For descriptions and analyses of this process, see Hanawalt, "Women and the Household Economy"; Wiesner, *Working Women*; and Howell, *Women, Production and Patriarchy.*

any work for the market or any assets they brought to the marriage under the umbrella of their husbands' business.[88]

This was the process Herlihy seemed to have had in mind and the one Stone described as part of the rise of "affective" relations in the family. However, it was only beginning in the sixteenth century, even in Douai where commerce had long reigned, and it would be another century at least before Stone's or Herlihy's idea that a nuclear family could be sheltered – either in practice or in ideology – from the daily business of commerce dominated. Then and only then did it become possible to imagine that *amour* alone sealed marriages. De Paradis and Vallain, however, thought no such thing. "Love" had indeed acquired new importance for them, so much so that they thought it necessary to explain their mutual donation – now coming to seem a bit old-fashioned – with the help of that concept, but love was by no means the antithesis of the market. It was the market's helpmate.

CULTURAL AMNESIA

Although not yet what Herlihy and Stone had in mind, the marriage of de Paradis and Vallain can nevertheless be seen as a distant ancestor of what scholars would label the companionate marriage of modern western culture. As scholars have defined this ideal, the companionate marriage was not just the union of an adult woman and man who had freely chosen to wed because they loved one another with a love that was romantic, personal, and sexual; it was also based on friendship, mutual interests, and shared activities. Made without regard for the expectations of parents, kin, and community and even without consideration of the property interests that had constituted marriage for centuries of European history, it was a private pact between the spouses alone.[89] Historians agree that by the dawn of the modern period this conception

---

[88] For a fuller discussion of this process, see Chapter 5.

[89] Stone's *Family, Sex and Marriage* provides perhaps the fullest account of this conception of the conjugal bond. Also see Edward Shorter, *The Making of the Modern Family* (New York, 1975). The "partnership" aspects of modern western marriages are particularly emphasized in Mitterauer and Sieder, *European Family*.

of marriage had become the ideological norm for Europe's emergent middle class. To be sure, property would long be considered the central issue in the marriage decision, but as the modern centuries unrolled its role would increasingly be questioned and, finally, the reality itself ideologically suppressed. Although the idealized companionate marriage of partnership, intimacy, and desire would be approximated only by middle-class people, and never fully realized even by them, this version of marriage has long seemed to most westerners, even to some scholars, a natural formation. It is the way marriage would be in the best of all possible worlds, if uncontaminated by illegitimate desires, by selfish ambitions, or by what westerners have often labeled backwardness or underdevelopment. After about 1700 and even until today in some countries, this ideal has functioned as the model against which middle-class Europeans measure any form of conjugality, whether in Europe or in parts of the world colonized by westerners, where it served to instruct the colonized on the supposed benefits of westernization.

Ravestissements like those written by de Paradis and Vallain, although seeming to express an early version of this narrative, also expose precisely what this romanticized version of conjugality hides: the link between property and love. The story of how this link came to be ideologically suppressed is complicated, but it was partially accomplished by cultural narratives crafted, for example, in novels that positioned brains, character, or beauty above mere money or that endlessly questioned how money was used and how the power to bequeath money was deployed. Eventually, the wealth that defined Europe's middle class would seem an insufficient or even an illegitimate basis of marriage. For example,

Among the many useful studies of the companionate marriage and its relationship to bourgeois culture in the eighteenth, nineteenth, and twentieth centuries, see the following: Leonore Davidoff and Catherine Hall, *Family Fortunes* (Chicago, 1987); Isabel V. Hull, *Sexuality, State and Civil Society in Germany, 1700–1815* (Ithaca, NY, 1996); Dagmar Herzog, *Intimacy and Exclusion* (Princeton, 1996); Jacques Donzelot, *The Policing of Families* (New York, 1979); Eli Zaretsky, *Capitalism, the Family, and Personal Life* (London, 1976); Michèle Barrett and Mary McIntosh, *Anti-Social Family* (London, 1982); Bonnie G. Smith, *Ladies of the Leisure Class* (Princeton, 1981); and Mary P. Ryan, *Cradle of the Middle Class* (Cambridge, 1981). For a discussion of the companionate marriage in its modern settings, see Hirsch and Wardlow, eds., *Modern Loves* and Collier, *From Duty to Desire*.

Figure 5. *Marriage and Money.*
Gérard Jean Baptiste Scotin (after William Hogarth), *The Marriage Settlement* (1745). Plate 1 from Marriage à-la-Mode. Etching, 38.3 × 46.1 cm. London, The British Museum. © Trustees of the British Museum.

Hogarth suggested such an opinion in his popular "The Marriage Settlement"; a copy of the print is reproduced above.

In this, the first of the images that make up the series called "Marriage a la Mode," we see the inaugural step in the protagonist's moral and social decline – the moment when he married for money.[90]

Although directed less at marriage itself than at Britain's class system, Hogarth's critique can be read, alongside the interrogations penned by

[90] Recent literature on this painting, the series, and the accompanying engravings include the following: David Bindman, *Hogarth and History Times: Serious Comedy* (London, 1997); Robert L. S. Cowley, *Marriage a la Mode: A Review of Hogarth's Narrative Art* (Manchester, 1982); Arthur S. Wensinger and William B. Coley, *Hogarth on High Life: The 'Marriage a La Mode' Series from G. C. Lichtenberg's Commentaries* (Middletown, CT, 1970).

novelists or poets, to help us trace the emergence of the amnesia that has long possessed the modern western cultural imagination. Middle-class moderns have long liked to think that property has been banished from the marriage decision, along with bossy parents, interfering kin, nosy neighbors, and "medieval" rules about exogamy, divorce, and marital sex. In the modern age, it has easily seemed that a good marriage is as van Leyden long ago portrayed it: a private pledge between two consenting adults who are in love.

But in reality, property's role in marriage has merely been hidden, not eliminated. Rather, in modern marriages, the *biens* that were so important to Vallain's and de Paradis's marriage have largely been commuted into cultural capital, one of the most important forms of property in advanced capitalism. Today, education, diction, health, bearing, "taste," skills, and looks (which are increasingly manufactured) can alone both mark and bequeath class. In the sixteenth century, cultural capital of this kind was in short supply, although hardly nonexistent, as the romances about beautiful princesses disguised as peasants or noble knights turned into frogs seem to suggest. But for most people, certainly for the hard-headed people who lived in cities like Douai, shops, tools, food stores, clothing, coin, hollowware, along with rents and land if the couple had any – all meticulously itemized in the typical marriage contract – constituted the principal basis of class position. Today, huge amounts of what de Paradis and Vallain called *labeur industrie et biens communs* – that is, years of parental attention enabled by leisure and wealth, along with steady infusions of communal resources in the form of schools, health care, and other public services – go into producing the cultural capital of modernity. By being invested in children's minds and bodies, these investments are transformed, as though magically, from what seem mere lucre into something attributable to forces separable from the market. In such "modern" marriages, property typically resurfaces only when the marriage fails or the estate is probated. But it is there, just as it was for de Paradis and Vallain.

3 Gift Work

Figure 6. *The Rituals of Giving.*
Rogier van der Weyden, *Jean Wauquelin Offers His Translation to Philip the Good*, from the *Chroniques de Hainaut* (c. 1448), Brussels, Bibliothèque royale de Belgique, ms. 9242, fol. 1. © Royal Library of Belgium.

GIFTS WERE THE FUEL OF SOCIAL INTERCOURSE IN MEDIEVAL Europe. Whether embedded in the period's patronage system, in religious culture, or in networks of friends and family, gifts bound people together – in political alliances, in faith, in families. In principle freely given as signs of liberality and largesse, they were the centerpiece of diplomacy and the stuff of dispute settlement in which, as the image above suggests, they incorporated the giver and receiver, whether as peer or retainer, in the elite circle. Gifts from the laity to the church or to charity expressed piety and helped pave the way to redemption, but they also sealed sociopolitical relationships between the donor and the ecclesiastical institutions that received the gifts. When circulated among neighbors and kin after someone's death; when given during courtship, at marriage, or after childbirth; or when exchanged on special holidays, gifts signaled friendship, loyalty, and membership in a family or community.

As the Middle Ages drew to a close, however, commerce changed the gift, in some scholars' opinion so corrupting it that it was relegated to a corner of the social world where it would be relatively safe from the cold logic of the market. Often delivered in coin or simply expressed as a price, gifts had come to seem little different from purchases, and the gift itself now seemed blatantly coercive. As other scholars have pointed out, however, gifts did not decline in importance in these centuries; on the contrary, the so-called gift economy exploded. This chapter explains the explosion and inserts it firmly in the history of the market economy. I argue that commerce not only expanded the possibilities for gift exchange but it also assigned new significance to the gift, for its ability to signal and confer honor was essential for the smooth functioning of the market.

Between about 1350 and 1450, the city of Ghent, then one of the northern continent's industrial and commercial giants, typically registered more than 20 percent of its total municipal expenses as gifts.[1] In 1366–7, for example, the account of presents (*prosenten*), one of three sections in the city's account books devoted to gifts distributed by the

[1] Selected years of those accounts are summarized in Table 3.1. The available fourteenth-century accounts have been edited and published as follows: N. de Pauw and J. Vuylsteke, eds., *De rekeningen der stad Gent: Tijdvak van Jacob van Artevelde, 1336–1349*, 3 vols. (Ghent, 1874–85); A. Van Werveke, ed., *Gentse stads – en baljuwrekeningen (1351–1364)* (Brussels, 1970); David Nicolas and Walter Prevenier, eds., *Gentse stads – en baljuwrekeningen (1365–1376)* (Brussels, 1999); J. Vuylsteke, ed., *De Rekeningen der stad Gent. Tijdvak van Philips van Artevelde, 1376–1389*, 2 vols. (Ghent, 1900).

Post-1389 accounts have not been published, but they are presented in summary fashion in Marc Boone, ed., *Geld en macht: De Gentse stadsfinanciën en de Bourgondische staatsvorming (1384–1453)* (Ghent, 1990) and Wouter Ryckbosch, ed., *Tussen Gavere en Cadzand: De Gentse stadsfinanciën op het einde van de middeleeuwen (1460–1495)* (Ghent, 2007).

aldermen, listed an apparently indiscriminate mix of wine, cloth, hollowware, coin, and simple expressions of monetary value. Aldermen gave
these gifts to citizens, their children, members of the count's court, and
the count himself as "courtesies," as rewards for services rendered, on the
occasion of marriage or taking of holy orders, or simply as accompani-
ments to hospitality.[2] Toward the end of the fifteenth century, the Duke
of Burgundy's chief financial officer similarly described about one-third
of the items in his accounts as gifts.[3] During the same two centuries,
citizens of Douai, another of the southern Low Countries' prosperous
cities, regularly used their wills to lavish individualized gifts on selected
friends and family members in expression of love and obligation.[4]

[2] See Table 3.1.

[3] Anke Greve and Émilie Lebailly, eds., *Comptes de l'argentier de Charles le Téméraire
duc de Bourgogne 1: Année 1468* (Paris, 2001); these calculations are reported in
Mario Damen, "Gift Exchange at the Court of Charles the Bold," in *In but Not
of the Market*, eds. Marc Boone and Martha Howell (Brussels, 2007).

   The accounts (kept by Charles's senior financial officer, the *argentier*) exclude
the expenses of certain domains, but they record the receipts and expenses for
the court itself and the central administration. Despite their frequency in the
accounts, gifts totaled only 7.2% of all outlays registered for that year, which
was more or less in accord with restrictions placed on the duke by his financial
counselors. During the next year, when the total budget had fallen by almost
50% (from about 659,901 *livres* [in the pound of 40 *groten*] to about 365,410
livres), gifts officially registered approximated 9.1% of the total: Anke Greve
and Émilie Lebailly, eds., *Comptes de l'argentier de Charles le Téméraire duc de
Bourgogne 2: Année 1469* (Paris 2002).

[4] Their gifts even occasionally so decimated the estate that only a small residue
was left for the usual heirs, who by customary law were due the bulk of it. For
a discussion of this custom and a fuller survey of the patterns of testamentary
bequests in the North, see Howell, "Fixing Movables."

   None of these donors was exceptional. During the fifteenth century, for
example, the city of Lille devoted five sections of its accounts to gifts: Alain
Derville, "Pots-de-vin, cadeaux, racket, patronage: Essai sur les mécanismes
de décision dans l'Etat bourguignon," *Revue du Nord* 56:222 (July–September
1974), pp. 341–64. Philip the Bold, the first duke of the Burgundian Netherlands, is reported to have spent about 15% of his demesne revenues on New
Year's gifts alone: Carol Chattaway, "Looking a Medieval Gift Horse in the
Mouth: The Role of Giving of Gift Objects in the Definition and Maintenance
of Power Networks of Philip the Bold," *Bijdragen en medelingen betreffende de
geschiedenis der Nederlanden* 114 (1999), p. 8; also see her *The Order of the Golden*

Literary and visual sources attest as eloquently to the ubiquity of gift-giving throughout the late medieval and early modern periods. For example, de Lannoy's *Instruction d'un jeune prince* of 1440 advised that "generosity and open-handedness belong above all to princes and great lords, for they are praised and loved for them . . . a prince who gives generously has no need of a fortified castle."[5] The paintings and drawings from the age tell us even more about the meaning of these practices. For example, courtly gift-giving was regularly depicted as an elaborate ritual in which the gift-giver knelt before the recipient, humbly presenting his offering, as in the image reproduced at the beginning of this chapter.

Although scholars have recognized that these traditions of gift-giving survived well beyond the early and central Middle Ages, they have nevertheless worried that the expansion of the commercial economy during the later Middle Ages impoverished the gift's cultural importance and thus its particular social power. When carefully itemized and priced in accounts or wills like those introduced here, they seemed like cold, impersonal market exchanges. Because many gift transfers appeared to demand immediate and commensurate return, some scholars have asked what distinguished a gift from the self-interested, calculated, and quantifiable exchanges of the marketplace. Indeed, some have argued

---

Tree: The Gift-Giving Objectives of Duke Phillip the Bold of Burgundy (Turnhout, 2007). For the period between 1394 and 1396, New Year's gifts alone apparently totaled about 6.5% of *total* revenues (based on figures provided by Richard Vaughan, *Philip the Bold: The Formation of the Burgundian State* [Woodbridge, UK, 2002], p. 227). For gift-giving via testament elsewhere see, for example, Philippe Godding, "La pratique testamentaire en Flandre au 13e siecle," *Legal History Review* 58:3 (1990), pp. 281–300; Paul Baur, *Testament und Bürgerschaft: Alltagsleben und Sachkultur im spätmittelalterlichen Konstanz* (Sigmaringen, 1989); Steven Epstein, *Wills and Wealth in Medieval Genoa, 1150–1250* (Cambridge, MA, 1984); Jacques Chiffoleau, *La comptabilité de l'au-delà: Les hommes, la mort et la religion dans la région d'Avignon à la fin du Moyen Âge, vers 1320–vers 1480* (Rome, 1980); Ahasver von Brandt, "Mittelalterliche Bürgertestamente: Neuerschlosssene Quellen zur Geschichte der Materiellen und Geistigen Kultur," in *Sitzungsberichte der Heidelberger Akademie der Wissenschaften, philosophische-historische Klasse*, Vol. 3 (Heidelberg, 1973), pp. 5–32.

[5] C. G. van Leeuwen, ed., *Denkbeelden van een vliesridder: De Instruction d'un jeune Prince van Guillebert van Lannoy* (Amsterdam, 1975), p. 48. Cited in Damen, "Gift Exchange," p. 81.

that in the later Middle Ages the boundaries between a gift and a sale were fatally blurred and others that the expanding market suppressed gift exchange. In discussing the twelfth century, when the commercial revolution was well underway, Lester Little concluded that "what remained of gift-economy behavior was complementary to commerce; it no longer opposed, or restrained, commercial activity."[6] Arnoud-Jan Bijsterveld put it this way:

> The period between 1050 and 1200, in which ... on top of [institutional and social changes] ... the monetary and market economy wholly expanded, seems to be the period in which the political and societal operation of gift exchange lost its strength. ... The mechanism of *do ut des* remained effective into the late Middle Ages (and possibly later still), with all its social, political, and religious implications, but on a more modest scale.[7]

Contemporaries seem, however, to have been unconcerned about the blurring of the particular boundaries noted by scholars. Furthermore, all available evidence indicates that they exchanged gifts even more exuberantly, in greater volume, and in more social arenas at the end of the Middle Ages than ever before. "The gift is everywhere" in this period, one scholar has said, and gifts were made with little apparent

---

[6] Lester Little, *Religious Poverty and the Profit Economy in Medieval Europe* (Ithaca, NY, 1978), p. 8, cited in Arnoud-Jan Bijsterveld, "The Medieval Gift as Agent of Social Bonding and Political Power: A Comparative Approach," in *Medieval Transformations: Texts, Power, and Gifts in Context*, eds. Esther Cohen and Mayke de Jong (Leiden, 2001), pp. 123–56, p. 144. In Little's understanding, money could form no permanent bonds because it is transitive, or as a recent scholar put it, money is "not something that can be enjoyed for its own sake, whose use is enjoyment (usufruct), it merely marks a passage": D. Vance Smith, *Arts of Possession: The Middle English Household Imaginary* (Minneapolis, 2003), p. 123. According to Little, it would not be until market exchange had absorbed more of the economic whole that Europeans would draw a clearer line between the gift and the sale, reducing the gift to the realm of sentiment and nostalgia.

[7] Bijsterveld, "The Medieval Gift," pp. 151–2. Stephen D. White, *Custom, Kinship, and Gifts to Saints: The Laudatio Parentum in Western France, 1050–1150* (Chapel Hill, NC, 1988) has explained that during this period property rights and the rules surrounding property transfers were formalized, a process that forced a sharp distinction between the sale and the gift and put the gift under new scrutiny.

self-consciousness about their relationship to commerce.[8] As Natalie Davis remarked in her study of gifts in sixteenth-century France, people then "drew on both self-definitions [as gift-giver or purchaser] in their daily dealings, moving, if need be, from one register [the gift or the market] to the other, as they collaborated, exchanged, and quarreled."[9]

However, this did not mean that contemporaries thought there was no difference between a gift and a market exchange. Rather, when they called something a "gift" they were labeling it a particular kind of exchange. They did so consciously, by no means mindlessly clinging to old routines or a desiccated, vestigial terminology that had been emptied of meaning by the gift's immersion in commerce.[10] Nor were they clumsily trying to disguise quasi-purchases as gifts. The treasurers who managed the finances of city or court were sophisticated men of the

[8] Alain Derville provided the "gift is everywhere" language in his "Les pots-de-vin dans le derniers tiers du XVe siècle (d'après les comptes de Lille et de St. Omer)," in *Le privilège général et les privilèges régionaux de Marie de Bourgogne pour les Pays-Bas 1477*, ed. Willem Pieter Blockmans (Kortrijk-Heule, Belg., 1985), pp. 449–71: "le don est partout," p. 451.

[9] Natalie Zemon Davis, *The Gift in Sixteenth-Century France* (Madison, WI, 2000), p. 53. For the medieval and early modern gift, see, in addition, Judith Bennett, "Conviviality and Charity in Medieval and Early Modern England," *Past and Present* 134 (February 1992), pp. 19–41; Felicity Heal, "Food Gifts, the Household and the Politics of Exchange in Early Modern England," *Past and Present* 199 (May 2008), pp. 41–71.

[10] In an analysis of marital prestations in late medieval northern Italy, Jane Fair Bestor has seemed to suggest that most people, including the rich, did not have a vocabulary sophisticated enough to capture the meaning of prestations that were not "really" gifts. In contrast, lawyers of the day could distinguish between "true" gifts and other kinds of nonmarket transfers of goods (like the wedding "gifts" Bestor was studying). See Jane Fair Bestor, "Marriage Transactions in Renaissance Italy," in particular pp. 33–4.

I suspect, however, that these people would have been capable of finding new words to capture new meanings and that they, just like the northerners I am studying, deliberately used the vocabulary of the gift to describe their marriage prestations because, in their minds, they did what they considered gift work. In any case, as Natalie Davis has pointed out, sixteenth-century Frenchmen had words for the "bad gift," and as I point out later, northerners in my period seem to have been inventing new vocabulary for one variety of the "bad" gift – the bribe. For Davis's references and my argument, see the pages to come.

market who could easily have hidden these distributions or made what we might think fake seem robustly gift-like.[11] The city people issuing the wills I describe here were not novices in the market; they needed no municipal clerks, notaries, or priests to explain the difference between a market transaction and a gift.[12] For them, just as for aldermen, court officials, and the duke himself, the boundary between the market and gift was not drawn where we might draw it. But it was drawn.

This chapter argues that all these people were using gifts to negotiate the contradictions of a life in commerce. Although they were preserving very old customs, they were also giving the gift new tasks. The gift's ability to seal personal bonds had special importance for them because a gift could materialize such relationships in ways a commercial exchange could not. A gift conferred honor, and in this culture personal honor, what was coming to be called a man's "credit," was not only the mark of social legitimacy but also the essential guarantor of market integrity. Gifts thus did important work in commerce.

GIFT THEORY AND GIFT HISTORY

Historians' understanding of the gift's significance has been powerfully shaped by social theory on "The Gift," which distinguishes a gift-like distribution from an exchange motivated either by direct command, as from a lord or state, or by the search for profit, as in a market exchange.[13]

[11] On the emerging bureaucracy of the central state and its urban connections, see J. Dumolyn, *Staatsvorming en vorstelijke ambtenaren in het graafschap Vlaandern, 1419–1477* (Antwerp, 2003); Walter Prevenier, "Officials in Town and Countryside in the Low Countries: Social and Professional Developments from the Fourteenth to the Sixteenth Century," *Acta Historiae Neerlandicae* 7 (1997); B. Schnerb, *L'État bourguignon (1363–1477)* (Paris, 1999).

[12] For a recent study exposing the financial sophistication even of ordinary citizens in cities of this region, see James M. Murray *Bruges: Cradle of Capitalism, 1280–1390* (Cambridge, UK, 2005).

[13] Although no scholar would argue that a particular act of exchange can be tidily contained by a single category alone, the general typology of "gift command-market transaction" has provided a sturdy framework for parsing the meanings of exchange itself. In addition to the specific references in this chapter, see, for a recent survey, a collection of articles by major theorists of the gift, and an

According to this model, a gift differs from a transfer of goods or services by command principally in that it is given as though it were a voluntary and spontaneous presentation, perhaps the expression of an unspoken duty but not the fulfillment of a formal obligation. Furthermore, a gift's route of transmission (i.e., its recipient) is determined by the social relations the donor wants to establish or maintain, not by the direct order of a superior. In this way, the giver is awarded agency that is explicitly denied the payer of tribute or taxes.

In the theorist's conception, the gift differs even more sharply from the classic market transaction. In the marketplace, an exchange terminates the relationship between buyer and seller, an effect literally conveyed on Wall Street today where a deal is said to be "done" or "closed" once the terms of sale have been agreed upon. In such transactions, buyer and seller need not know each other; in fact, in principle they should not know each other. So clear is this norm that in many modern market settings, buyer and seller struggle to create the conditions of "arm's-length" dealing if they are perchance acquainted. In contrast, the gift (as scholars have described the classic model) does not terminate, but rather deepens, personal relationships. Gifts generate an endless cycle of exchange that nourishes ongoing social bonds, not just between the original giver and receiver (who are necessarily known to one another) but potentially also among subsequent recipients of the object in circulation.

Gift exchanges also contain an element of mystery unknown to a market exchange. Although a gift is generally understood to compel a counter-gift and can therefore seem like a market exchange, the ambiguity of both the timing and the form of the gift's return gives it a power that the calibrated quid pro quo of a market exchange can never possess. As one recent commentator put it, "Gifts are disinterested not because there is no return, but because what comes back often violates or transcends the rules of mercantile equivalence."[14] Bourdieu

---

extensive bibliography, Aafke E. Komter, *The Gift: An Interdisciplinary Perspective* (Amsterdam, 1996); also see, for recent discussions of theory, Mark Osteen, ed., *The Question of the Gift: Essays across Disciplines* (New York, 2002).

[14] Jacques T. Godbout, with Alain Caillé, *The World of the Gift*, trans. Donald Winkler (Montreal, 1998), cited in Osteen, *Question of the Gift*, p. 25.

made a similar point in speaking of gifts: "the most ordinary and even the seemingly most routine exchanges of ordinary life [i.e., gifts]... presuppose an improvisation, and therefore a constant uncertainty which, as we say, make all their charm, and hence all their social efficacy." Elsewhere he commented that "to reduce to the function of communication... the exchange of gifts, words, or women, is to ignore the structural ambivalence which predisposes them to fulfill a political function of domination."[15]

In further contrast, a good exchanged on market terms has a specific "utility" value; in neoclassical economic theory, this value is a fundamental element of its price. The terms of a classic gift exchange, however, do not reflect the utility of the object or service proffered, at least not as it would be measured by neoclassical theory. In extreme cases gifts seem even to have no apparent material use at all. The point of their production is exchange, and the point of exchange is, on the face of it, just exchange. For example, the Kula system famously described by Bernard Malinowski appeared to consist simply of the ritualized and continuous exchange of shell jewelry among elites in a chain of islands, none of it having any productive capacity or material value as a consumption good, for the shells could not be eaten and they kept no one dry or warm.[16]

Such an understanding of the gift originated nearly a century ago. Malinowski's well-known *Argonauts of the Western Pacific* distinguished a "pure" gift, which created no expectation of return, from a "ceremonial" gift, in which an element of quid pro quo was visible, although Malinowski emphasized that in practice most gift-like transfers could not be tidily contained by either subcategory alone. In contrast, Marcel Mauss's even more famous *Essai sur le don* argued that the logic of compulsive reciprocity underlies all gift exchange; he insisted that the principle of *do ut des*, although often obscured, is always

[15] Pierre Bourdieu, "The Work of Time," in *The Gift*, ed. Aafke Komter, pp. 135–47, and *Outline of a Theory of Practice*, trans. Richard Nice (Cambridge, UK, 1977), p. 14.

[16] Bernard Malinowski, *Argonauts of the Western Pacific*, 3rd. ed. (orig. 1922; London, 1950); this cycle of exchange was, however, accompanied by – and in effect enabled by – a separate and simultaneous exchange of subsistence goods.

operative.[17] Mauss also made the object that is given central to the gift's meaning, for in his interpretation the object or "thing" given is the force that compels reciprocity.[18] This feature explains, scholars have emphasized, why the ideal gift is concrete and personal; it then carries specific meaning associated with the donor – the *hau* in Mauss's study – that sets the terms of the social relationship thus established. A gift of a book has one meaning, a jewel another, a personal service another, and the meaning of each is inherent not just in the book, jewel, or service but also in the personality or status of the person who gave it.[19] In utter contrast, the thing bought or sold in a market exchange is nothing but an expression of exchange value – a commodity. It is entirely fungible, always potentially something else, anything at all.

Jane Fair Bestor has understood Mauss's work on gifts as a rejection of Durkheim's view about the relationship between persons and things. According to Durkheim, it is not people who give value to things (especially to land, the premier "thing" in premodern cultures), as the labor theory of value has it. Using the early modern French nobility's commitment to patrimonial land as his example, he spoke of the "moral community between the thing and the person," claiming that "people are possessed by things at least as much as things by people."[20] Bestor

---

[17] Marcel Mausss, "Essai sur le don: forme et raison de l'échange dans les sociétés archaiques (1923–1924)," *Sociologie et anthropologie* 9 (1950), pp. 143–279; in English as *The Gift: The Form and Reason for Exchange in Archaic Societies*, trans. W. D. Hall (New York, 1990).

[18] For Mauss's predecessors and a commentary on the originality of his thesis, see Beate Wagner-Hasel, "Egoistic Exchange and Altruistic Gift: On the Roots of Marcel Mauss's Theory of the Gift," in *Negotiating the Gift: Pre-Modern Figurations of Exchange*, eds. Gadi Algazi, Valentin Groebner, and Bernhard Jussen (Göttingen, 2003), pp. 141–71. Also see Bernard Malinowski, "The Principle of Give and Take," in *The Gift*, ed. Komter, pp. 15–18. On generalized and balanced reciprocity, see Marshall Sahlins, *Stone Age Economics* (London, 1972). See, however, Annette B. Weiner, *Inalienable Possessions* (Berkeley, CA, 1992) for a critique of this structuralist notion of reciprocity.

[19] Weiner, *Inalienable Possessions*, points out that some goods are not "easy to give," because the "object 'is' the person, like the crown 'is' the king" (p. 7). Thus those things *not* given are as significant measures (and creators) of social status as those that are.

[20] Émil Durkheim, *Leçons de sociologie: Physique des moeurs et du droit* (first publ. Paris, 1950; repr. Paris, 1969), p. 175; cited from Bestor's translation in "Marriage Transactions," p. 12.

argued that Mauss rejected "the invariant character of the categories of 'person' and 'thing'" on which Durkheim had insisted; the relationship, Mauss reasoned, is historical and thus changeable. It is this move that gave him a history of the gift, and Roman law gave him the explanation of how westerners came to abstract economic relations from social relations and thus abandoned the idea that a thing given bears the personality of the giver (the *hau*) and must be returned.[21] For Mauss, reciprocity is a necessary feature of gift exchange – not as a result of legal rights and obligations (as under property law) but as a result of the "tie between souls" engendered by the gift.[22] Mauss also reasoned that the radical differences between gift exchange and market exchange put them in an inversely proportional relationship: to the extent that one form of exchange expanded, the other would tend to diminish. It followed that the gift had a history that was tied to the history of the modern western market economy. Although Mauss did not argue that the gift played no role in the modern West – in fact, he hoped that its vigor could be restored – he nevertheless concluded that the gift's power had been eroded by the capitalist market.

Mauss's model of the gift and its history has remained paradigmatic, despite the many amendments and qualifications to it that scholars have offered over the years. European historians have made especially

---

[21] Bestor, "Marriage Transactions," p. 13.

[22] For this discussion see Bestor, "Marriage Transactions, pp. 17ff. According to Bestor, Mauss used the terms "property" and "alienation" inconsistently, which has produced serious confusion in the scholarly literature. In particular, Bestor questions Annette Weiner's influential *Inalienable Possessions*, which argued that a good is never securely inalienable, but acquires that position only in politics. Bestor counters, in part quoting Marilyn Strathern's *Gender of the Gift*, that "'inalienability signifies the absence of a property relation,' at least in the sense of the absolute control over a thing characteristic of western folk models of property, namely, control over the conditions of its alienation" (p. 19); the phrase from Strathern can be found on p. 161 of her *Gender of the Gift*.

Because, following this logic, the gift (predicated on inalienability) and property cannot coexist, Bestor concludes that "true" gift exchange is impossible in market societies like the late medieval Italian cities she studied; see in particular p. 20. I am arguing, however, that we need not use Mauss's (or anyone else's) theory as a template to measure whether a gift is "really" a gift. Rather, we need to understand what people meant when they called something a gift.

good use of it in studies of the early and central Middle Ages, when priced exchange was but a tiny part of the economic whole and gifts played a central role in forming and cementing social and political relations.[23] More generally, gifts were also an expression of medieval culture's concerns about material abundance. What was thought "surplus" in medieval society was considered morally dangerous, and gift-giving was one of its remedies: the wealthy gave in expiation of superfluous possession itself.[24] If the classically "medieval" gift drew its power in part from the relative insignificance of the commercial sphere, it follows that the sphere of gift exchange should have lost significance as the market economy expanded during the last centuries of the medieval era. Georges Duby long ago came to that conclusion; as early as the year 1000, when Europeans had just begun to monetize their exchanges and express value as money, he reasoned that the gift economy began a decline.[25] As mentioned earlier, Lester Little concluded that the

[23] For a review of the literature on the medieval gift, see, in addition to Little, *Religious Poverty*; Bijsterveld, "The Medieval Gift"; idem, *Do ut des: Gift Giving, Memoria, and Conflict Management in the Medieval Low Countries* (Hilversum, 2007). Also see Esther Cohen, *Gift, Payment and the Sacred in Medieval Popular Religiosity* (Wassenaar, Ger., 1991) and Brigitte Buettner, "Past Presents: New Year's Gifts at the Valois Courts, ca 1400," *Art Bulletin* 83, no. 4 (December 2001), pp. 598–625. For another recent discussion of the scholarly literature regarding the "medieval" gift and an argument that gift-giving among elites in Merovingian and Carolingian Europe was essentially "a political phenomenon, instead of an economic strategy or a mere mechanism for maintaining social stability," see Florin Curta, "Merovingian and Carolingian Gift Giving," *Speculum* 81, no. 3 (July 2006), pp. 671–700, p. 677.

Important early studies on the medieval gift include Philip Grierson, "Commerce in the Dark Ages: A Critique of the Evidence," *Transactions of the Royal Historical Society*, 5th series, 9 (1959), pp. 123–40; Georges Duby, "Prendre, donner, consacrer," in idem, *Guerriers et paysans, VIIe–XIIe siècle: Premier essor de l'économie europénne* (Paris, 1973), pp. 60–9. In the last quarter-century the literature has multiplied exponentially. Notable among these studies are Barbara Rosenwein, *Rhinoceros Bound: The Abbey of Cluny in the Tenth Century* (Philadelphia, 1982) and idem, *Be the Neighbor of Saint Peter: The Social Meaning of Cluny's Property 909–1049* (Ithaca, NY, 1989); White, *Custom, Kinship, and Gifts to Saints*; Philippe Jobert, *La notion de donation: Convergences: 630–750* (Paris, 1977).

[24] Smith, *Arts of Possession*, p. xvi.

[25] Duby, "Prendre, donner, consacrer,"; also see Marc Bloch, *Feudal Society* (Chicago, 1964).

boundary between the gift and the market was eroding in these centuries, and medievalists have generally agreed that the result was the gradual marginalization of the gift.

There can be no doubt that gifts did somewhat different work in 1300 or 1500 than they did, say, in 900 or 1100. But during the late medieval and early modern periods, the gift was by no means relegated to a "modest" role in politics, religion, or social life more generally; nor did money come to mark the boundary between the gift and the sale. As Gadi Algazi remarked in a recent essay, "if the processes of modernization of economic, social, and political relations are significantly related to the use of gifts, the link does not seem to consist in the withering away of gift exchange."[26] Algazi even suggested that we may have to give up "The Gift" as a category of analysis: it is not clear that in the late medieval and early modern ages "specific acts of transfer and exchange that are occasionally termed 'gifts' in historical sources can easily be identified with concepts of 'The Gift' in social and ethnological research."[27]

My study takes the pragmatic approach suggested by Algazi's comment. Although hardly innocent of theory, it does not ask whether the *dons, prosenten, gifte,* and the like that people then distributed were "really" gifts according to some abstract model.[28] Instead, I have

---

[26] Gadi Algazi, "Introduction: Doing Things with Gifts," in *Negotiating the Gift,* eds. Algazi et al., p. 25.

[27] Algazi, "Doing Things with Gifts," p. 10. Patrick Geary recently posed a similar question: "Are they [social science models of gift exchange] . . . anthropologists' mental constructs derived from the very European tradition we seek to illuminate, but projected by the anthropologists onto other cultures[?]": Patrick J. Geary, "Gift Exchange and Social Science Modeling: The Limitations of a Construct," in *Negotiating the Gift,* eds. Algazi et al., pp. 129–40, esp. p. 131. Indeed, anthropologists themselves have increasingly warned about the hazards both of the rigid taxonomy and of any evolutionary model equating gifts with nonmonetized, noncommercial, (and egalitarian) societies. See, for example, C. A. Gregory, *Gifts and Commodities* (London, 1982) and Jonathan Parry and Maurice Bloch, "Introduction: Money and Morality of Exchange," and Jonathan Parry, "On the Moral Perils of Exchange," both in idem, eds., *Money and the Morality of Exchange* (Cambridge, 1989).

[28] Social scientists tend to take a different approach, searching for the precise definition that will capture the essence of the gift. In an interesting recent study, for example, Alain Testart has argued that the fundamental distinction between a gift and "exchange" (*échange*) is whether the person transferring the object or

searched for the meaning of what they called gifts, taking the sources in which people recorded their distributions as my guide. As E. P. Thompson once cautioned, because gift-giving "always emerges within the historical peculiarity of the ensemble of social relations of its age," gifts acquire their meaning not in theory, but in practice, or what Arjun Appadurai called their "social life."[29] To understand the work of gifts, we must follow each gift's trail as it was passed from hand to hand, examining its form and considering the situation in which it was given.

In taking this approach, I have not relied principally on visual or narrative sources, as do many historians. Instead, I have based my study on the financial and legal documents that listed, counted, and priced gifts during the later medieval centuries in the North. These kinds of sources not only expose how deeply the gift economy was inflected by its intersections with commerce, but they also take us to the heart of commercial society. They were authored and given particular form by ordinary householders, artisans, and shopkeepers, as well as by merchants and the financiers who worked between the courts or town halls and the commercial economy of the day. By studying what kind of gifts such people gave, when and how they distributed them, and the people or

service has a <u>right</u> (*droit*) to a return. If not, we are in the sphere of the "gift" (similar to Malinowski's "pure" gift); if so, we are in the sphere of exchange, not of gift and counter-gift; see Alain Testart, "Échange marchand, échange non marchand," *Revue française de sociologie* 42, no. 4 (October–December 2001), pp. 719–48. Also see his "Les trois modes de transfert," *Gradhiva* 21 (1997), pp. 39–58.

[29] Edward P. Thompson, "Folklore, Anthropology and Social History," *Indian Historical Review* 3 (1977), pp. 252–72, p. 258, cited in Wagner-Hasel, "Egoistic Exchange," p. 163. Arjun Appadurai, "Commodities and the Politics of Value," in idem, ed., *The Social Life of Things: Commodities in Cultural Perspective* (Cambridge, UK, 1986). For a general argument about the ways goods acquire meaning in social intercourse, also see Jean Baudrillard, *For a Critique of the Political Economy of the Sign* (St. Louis, 1981).

As Barbara Sebek has commented, gifts "take shape differently in different historical and cultural contexts . . . [and] are *relational* [her emphasis.]: Barbara Sebek, "Good Turns and the Art of Merchandising: Conceptualizing Exchange in Early Modern England," http://emc.eserver.org/1–2/sebek/html (accessed September 4, 2009).

institutions on whom they bestowed their favors, we learn a great deal about the work gifts were called upon to do in a world where so much was for sale.

By casting my net so widely in the social world, I have included many kinds of gifts in my study – both "official" distributions of cash, plate, or cloth that show up in formal accounts and postmortem bequests of money or things to the church, to charities, to family, and to friends or co-workers. Obviously, these distributions are not all alike. The dress or silver cup distributed after someone's death by the estate's executor and the jewel-encrusted reliquary publicly presented to royalty in a pompous ceremony are different creatures; the impulses that drove an aged widow to make her gifts might seem entirely unlike the calculations that were made as a prince's gift-giving was being planned. In key respects, however, these gifts were similar: they sealed a social bond, identified and honored both giver and recipient, and derived much of their power and significance from commerce. It is those similarities that interest me.

THE COMMERCE IN GIFTS

Even a cursory look at the records I have used leaves no doubt about commerce's effects on gifts. The most concrete measure was the gift's monetization. For example, consider that nine of the thirty entries in Ghent's *prosenten* account of 1366–7 were made in coin, in this case the *lion*.

> *Item*, sent to Petren van Zele, when he married, 9 *lions*, which makes 60 lbs.
>
> *Item*, sent to Meester Jans Marscalx zone, when he married, 100 *lions*, which makes in pounds payement 666 lbs., 13s., 4d.
>
> *Item*, sent to Janne de Mery in Bruges, when he married the Sunday before St. Symoens and St. Juden's day, 10 *lions*, which makes in lbs. payement 66 lbs. 13s., 4d.
>
> *Item*, sent to my lord Goesins Wilden zone, the Receiver of Flanders, when he married, 30 *lions*, which makes 200 lbs.
>
> *Item*, to Arem Jan, the falconer of My Lord of Flanders [the count], when he married, 2 *lions*, which makes 13 lbs., 6s., 8d.

> *Item*, to one of the daughters of My Lord's [the count] pipers, when she married, 1 *lion*, which comes to 6 lbs., 13s., 4d.
>
> *Item*, to Louwerse, the *duerwaerdre* [a judicial official] of My Lord of Flanders [the count], on Christmas eve, 1 *lion*, which comes to 6 lbs., 13s., 4d.
>
> *Item*, to the falconer, 1 *lion*, which makes 6 lbs., 13s., 4d.
>
> *Item*, to the pipers, 1 *lion*, which comes to 6 lbs, 13s., 4d.

Commerce left an even clearer trace when gifts were expressed simply as money of account. This was an abstraction of an abstraction; no object at all but simply a price, a money of account was utterly unable to bear any concrete meaning. When actually delivered, a gift originally expressed as money of account could be anything – a coin, a dress, an hour's labor, even a favor. The same *prosenten* account contained nine such money of account entries, of thirty.

> *Item*, to the chamberlains of my lady of Borgoengien, on Christmas eve, in "courtesy," 20 lbs.
>
> *Item*, to the chamberlain of my lord of Borgoengien, when he married, 20 lbs.
>
> *Item*, to the "upper" messengers of My Lord [the count], 12 lbs.
>
> *Item*, to the "under" messengers, 8 lbs.
>
> *Item*, to the pages of My Lord [the count], 8 lbs.
>
> *Item*, to the "little" pages, 3 lbs., 6s., 8d.
>
> *Item*, to the Master of My Lord's [the count] summer's wardrobe [*soemers*], 4 lbs. 13s., 4d.
>
> *Item*, to the Bailiff's servants [*cnapen*], on Christmas eve, 8 lbs.
>
> *Item*, to the nephew of the "high" Bailiff, when he married, 4 lbs. 10s.

It was the same in each of the three major gift accounts from Ghent, a summary of which from selected years is presented in Table 3.1.[30]

The second of the accounts in 1366–7, which registered thirty-one separate donations of alms and other charitable gifts and totaled 17,916 d. *groten*, included nine that were expressed only in money of account. The city's third and largest of the major gift accounts (totaling 88,122

---

[30] Taken from the sources cited in note 1 above.

Table 3.1. Municipal Accounts, City of Ghent

YEAR	1353–4 amt. in d. gr.	1353–4 % of total	1360–1 amt. in d. gr.	1360–1 % of total	1365–6 amt. in d. gr.	1365–6 % of total	1366–7 amt. in d. gr.	1366–7 % of total
GIFT ACCOUNTS								
"presents"	10,974	3.3%	31,422	3.7%	24,978	4.4%	29,194	4.9%
"alms"	8,864	2.6%	11,892	1.4%	14,448	2.5%	17,916	3.0%
"gifts and pensions"	60,372	18.0%	86,322	10.2%	85,134	15.0%	88,122	14.8%
"gifts to messengers"	5,076	1.5%	5,754	0.7%	2,208	4.0%	2,010	0.3%
TOTAL GIFTS	85,286	25.4%	135,390	16.0%	126,768	22.3%	137,242	23.0%
DEBTS AND RENTES	101,460	30.2%	51,024	6.0%	31,9284	56.1%	30,8214	51.7%
OTHER EXPENSES	149,236	44.4%	661,212	78.0%	122,904	21.6%	150,494	25.3%
TOTAL EXPENSES	33,5982	100.0%	84,7646	100.0%	56,8956	100.0%	59,6010	100.0%

YEAR	1372–3 amt. in d. gr.	1372–3 % of total	1410–11 amt. in d. gr.	1410–11 % of total	1425–6 amt. in d. gr.	1425–6 % of total	1443–4 amt. in d. gr.	1443–4 % of total
GIFT ACCOUNTS								
"presents"	44,964	9.0%	36,480	5.4%	65,962	5.3%	13,6776	9.6%
"alms"	25,746	5.1%	20,649	3.1%	29,928	2.4%	83,720	5.9%
"gifts and pensions"	120,474	24.0%	105,935	15.6%	143,115	11.6%	154,812	10.8%
"gifts to messengers"	1,428	0.3%						
TOTAL GIFTS	192,612	38.4%	163,064	24.1%	239,005	19.3%	375,308	26.3%
DEBTS AND RENTES	120,162	24.0%	59,277	8.8%	31,7093	25.6%	65,0799	45.5%
OTHER EXPENSES	188,364	37.6%	454,577	67.2%	680,565	55.0%	403,589	28.2%
TOTAL EXPENSES	50,1138	100.0%	676,818	100.0%	1,236,683	100.0%	1,429,696	100.0%

d. *groten*) contained even more such gifts. Alongside the outlays for the cloth and clothing given to city officials and administrators that, I argue, had huge symbolic importance were what Gentenaren already called "pensions" (*pensioen*). These were standardized distributions expressed as price and given to individuals according to their particular function. There were sixty-five such money of account entries in 1366–7, compared to forty that listed distributions of cloth and clothing, all but a few specifically described as "pensions." They ranged from 10 lbs. *payement* (60 d. gr.) for someone like "Turreman, who maintained the place of the fish market" to 640 lbs. (3,840 d. gr.) for Janne van der Rake, the senior alderman, and 560 lbs. for Justase van den Hole, dean of the weavers. The small stipend of 60 d. gr. received by Turreman, the man who oversaw the fish market, was no living wage (equivalent to only about six days' work by a skilled craftsman), and even the top pension of 3,840 d. gr. (2.5 years' work), although generous, could not have supported the lifestyle of a man so high in the city's social hierarchy as its senior alderman.[31]

Although a significant number of gifts in these accounts were paid in coin or expressed only in price, some were delivered in kind, as cloth for official vestments. But in these accounts even the city's best "scarlet," the cloth worn only by the most distinguished citizens and ritually bestowed annually on all high officers, was necessarily reduced to price. The orderly and monotonously repetitive rows of *item*, object, name, and price intensified the effect of quantification and abstraction.

---

[31] For the conversion of money values to craftsmen's wages, see Appendix II. Although we would surely label these "pensions" a kind of stipend, bonus, or tip, in Ghent they were grouped with distributions of cloth that had enormous political and social meaning independent of their cash value. Rhetorically at least, the "pensions" belonged to what Gentenars thought of as a gift register. In fifteenth-century Lille, according to Derville, "pensions" were not grouped with gift-like distributions, but had made their way into regular expense accounts as though they were considered straightforward salaries. In fourteenth-century Ghent, however, this was not yet the case (although by the next century it was), and in any case they were not sufficient to constitute a salary in any modern sense of the term, not in Ghent, and not in Lille. For Derville's comments, see "Pots-de-vin, cadeaux, racket," p. 345.

Consider, for example, the first few entries in the account of 1366–7:

- To Justase van den Hole [was paid] 50 lb. 12.d. gr. for 4.5 *roeden scaerlakenen*; to Mathise van den Winckele, [was paid] 36 lbs. gr. *halle paye* for 3 *gheleiden lakenen*; together that makes 3,550 lbs in *payement*, so that the aldermen of both benches could have clothes made by Master Jan van der Rake and Meester Lievin de Buc.
- *Item*, for 26 sets of linings [for the above garments], each 4 s. gr., which comes to 208 lbs.
- *Item*, to Janne Ondertmaerc [was paid], for 3 *dickedinnen*, each 26. d., and to Jacoppe Berdekin, for 3 white "striped" each 41 gulden; in *payement* that comes to 864 lbs., 6s., 8 d., for the summer dress of the aldermen.
- *Item*, for 12 ellen brown scarlet, each 5s. 6 d gr, and [was paid] to Willem Everboud, for 12 ellen striped, each 33 gr., both together come to 198 lbs, so that Justaes van den Hole ende Aernoud van der Varent [aldermen and deans] could have vestments.

As we move down the long list of entries, reading line after similar line, all gifts seem exactly the same, their only difference being their monetary value. By the time we arrive at the thirty-seventh entry, in which four minor officials, only two of them actually named – Willem de Blacke, an unnamed man described as *de costre in de cappelle*, another unnamed man described as *de clerke van den wercke*, and "Jan *de die werclocke luut*" – share one *smaelre dickedinne* worth 22.5 d. gr., no gift has retained individuality. In the next year and for decades to come, the entries are virtually the same. Only the names change.

It was the same in the ducal court, for Charles expressed the bulk of his gifts in cash or money of account alone.[32] Although he handsomely rewarded the messengers and courtiers who coordinated his diplomatic relations with Louis XI, he delivered the gifts as prices; for example, ordering that the servants who brought Louis's gift horses to him receive 50 pounds each.[33] The same pattern appears in wills from the period.

---

[32] Damen, "Gift Exchange," provides the information about the relative number of gifts in kind.

[33] These data are taken from Damen, "Gift Exchange." On his *joyeuse entrée* through Holland and Zeeland, he gave 30 *Rheingulden* (about 6.5 months' work) to the

The bequests of Marie Le Grande of Douai included "a royal crown or the equivalent of 40 d. gr. in other coin" each for three men, one of them the executor of her will.[34] Ralph Cornish, a tailor in late-sixteenth-century Bristol, England, left his brother 20 gold nobles in trust for his apprenticeship.[35]

It was even more common for testators to express their bequests in money of account alone. In 1438, Miquel Du Four, citizen of Arras but testator in Douai, used his will to arrange his funeral and burial as was customary in the age and then went on to scatter small cash bequests for the maintenance of various chapels, for funeral masses for himself and his family, and for his *curé*. The bequests for his two children were also expressed in money terms ("40 *francs* each, valued at 33 d. gr. *monnaie de flandre* [*mdf*] to the *franc*," he carefully explained). Unlike most testators, he bothered to specify that the money for the latter bequests would be raised by selling "his most accessible goods" (*plus apparans biens*). Such a detail was hardly necessary, however, for an executor had no choice but to sell the testator's goods, easily accessible or not, to deliver bequests expressed in money.[36] Thomas Beese, a clothworker in Bristol, left "two fine graye Cottens" to his brother, instructing him to sell them to "paye my daughter Margaret 4 lbs. and my daughter Martha fourty shillings."[37] Agnes, wife of a painter and alderman in Basel, left her

steward of Frank van Borselen at Brielle, one of his hosts during the trip. Coin or simply an expression of value as price was also the preferred gift at the lower end of the social scale, although the amounts given were tiny in comparison.

[34] Margheritte Darre, also a Douaisien widow, similarly included a bequest of two royal crowns among the longer list of personal goods she distributed. Catheline Quoitre left two gold crowns; Jacquez Vallans, a tanner, listed 200 royal crowns for his son and 10 royal crowns each for other relatives, along with special bequests of real estate and personal goods: AMD, FF 869, 25 March 1405; FF 869, 3 August 1402; FF 869, 19 September 1403.

[35] Sheila Lang and Margaret McGregor, eds., *Tudor Wills Proved in Bristol 1546–1603* (Stroud, UK, 1993), no. 58, pp. 25–6.

[36] FF 448/fol. 1; Du Four left the remainder of his estate to his wife (who appears to have remarried within six months): AMD, FF 615/2208 [1439].

　　Agnes Loubard simply assumed such a process, stipulating only that 5 lb. *mdf*. go to her nephew and that he be forgiven another 5 lb. *mdf* he owed her: AMD, FF 448, 16 Dec. 1438.

[37] Lang and McGregor, eds., *Tudor Wills*, no. 134, pp. 63–4. In the same city, William Yeman, a glover, left 20 lbs, three houses, and his best goblet to his

nephew her best robes or, at his choice, the equivalent 12 lb. in the local money of account. As Gabriela Signori dryly commented in reporting this information, "the boundaries between an object possessing its own history and an object regarded as an investment . . . were occasionally fluid."[38]

These people had good practical reasons for choosing to make their gifts in cash or simply as price. Coin was easily transported; peripatetic rulers needed to be able to distribute gifts en route, whether to hosts, allies, or retainers, and their treasurers surely found it easier to travel with a chest of silver *groten* or golden florins than with trunks full of the clothing and jewels or trains of horses and mules that might be used as gifts.[39] By Charles the Bold's day it was not even necessary to transport the coin, however, for his treasurers could convert price into cash along the way with the help of local moneychangers and credit instruments.[40] Managers of city treasuries would also have been glad to avoid the bother and expense of commissioning the silver bowl,

son, 20 lbs each to his legitimate daughters, and 5 lb. to his "base" daughter, all to be paid when they were twenty years old: no. 22, pp. 9–10. In 1240, in Genoa, Bernardo de Nuxiga left 2 lbs, 2 s. 7d. "for his soul" and 40 *soldi* for his nephew, stipulating that his widow was to have her clothing and the rest of his goods, so long as she remained unmarried and kept the children with her (Epstein, *Wills and Wealth*, p. 211); also see p. 208 where Stefano, a shopkeeper in the same city, left 20 lb. "for his soul," naming eighteen individual recipients of that bequest.

A merchant in Basel reserved all his clothes, armor, and "everything which belonged to his body," along with three silver cups and 100 florins for distribution as bequests out of his estate: Gabriela Signori, "Family Traditions: Moral Economy and Memorial 'Gift Exchange' in the Urban World of the Late Fifteenth Century," in *Negotiating the Gift*, eds. Algazi et al., pp. 285–318, p. 315.

In far-away Genoa as early as the thirteenth century, gifts that were expressed simply as price occupied the same status in the list of bequests as a dress or armor: Steven Epstein, *Wills and Wealth in Medieval Genoa, 1150–1250* (Cambridge, MA, 1984). The phrase *in pecunia numerata* in the wills indicated that the bequest was to be paid in coin, but the coin was not specified.

[38] Signori, "Family Traditions," p. 313.

[39] This is Damen's point in "Gift Exchange."

[40] For close studies of these operations in the court of Philip the Bold, see A. Van Nieuwenhuysen, *Les finances du duc de Bourgogne Philippe le Hardi, 1384–1404* (Brussels, 1990).

ordering up the bolt of cloth, and overseeing the wine purchases; they would surely have found it much easier to order the transfer of some coin. The lucky recipients of royal largesse may well have been equally glad to receive coin so that they could, for example, choose their own horse rather than have one chosen for them by the prince's stable master. Even an individual writing a will – or the executor of the will who had the task of handing out the bequests – would have recognized the advantages of simply dividing up the money received after a liquidation sale of household goods and distributing it among priests and curates, charities and monasteries, friends and family as ordered. No need to decide which ring went where, which set of linens would best please, or the relative merits of each silver bowl. Better to let the market decide, and better to give the priest money for the church roof, to let the beguine determine how the poor would best be helped, or to allow a favorite niece to pick the fabric for her new gown.

Commerce provided not only convenient ways of making gifts but also powerful tools for quantifying the relationship between giver and receiver, another sign, we might conclude, that the gift had been degraded or so elided with the market exchange to have lost meaning. A coin or a price ineluctably and unmistakably made that calculation, but people could almost as easily make the evaluation themselves. Everyone would have known that a plain silver cup of the kind regularly distributed in wills or by governments cost the equivalent of at least ten days' work by a master mason; a "best bed" in the typical merchant's home could have cost about 25 pounds *parisis mdf* (500 d. gr., or about fifty days of work); an ordinary frying pan was the equivalent of two days' work; a *houppelande* (a long cloak) of wool cloth, sparingly trimmed with common fur, adorned with simple closures, and lined with ordinary fabrics, the kind worn even by prosperous urban folk, was regularly valued between 8 and 30 lbs. *parisis mdf.* (160–600 d. gr., or sixteen to sixty days of work). A "cremsyn gown" left by an English pewterer around 1500 was valued at 38s. 4d. sterling, the equivalent of about 76 days work.[41] A *longue robe* ordered by a young noble in the court of Philip the

---

[41] The daily wage of a master artisan in England around 1500 was about 6 d: John Munro, "Money, Wages, and Real Income in the Age of Erasmus: The Purchasing Power of Coins and of Building Craftsmen's Wages in England and

Good cost 45 lbs. (in the pound of 40 *groten;* equal to about 160 days of work).[42] The gown given by the son of a Florentine businessman to his bride in 1447 apparently cost 260 florins, not counting some 80 florins for decorations of feathers and pearls.[43] Even lesser goods had significant market values. In sixteenth-century England, for example, a dozen yards of uncut and unsown linen – the kind used for smocks, underwear, and bedclothes – cost 7.6 shillings (in the pound sterling), the equivalent of three weeks' work. There, a good-quality broadcloth went for about 50 pence a meter, making each meter the equivalent of eight full days of work. Such prices reveal that Edith Mason's gifts of aprons, smocks, and bed linens were more than merely the odds and ends of her chests.[44]

the Low Countries, 1500–1540," in *The Correspondence of Erasmus*, Vol. 1, *Letters 1–151, 1484–1500*, eds. Sir Roger Mynors et al. (Toronto, 1974), pp. 311–48.

[42] Marie-Thérèse Caron, "Les choix de consummation d'un jeune prince à la cour de Philippe le Bon," in *La vie matérielle au moyen âge: l'apport de la pratique*, eds. Emmanuelle Rassart-Eeckhout et al. (Louvain-la-Neuve, Fr., 1997), pp. 49–65.

[43] Bestor, "Marriage Transactions," pp. 6–7. At the bride's death, her widower got 68 florins for a gown, an overdress, a piece of cloth, and a pair of sleeves that had been hers. At very roughly calculated exchange rates between the Florentine florin and the Flemish *groten* in 1447 and 1490, respectively, these prices work out to 12,000 *groten* and 4,000 *groten*, the first equivalent to about 1,000 days' work by a master mason and the second to about 330 days; both prices and wage rates are adjusted for the decline of the Flemish *groot* relative to the florin and the rise in wage rates during the period; for more on the debasements of the Flemish *groot* in the later fourteenth and fifteenth centuries, see John H. Munro, "Warfare, Liquidity Crises, and Coinage Debasements in Burgundian Flanders, 1384–1482: Monetary or Fiscal Remedies?" University of Toronto Department of Economics Working Paper 335, http://repec.economics.utoronto.ca/files/tecipa-355.pdf (accessed June 9, 2009).

[44] Prices and wages taken from John H. Munro, "Money, Wages, and Real Incomes in the Age of Erasmus: The Purchasing Power of Coins and of Building Craftmen's Wages in England and the Low Countries from 1500 to 1540," in *Erasmus: Letters 1668 to 1801 (January 1526–March 1527)*, trans. by Alexander Dalzell, annotated by Charles G. Nauert, Jr. (Toronto, 2003), pp. 551–702, pp. 688–9.

Wills and inventories from the small city of Darlington (near Durham) in England priced representative household goods similarly: beds ranged from about L6 13s 4d to 3s 4d sterling (the latter for a simple trundle bed); blankets

Although testators rarely actually priced the goods they named for distribution, they often indirectly referred to their market values, at least in a relative sense. For example, in 1364, Nicaise De La Desous of Douai left, among other bequests, a *robe*, "the best that he owns on the day of his death," to his brother; his "best bed," "completely furnished" but without pillows, one copper pot, and his "best" bronze frying pan to his godson; a feather bed, a pair of linens, his "best after those already named," to his nephew; two pillows trimmed in *"chandal d'une maille dor"* to his niece; and a bronze frying pan, the "best after that mentioned earlier" to his grand-niece.[45] De La Desous did not explicitly equate "best" with expensive or tell us that pillows trimmed in a gold lace-like tissue were worth a lot of money, but it is hard to know what other standard the executor (or the beneficiaries) would have been able to apply in parceling out the pillow, bed, or clothing.[46]

Directly or indirectly, we see, the gifts recorded in sources such as these gave a market measure of the personal relationship that was sought, solidified, and announced by the gift. This quantification was a relatively new feature of gift-giving, for it was only around 1300 that in northern Europe propertied people of all social ranks – princes, courtiers, urban citizens, tenant farmers, and even some peasants – began keeping accounts like those presented here.[47] Although hardly as

were valued at around 7s 6d and linen sheets at 8s per pair. As a frame of reference, note that the median valuation of the fifty-seven inventories in this collection was L46 8s 4d; the range was L2 17s 10d to L816 17s 5d: J. A. Atkinson, "Introduction" idem, ed., *Darlington Wills and Inventories, 1600–1625* (Newcastle upon Tyne, UK, 1993).

[45] AMD, FF 862, 20 December 1364.

[46] Hugh Cicill, a carpenter in Bristol, left his son his "best" cloak, his "best doublet," but only his "least kettle saving one"; he left one daughter "my wyves [best Showes] and hosen"; another daughter "my wyves best Cassacke; and a third daughter "my wyves best and second petticotes": Lang and McGregor, eds., *Tudor Wills*, no. 56, pp. 24–5. In Basel, Ennelit Schererin and Margreth Winnmännin reserved their best veils (*jr beste ufflegi tüchlin*): Signori, "Family Traditions," p. 314.

[47] According to Christopher Dyer, "Do Household Accounts Provide an Accurate Picture of Late Medieval Diet and Food Culture?" in *La vie matérielle*, ed. Emmanuelle Rassart-Eeckhout, pp. 109–27, the first English household accounts appear about the same time as estate accounts – the end of the twelfth

ruthlessly numerate as financial accounts had to be, wills also provided a convenient way to quantify gifts, and they too were new to the North in this period. There inheritance was typically governed by customary law, most of it unwritten, and the law usually required the bulk of property to be passed to the next of blood kin or to the survivor of the marriage. *God chooses heirs* went the adage of the day.[48] Hence, testaments had long been used almost exclusively for gifts *pro anima*, made orally at death, and it was not until after 1200, or even later in most places in the North, that we have good collections of wills detailing bequests to friends and family, many if not most written long before death. Such changes had come earlier to the commercial areas of the South, but even there it was not until after 1100 (after 1200 in most areas) that many documents of this kind were produced.

The Europeans who wrote such wills or who kept accounts detailing their receipts and expenditures thus participated in a cultural revolution arguably as important as the earlier – and much studied – shift from

century – but it is not until the first half of the thirteenth century that we have more than a few and it is not until after 1300 that they become plentiful. Also see Dyer's *Everyday Life in Medieval England* (London, 1994). In addition, C. Woolgar, ed., *Household Accounts from Medieval England* (Oxford, 1992–3) and the discussion among Muldrew, Benders, van der Wee, and Smith in Simonetta Cavaciocchi, ed., *Fieri e mercati nella integrazione delle economie europee, secoli 13–18* (Florence, 2001) pp. 391–2.

[48] Although by the late medieval period, that restriction had been loosened in most parts of the North, everywhere custom set limits on the kind and amount of goods that could be diverted from the estate and passed to selected beneficiaries by means of a testament.

For the history of the medieval will in the southern Low Countries, see Howell, "Fixing Movables"; Monique Mestayer, "Testaments douaisiens antérieurs à 1270," *Nos Patois du Nord* 7 (1962), pp. 64–77; Philippe Godding, *Le droit privé dans les Pays-Bas méridionaux du 12e au 18e siecle* (Brussels, 1987); idem, "La pratique testamentaire"; idem, "Le droit au service du patrimoine familial: Les Pays Bas méridionaux (12e–18e siècles)," in *Marriage, Property and Succession*, ed. L. Bonfield (Berlin, 1992), pp. 15–35. On the general history of the medieval will in western Europe and France in particular, see Paul Ourliac and Jehan de Malafosse. *Histoire du droit privé*, Vol. 3, *Le droit familial* (Paris: 1969); J. Vanderlinden, ed., *Actes à cause de mort/Actes of Last Will*, 4 vols. (Brussels, 1992–4); H. Auffroy, *Évolution du testament en France des origines au XIII siècle* (Paris, 1899).

orality to literacy of the central Middle Ages.[49] They were learning to express social and cultural values in monetary terms, not only rendering value in terms of money – equating a dress with a coin, a service with a price, or a friendship with either – but also indicating that both the goods and the relationships acquired meaning when registered in this form. The written records not only evidenced those equations but they also brought them into being by "pricing" a dress, a coin, or a friendship. Even the dress pulled out of the unarticulated mass of the estate, lined up and itemized alongside coins and entries expressed only in money of account, enabled such quasi-priced gifts, like a coin or a money of account, to quantify a social bond.[50]

Other scholars have similarly described the effects of quantification on people's conceptions of value, exchange, and the social relations created by exchange, but most have argued that these effects were not felt among ordinary people and even among most elites until much later.[51] According to this scholarship, only after 1600, even in England, is there good evidence of such a cultural change and still later that women reflected the quantifying logic in ordinary practice. There is

---

[49] The classic study is J. Goody and I. Watt, "The Consequences of Literacy," in *Literacy in Traditional Societies*, ed. J. Goody (Cambridge, 1968). Also see B. V. Street, *Literacy in Theory and Practice* (Cambridge, UK, 1984); Brian Stock, *Implications of Literacy: Written Language and Models of Interpretation in the 11th and 12th Centuries* (Princeton, 1987); Rosalind McKitterick, *Carolingians and the Written Word* (Cambridge, UK, 1989); M. Clancy, *From Memory to Written Record: England 1066–1307*, 2nd ed. (1979; Repr., Oxford, 1993); D. H. Green, "Orality and Reading: The State of Research in Medieval Studies," *Speculum* 65, no. 2 (Apr. 1990), pp. 267–80; Matthew Innes, "Memory, Orality and Literacy in an Early Medieval Society," *Past and Present* 158 (Feb. 1998), pp. 3–36; Adam Kosto, "Laymen, Clerics, and Documentary Practices in the Early Middle Ages: The Example of Catalonia, *Speculum* 80, no. 1 (2005), pp. 44–74.

[50] The tendency to render value this way was not confined to merchants and others expert in high finance. See Joel Kaye, "Money and Market Consciousness in Thirteenth and Fourteenth Century Europe," in *Pre-Classical Economic Thought*, ed. S. Todd Lowry (Leiden, 1998).

[51] See Alfred W. Crosby, *The Measure of Reality: Quantification and Western Society, 1250–1600* (Cambridge, UK, 1997) and Keith Thomas, "Numeracy in Early Modern England," *Transactions of the Royal Historical Society* 37 (1987), pp. 103–32.

no doubting these scholars' evidence, and there is also no doubt that few of the people I observed, especially those writing wills, were fully numerate. Either city clerks or notaries drafted the testaments we have from this period, and the documents they wrote adhered to rhetorical formulas that were not the purported author's own. Thus, a woman who gave her beneficiary a choice between a belt and its price, as did Agnes, the alderman's wife from Basel, may not have "authored" that equation in a robust sense.[52] Her clerk, not she, may have been the one to imagine that a belt could be rendered as price, and it may have been that only he could actually price it. Even so, the fact that her gift was expressed both as thing and as price is certain evidence that the clerk was able to conceive of value in this way, and at a minimum it is certain evidence that she was being introduced to and learning to accept that logic.[53] It thus seems clear that people who lived in commercial societies of the day, even ordinary householders, were not only able to quantify social relations but also regularly did so, even if they required the help of others in doing so.

GIFTS OF THINGS

Nevertheless, even as donors regularly assigned prices to the objects they gave and delivered their gifts in the form of coin or simply expressed them as price, they also used unpriced objects, animals, or even services for certain instances of gift-giving. The choices they made leave no doubt that they still imagined a concrete thing to be a different kind of gift. In these instances, they seem to have lived in the world Mauss described, in which, as James Carrier has said, "the object is not a neutral thing

---

[52] For her will, see Signori, "Family Traditions."

[53] Beverly Lemire, *The Business of Everyday Life: Gender, Practice and Social Politics in England, c. 1600–1900* (Manchester, UK, 2005), provides evidence of women's numeracy in the centuries she studies, but argues that women were slow to become incorporated into the culture of numbers and quantification. My own evidence suggests that women testament writers were indeed slower than men to reduce social relations to numbers (based on a comparison of men's and women's wills in fourteenth- and fifteenth-century Douai), but that they were certainly capable of doing so, as the examples I have provided here suggest.

but a part of the group itself, carrying and defining the group's being or substance.... Likewise, the object transacted... bears the identity of the giver, and after it is given it bears as well the identity of the recipient and of the relationship between recipient and giver."[54]

Even Charles the Bold's gift-giving betrays such reasoning, for when he made gifts in kind he seemed to do so with full knowledge of the supplemental worth they had as objects. Silver cups and bowls, sometimes raw silver itself, all of relatively insignificant market value, were routinely handed out to members of his own entourage and to those of his allies and clients on special occasions such as marriage, baptisms, or appointments. Although close to cash, because the silver plate could be melted down for coin or easily pawned, the hollowware was typically personalized with engravings of the duke's arms or some other symbol of ducal status that supplemented the material value of the gift. The silver flagon worth more than 130 lbs. given to the Portuguese ambassador or the elegant piece priced at 360 lbs. given to the English ambassador (both in the pound of 40 *groten*; equivalent to 472 and 1,309 days of work, respectively) even more clearly bespoke a personal relationship and the recipient's distinction.[55]

Although often distributed in a similarly conventionalized way (with Charles's standard gift having been about 20 yards of black velvet or

---

[54] James G. Carrier, *Gifts and Commodities: Exchange in Western Capitalism since 1700* (London, 1994), p. 9. On the capacity of gifts, even at death, to forge social relations, also see Osteen, *The Question of the Gift*, p. 33: "We cannot understand the gift if we persist in the idea that gifts are given and reciprocated by autonomous individuals... in giving and receiving we expand the self, paradoxically, by firmly attaching it to social relations. In doing so, we render economic concepts of loss and gain [i.e., calculated reciprocity] inadequate."

[55] Nevertheless, such objects could be sold and pawned. Spectacular examples include the famous "Goldene Rössl," a tabernacle featuring the virgin and child in a garden, with donors and a courtier (along with his horse). It was pawned by Charles VI shortly after it was given him by his wife, Isabeau of Bavaria, in 1405. The Royal Golden Cup given to Charles VI by his uncle, Jean de Berry, in 1391 was pawned in 1449 and again in 1451: Buettner, "Past Presents," pp. 604–5 and 608. More generally on the way that gifts of objects could be converted into money, see Philippe Henwood, "Administration et vie des collections d'orfèvrerie royale sous le règne de Charles VI (1380–1422)," *Bibliothèque de l'Ecole des Chartes* 138 (1980), pp. 179–215.

damask), cloth probably carried greater cultural weight than other physical objects. Unlike silver plate, which was distributed widely across the
social spectrum, cloth seems to have gone only to adorn elegant chapels,
to honor high administrators of Charles's most valued allies, or to dress
his own courtiers. In 1468, for example, Charles spent the incredible
sum of 30,000 lb. (in the pound of 40 *groten* – over 400 *years* of work!)
on cloth to dress his and his bride's courtiers for his wedding (not all of
which was distributed as gifts). If made into livery, such cloth carried
more specific meaning than plate, for it identified the duke's circle in
the most public way possible, both honoring the recipient and signaling
the duke's own power. Unlike plate, however, its market value was not
readily available to the recipients, for personal livery was not easily sold;
having received more social and political status than cash value from
their gift, Charles's courtiers and servants probably intended to hold on
to it. Charles also frequently gave gifts in kind to religious institutions.
Wax, candles marked with his personal seal, expensive cloth for clerical
vestments or for the altar, and, most spectacularly, stained glass windows were all signs of his protection and devotion and also, inevitably,
evidence of his might. Perhaps least conventionally of all, Charles gave
horses to his peers – not the money to buy them. In some wordless game
of male one-upmanship, he and Louis XI, king of France, exchanged
(presumably different) horses and tack at several occasions in 1468.

   In cities like Ghent, objects mattered even more, even if, as we have
seen, the city's officers could also equate gifts with money just as easily
as could the duke's. As in the ducal court, cash was used for the most
conventionalized distributions, as when Ghent city officials distributed
pensioen to its municipal administrators or gave *almoesen* (alms) to the
poor. Cash was also often given at weddings, but interestingly, cash
wedding gifts were mostly reserved for people living outside the city,
going in small amounts to minor officials of the count's entourage; in
contrast, citizens usually received wedding gifts in kind, often in the
form of plate.[56] Ghent aldermen ritually distributed wine as well. A

---

[56] In 1367–8, for example, Ghent presented three cash wedding gifts and six gifts
of plate. Two of the cash gifts went to the court (9 and 20 lbs. respectively, or
54 d. gr. to 120 d. gr.; about seven to sixteen days of work), and the third went
to the nephew of a citizen who was marrying in Ypres (at 30 lbs., 180 d. gr.

specially appointed officer managed the distributions registered in the *prosenten* account, and we have no record of who got the wine; we know only how much he spent in the course of the year. But wine was also regularly distributed to charitable organizations along with food, fuel, and cash, and we have specific records of those distributions.[57] Wine also went to visiting dignitaries: for example, the Bishop of Tournai received two *amens* worth 100 lbs. (600 d. gr. or eighty-one days of work) when he visited the city in 1366–7.

However, the gift in kind that had the greatest value in Ghent was neither wine nor plate: it was cloth. Ghent was a great cloth town, maker of some of northern Europe's finest woolen drapery, which sold on international markets at prices approaching the best silks, damasks, and velvets from Italy and the East. When the city officials distributed the city's cloth to aldermen, deans, or to visiting dignitaries, they were not just showing respect or demarcating their political circle, as Charles was doing when he gave cloth to ambassadors or dressed his courtiers. They were also expressing Ghent's identity. It is no wonder, then, that cloth dominated the gift registers in Ghent. In total, gifts of cloth accounted for 45 percent of the entire cash value of gifts in 1365–6 and comparable proportions in each of the subsequent four years I have investigated in detail.

Annually, the aldermen and high officials of the city received gifts of cloth worth a year of a skilled craftsman's labor. Cloth was also given to ordinary citizens on special occasions. In 1365–7, Brother Janne van Daelpitte received twelve ells of white cloth worth 68 lbs., and Annin

or 24 days of work). All the gifts of plate (valued at between 54 lbs. and 100 lbs.; 324 d. gr. and 600 d. gr.; forty-four to eighty-one days of work) went to citizens. Similarly, in 1365–6, the city sent six cash wedding gifts to various minor officials at court and one to a Gentenar, "the cnape" of an administrator; in 1366–7, the city registered another six cash wedding gifts, four of them for minor court officials and two very large cash gifts for distinguished citizens. In the latter year, however, two citizens of Ghent received expensive plate when their children married, and another was similarly honored when his daughter entered a religious order. Also see Marc Boone, "Dons et pots-de-vin, aspects de la sociabilité urbaine au bas moyen age: Le cas Gantois pendant la période bourguignonne," *Revue du Nord* LXX (1988), pp. 471–87.

[57] In 1366–7, twenty of the gifts listed in that account were in the form of wine, fuel, or food, together counting for about 85% of the value of the distributions.

Gloriaerd was given six ells of striped cloth, some linen, and some embroidered crests of the city, all to make the outfit she would wear as head of one of the charities in Ghent. But the most important use of cloth, beyond that given for the livery of the city's high officials, was to honor Ghent's most distinguished political associates. In 1366–7, the comptal court received four gifts of cloth, totaling more than 1,200 lb. *payement* (7,200 d. gr.); in 1365–6 they received 2,400 lb. *payement* (14,400 d. gr) and, in 1367–8, 1,500 lb. *payement* (9,000 d. gr.). These were the city's best cloths; unlike the plain textiles that went to the curé or to the manager of a hospital and sold for only 20, 30, or 60 lb. *payement*, one half of a "scarlet" of the type given to princes cost 200–300 lb. *payement*, the equivalent of about a year's work by a skilled craftsman. As valuable as these cloths were on the market, they were the least fungible of all the gifts distributed by the city. Unlike the plate and jewels given to the count or duke that then might have been pawned or sold, cloth received as an honorific gift in Ghent would rarely have been returned to the market. Even the members of the count's entourage or a visiting noble would probably have recirculated it in their own domestic gift economy rather than sell it.[58]

Like high officials, ordinary people made careful distinctions among their recipients, personally parceling out specific items to named individuals when they distributed the portion of their estates not reserved for customary heirs. For example, Catheline Quoitre, a Douaisien widow of moderate means, left a bed, its coverings, pillows, and linens to her niece; the *drapiaux* that she wore daily to her sister; her best *court mantel* and *cotte hardie* to another sister; a rosary decorated in silver and a reversible cloth to a woman friend; and another piece of cloth along with a box decorated in coral to still another woman.[59] Jehene Malarde chose even more scrupulously. She not only bequeathed sumptuous clothing, linens, and draperies to a long list of legatees, but she also laboriously

---

[58] We have, however, good records of resales of clothing in Italy. There, scholars have demonstrated that men regularly pawned, loaned, or sold the elegant clothing they had "given" their wives as marriage prestations. For this pattern, see Carole Collier Frick, *Dressing Renaissance Florence: Families, Fortunes, & Fine Clothing* (Baltimore, 2002), and for a careful study of the legal and social logic of these prestations, see Bestor, "Marriage Transactions."

[59] AMD, FF 869, 3 August 1402.

inventoried her kitchen, her chests, and her public rooms. More than a dozen beneficiaries received separately itemized calibrated pots made of tin, kettles, frying pans, bolts of cloth, tablecloths, napkins, pillows and cushions, bedspreads, quilts, draperies, tables, chests, benches, silver hollowware, coats, dresses, purses, belts, hats, and scarves.[60]

From Bruges to Bristol, London to Lübeck; from Constance to Basel, Avignon to Genoa, people did the same.[61] Edith Mason, a widow in Bristol, devoted the bulk of her will to parceling out her personal possessions between two daughters, but she left only perfunctory cash gifts to another daughter and to her son.[62] In Basel, Agnes gave her coral rosary to Brida von Genheim, her gilded belt to her half-brother, and another to his sister; her best robes (or 12 lbs. in local money, as we have already seen) went to a nephew.[63]

[60] AMD, FF 862, 26 January 1355. Pierre Toulet, a tanner who first registered his will in July 1443 and added two codicils to it in the next few months, left his wife the 300 *florins d'or* promised in their marriage contract but went on to list dozens of cups, vases, beds, linens, benches, calibrated pots, table linens, and other goods that would be hers and then provided a similarly explicit list of household objects that would go to his son: AMD, FF 875, 15 July 1443.

[61] For the southern Low Countries, see in particular Godding, "La pratique testamentaire"; for additional references see note 4.

[62] Daughter Suzan got her best gown and two partells, one gorget, four kerchiefs, one white apron, two smocks and a coffer "she hath in the country"; Suzan's own daughter got a gown that had already been made for Suzan, three smocks, five kerchiefs, two partells, one band, and a gorget, along with "my Stamell wascotte," one black apron, "my best petticote, two white aprons and one dyed apron and one coffer at Bristol": Lang and McGregor, eds., *Tudor Wills*, no. 178, pp. 88–9. No. 179, pp. 89–90 describes Simon Mayne, a yeoman. He had different kinds of goods to distribute, but he was almost as meticulous as Edith Mason. He gave 2s. to the poor, but a cow, a bedstead with flockbed, bolster, coverlet and blanket, a pair of sheets and chest, his biggest kettle "but one," a frying pan, a spit, and six pieces of pewter to his daughter Elizabeth; his wife, also called Elizabeth, got a cow as well, along with "the featherbed next to the stairs" with bedstead, bolster, coverlet, and blanket belonging, and a pair of sheets. His wife also got use of his house for ten years, but his son Richard got the house and 4d a year from his mother so long as she was in the house.

[63] Signori, "Family Traditions," p. 313. A baker left his great-nephew armor, clothes, and a silver cup, whereas another Agnes, the wife of a tailor, left her "Arras robe," her veils, and her silver plate to her brother: Signori, "Family Traditions," p. 316.

Among the collections of wills I have studied, those from Douai and Bristol are rich enough to reveal the social map that testators implicitly drew as they chose a bed, a dress, or coin for particular recipients. These testators had four distinct groups of beneficiaries, each not only receiving different amounts but also different *kinds* of goods.

(1) Charities and the parish church typically did not receive objects; they got cash. Some testators were very generous with their bequests *pro anima*, but most people in both cities were stunningly parsimonious, making only perfunctory offerings to local charities, the parish priest, and the church *fabrique*.[64]

(2) An eclectic mix of coin, money of account, and plate went either to the legal heirs, as though in obedience to the dictates of custom, or to more distant kin, as though to acknowledge their residual rights to the estate, perhaps as consolation for the fact that they did not stand close enough in line to share in the estate. These bequests too have a perfunctory, business-like tone, as though the testator was simply doing his or her duty by the kin group.[65]

[64] Bernard Hucquedieu, a prosperous Douaisien tanner, for example, left a total of 9¾ *francs* to his parish church and 18 *francs* to hospitals and charities in the city, but he left 200 *francs* to his children, another 200 *francs* to nieces and nephews, 200 *francs* to his wife, his best "hanap" to a certain Simmonet de Bregez, and his second-best to Bernard in Hucquedieu, apparently a nephew. He also left all his "surplus" to his widow, stipulating that if she remarried she was to give 50 *francs* to the children. Some people gave nothing at all to the church, at least to judge from the written testament. In 1270, Jakemon de St. Dierce of Douai left nothing; in 1303 Colars dou Panerel and Gillate, his wife, made the same choice, as did Wagquenes dou Mares in 1328. AMD, FF 861 (August 1270); FF 861 (December 1303); FF 862 (August 1328). Wills from later years commonly include some kind of gift to the church or charities, but many were very small.

It was even worse for the church in Bristol. The Reformation was under way in the second half of the sixteenth century, so it perhaps is no surprise to find that testators there were abandoning "Catholic" practices of buying masses for the dead, donating to altars, and the like; indeed some of the wills indicate that the testator had taken up Protestant ways of worship. But even those who clung to the old formulas of gifts *pro anima* seldom gave more than a few pennies to the church.

[65] John Adeane, a soap maker in Bristol, took a particularly no-nonsense approach. He first counted out four gold rings, each worth, he announced, 20 shillings,

(3) Servants sometimes received such perfunctory gifts, rather as the parish poor did, but the occasional will made it clear that the servant was a cherished companion who had earned the testator's gratitude and loyalty. For example, Mary Kemble of Bristol quickly dispensed her gifts to the church, the poor, and a few friends or relatives, but then went on to name, in excruciating detail, the many and relatively valuable objects that should go to Elizabeth Hobbs, her servant.[66]

(4) However, the bulk of the individually described objects went not to servants, but to two intermingled groups of carefully selected individuals: first, immediate family members, usually children or nieces and nephews, who were chosen for special recognition *beyond* that which might have been due them as residual heirs; and second, godchildren, illegitimate children, co-workers, and friends who would otherwise have received nothing.[67]

and gave them to his mother, mother-in-law, an aunt, and a cousin. To his brother's seven children he then gave 20s twice, 40s once, and 50s four times. To his other brothers' two children he gave 40s each; to his living brother he gave 10 lbs. and to his sister, 5 lbs. Two uncles got 40s each; a godson got 20s; the maidservants of his father 10s, his apprentice got 40s, and a woman named Ellen Pickerel got another 20s. The poor of two parishes got 40s each. This severely business-like will gives the appearance of having been drafted dutifully and with thought only to money (except for the gold rings, all as monies of account); other than these mechanical distributions, it contained no other bequests at all – not a single cloak or silver bowl, not even a gold coin: Lang and McGregor, eds., *Tudor Wills*, no. 132, p. 62.

[66] Elizabeth got a flock bed, a little feather bed, a feather bolster, a flock bolster, a rug, a red coverlet, a blue blanket, a pair of old white blankets, a cotton blanket, a truckle bed, a pair of old sheets, a down pillow, all her "wearing clothes," woolen and linen, a great chest in her bedchamber, a little chair "that I was wont to sitt in by the Fyre," a little low joined stool, two high joined stools, a cupboard board in her bedchamber, a brass kettle, her second-best cupboard, a half-cupboard of joined work, a little press of joined work, a pewter pin pot, a "tunne" pewter cup, a brass candlestick, a green curtain of "sayes," a little box, and a yellow cushion: Lang and McGregor, eds., *Tudor Wills*, no. 177, p. 88.

[67] For examples of illegitimate children's bequests, see in particular Myriam Carlier, *Kinderen van de minne? Bastaarden in het vijftiende-eeuwse Vlaanderen*, Koninklijke Vlaamse Academie van België voor Wetenschappen en Kunsten 3 (Brussels, 2001).

The early-fifteenth-century will of Marie Narrette dit De Sandemont, a prosperous Douaisien spinster, exemplified the last pattern almost perfectly. Nine of her twenty-eight named beneficiaries were related to one another and may have been related to her, although they bore the family name of De Haricourt or Birchard, not Narrette, and they were not referred to with the sobriquet of Sandemont. For example, Jehan De Haricourt De Durr the Elder got a vase with marbled feet; a man who may have been his son got one *franc* (a money of account). Hannette Birchard, daughter of Jakemon Birchard, and Marguerite, his wife and mother of Hannette, received expensive accessories; the first got the testator's best silk belt, which was decorated in silver, and the second was given Marie's best amber rosary, which was decorated with silver scarabs. Another thirteen beneficiaries appear to have had no relation to Narrette or to one another. Among that group was a certain Jeanne De Bourech, who received Narrette's best long *drap* in bright blue, which was lined with fur from the backs of squirrels and 4 *raisères* of wheat. Three of the beneficiaries were spiritual kin; one was described as a "poor woman" (she received a cloth of coarse, undyed wool). Four other women received night kerchiefs.

Significantly, twenty-three of Narrette's twenty-eight beneficiaries were women.[68] Her decision to parcel out individual goods to specially chosen friends and relatives seems a distinctly feminine characteristic of Douaisien testamentary practice.[69] Although men also distributed

---

[68] AMD, FF 869, 4 June 1405.

[69] For details regarding the gender of gifts and giving in Douaisien wills, see Howell, "Fixing Movables." Customs elsewhere often directly expressed the gender of things. The custom of late medieval Genoa, for example, always assumed that a woman's personal clothing and adornments were hers (as *parapherna*), and they were returned to the widow along with her dowry and *antefactum* (*donatio propter nuptias*). In keeping with the tradition that linked women to personal goods, Genoese men also often gave their widows household possessions – clothes, cookware, and the bed – (the *massaricia*) as legacies, in addition to the *parapherna*, dowry, and *antefactum* proper: see Epstein, *Wills and Wealth*.

Custom in Basel also traditionally distinguished "male" goods from "female," expecting the former to flow to sons and the latter to daughters. Although these particular lines of transmission were apparently not rigidly honored in fifteenth-century Basel, the wills we have reveal that there was, nevertheless, a distinction made between female gifts and male gifts. In Bristol,

personal property, their circle of beneficiaries was typically more clearly dominated by lineal relations or by craft and professional ties.[70] For example, Jehans Hans de Cuer of Douai gave several cash gifts to his parish, the city's mendicant friars, and hospitals; the rest went to kin, the church, his executor, or heirs. He left 30 *livres* to his sister, he released his godson from a debt, and he gave each of his godson's sons "a loom for weaving long drapery, with accompanying apparatus"; to the table of St. Nicholas (a charitable organization) he gave his best *robe*, and to each of his executors, he gave one *hanap*; the surplus went to his heirs.[71] Whether male or female, however, testators who selected

men regularly gave women's clothes to women (even when their wives were still alive), and they seem to have been as eager as women were to parcel out their own personal goods. Women wrote so few wills in Bristol, however, that it is hard to be sure about the significance of that pattern. Only 47 of 192 (24%) wills were written by women, 40 of whom were widows (hence, only 4% were either single or married, and the remaining 20% were widows). Men who distributed women's goods may have been expressing their wives' wishes so that in effect the will was co-authored.

[70] Testamentary rights for men and women always differed, but the pattern in a particular place depended on local law. In Douai, women made up almost half of the testators I sampled, a measure of their freedom as widows and the strength of their property rights. In contrast, only about 20% of fourteenth-century Lübeck's testators were female (Von Brandt, "Mittelalterliche Bürgertestamente," p. 11), only about 18% of Freiburg's, 15% of Ravensburg's, and 33% of fourteenth-century Constance's (Baur, *Testament und Bürgershaft*, p. 60). In Avignon, about 35% of testators were female (Chiffoleau, *La comptabilité*, p. 50), and in Cologne, about 53% (Baur, *Testament und Bürgerschaftt*, p. 64).

[71] FF 862, May 1327. Pierre De Le Bacye, an apothecary, left his shop to his brother and made him the residual heir of his estate after his wife's death, excepting some real estate that had come jointly to him and his sister; she was to have that property. His wife, however, was to have all property except the shop for her use during her life: AMD, FF 488 (ca. 1430). Men in Bristol seem to have made similar choices. Edmond Auflitt, a chandler, gave his son his "furnace" (i.e., his workshop), providing that if his son were to die before coming of age his wife could keep it until her death, at which time it was to be sold and the profits distributed equally among the remaining children; Thomas Hayward, a shearman, left his brother Edmond his shop, giving all the tools and goods "whatsoever therein" and his house to his two brothers together, but requiring only that his brothers provide "his 'now' wife Joan Hayward with sufficient maintenance for a woman of her degrees or else paying her 5 lbs. for

individual objects and distributed them so carefully to selected friends and relatives were assigning values to their gifts that differed from the market values they represented. At least imaginatively, they were rendering them personal in a way that mere commodities never could be. A silver-footed vase, an illuminated book of hours, a fur-trimmed cloak, a silk dress, a weaving loom, even a stack of linens or a soup pot – each placed its owner socially, each resonated with cultural significance, each forged a link between giver and receiver, each told a life story.[72]

Things evidently carried cultural weight that could exceed their commercial worth, but it does not necessarily follow that testators considered the two regimes of value incompatible. As we have seen, people seemed not only to move between the two systems surprisingly comfortably but also not to bifurcate them as we are inclined to do. There is no doubt that, for them, an object could contain *both* symbolic and commercial value.[73] Still, the difference between a gift as object and a gift as money did matter to them; else they would not have chosen to give things at one moment, and coin or simply price at another. Yet they clearly did not think that a gift of money, or one expressed in monetary terms, was the same as a market transaction.

GIFT AND COUNTER-GIFT

Whether delivered as price, coin, or object, gifts were expected to elicit a reward. Charles the Bold's accounts made the calculus especially

life, at her choice": Lang and McGregor, eds., *Tudor Wills*, nos. 133, pp. 63 and 95, p. 44. Women were equally careful to make sure that their children were cared for, and in Douai, where widows often had full control of the entire estate (not just personal property), they dutifully passed it down to customary heirs.

[72] More generally on the power of objects as gifts, see Oleg Grabar, "The Shared Culture of Objects," in *Byzantine Court Culture from 829 to 1204*, ed. Henry Maguire (Washington, DC, 1997).

[73] Kathleen Ashley, "Material and Symbolic Gift-Giving: Clothes in England and French Wills," in *Medieval Fabrications: Dress, Textiles, Clothwork, and Other Cultural Imaginings*, ed. E. Jane Burns (New York, 2004), pp. 137–46, has argued that in this period, rich people's clothes were given more in recognition of their symbolic value than their commodity value, but that for all classes clothing was simultaneously a thing of monetary value (this is what Ashley considers its "commodity" meaning) and an object laden with symbolic meaning.

clear. For example, when he gave 1,000 lbs. to Jean de Luxembourg, his councilor-chamberlain, it was for "services" and as his portion of money collected from Liège after a successful siege; when he later gave Luxembourg another 400 lbs. it was "to bring him into service in his army." At the war's end Charles gave five stewards 90 pounds each "for services performed (and to perform) in the present army and in order to serve the duke even better and more honourably." A group of English ambassadors who helped negotiate the duke's own marriage to Margaret of York also got substantial cash gifts, in explicit thanks for their help.

Occasionally, Charles's financial officer even equated his gifts with wages. For example, an ordinance of 1469 explained that "because his chamberlains and gentlemen are more inclined to reside and serve in the *hôtel* of my lord if the status of their retinues is maintained, my lord has ordered . . . [that they] will have from my lord a month's extra wage."[74] Sometimes the duke's followers directly asked for gifts, a practice that his financial advisors sought to end with a 1474 ordinance forbidding courtiers to approach the duke after dinner to request gifts "whether of offices and benefits such as cloth of gold, silver or silk"; instead, they were required to submit their requests in writing to the duke's financial officers.[75] The duke was just as anxious to receive gifts as were his courtiers, and he unashamedly used his power to do so. By serving as official hosts of his clients' weddings, the duke provided them a way to stage elaborate ceremonies that would have been forbidden by sumptuary legislation of the day. In doing so, however, he also

[74] Ordonnance d'hôtel de Charles le Téméraire, no. 3.1 (1469), section 212, in *Die Hofordnungen der Herzöge von Burgund*, Vol. 2, *Herzog Karl der Kühne 1468–1477*, eds. Torsten Hiltmann and Werner Paravicini (forthcoming, Paris: Deutsches Historisches Insitut).

Another ordinance a few years later explained that his chamberlains and various gentlemen in his retinue would be given cash gifts (of 100 *écus* and 100 *livres*, respectively) "in the form of gift, over and above their ordinary wages" because they had not otherwise asked the duke for "a gift or compensation for expenses": Ordonnance d'hôtel de Charles le Téméraire, no. 5 (1474), section 1400, in *Hofordnungen*, Vol. 2, *Herzog Karl der Kühne*, I am grateful to Dr. Hiltmann for sharing these references and the one in the next note.

[75] Ordonnance d'hôtel de Charles le Téméraire, no. 5 (1474), section 1380, in *Hofordnungen*, Vol. 2, *Herzog Karl der Kühne 1468–1477*. On this point, also see Damen, "Gift Exchange."

manifested his authority and collected riches, for with the invitation to the wedding went a clear call for a generous gift.[76]

The ducal court was not alone in using the gift for political and financial gain. A large part of Ghent's gift budget was allocated for "extraordinary" gifts registered as *prosenten* (presents) in 1366–7, most of them as favors, rewards, bonuses, or compensation. About one-third of the total went to the count, his entourage, and other high nobility in the region. City officials – deacons of the drapery and the small trades, principal aldermen, financial and legal officers, clerks, and sometimes even watchmen and messengers – received approximately another third.[77] It

[76] Werner Paravicini, *Les invitations au mariage: pratique sociale, abus de pouvoir, intérêt de l'Etat à la cour des ducs de Bourgogne 1399–1489* (Stuttgart, 2001).

We do not have a full accounting of the amounts collected in this way, but the assembled evidence leaves little doubt about the extent of the burden imposed on the cities who were expected to send representatives and expensive presents to the weddings. One observer claimed that at a marriage in 1472, 100,000 *écus* were collected (the equivalent of 4,800,000 d. gr.). This was surely an exaggeration – St. Omer registered only 40 *écus* (about one year's work) for that wedding, and the much richer city of Ghent only 25 pounds gr. (120 *écus*, or about three years' work) – but scholars are convinced that the collect for these festivals far exceeded their cost: Paravicini, *Les invitations*, p. 32 and note 167.

Few could resist, not even the most powerful cities like Bruges and Ghent. They too, along with lesser urban centers like Ypres or Lille, needed to build relationships with the duke's circle, and they had much to gain by attending these ceremonies where they could rub shoulders with the people who had direct access to the duke. Those that did resist lay on the borders of the duke's realm and had other protectors. In 1447, for example, Amiens, only recently having been ceded to the Burgundians and soon to be returned to the French, dared decline such an invitation, claiming to be "chargie de trop grans charges, rentes et debtes": Amiens, AV, BB 6, fol. 56v; cited in Paravincini, *Les invitations*, p. 22 and doc. 61.

[77] The rest went for wine that was distributed to unnamed recipients during the year, presumably to many of the same people. In 1366–67, 1,737 pounds *payement* (10,422 d. gr.) went for unspecified gifts of wine (almost double the previous year's total), another 1,516 (9,096 d. gr.) to the citizenry, and 1,611 (9,666 d. gr.) to outsiders; for these figures, see Nicholas and Prevenier, eds., *Gentse stads – en baljuwsrekeningen (1365–1376)*.

Although hardly new in 1366, gifts of this kind were then becoming increasingly important, and their size would rise into the next century, reaching

was the same in Lille and St. Omer. In 1468 alone, the same Anthony to whom Charles the Bold gave lavish gifts, got 420 pounds *mdf* in cash from Lille *sur sa requete* (8,400 d. gr.; 3.5 years' work); the chancellor got 105 pounds *mdf*. (2,100 d. gr.) *sur sa requeste*; and a group of unnamed recipients were paid 248 pounds *mdf* (4,960 d. gr.) "in fulfillment of certain promises."[78]

Scholars have often suggested that gifts openly solicited, given in so calculated quid pro quo or used so instrumentally, had exited or were exiting the medieval gift economy, or at least ought to have been banished from it. Natalie Davis argued that in sixteenth-century France, a rapacious monarchy was steadily eliding the gift too closely with what she called the "sale mode." Although she emphasized that such gifts were necessary, they were also "the source of intolerable obligation and of accusations of corruption. For some, the language of gift courtesy was adulterated or mendacious, and the meaning of words like 'service,' 'merit,' and 'reward' strained.... By requiring payment for royal office, the monarchy was introducing a sale mode into an already contested gift mode for distributing the honors, benefits and profits of the republic."[79] Also referring to early modern France, Sharon Kettering commented that "[although] the language of patronage contained numerous terms for the voluntary, spontaneous, and disinterested bestowal of patronage as a gift, [these were] terms concealing its obligatory nature."[80]

Contemporaries themselves also frequently complained about these kinds of gifts. For example, a 1433 Privilege granted by Duke Philip the Good to the third member of Ghent's corporate body [the "small crafts"] ordered that

> an average of 123,768 d. gr. in 1440–5. Even adjusting for the decline of the Flemish *groot* (in the 1440s it had only 40% the purchasing power of the 1350s), the account had more than tripled in size and had risen from 3.3% of total expenses in 1353–4 to 15.7% of nonextraordinary expenses and 7.6% of all expenses in the 1440s.

[78] Derville, "Les pots-de-vin dans le dernier tiers du XVe siècle," pp. 464–5.

[79] Davis, *The Gift*, p. 99.

[80] Sharon Kettering, "Patronage in Early Modern France," *French Historical Studies* 16, no. 2 (1989), pp. 408–35, p. 844.

because the good men of these trades have had many expenses on account of marriages and other festivities which were held by the aldermen, deans, and other officers of this, our city, about which they have complained to us, it is thus that we command, in order to save these good men from these expenses, that hereafter no one must be constrained to give anything to defray the expenses of these weddings, or for the wedding and festivities.[81]

The Grand Privilege of 1477, issued by Mary of Burgundy (heir of the last Burgundian duke) to restore the privileges of the estates that her father and grandfather had abrogated, dedicated 60 of its 264 articles to what was labeled "corruption," each of which named gifts among the "abuses."[82] In 1469, the duke himself ordered that no member of his Council should "accept gifts or promises that might corrupt" from individuals whose legal cases were before the Council.[83]

Indeed, Alain Derville argued that what had once been an honorable way to do political business had become a mendacious system in the late medieval Low Countries. He concluded that few of the gifts that circulated in official circles were sustaining long-term, stable, and personal relationships between the city and its lord or protector in the traditional manner.[84] Instead, what Derville approvingly characterized as *patronage*

---

[81] Paravicini, *Les invitations*, p. 27. In the same year, Philip ordered his agents to reduce the expenses in the Franc of Bruges with respect, among other things, to the "gifts of jewelry and silver on the occasion of the weddings of various persons": Paravicini, *Les invitations*, 27.

[82] See Blockmans, ed., *Le privilege* for these details. Similar complaints issued from other sites in the same period. See, for example, Henri Moranville, "Remonstrances de l'Université et de le Ville de Paris à Charles VI sur le gouvernement du royaume," *Bibliothèque de l'École des Chartes* 51 (1890), pp. 420–42.

[83] Ordonnance d'hôtel de Charles le Téméraire, no. 3.1 (1469), section 249, in *Die Hofordnungen der Herzöge von Burgund*, Vol. 2, *Herzog Karl der Kühne 1468–1477*. I am grateful to Dr. Hiltmann for sharing this reference.

[84] For this model, see Derville's "Pots-de-vin, cadeaux, racket" esp. the appendix, p. 364. Also see his later "Les pots-de-vin dans le dernier tier du XVe siècle."
   Derville's model resembles those of Roland Mousnier and Yves Durand, who distinguished what they called relationships of "fidélité" in French political culture from mere clientage, although Derville used different terminology. For Roland Mousnier, see his *La vénalité des offices sous Henri IV et Louis X*, 2nd. ed. (Paris, 1971) esp. pp. 531–2; for Yves Durand, see his "Clientèles et fidélités

or "true gifts" were being replaced by *pots-de-vin*, in which a weaker party offered gifts in an attempt to elicit the support of the stronger; these "gifts" smelled too much of precisely calculated quid pro quo. The third and worst kind were blatantly extortionist payments (his term was *racket*) that flowed when the subordinate and virtually powerless "partner" in the relationship was aggressively pursued for "gifts" by his so-called patrons.

Gifts could undoubtedly be crudely exploitative as Derville described, and the market did indeed facilitate the calculation and expose the instrumentality that made them seem so. But calculation, instrumentality, and exploitation are endemic to gift exchange everywhere, certainly not the invention of this age and certainly not attributable to commerce alone. As Alain Guéry put it, throughout the Middle Ages princes were fully aware that to give a gift was, ambiguously, both to command a counter-gift and to claim authority over the recipient: "donner de l'or, c'est bien ordonner."[85] Natalie Davis also reminds us that the gift mode "is inevitably a contentious one" and always elicits complaints.[86] The "voluntary" transfers of property rights, services, or goods that settled disputes and formed alliances in the early and central Middle Ages were, for example, easily and often labeled plunder or robbery if the transfer had been forced or the political relationship turned hostile. Throughout the entire Middle Ages, aldermen, princes, and commentators alike could always be counted on to charge extortion or fraud when the gift did not elicit the expected favor, when it went to the wrong person, or when it was thought too valuable for the uses to which it was put.

To the extent that *dos ut des* caused special outrage in the late medieval Low Countries, politics, not commerce, was the likely culprit. Although no one then and no scholar since have doubted that gifts were essential tools of politics everywhere in premodern Europe, the Burgundian

---

dans le temps et dans l'espace," in *Hommage à Roland Mousnier: Clientèles et fidélités en Europe à l'époque moderne*, ed. Yves Durand (Paris, 1981).

[85] Alain Guéry, "Le roi dépensier: le don, le contrainte, et l'origine du système financier de la monarchie française d'Ancien Régime," *Annales: économies, sociétés, civilisation* 34 (1984), pp. 1241–64, p. 1247.

[86] Davis, *The Gift*, p. 99.

state was especially dependent on gifts, which worked not just to solidify central power but also to create it. The gift's capacity to cement
alliances, calm fears, and repair ruptures helped keep what was a weak,
if fabulously rich, state together.[87] The Burgundian empire was made
up of counties, bishoprics, and powerful cities that were only loosely
bound by economic ties. Having taken shape in the second half of the
fourteenth century with the union of the houses of the Valois Dukes
of Burgundy and the Flemish count, the empire spread north during
the fifteenth century, into what is now the Dutch state, under the first
duke's grandson, Philip the Good. It would pass to the Hapsburgs after
the 1477 marriage of Mary, the last duke's only heir, to Maximilian
of Austria (later the Holy Roman Emperor).[88] However, it would be
almost two decades before Maximilian established control over this rest-
less realm, and in the process he lost Picardy and the duchy of Burgundy
itself, which lay further to the south, to the French crown. Even then,
the region was not quiescent, and the northern provinces would win
independence from the Hapsburgs, then centered in Spain, during the
Dutch Revolt that began in the second half of the next century.[89]

Governing the often fiercely independent counties and rich cities of
their realm was no easy task, and the Burgundian dukes did not have
a well-organized administrative apparatus or clearly defined rights to
make, interpret, and execute law; to collect taxes; or even to organize
the defense. They were thus always in negotiation with their subjects
and sometimes at war with them. For their part, any of the cities in
the region, even the most powerful like Ghent, Bruges, or Antwerp,
were also in negotiation with the duke. To some extent rivals of one

---

[87] For a recent comparative study, see Antoni Maczak, ed., *Klientelsystem im Europa
der Frühen Neuzeit* (Munich, 1988); for a systematic review of the literature on
patronage in early modern France, with references to other regions; also see
Kettering, "Patronage."

[88] See Antoni Maczak, "Patronage im Herzen des frühneuzeitlichen Europa," in
Klientelsysteme in Europa, ed. Antoni Maczak, pp. 83–9, for a discussion of the
peculiarities of this political system and its particularly complex and unstable
patronage-clientage relationships.

[89] For a general history of the region and its political culture, see W. Blockmans
and W. Prevenier, *The Promised Lands: The Low Countries under Burgundian
Rule* (Philadelphia, 1999). Also see Peter Arnade, *Beggars, Iconoclasts, and Civic
Patriots: The Political Culture of the Revolt of the Netherlands* (Ithaca, NY, 2008).

another, which impeded efforts to mount organized resistance to his rule, they were also in need of his support, above all to protect the industry and trade on which their wealth depended. Both sovereign and subject were thus engaged in a tense dance, constantly seeking both to please and to use one another, and both were doing so without a well-oiled administrative structure, well-understood rules, well-marked boundaries, and well-defined powers.

Personal relationships of the kind established or solicited by means of gifts were thus considerably more than grease for the wheels of politics-as-usual or a temporary symptom of the bumpiness of the "transition" from medieval to modern, as some scholars have dismissed them.[90] Gifts linked these disparate political units together and provided the means for communicating, keeping peace, sharing resources, and building reliable lines of command across far-flung and disconnected territories. They

[90] For this argument, see Wim Blockmans, "Corruptie, patronage, makelaardij en venaliteit als symptomen van een ontluikende staatsvorming in de Bourgondisch-habsburgse Nederlanden," *Tijdschrift voor Sociale Geschiedenis* 11, no. 3 (August 1985), pp. 231–47. In English, in Maczak, *Klientelsysteme im Europa* as "Patronage, Brokerage and Corruption as Symptoms of Incipient State Formation in the Burgundian-Habsburg Netherlands," pp. 117–26. On this point, also see Paravicini, *Les invitations*, who hesitates between calling such a gift "un impôt déguiseé" and insisting on its social usefulness; esp. pp. 22–37; also see John Bartier, *Légistes et gens de finances au XVe siècle* (Brussels, 1955): "Ces pratiques peuvent nous étonner, elle ne choquaient au XVe siècle que quelques moralistes grincheux," p. 137; quoted in Paravinci, *Les invitations*, note 108. Indeed, as Derville himself admitted in discussing political gifts, what might seem bribes to us were "rather, necessary for bringing order to a mosaic of particularisms." Derville, "Pots-de-vin, cadeaux, racket," p. 363.

Wim Blockmans has pointed out that the most effective form of clientage in this region was not, however, the traditional patronage relationship; instead, "brokers" – go-betweens who represented the suppliant to the prince – were the cogs in the political wheels here: Blockmans, "Corruptie," p. 242. In "Patronage," Maczak himself points out, however, that Blockmans' study is concentrated on a particularly charged moment in the history of that state, the period after the death of Charles the Bold in 1477. Helmut Koenigsberger's study in the same volume, "Patronage, Clientage and Elites in the Politics of Philip II, Cardinal Granvelle and William of Orange," pp. 127–48, describes a slightly different pattern, although that study, too, Maczak points out, focuses on a particularly charged period of history in the subsequent century.

did additional work as well by helping constitute the elegance of the Burgundian court, where music, arts, dress, food, and chivalric feats were vital mechanisms of rule. The New Year's gifts, called the *étrennes*, that circulated in this court are a case in point. As Jan Hirschbiegel has recently argued, they were powerful communication devices, ways of signaling membership and honor in court.[91]

Political gifts in fourteenth- and fifteenth-century Ghent itself did similar work. The city was then governed under a corporative structure that uneasily combined the old elite (the *poorters*), the weavers' guild led by newly rich and ambitious merchant-drapers, and a third body of the fifty-three "small crafts." So unwieldy a structure required extraordinary supports, and the gifts meticulously recorded in the *prosenten* account gave all parties a stake in the system; they served to quiet protest, heal wounds, and co-opt the reluctant.[92] Thus, rather than sending most of their gifts up the ladder of political hierarchy, Ghent used most of its gifts intramurally to fuel its own political machine.

Gift-giving was just as openly instrumental in ordinary life as in politics, and it was sometimes just as coercive. Like many of her contemporary testators, for example, Marie Narrette of Douai asked her beneficiaries to "pray for her" in implicit compensation for the bequests she made: "to demoiselle Jeanne De Boucren, widow of Jehan Gascourt, [she gives] her best long *drap* of fine wool trimmed in thick fur and 4 *raisières* of wheat, *with the request that she pray for her*" [emphasis added].[93] Margarite Darre left 20 *sous* in explicit exchange for eight requiem masses – for her, her parents, her husband, and other named

---

[91] Jan Hirschbiegel, *Étrennes: Untersuchungen zum höfischen Geschenkverkehr im spätmittelalterlichen Frankreich der Zeit König Karls VI (1380–1422)* (Munich, 2003) and Buettner, "Past Presents." Also, more generally, see Elodie Lecuppre-Desjardin, *La ville des cérémonies: Essai sur la communication politique dans les anciens Pays-Bas bourguignon* (Turnhout, 2004); Peter Arnarde, *Realms of Ritual*.

On largesse in medieval courtly life, see Marian Parker Whitney, "Queen of Mediaeval Virtues: Largessse," in *Vassar Mediaeval Studies*, ed. Christabel Forsyth Fiske (New Haven, CT, 1923), pp. 183–215; for the continuation of the traditions into the Renaissance, see, for example, Margaret Greaves, *The Blazon of Honour: A Study in Renaissance Magnanimity* (London, 1964).

[92] I owe this argument to Boone, "Dons et pots-de-vin." Also see his *Geld en macht*.

[93] AMD, FF 869, 4 June 1405.

individuals.[94] Although neither of these Douaisien wills expresses the quid pro quo quite as crudely as one from fifteenth-century Regensburg, in which a man ordered his executors to "buy him four brotherhoods," the same spirit permeates all the Douaisien wills of the period.[95] In the region of Avignon, testators specifically priced the cost of salvation and release from Purgatory, calibrating their bequests to match the expected return.[96] Gifts made to friends and family were no different in this respect. The same Marguerite Darre, who so carefully extracted counter-gifts from the church and the divinity himself, also gave her niece a long list of valuable objects and coin "for god and for charity and *in remuneration of the good and kind services which she provided*" [emphasis added].[97] Even though individual testators could not have hoped for so explicit a return as the city of Lille might have expected from the Burgundian duke, they certainly thought that their gifts brought returns, some in life, some in death, and some in a sphere that connected both worlds.

MATERIALIZATIONS OF HONOR

However instrumentally they used gifts, however often they complained about the abuses that could attend gift exchange, and however easily

---

[94] AMD, FF 869, 22 May 1403: In addition, among her gifts *pro anima*, she listed purchases of candles to be used at her funeral and during subsequent masses along with the shroud in which she would be buried; to her curé she left 2 *sous* with the instructions that he pray for each of the people named on each Sunday of the year; for a year of masses she paid another 24 *francs*.

[95] F. Bastian, ed., *Das Runtingerbuch, 1383–1407, und verwandtes Material zum Regensburger-südostdeutschen Handel und Münzwesen*, 3 vols. Deutsche Handelsakten des Mittelalters und der Neuzeit, Vols. vi–vii (Regensburg, 1935–44), Vol. vi, pp. 4–5; cited in von Brandt, "Mittelalterliche Bürgertestamente."

[96] Chiffoleau, *La comptabilité*. Samuel Cohn's studies of testamentary bequests in late medieval and early modern Italy, although taking a broader thematic and chronological frame, similarly expose the way the will expressed testators' efforts to elicit specific returns in the afterlife: Samuel K. Cohn, *Cult of Remembrance and the Black Death: Six Renaissance Cities in Central Italy* (Baltimore, 1992); idem, *Death and Property in Siena, 1205–1800: Strategies for the Afterlife* (Baltimore, 1988).

[97] AMD, FF 869, 22 May 1403.

they crossed what we might consider the boundary between the gift and the sale, people in this age rigorously preserved the category of the gift. They carefully distinguished a "gift" from wages, studiously labeled as "alms" what seem to us crude purchases of requiem masses and prayers, and meticulously separated the distribution of cloth to retainers from the reimbursements or salary owed them. There can be no doubt that they did not think of gifts as just another way of buying what they wanted.

The reason they so carefully nurtured a gift register is revealed by language, by image, and by the ways they recorded their distributions: gifts conferred honor. Contemporaries often said so explicitly, as when the city of Lille said that it was making "honorable gifts . . . in honor of the said city and of the people to whom the gifts are given."[98] It was the same outside official circles, where to give, not just to receive, a gift was to earn honor.[99] The language of honor had long surrounded gift-giving in Europe, for gifts were an essential feature of the medieval aristocracy's culture of honor, but in this age honor had new work to do, and it had acquired new importance throughout society.

Julian Pitt-Rivers has called honor the "nexus between the ideals of a society and their reproduction in the individual through his aspiration to personify them."[100] As a general rule, that definition holds everywhere, but during the last centuries of the Middle Ages, particularly in the commercialized regions of northwestern Europe and Italy, what it meant to be "honorable" was no longer as clear as it had once been. Although it was fully understood that honor "reflected the ways in which individuals

---

[98] Derville, "Pots-de-vin, cadeaux, racket," p. 345. There he continued, "a study of the gift compels us to reflect on honor, a notion central in a society governed by aristocratic values."

[99] On this point in particular, see Bestor, "Marriage Transactions," p. 38.

[100] Julian Pitt-Rivers, "Honor," in *International Encyclopedia of the Social Sciences*, ed. David Sills, 18 vols. (New York, 1968), 6:503–11, p. 505. On honor generally, also see his "Honor and Social Status," in *Honour and Shame: The Values of Mediterranean Society*, ed. J. G. Peristiany (Chicago, 1966) and "The Anthropology of Honour," in *The Fate of Shechem, or, the Politics of Sex: Essays in the Anthropology of the Mediterranean*, ed. Julian Pitt-Rivers (Cambridge, UK, 1977), 1–17; also see Friedrich Zunkel, "Ehre," in *Geschichtliche Grundbegriffe: Historisches Lexikon zur politisch-sozialen Sprache in Deutschland*, eds. Werner Conze, Otto Brunner, and Reinhard Koselleck, 8 vols. (Stuttgart: 1972–97), 2:1–63.

were evaluated in the eyes of the societies to which they felt they belonged," as Richard Cust recently put it, it was not clear just which society certain individuals belonged to or, to cite Pitt-Rivers, what the "ideals" of that society were.[101] The knightly code of honor, traditionally based on military exploits, heroism, lineage, and passion (volonté in French texts of the period), no longer qualified men for membership in court circles in these regions. Instead, a new model was in formation. Although indebted to the old medieval ideal, it betrayed the effects of commerce by its insistence on display, performance, and taste. The result was the courtier so famously depicted by Castiglione, a type in eager attendance at the Burgundian court.

Howard Kaminsky has proposed another model of elite honor that comes closer to the urban world of Ghent's aldermen. These men belonged to what he labeled "noble estate," in which honor consisted of property and "preferences" (such as public office, privileges of various kinds, or acceptance in certain social circles).[102] Although not using Kaminsky's term, Felicity Heal added generosity to that definition, arguing that this "medieval" virtue had been taken up by the English gentry of the Tudor period, who made lavish and open hospitality a key source and sign of their honor.[103] There were still other variations on the theme. In industrial cities like Ghent, Leiden, Nuremburg, or Lyon, artisans and tradesmen were simultaneously claiming honor on the basis of skill, financial independence, and political rights. According to their code, a man of honor was hardworking, responsible, and clever; he headed and provided for a well-run household and, at full maturity, helped govern his guild, confraternity, or neighborhood.[104]

---

[101] Cust, "Honor and Politics in Early Stuart England," *Past & Present* 27, no. 149 (1995), pp. 57–94, esp. pp. 58–9.

[102] Howard Kaminsky, "Estate, Nobility, and the Exhibition of Estate in the Later Middle Ages," *Speculum* 68, no. 3 (July 1993), pp. 684–709, pp. 684–5.

[103] Heal, "The Idea of Hospitality in Early Modern England," pp. 74–5.

[104] For this typology, see Zunkel, "Ehre"; Merry E. Wiesner, "Wandervogels and Women: Journeymen's Concepts of Masculinity in Early Modern Germany," *Journal of Social History* 24, no. 4 (Summer 1991), pp. 767–82; Ruth Mazo Karras, *From Boys to Men: Formations of Masculinity in Late Medieval Europe* (Philadelphia, 2003), esp. Chapter 4. For literary expressions of this code, see Herman Pleij, "Restyling Wisdom, Remodeling the Nobility, and Caricaturing the Peasant: Urban Literature in the Late Medieval Low Countries," *Journal of Interdisciplinary History* 32–4 (Spring 2002), pp. 689–704.

A hybrid model of merchant honor was also taking shape, unstably combining the traditional knightly honor, its transformation into the honor accorded sufficiently elegant and skilled courtiers, Kaminisky's "noble estate," and the artisanal ideal of self-reliance and practical acumen. Hakluyt's famous collection of travel narratives and similar texts gave eloquent voice to this image.[105] The English merchants who roamed the world for adventure and gain in these stories are recognizable descendants of the brave, loyal, and curious knights-errant of medieval romance; they admire and seek elegance like the courtiers of their day, and they compete for public preferences just as Kaminsky described; they are also clever and materially ambitious, qualities that bespeak their immersion in trade and fit them for leadership in commercial society.

However different the particular features constituting honor in each of these codes, all of them assumed that honor was achieved in, constituted by, and entirely dependent on the public.[106] None knew anything of a later bourgeois conception that internalized honor as wisdom, conscience, and temperance and evidenced it only as soberly performed

---

[105] Richard Hakluyt, *Voyages and Discoveries: The Principal Navigations, Voyages, Traffiques and Discoveries of the English Nation*, ed. Jack Beeching (Hammondsworth, 1972)

[106] On honor as a public good, see, in addition to the references in notes 100 and 104, Martin Dinges, "Die Ehre als Thema der Historischen Anthropologies: Bemerkungen zur Wissenschaftsgeschichte und der Konzeptualisierung," in *Verletzte Ehre: Ehrkonflikte in Gesellschaften des Mittelalters under der frühen Neuzeit*, eds. Klaus Schreiner and Gerd Schwerhoff (Cologne, 1995), pp. 29–63. He reminds us that "der Charakter der Ehre als eines Gutes, das öffentlich hergestellt wird, findet seine Stütze in der zeitgenössischen Theorie und Praxis. So verlangt die öffentliche Ehrschädigung nach einer öffentlich angekündigten Rache oder einer öffentlich vollzogenen Ehrenstrafe. Erst die konstitutive Bedeutung des Öffentlichkeitscharakters der Ehre sichert auch deren Erforschbarkeit anhand objektivierbarer äußerer Zeichen," p. 50. (Loosely translated as: "Contemporary theory and practice gives support to the idea that honor is a good constituted in public. Hence, a public injury to honor demands a publicly announced revenge or a publicly executed shaming [literally, "honor punishment"]. Morever, because honor is a public good, it can be known only by means of objective, external signs.") Also see Martin Dinges, "Die Ehre als Thema der Stadtgeschichte: Eine Semantik im Übergang vom Ancien Régime zur Moderne, *Zeitschrift für Historische Forschung* 16 (1989), pp. 409–40.

public service.[107] Instead, honor was flamboyant, achieved through performance; it was an assessment, to cite Cust again, of "the ways in which individuals were evaluated in the eyes of the societies to which they felt they belonged." Courtiers exhibited themselves proudly, fully aware that they were accorded honor only if they could display its accoutrements. Kaminisky's "noble estate" was won through comportment, dress, lifestyle, and the like and enjoyed as "preferences" and privileges, all immediately recognizable and all conceived of as things to be presented to the public – to be worn, shown, talked about. Ordinary people similarly equated their honor with public regard. In Douai, for example, parents writing marriage contracts regularly explained that they would dress their daughters and sons for their weddings "according to estate," in effect defining estate as the way the bride and groom would look.[108] It was precisely this conception of honor, let us recall, that made livery such a treasured gift in this age.

These exterior symbols were not just the trappings of honor; they were its essence. As the next chapter discusses in detail, in this cultural logic the exterior was the sign of the person and inseparable from it; the social, visible self was the entire self. Honor even extended to the sexual self. As

---

[107] For a discussion of "bourgeois" honor and its emergence in early modern England, see in particular M. E. James, "English Politics and the Concept of Honor 1485–1642," *Past and Present Supplement* III (Oxford, 1978); also see Reta A. Terry, "'Vows to the Blackest Devil': Hamlet and the Evolving Code of Honor in Early Modern England," *Renaissance Quarterly* 52, no. 4 (Winter 1999), pp. 1070–86; and Richard Cust, "Honor and Politics in Early Stuart England," pp. 57–94.

More generally, see Albert O. Hirschman, *The Passions and Interests: Political Arguments for Capitalism before its Triumph* (Princeton, 1977), esp. pp. 10–12. Lecuppre-Desjardin pointed to the tension between the honor code(s) of this age and those of a later, "bourgeois" period, commenting that "the nature of honor [in elite circles of the late medieval Low Countries] is incessantly to claim rights [preferences] and distinctions," behavior that would seem "pernicious" were it to take place in a republic: Lucuppre-Desjardin, *La ville des cérémonies*, p. 47.

[108] It was the same in contemporary Dijon, where the daughter of a former mayor was promised to be dressed "bien et honorablement selon son état et celui de son père": Thierry Dutour, "Le mariage, institution, enjeu et ideal dans la société urbaine: le cas de Dijon à la fin du moyen âge," in *Le marriage au moyen âge (XIe–XVe siècle)*, ed. J. Teyssot (Montferrand, Fr., 1997), pp. 29–54, p. 33.

Pitt-Rivers has pointed out, honor, although a measure of the seen, was "allied to the conception of self in the most intimate ways . . . linked to the physical person in terms of the symbolic functions attached to the body: to the blood, the heart, the hand, and the genitalia."[109] The visible, being material, was corporeal, and the interior corpus was known by its exterior. It was for this reason that defamation suits explicitly linking sex and honor exploded in this period. Sex was no private matter.[110]

In commercial settings, the honor of men who populated Hakluyt's narratives, of citizens who achieved Kaminsky's "noble estate," or of artisans who demanded their fellow burghers' respect was coming to be explicitly elided with "credit," so that a man of honor was simultaneously a man of credit. However, credit was more than a personal virtue; it was the guarantor of the market's smooth functioning and of commercial society itself. Although the product of public regard – what contemporaries often referred to as reputation or repute – credit was entirely immaterial; it was nevertheless able to guarantee the equally amorphous promise to pay. Perhaps inadvertently reproducing this circular logic, Gervase Rosser put it this way: "until good repute could be vindicated, it would be impossible to obtain credit."[111] In speaking of a later but still premodern time, Peter Mathais used the example of female honor to emphasize just how amorphous that quality was. Because, he said, "reputation, standing, stakes in the trade . . . depended [entirely] on the perceptions of others . . . credit was like a lady's honor . . . once

---

[109] Pitt Rivers, "Honor," p. 505.

[110] For a study of this process, see Cust, "Honor and Politics." On guild culture and sexual mores, see Knut Schulz, "Die Norm der Ehrelichkeit im Zunft – und Bürgerrecht im spätmittelalterliche Städte," in *Illegitimität im Spätmittelalter*, ed. Ludwig Schmugge (Munich, 1994), pp. 67–84. On defamation and gossip in this period, see, for example, L. Gowing, "Gender and the Language of Insult in Early Modern London," *History Workshop* 35 (Spring 1993), pp. 1–21; J. A. Sharpe, *Defamation and Sexual Slander in Early Modern England: The Church Courts at York* (York, UK, 1980).

[111] Gervase Rosser, "Crafts, Guilds and the Negotiation of Work in the Medieval Town," *Past and Present* 154 (Feb. 1997), pp. 3–31, p. 9. Also see Alexandra Shepard, "Manhood, Credit and Patriarchy in Early Modern England, c. 1580–1640," *Past and Present* 167, no. 1 (2000), pp. 75–106. For more on the link between credit and honor in these cultures, see the Introduction to this book.

forefeited, it could never be regained. . . . It could not be asserted, bought or acquired in the short run."[112]

Matthais's use of female honor to characterize credit unintentionally exposes the fact that "credit" was an exclusively male virtue. Women's honor, like men's, depended on the public and embraced the entire self – sexual and social – but it was not conflated with credit because the market was culturally gendered male and, as I argue in Chapter 5, was increasingly acquiring that meaning in practice. This did not mean that women had no role in market production; indeed, in cities like late medieval Ghent, as we have seen, they regularly bought and sold, borrowed and lent. However, they did their business on the assumption that they were representing the patriarchal household. Sometimes the equation was made explicit, as in regions where women were under effective coverture during marriage. As the convention of the "feme sole" reveals, an independent businesswoman – someone acting on her own "credit" – was an oddity created only with her husband's permission, which was given not to "free" her but to protect him from her creditors. Women not so positioned, either as representative of the patriarchal household (as mistress or widow) or as "feme sole," earned no "credit." Inevitably they were poor, and their "businesses" consisted of peddling, piecework, personal services, and the like. In this age, we thus hear no talk of "women of credit," only of "female honor," and everyone knew that such honor derived from women's submission to patriarchal authority and protection.[113]

---

[112] Peter Mathias, "Risk, Credit, Kinship in Early Modern Enterprise," in *The Early Modern Atlantic Economy*, eds. John J. McCusker and Kenneth Morgan (Cambridge, UK, 2000), pp. 15–36, p. 29.

[113] For a discussion of the "feme sole" and references to literature, see Chapter 2, note 32. On the particularly gendered/sexed nature of honor in the late medieval and early modern period, see Martin Dinges, "Ehre und Geschlecht in der Frühen Neuzeit," in *Ehrkonzepte in der Frühen Neuzeit: Identitäten und Abgrenzungen*, eds. Sibylle Backmann, Hans-Jörg Künast, Sabine Ullmann and B. Ann Tlusty (Berlin, 1998), pp. 123–148; and Helmut Puff, "Die Ehre der Ehe – Beobachtungen zum Konzept der Ehre in der Frühen Neuzeit an Johann Fischarts, 'Philosophisch Ehzuchtbüchlein' (1578) und anderen Ehelehren des 16. Jahrhunderts," also in *Ehrkonzepte in der Frühen Neuzeit*, pp. 99–119. Most scholars take it for granted that honor is always gendered because honor is an attribute of a social self, and the self is by definition gendered. However, gender,

The irreducible insubstantiality of honor, whether male or female, provides us the conceptual link to gifts. Gifts materialized honor. They gave public, concrete evidence of the status of particular individuals and of their relationship to others, locating them in the social whole. A recent study of gift-giving rituals by Brigitte Buettner helps us see how this connection was imaginatively made. Using portrait miniatures of the period, Buettner argued that gifts acquired their power not only as objects or as embodied market values but also through their public presentation, individual to individual.[114] In the usual depiction, the donor was shown kneeling to present his gift, with both donor and prince surrounded by witnesses, as in the image that introduced this chapter and as in the image here, which she included in her study.

To judge from this and countless equally stereotypical scenes, Buettner reasoned, "full visibility was the precondition for the ritually correct giving of gifts" because "seeing and being seen were of paramount importance [in court circles]."[115] The miniatures also deployed a specific vocabulary of bodily gestures. Whereas writers and painters presented their works by kneeling before the prince, as in this image, equals were usually depicted as standing face to face when giving or receiving a gift.[116]

Gifts, we learn, must be given personally, individual to individual, in full view of observers, for only then can they do their social work.[117] Buettner's study not only exposed the grammar of gift-giving rituals,

as Garthine Walker has recently pointed out, cannot be reduced to sexuality; nor can gendered honor be seen in terms of static binaries in which men "do" and women "are" (my terms). See Garthine Walker, "Expanding the Boundaries of Female Honour in Early Modern England," *Transactions of the Royal Historical Society*, 6th series, Vol. 6 (1996), pp. 235–45.

[114] Buettner, "Past Presents." On the gifts themselves, also see Hirschbiegel, *Les Étrennes*. On the gestures and rituals of medieval political culture, see Marc Bloch's classic *Feudal Society*.

[115] Buettner, "Past Presents," p. 609.

[116] For examples, see Buettner, "Past Presents."

[117] These images are only representations of meaning, not portrayals of actual events. Donors would normally not have been allowed to approach the throne to offer their books, and Charles the Bold and Louis XI did not meet face to face to exchange the horses and tack listed in Charles's financial accounts.

Figure 7. *The Gift's Public.*
Jean Fouquet, *Pierre Salmon Presents His Book to Charles VI*, from Pierre Salmon, *Réponses à Charles VI et Lamentation au roi sur son état* (c. 1409). Paris, Bibliotheque National, ms fr. 23279, fol. 53r. Photo Credit: Snark / Art Resource, NY.

but it also proposed that it was precisely these social features that sequestered gift distributions from the market. Buettner reasoned that the abstraction of material value created by commercialization forced the manifestation of the concrete so that, even as people enacted the logic of a market economy, systematically counting and measuring and pricing their gifts, they also bracketed the market by cataloguing distributions that might seem to us outright purchases, bribes, extortionist payments, and the like as gifts. The fabulous New Year's gifts exchanged in courts of the day on which she concentrated (the *étrennes*) allowed, she concluded, "late medieval nobility to counteract the values attendant on the growth of a cash economy by stressing the social functions over economic aims."[118]

However, this cultural logic was not exclusive to the princes whom Buettner described. It was not even the province of elites more generally, whether merchants or aldermen.[119] Simpler people who wrote wills,

---

[118] Buettner, "Past Presents," p. 619. In Hirschbiegel's view, the *étrennes* escaped the logic of reciprocity; they belonged instead to the particular cultural logic of the late medieval court (Hirschbiegel, *Etrennes*, p. 126). He quotes Harold Haferland, *Höfische Interaktion: Interpretationen zur höfischen Epik und Didatik von 1200* (Munich, 1989), pp. 151ff., who explains that "a courtly gift must be a gift of honor and thus must be freely given. It may be given neither in expectation of a return gift nor of requisite expression of gratitude, nor out a simple duty to a prior relationship." Even more significant in Hirschbiegel's view, *étrennes* were typically exchanged only among equals – family members, high officials, powerful barons. Although people lower in the social order might receive an *étrenne*, they did not return one in the form of an object. I argue, however, that although the *étrennes* may not have functioned to "compensate" or "reward" in a literal expression of reciprocity, they nevertheless identified and responded to existing social bonds, thereby strengthening them. Nor did the gifts that went down the social hierarchy fail to confer honor; even if they more explicitly functioned to elicit or reward loyalty and service, they also honored by materially placing the recipient under the protection of his lord and made the patronage relationship visible. One function (quida pro quo) did not necessarily exclude the other (honor).

[119] This culture's need to manifest the personal by means of the concrete gift was not confined to commercial realms, but seems to have been more broadly characteristic of the age. Jeffrey Hamburger has suggested that a similar logic informed the thought of Seuse, the fourteenth-century author of the *Horologium Sapientiae*. In an essay on friendship, Seuse conceded that friendship may have

passing out their cooking pots, bed linens, or garments, exhibited the same logic. "This is who I am; these are my things and my people," they seemed to announce, thereby reassuring themselves about their person as well as inserting themselves in the material world where their memory would live on. Whether an elegant silver flagon given as *étrenne* or simply the *sous* given to a niece "in compensation for good and pleasant services," as Marguerite Darre of Douai phrased it in her will, gifts were ways of rendering concrete what the market dangerously abstracted.

Although the magic worked best, we have seen, when the gift came as an actual object, even gifts of coin or gifts as price, if publicly announced, could do that work too.[120] As Marc Boone has pointed out, some of the gifts registered in Ghent's official accounts were never actually made; they existed *only* as an entry in the accounts, and the registration alone created the necessary effect.[121] Similarly, when a Douaisien testator wrote in her will that a specific dress from her wardrobe should go to her favorite niece, even when she counted out coins or named a price in the form of so many *livres parisis monnaie de flandre* that were to go to a nephew, she was implicitly positioning these transfers in a sequestered category distinct from the dictates of law and number that the document itself was intended to serve. They were gifts, she was insisting, things she had specially chosen for special people; they were no longer an abstracted share of a monetized estate.

been an invisible bond between equals, as moralists had traditionally argued, but he also mused that it became "knowable" only "in the realm of the visible," by means of gifts of objects: Hamburger, "Visible, yet Secret: Images as Signs of Friendship in Seuse," *Oxford German Studies* 36, no. 2 (2007), pp. 141–62, p. 9.

[120] Hirschbiegel reports that only about 10% of the *étrennes* he catalogued were given as money (pp. 298–9); instead they came as carefully chosen works of art – elaborately worked silver, gold, and bejeweled vases, plates, cups, flagons, salt cellars; elegant jewelry in the form of necklaces, pendants, brooches, clasps, and rings; altarpieces, reliquaries, and religious images; and animals such as horses, dogs, and falcons. For further discussion of gift-giving practices in the court, see Hugo van der Velden, *The Donor's Image: Gerard Loyet and the Votive Portraits of Charles the Bold* (Tounhout, Belg., 2000).

[121] The point of recording them was less to effect the transfer of monetary value than to register the relationship established by the promise of the gift: Boone, *Geld en macht*, Part II, Chapter 2.

In effect, the quantification of value produced its cultural opposite. It did more, however. Its ability to preserve, even define, individuality was essential to the smooth functioning of the market. Commerce depended on trust – on the promises of known individuals who were accountable to the public as well as to their creditor – but commerce itself could not do the work of creating the trustworthy (the "credit-worthy") person. Rather, as I discussed in the Introduction, it was the "credit" of participants in the marketplace that gave substance to credit instruments, not the market itself, certainly not in an age when risk was so difficult to assess, asset structures hard to measure, debts hard to track, laws often incommensurate and unevenly applied. In fact, the logic of a market exchange denied the individuality that made credit arrangements possible by rendering both things and people fungible. It was for this reason that "repute" or "credit" became such charged categories in this age. Thus for all that the line separating the market from the gift was unstable, sometimes hard to see, and often easy to cross, it existed and was respected; without it, there could have been no expansion of commercial networks.[122] Only when methods of accounting and record keeping could reliably quantify and specify risk, only when legal institutions were capable of systematic enforcement of commercial agreements, and only when commerce itself had been sufficiently cleansed, brought into public view, and positioned as an agent of public good could its actors claim automatic membership in the moral order and could a market exchange seem itself "creditable." In the late sixteenth century, Montaigne seems to have anticipated that change when he condemned gifts and the honor they bestowed as chains that bound, and he celebrated commerce as liberation:

I believe that one must live by law and authority, not by reward and grace. I flee from submitting myself to any kind of obligation, especially one that attaches me by the duty of honor. I find nothing so costly as that which is given me, for then my will is mortgaged by a title of gratitude. I would rather buy a [royal] office

---

[122] As Barbara Sebek has remarked in speaking about this age, "gift-giving practices [had become] . . . a highly charged arena of cultural work, and the distinction between gifts and commodities . . . [had become] an important ideological question as various social relations – between friends, family members, husbands and wives, masters and servants, rulers and subjects – were being reconfigured": "Good Turns," p. 2.

than be given one, for buying it, I just give money. In the other case, I give myself. The knot that ties me by the law of honor seems much tighter than the knot of civil constraint. I'm throttled more gently by a notary than by myself.[123]

But Montaigne did not abandon the gift. As Natalie Davis has told us, he was in practice as fully immersed in gift exchange as his contemporaries, apparently as committed as they were to the notion that the best way to solicit, seal, and reward service or to bestow and exhibit status was with the gift. Able to articulate the ethic of a later epoch, he nevertheless lived the ethic of his own.[124]

The day would come, however, when gifts would be relieved of the burden of conferring honor. Then the virtues constituting honor would be internalized so that the honorable man would be distinguished by his wisdom, conscience, and temperance rather than by ostentatious display; then public service rather than "preferences" would earn the regard of the public.[125] Then soldiers and bureaucrats would openly be paid salaries, central governments would rely on a secure tax base rather than gifts, and the bulk of inheritances would be expressed simply as exchange value and be delivered as cash. According to scholars of the early modern Dutch state, that day arrived as early as the seventeenth century.[126] Readers

---

[123] From a 1588 edition: Michel de Montaigne, *Essais*, 3:9, in *Oeuvres completes*, eds. Albert Thibaudet and Maurice Rat (Paris, 1962), p. 943; cited and translated in Davis, *The Gift*, p. 74.

[124] Davis also notes that "as always with Montaigne, his thought is full of paradoxes, and in other situations he can be critical of buying and selling as a threat to his honor": *The Gift*, n. 22, p. 155.

[125] See note 107 for literature concerning bourgeois honor.

[126] See Yvonne Bos-Rop, "The Power of Money: Financial Officers in Holland in the Late 15th and Early 16th Century," in *Powerbrokers in the Late Middle Ages: The Burgundian Low Countries in a European Context*, ed. Robert Stein (Turnhout, Belg., 2001), pp. 47–66, who comments that "new bodies of government were created – informally and ad hoc at first, but gradually growing into permanent, specialized, professional institutions. . . . The methods and practices of central and regional institutions came to resemble each other more and more" (p. 48). In effect, she concludes, Weberian bureaucracies were taking shape, where "full-time, salaried individuals . . . work in a hierarchy with clear rules . . . [and] get promotions on the grounds of seniority or performance" (p. 49).

According to Wim Blockmans, such standards would become normative in the Low Countries by the end of the sixteenth century: "In the southern

will also have noticed signs of that future in my sources. Some wills summarily lumped all distributions into a priced sum and mechanically passed them out among broadly defined categories of recipients, just as many testators typically do today.[127] People were already typically making charitable gifts simply by naming the monetary value to be distributed, and like people today all they wanted from the gift was recognition of having made it. Furthermore, *pensioen* in Ghent were rigidly fixed in accord with some unarticulated bureaucratic sense, and the treasurers in the duke's court apparently even sought – mostly in vain – to shift money from the gift accounts to "ordinary" expenses for salaries.[128] But this was not yet the future; practices that to us look nothing like gifts still abounded and they were *gifts* as people then understood them.

The public and personal quality of the gift was, for them, its essential feature, the quality that gave it such social power. It was thus during this period that people began, carefully but firmly, to exile from their gift register transfers of objects or money that did not meet this standard. In effect, they were learning new ways to distinguish the "good" gift from the "bad." The dividing line was not determined, as scholars have generally assumed, by the degree of instrumentality, quid pro quo, or

Netherlands after the central state's seizure of power in 1585 brokerage was put to a stop. Its place was taken by new systems of recruitment in which professional education in universities and colleges came to play a greater role. In the North, urban bourgeois, with their strict Calvinist ideas, introduced new ideas into political "life.": Blockmans, "Corruptie" (p. 245). Antoni Maczak has suggested that the change came about with modernization itself – produced by a combination of commercial development and state building: Maczak, "Patronage."

[127] Ernoul Passet, for example, left "the usual small amounts to the church" [sic], and 40 *francs* to each of his three children. To his wife he left one house as her own property, along with the "surplus et remanant," except that all the other houses in the estate were to be hers only during her lifetime; after that they went to the children. He made no other bequests, seeming to consider his will simply a tool for dividing up his extensive real properties, giving his children a portion of his movables in the form of cash, and ensuring that his wife got the "rest": AMD, FF 448, 16 Dec. 1438.

[128] Damen, "Gift Exchange," describes the efforts in the ducal court to change the methods of accounting.

even coercion alone. Nor was the line drawn at the point where gifts began to resemble purchases. Rather, it was drawn where the gift went underground. The bad gift was bestowed in private and taken for private benefit rather than in reward for public service or in public recognition of a personal relationship.

We owe this understanding of the bad gift to Valentin Groebner's study of cities of the upper Rhineland during the late medieval centuries, where such a gift acquired meaning as the inverse of the official *schenk*. The term employed there for a "bad" gift was *miet*. In its original meaning, *miet* had implied compensation for a service and was closely associated with ransoms; in late medieval Strasbourg, however, it came to be used to describe "the cloak and hidden counterpart to the demonstrative public gifts that were so much the focus of municipal self-representation and political registration."[129] *Miet* could come in any form – coin, price, or thing. A Strasbourg ordinance of 1433 specifically described *miet* as "horses, clothing, suits of armor, coins, gold, silver, salt, any kind of game meat, victuals and other things, small or great, in money or cash value, that is liable to soften a man and is used to prevent the city from doing something or to promote or disadvantage certain persons."[130] *Miet* thus distinguished what we might call a public servant from someone's "man," a distinction that turned on whether the gift was public or secret. *Miet* played evil twin to the kinds of gifts openly registered as *prosenten* in Ghent, dutifully sent up to the prince by Lille, and called up by the sovereign himself as a "marriage gift." Such gifts were an extreme case of what Natalie Davis has referred to as "gifts-gone-wrong" – wrong, however, not because they were made in money or because they were excessive, coerced, calculated, or instrumental, but because what was returned was a person's private service, not a public good. The bad gift was, in short, a bribe.

It is surely a measure of the cultural shifts under way in this age that people across northwestern Europe were just beginning to formulate a

[129] Valentin Groebner, *Liquid Assets, Dangerous Gifts: Presents and Politics at the End of the Middle Ages* (Philadelphia, 2002), p. 75.

[130] Groebner, *Liquid Assets*, p. 72. Also see Jacob and Wilhelm Grimm, *Deutsches Wörterbuch*, Vol. 12 (L – Mythisch), ed. Moriz Heyne (Munich, 1984) [orig., vol. 6, Leipzig, 1885].

robust vocabulary for the concept of a bribe.[131] The word *miet* used in the upper Rhineland would soon lose out to the modern German verb *bestechen* (noun: *die Bestechung*), but when appearing in medieval sources, *bestechen* meant only "to stick" or "to prick," and the earliest use of the term in the modern sense dates only from the sixteenth century.[132] English had the word "bribe" by Chaucer's time, but it meant something given or taken dishonestly, and it was not until the sixteenth century that its modern sense of "secretly buying favors" stabilized.[133] By the late Middle Ages, the Dutch began to use *omkoping* in the sense of bribe, and they had *steekpenning* as well, but it meant "hush money," not quite bribe, and they did not yet have the modern *smeergeld*.[134] The French were even later in developing a specific term for bribe. The modern term *pot-de-vin* existed, but it then meant only a gift of wine or a conventionalized gift, not necessarily of wine. It was not until the modern centuries that it acquired the clearly pejorative meaning it has today.[135] *Soudoyer*, the modern French verb for bribe, had not yet entered the vocabulary in that sense.[136]

To judge from this linguistic history alone, the bribe was emerging as the boundary marker of the political gift, the place the gift lost honor

[131] Medieval judicial authorities did have a Latin term that contained both good and bad gifts: *munus*. It meant both an office and the income deriving from an office, which could consist both of licit and illicit gifts. For this discussion see Valentin Groebner, "Accountancies and Arcana: Registering the Gift in Late Medieval Cities," in *Medieval Transformations: Texts, Power, and Gifts in Context*, eds. Esther Cohen and Mayke De Jong (Leiden, 2001), pp. 219–44, p. 223.

[132] Grimm, *Deutsches Wörterbuch*, Vol. 1 (A – Biermolke) (Munich, 1984) [orig., vol. 1, Leipzig, 1854]. Also see Robert R. Anderson, Ulrich Goebel, and Oskar Reichmann, *Frühneuhochdeutsches Wörterbuch* (Berlin, 1986).

[133] "bribe, n.," *Oxford English Dictionary*, 2nd ed., *OED Online* (Oxford, 1989).

[134] Eelco Verwijs and Jacob Verdam, eds., *Middelnederlandsch Woordenboek* (The Hague, 1885).

[135] Maurice Arnould, "L'origine historique des pots-de-vin," *Bulletin de la classe des lettres et des sciences morales et politiques*, 5th series, LXII (1976), pp. 216–67.

[136] In medieval French, *soudoyer* existed as *soldoier*, either as noun or verb; as a verb it simply meant "to pay" or "to support," almost always with reference to mercenary soldiers; thus its meaning as a noun. For this see "soldoier, s.m." Fréderic Godefroy, ed., *Dictionnaire de l'ancienne langue française et de tous ses dialectes du IXe au XVe siècle*, Vol. 7 (Paris, 1892) [This edition is available electronically through the Bibliothèque nationale de France, "Gallica," http://gallica.bnf.fr].

by going underground. Born in the period when the gift itself was being so heavily invested with the cultural freight of honor and when honor was so unambiguously a public good, the bribe had important work to do as the gift's foil. It put the spotlight on what made a "gift" a gift. Although created in political culture and still mostly associated with that domain, secret gifts were even then suspect, however, just as they are today, because they somehow seemed to disguise and to deform rather than to display a personal relationship. A love token given in private might be nothing but a way of paying for sex; a present sent anonymously might frighten as much as please; a glass of wine shared by two merchants in the dark might close a shady deal, not seal their "credit."

Although functioning conceptually as the gift's counterpoint, the bribe also indirectly expressed, and in the end helped contain, the market's dangers. It was not unambiguously the inverse of commerce, for commerce's dangers were multiple, its mystery or obscurity being only one of them. But secrecy, the very thing that distinguished the bribe from the gift, was an important aspect of commerce's dangers. By abstracting and depersonalizing things and people, commerce enabled secrecy, thereby opening the door to fraud, cheating, and illicit gain. The bribe implicitly called attention to that danger by rigorously positioning the "good" gift in the public and labeling that domain the field of honor. Today, it is almost the opposite. In the celebratory discourse of modern market society that still, even as I write in 2009, dominates in the West, commerce can be imagined to do the work of honor because its very ability to depersonalize and abstract – to make one person just like another, one good just like another – can seem to create open spaces, to allow trade to escape dark places where the terms of exchange are not quite clear and the players hard to see. As Braudel warned, however, and as the 2008 collapse of the U.S. financial markets reminds us, that abstraction provides no guarantee of honor. It can, in fact, be a cover for corruption.

For the modern market economy to be praised as modern western-ers have done, a lot more needed to happen than had been possible in

The modern sense of the term seems to have developed only during the eigh-teenth and nineteenth centuries. For this see "Dictionnaires d'autrefois," *The Artfl Project* (Chicago), http://artfl-project.uchicago.edu/node/17.

the world before 1600. Mandeville and his contemporaries had to provide Europeans a moral defense of luxury spending, and Adam Smith, along with fellow economists and moralists, had to provide a basis for believing that the unrestrained pursuit of individual gain could serve the commonweal. Only then could commerce or "the market" be seen as the site of social and moral good and could gifts be relegated to a more private place.[137] There they would serve, just as they serve modern westerners today, principally as tokens of affection and gratitude and as signs of civic consciousness. As an ideological space sequestered from the logic of the market, gifts today can seem a safe port for values that the market excludes – what Gabriela Signori has characterized as "the modern age's yearning for paradise lost."[138] In premodern Europe, however, commerce was simultaneously locating the gift both in the market, where its exchange value could be precisely calculated, and in a world of stable meanings, where it linked giver and receiver in a bond of honor. That bond helped make commerce possible and, in fact, ushered Europeans into a world where it could be ideologically positioned as an unequivocal good.

[137] Even as early as the fifteenth century some moralists were beginning the discourse by lauding riches themselves, arguing that the private accumulation of wealth brought virtue and implying a link between private virtue and public good. In the preface to his translation of the pseudo-Aristotelian *Economics* (c. 1420), for example, Leonardo Bruni commented that "as health is the goal of medicine, so riches are the goal of the household. For riches are useful both for ornamenting their owners as well as for helping nature in the struggle for virtue." See, for this and similar examples from Italian humanists of the period, Diana Wood, *Medieval Economic Thought* (Cambridge, UK, 2002), p. 52. On the ambiguities that still attended wealth in this culture, also see, however, Frick, *Dressing Renaissance Florence.*

[138] Signori, "Family Traditions, p. 287; also see Carrier, *Gifts and Commodities*, esp. pp. 190–206, on the way the gift works to define the market in modern western economies. Geary similarly remarks, "The gift was never about the 'other,' but always and essentially about ourselves." ("Gift Exchange," p. 140).

4 The Dangers of Dress

THE PERIOD BETWEEN ABOUT 1300 AND 1600 WAS EUROPE'S
great age of sumptuary legislation, a time when princes, urban
magistrates, and church officials alike relentlessly sought to control
display, especially the display of dress. Scholars are agreed that commerce
was principally responsible for this legislative furor. Commerce not only
gave new people access to luxuries that had once been the sole preserve of
the nobility; it also radically increased the supply of such goods, dress
above all. As legislators repeatedly complained, the result was not only
social disorder but also moral rot.

This chapter argues that even more was at stake in sumptuary
legislation's obsession with dress. The problem was not just the threat to
social order or morals. It was the disruption of the presumed relationship
between the material and the immaterial. Dress was the central target of
sumptuary laws because commerce eroded the ability of dress to do what it
had traditionally been thought able to do: reliably express identity. Under
the pressure of commodification, dress was abstracted as price, thereby
losing specific material meaning, and at the same time it was endlessly
rematerialized in ephemeral forms – as fashion. It was therefore not just
the link between appearance and social status that was at issue, and not
even simply the link between appearance and personhood. The worries
about dress were an expression of Europeans' uncertainty about the link
between the material and the immaterial.

In 1373, the city of Florence ordered that "all women and girls, whether
married or not, whether betrothed or not, of whatever age, rank and

Figure 8. *Sleeves.*
Raffaello Sanzio, *Jeanne d'Aragon, Queen of Naples* (1518). Oil on canvas,
120 cm × 96 cm. Paris, Musée du Louvre. Photo: Hervé Lewandowski. Photo
Credit: Réunion des Musées Nationaux / Art Resource, NY.

condition . . . who wear – or who wear in future – any gold, silver, pearls,
precious stones, bells, ribbons of gold or silver, or cloth of silk brocade on
their bodies or heads . . . for the ornamentation of their bodies . . . will be
required to pay each year . . . 50 florins."[1] In 1415 the same city decreed
that the sleeves of a woman's undergowns not be of silk or velvet, and

---

[1] Gene Brucker, *The Society of Renaissance Florence: A Documentary Study* (New York,
1971), p. 180. This was a huge tax, equivalent to the annual earnings of a well-
paid craftsman. For more on sleeves and sumptuary laws in Italy, see Evelyn
Welch, "New, Old, and Second-Hand Culture: The Case of the Renaissance
Sleeve," in *Revaluing Renaissance Art*, eds. Gabriele Neher and Rupert Shepherd
(Aldershot, UK, 2000).

Figure 9. *Royal Splendor.*
Jean Clouet, *François I, King of France* (c. 1525). Wood on panel, 96 × 74 cm.
Paris, Musée du Louvre. Photo Credit: Erich Lessing / Art Resource, NY.

in 1456 it forbade any woman to have more than one pair of brocaded sleeves worth more than 10 florins.[2]

Painters elsewhere in Europe could easily imagine costumes of the kind described in the Italian laws and depicted above, but the legislators in northern lands did not typically concentrate on women's sleeves, nor even on women, in writing their sumptuary laws. Men were their principal concern, and legislators there worried about more than sleeves or undergowns. A French royal ordinance dating from 1279 ordered that no duke, count, prelate, baron, or others may have more than four pairs of robes made of squirrel or any robes of cloth costing more than 30

---

[2] Carole Collier Frick, *Dressing Renaissance Florence*, pp. 194–7.

sous tournois per Parisian yard. The legislation seemed almost desperate to ensure that the king must be recognizable as king.[3]

Across the channel in England, the crown passed the first such law in 1337; it forbade fur on clothes for all except the royal family, prelates, earls, barons, knights, and ladies and "people of the holy church."[4] In 1497, Archduke Philip the Fair issued a similar regulation for the county of Flanders that generally prohibited the wearing of velvet and silk, except for wives and daughters of the knights of the Golden Fleece, along with barons and baronets.[5] Other legislators targeted the urban

[3] For this ordinance (and that of 1294), see Sarah-Grace Heller, "Anxiety, Hierarchy, and Appearance in Thirteenth-Century Sumptuary Laws and the *Romance de la Rose*," *French Historical Studies* 27, no. 2 (Spring 2004), pp. 311–48. According to Heller, there was one earlier ordinance, of 1188, issued to regulate Crusaders' apparel; another early regulation of 1283 that is often mentioned in scholarly literature is, she reports, lost. The French crown issued eighteen such ordinances between 1485 and 1660.

[4] John Scattergood, "Fashion and Morality in the Late Middle Ages," in *England in the Fifteenth Century*, ed. Daniel Williams (Woodbridge, UK, 1987), p. 260. In 1463, the same crown ordered that "no person under the estate of a lord [may] wear any manner of cloth or silk being of the color of purple." 3 Edw. IV; c.5; SR 2; pp. 399–402; cited in Alan Hunt, *Governance of the Consuming Passions: A History of Sumptuary Law* (New York, 1996), p. 128. The restriction was repeated in what was probably the most extensive of the English royal legislation of this type, the 1533 "Act for the Reformation of Excess in Apparel." It forbade crimson, scarlet, or blue velvets to any but dukes, marquises, or earls.

[5] Raymond van Uytven, "Showing off One's Rank in the Middle Ages," in *Showing Status: Representations of Social Positions in the Late Middle Ages*, eds. Wim Blockmans and Antheun Janse (Turnhout, Belgium, 1999), pp. 19–35, 28–30. Men "living as noblemen or men of standing" were also permitted 8 ells of such cloth, whereas the wives and daughters of officers in the ducal household and other "truly noble" women were allowed velvet, satin, and damask for their accessories. Also see Raymond van Uytven, *De zinnelijke middeleeuwen* (Leuven, 1998), pp. 121–49. For additional information about sumptuary legislation in the Low Countries (where the record seems to be extraordinarily slight in comparison to England or Italy), see Wim Blockmans, "Vete, partijstrijd en staatsmacht," in *Bloedwraak, partijstrijd en pacificatie in laat-middeleeuws Holland*, ed. J. W. Marsilje (Hilversum, Neth., 1990), pp. 29–30; in the same volume, see remarks by Hanno Brand, "Twistende Leidenaars: Verkenningen naar het voorkomen van clan en kerngezin, partij en factie aan de hand van drie oproeren in een Hollandse stad in de 15e eeuw," p. 103, and M. J. van Gent, "De Hoekse

population. In 1470, Duke Ludwig the Rich of Bavaria forbade all furs to ordinary citizens in the city of Landshut and the region of Oberpfalz, specifically denying artisans the right to wear "the feathers of herons and ostriches."[6] Dress was not the sole target of such legislation; other significant objects of the laws were public events like funerals, weddings, and christenings, but these ceremonies were frequently linked to the dress regulations, as though the two forms of display posed similar dangers.[7]

Sumptuary legislation did not originate in late medieval Europe. The classical Greek and Roman worlds knew such laws, and a few texts

factie in Leiden circa 1445–1490: Het verhaal van verliezers," pp. 131–2. On Burgundian costume in general, see Michèle Beaulieu and Jeanne Bayle, *Le costume en Bourgogne, de Philippe le Hardi à Charles le Téméraire* (Paris, 1956) and on dress and marginality, see Marleen Maes, "Kledij als teken van marginaliteit in de late middeleeuwen," in *Sociale structuren en topografie van armoede en rijkdom in de 14e en 15e eeuw*, eds. Walter Prevenier and Raymond Van Uyven (Ghent, 1985), pp. 135–56.

[6] The same law permitted sons of the town's councilmen to sport a knife with a silver handle, a silver belt, and a silver (neck) chain: Veronika Baur, *Kleiderordnungen in Bayern.vom 14. bis zum 19. Jahrhundert* (Munich, 1975), p. 42.

[7] Many fewer – perhaps less than 1% – regulated possessions such as horses, armor, and servants, or they restricted the size or design of buildings, often by limiting the number and size of windows. However, it is impossible to precisely quantify the legislation by type. Some of it was embedded in regulations about public order more generally, so that it is hard to find a basis for measuring statistical significance. Most was included with other sumptuary rules, but the articles of these ordinances were so variously detailed that one law cannot be compared to another in terms of the items named, the people addressed, or the costs itemized. However, it is obvious that dress dominated.

Neithard Bulst, "Kleidung als sozialer Konfliktstoff: Problem kleidergesetzlicher Normierung im sozialen Gefüge," *Saeculum* 44 (1993), pp. 32–47, estimates that in the German Empire some 1,350 clothing laws were issued between 1244 and 1816 by 150 municipalities and 30 territorial sovereigns. Laws regulating weddings, funerals, and christenings were even more numerous in that part of Europe (2,300 laws by 650 issuers), but many of them also included clothing regulations. Also see his "Zum Problem städtischer und territorialer Kleider-, Aufwands – und Luxusgesetzgebung in Deutschland (13.–Mitte 16. Jahrhundert)," in *Renaissance du pouvoir legislative et genèse de l'état*, eds. André Gouron and Albert Rigaudière (Montpellier, Fr., 1988). For further estimates on the number and type of these ordinances in the German-speaking territories, also see his "Les ordonnances somptuaires en Allemagne: expression de l'ordre social urbaine (XIVe–XVe siècles)," *Comptes-rendus des séances de l'Académie des inscriptions et belles-lettres* 137, no. 3 (1993), pp. 771–81.

have survived from the Church and royal courts of the early and high Middle Ages that similarly restricted dress or the expenses of funerals, weddings, and the like.[8] Still, late medieval and early modern governors wrote a distinct and dramatic chapter in the history of sumptuary law. In no other period did lawmakers give dress and the display associated with rites of passage such as weddings and funerals such frenzied attention, and nowhere was the legislation so abundant, detailed, and repetitive.[9]

[8] On the Greek and Roman legislation, see N. B. Harte, "State Control of Dress and Social Change in Pre-Industrial England," in *Trade, Government and Economy in Pre-industrial England: Essays Presented to F. J. Fisher*, eds. Donald Cuthbert Coleman and A. H. John (London, 1976), pp. 132–65, p. 133. On the classical and medieval, see Baur, *Kleiderordnungen*, p. 2, and James A. Brundage, "Sumptuary Laws and Prostitution in Late Medieval Italy," *Journal of Medieval History* 13 (1987), pp. 343–55, pp. 343–4.

Non-European populations were also subjected to sumptuary laws. From medieval and early modern China and Japan we have particularly good records of such practices, and spottier evidence from elsewhere leaves little doubt that ecclesiastical and secular governments alike frequently thought it necessary to tell people what and how much to eat and drink on certain public occasions, or what to wear and what not to wear. There are also scattered examples of such legislation from later centuries in western Europe, beyond the late medieval and early modern periods.

Sumptuary legislation survived well into the nineteenth century in many places, although it was then increasingly incorporated into general "police" ordinances. Some scholars have argued that this regulatory impulse extends into our own age. Although western governments today do not tell people what to wear or how much to spend on their weddings or funerals, they do seek to control alcohol consumption and the use of drugs and tobacco, prescribe the use of seatbelts and motorcycle helmets, promote good nutrition, and in general celebrate the sound body and mind, all in an energetic effort to "govern" the civic whole. For this argument see Hunt, *Governance*, pp. 410–28, and esp. Alan Hunt, "The Governance of Consumption: Sumptuary Laws and Shifting Forms of Regulation." *Economy and Society* 25, no. 3 (1996), pp. 410–27.

[9] Catherine Kovesi Killerby, "Practical Problems in the Enforcement of Italian Sumptuary Law, 1200–1500," in *Crime, Society and the Law in Renaissance Italy*, eds. Trevor Dean and K. J. P. Lowe (Cambridge, UK, 1994), pp. 99–120, reports that more than forty Italian cities issued such laws between 1200 and 1500. Included among them, in addition to Bologna and Florence, were Genoa, Rome, Milan, Venice, Lucca, and Siena. Countless German and Swiss cities did so as well, as did most of the territorial principalities or national monarchies, including England, France, Castile, Catalonia, Aragon, Poland, and Russia. Bulst, "Kleidung als sozialer Konfliktstoff," p. 32, reports that the earliest

To judge from the quantity and the intensity of the surviving legislation, in that age a good governor had no more urgent task than to ensure that the population was appropriately attired. In the minds of those princes, their counselors, and the urban magistrates who issued these laws, dress was dangerous, and it somehow compounded the dangers associated with ceremonies of marriage, burial, and christening.

Legislators themselves regularly insisted that sumptuary laws were intended to prevent social, moral, and economic decay. Historians have generally adopted the same explanations for the laws, usually concluding that the basic problem was a threat to social hierarchy: commerce had made clothing an unreliable signifier of social status.[10] This chapter argues, however, that more was at stake: dress had become an unreliable identifier of the self. Although its traditional capacity to establish both social and personal identity had been magnified as commerce brought new fabrics, styles, and ornamentations from workshops near and far, the expansion of possibilities for display came at a huge cost. Thanks to its abundance and variety, dress was losing its ability to do its traditional cultural work, and the erosion of the presumed equation between appearance and personhood raised doubts about the relationship between the material and the immaterial more generally.

SUMPTUARY DISCOURSES

Contemporaries justified their legislation with the help of several discourses, the most general of which was an age-old critique of superfluous wealth and luxury drawn from Judeo-Christian and classical moralist tracts.[11] Refusing the usual medieval justification that such wealth both

> known law dates from 1157 in Genoa and that the German areas, although later to adopt the practice, clung longest to the agenda.
>
> [10] Neithard Bulst has offered a more complex explanation of these laws that turns in part on chronology, particularly in the Germanic areas on which his research has concentrated. For his general argument, see the references in note 9 and the further discussion in the section "The Body on Display" in this chapter.
>
> [11] For the general critique of wealth, see Chapter 5. Luxury was associated with original sin and disruption of a hierarchy established by the divine, for Eve's crime was to seek that to which humans had no right. For this discussion, see in particular John Sekora, *Luxury: The Concept in Western Thought, Eden to*

permitted the charity expected of Christians and financed the *largesse* and *liberalité* that secured rule and social order, legislators flatly charged that luxury was a mark of pride, incontinence, lust, and envy – in short, a breeding ground for moral collapse.[12] For example, English laws of 1522–33 forbade "costlye arraye and apparel" because it led to the "utter impoverysshement and undoing of many inexpert and light persons inclined to pride, moder [mother] of all vices."[13] A law from Nuremberg in 1654 spoke of the "immoderate costly display" that grieved "virtue-loving persons."[14]

A closely associated discourse concerned gender. Some laws, especially in Italy, were laden with the misogynist rhetoric of the age. As the priors of Florence's *Officiale della donne* set out to "dress women down," to employ Ronald Rainy's felicitous phrase, they charged women with "barbarous and irrepressible bestiality" and a "reprobate and diabolical

Smollott (Baltimore, 1977), Chapter 1. For a general discussion of the history of ideas about luxury's dangers (and benefits), see Maxine Berg and Elizabeth Eger, "The Rise and Fall of the Luxury Debates," in *Luxury in the Eighteenth Century: Debates, Desires, and Delectable Goods*, eds. Maxine Berg and Elizabeth Eger (Hampshire, UK, 2003). Also see Hans Baron's argument that Bruni's translation of the pseudo-Aristotelian *Economics*, which defended the role of wealth in public life, challenged the old argument about poverty's virtue and gave early form to an argument about the social usefulness of commerce: Hans Baron, "Franciscan Poverty and Civic Wealth in Humanistic Thought," *Speculum* 13 (1938), pp. 1–37, and, more generally, Wood, *Medieval Economic Thought*, p. 52. The debate about luxury would continue for centuries and in the eighteenth century entered French political discourse with a vengeance. For this discussion, see John Shovlin, *The Political Economy of Virtue: Luxury, Patriotism, and the Origins of the French Revolution* (Ithaca, NY, 2006), esp. Chapter 1.

[12] As a seventeenth-century French legist put it in making the traditional argument for consumption by elites, "this splendor ... is necessary to uphold the dignity of their [the nobility's] birth, to impress upon the people the respect [due them], and to maintain business and the arts": Nicolas Delamare, *Traité de la police* (Paris, 1713–38), Vol. 1, p. 413; cited in Michèle Fogel, "Modèle d'état et modèle social de dépense: Les lois somptuaires en France de 1485 à 1660," in *Genèse de l'état moderne Prélèvement et redistribution*, eds. J. Ph. Genet and M. Le Mené (Paris, 1987), p. 228.

[13] Scattergood, "Fashion and Morality," p. 263.

[14] For the Nuremberg material, see Kent Roberts Greenfield, *Sumptuary Law in Nürnberg: A Study in Paternal Government* (Baltimore, 1918), p. 127.

Figure 10. *Bosoms.*
Lucas Cranach the Elder, *Portrait of a Young Woman* (c. 1530). Oil on wood,
42 × 29 cm. Florence, Uffizi. Photo Credit: Alinari / Art Resource, NY.

nature." Accordingly, they claimed, women used "honeyed poison" to
trick their husbands into buying them more finery.[15] More generalized concerns about the sexualized body also made an appearance. An
ordinance from Strasbourg in 1370 banned corsets that "pushed up
the bosom."[16] Men's bodies were also under surveillance. A Heidelberg

[15] In Ronald Rainey, "Dressing down the Dressed-Up," p. 232. Also see Ronald
Rainey, "Sumptuary Legislation in Renaissance Florence."
[16] Veronika Bauer, "Korsettähnlichen Unterkleidern, die den Busen hohen," in
Kleiderordnungen, ed. Baur, p. 3. Others from the Germanic area sought to ensure
that peasant women's skirts were long enough: Baur, *Kleiderordnungen*, pp. 3,

Figure 11. *Male Anatomy.*
Titian, *Portrait of Charles V* (1533). Oil on canvas, 192 × 111 cm. Madrid, Museo del Prado. Photo Credit: Scala / Art Resource, NY.

police ordinance from 1465 set minimum lengths for men's jackets, and one from the same period in Nuremberg ordered that a man's coat "not

40–50, 65–6; also see Greenfield, *Sumptuary Law in Nürnberg*, p. 114. The worry about women's modesty was not confined to German-speaking areas. In the 1470s, the Florentine commune commanded that a widow not expose her breasts: for this see Isabelle Chabot, "'La sponsa in nero': La ritualizzazione del lutto delle vedove fiorentine (secoli XIV–XV)," *Quaderni storici* 86, no. 2 (August 1994), pp. 421–62; cited in Frick, *Dressing*, p. 90.

be cut out too deeply, or be left open, in order that everyone's shame may be covered, and he may not be found unchaste therewith."[17]

Some of the texts took another approach as well, claiming that lavish spending brought economic ruin, thus implicitly equating sober dress with economic prudence.[18] English royal legislation of 1363 ranted about "the outrageous excessive apparel of divers people, against their estate and degree, to the great destruction and impoverishment of all the land."[19] A law issued in Bavaria in 1599 complained that nobles spent so much on their weddings that the debts burdened heirs for years afterward.[20] Many of these laws had a distinctly mercantilist cast, for they targeted imported goods and seemed to equate such purchases with bad citizenship, even with treason. For example, an English ordinance of 1463 accused those who wore "excessive and inordinate array and apparel" of "impoverishing . . . the realm of England and . . . enriching . . . other strange realms and countries to the final destruction of the husbandry of this fair realm."[21] A Strasbourg regulation of 1660 attacked "clothing from foreign, non-German nations" that had little of "the commendable steadfastness for which our old German forefathers had a singular reputation in other things as well as in clothing."[22] Florentine ordinances of the fifteenth century banned necklines "in the French

---

[17] Greenfield, *Sumptuary Law in Nürnberg*, p. 115; also see Lyndal Roper, "Blood and Codpieces: Masculinity in the Early Modern German Town" in idem, *Oedipus and the Devil: Witchcraft, Sexuality, and Religion in Early Modern Europe* (London, 1994), pp. 107–25.

[18] Hunt, *Governance*, pp. 207–8.

[19] *Statutes of the Realm* 1, pp. 280–1, cited in Scattergood, "Fashion and Morality," p. 260. An Act of 1509–10 repeated the litany: "The greate and costly array and apparel used within this realme . . . hathe be the occasion of grete impoverishing of divers of the kinges subjectes": Scattergood, "Fashion and Morality," p. 262.

[20] Baur, *Kleiderordnungen*, p. 122.

[21] Scattergood, "Fashion and Morality," p. 261. Another English law in effect between 1571 and 1597 required that all nongentry men wear an English-made wool cap on Sundays and holy days: Harte, "State Control," p. 138.

[22] John Martin Vincent, *Costume and Conduct in the Laws of Basel, Bern, and Zurich, 1370–1800* (Baltimore, 1935), pp. 68–9. Similarly, a Bavarian text from 1616 spoke of the "reason why more money flows out of than into our land": Baur, *Kleiderordnungen in Bayern*, pp. 122–3.

style" or saddle-shaped headgear "in the Flemish or French style."[23] A 1543 French law denounced "excessive and superfluous expense on cloth and ornaments of gold and silver . . . the means by which huge sums of money are sucked from the realm," which permits foreigners to "enrich themselves from the fat of our realm and give aid to our enemies."[24]

Alone or together, however, these justifications do not sufficiently explain why dress was singled out above almost all other forms of consumption or exactly what it was about dress that so disturbed legislators of the day. The critique of luxury was a centuries-old script, and late medieval sumptuary legislation's only contribution to the rhetoric was a specific focus on dress rather than more generally on "excess."[25] Women's vanity, their passion for personal adornment, their frivolity, and wastefulness – these too were all old canards, tired tropes that had circulated in every decade of western European history.[26] In any case, in

[23] In Rainey, "Dressing down the Dressed-Up," p. 219, notes 8 and 9.

[24] "L'excessive et superflue dépense en draps et ornaments d'or et d'argent . . . le moyen de quoy grandes sommes de deniers se tirent de cestuy royaume," which permit foreigners to "d'eux enrichir de la graisse de notre royaume . . . [and] d'en pouvoir ayder auxdits ennemis"("the excessive and superfluous expense for cloth and ornaments of gold and silver . . . the means by which huge sums of pennies are pulled from this realm," which permit foreigners to "enrich themselves from the fat of our realm . . . and makes it possible to aid our enemies with it"): in Delamare, *Traité de la police*, Vol. I, p. 418; cited in Fogel, "Modèle d'état," p. 231.

[25] Claire Sponsler points out that the discourse on "luxury" provides no measure of what is enough, what is too much, or what kind of goods constitute the "excess" or particularly feed vanity. Instead of attacks on luxury, she argues, these regulations were "clothing laws," not sumptuary legislation or attacks on generic consumption, and the laws should be read as "narratives responding to pressing social needs by sketching out a vision of a society ordered in a particular way": Claire Sponsler, "Narrating the Social Order: Medieval Clothing Laws," *CLIO* 21 (1992), pp. 265–83, p. 269. For more on arguments about the equation between social ordering and dress, see pp. 220–26 following.

[26] For a discussion of how the misogynist text worked and how it circulated in medieval culture, see Howard R. Bloch, *Medieval Misogyny and the Invention of Western Romantic Love* (Chicago, 1991). The notions about women's frivolity and lust for finery seem to have infected modern scholarship as well. For one example from the nineteenth century, see Henri Baudrillart, *Historie du Luxe Privé et Public depuis l'antiquité jusqu'à nos jours*, Vol. 3, *Le Moyen âge et la*

Figure 12. *Male Elegance.*
Hans Holbein the Younger, *Portrait of Henry VIII of England* (1540). Oil on panel, 75 × 89 cm. Rome, Galleria Nazionale d'Arte Antica. Photo Credit: Scala/Ministero per I Beni e le Attività culturali / Art Resource, NY.

this age men were every bit as devoted to extravagant dress as women were. Indeed, most laws showed more concern with men's dress than with women's.[27]

> *Renaissance*, 2nd ed. (Paris, 1881), p. 251. "It is only too often in the history of luxury that we have cause to regret the deplorable influence exercised by women": cited in Heller, "Sumptuary Law," p. 336.

[27] For example, in Renaissance Florence, men were in fact as richly dressed as women, and they often took charge in ordering and designing the costumes worn by their wives and daughters: Frick, *Dressing*, esp. pp. 215–19. Duke Philip the Bold of Burgundy spent between 15,000 and 20,000 *francs* per year on silks, wools, furs, and luxury cloths of other materials for his own wardrobe: A. van Nieuwenhuysen, *Les finances du duc de Bourgogne*, pp. 394–5. René d'Anjou's budget for clothing and apparel was twice his queen's: Françoise Piponnier, *Costume et vie sociale: la cour d'Anjou, XIVe – XVe siècle* (Paris, 1970), pp. 97–105. Harte, "State Control," emphasizes that the "labyrinthine control

A 1483 English act, for example, included women in only two of seven targeted groups, almost as afterthoughts. The wife, mother, or sisters of the king (who were permitted cloth of gold, silk, or the color purple) were named in the first group, and the last of the seven included the wives of servants of husbandry, of common laborers, and of servants to artificers outside any city or borough.[28]

Laced throughout much of the legislation was the even more specific complaint that people were dressing above their station, and scholars have generally agreed that this was the legislation's fundamental impetus. Lawmakers were struggling to reestablish a traditional equation between luxurious dress and rank in response to the new abundance of luxury goods and the rise of new social classes now able to participate in luxury consumption. As they ruled that the wife of a simple artisan in Bologna could wear only crimson sleeves, whereas a woman married to a notary could own sleeves of gold, or that an English lord could wear purple silk but a commoner could not, lawmakers implicitly assumed that the cut of a costume, the materials from which it was made, the decorations it bore, and even its color signified social place.[29] In late medieval England, Claire Sponsler argues, it was thought that "clothing

over both fashions and fabrics was aimed more at men than at women" and notes that "men were the more brightly and elaborately dressed of the sexes," p. 143.

[28] Sponsler, "Narrating," p. 279. Women made no other appearance in the legislation, however, and the clothing they were allowed was described only cursorily. In contrast, some English laws described men's clothing in excruciating detail. For example, an especially odd Proclamation of 1561 took on men's trousers (*hosen*): "no Taylour, Hosier, or other person . . . shall put any more cloth in any one payre of hosen for the outside, then one yarde and a halfe, or the moste, one yearde and three quarters of a yearde of karsey or any other cloth, lether, or any other kinde of stuffe above at quantitie. . . . Neyther any man under the degree of a Baron, to weare within his hosen any velvet, Sattin, or any other stuffe above the estimation of Sarcenet, or Taffata": Wilfred Hooper, "Tudor Sumptuary Laws," *English Historical Review* 30:119 (July 1915): pp. 433–49, p. 440.

[29] A 1474 law from Bologna was similarly worried about women's sleeves. It reserved gold gowns for the daughters and wives of knights, sleeves of gold for those of notaries and bankers, crimson dresses for the wives and daughters of artisans in the senior guilds, but only crimson sleeves for women whose fathers or husbands were in humbler trades. From Diane Owen Hughes, "Sumptuary

Figure 13. *Merchant Splendor.*
Hans Holbein the Younger, *Portrait of a Young Merchant*, probably the Nurem-
berg patrician Hans von Muffel (1541). Oil on canvas, 47 × 35 cm. Vienna,
Kunsthistorisches Museum. Photo Credit: Erich Lessing / Art Resource, NY.

could actively *produce* status, not just passively reflect it."[30] A Venetian
diarist of the early sixteenth century put it directly: the city suffered
"because . . . everyone is wearing robes of dogal sleeves, those which
were first worn by the Doge and doctors alone."[31] Even merchants,
practitioners of a trade once condemned in moralist legislation, could
wear elegant clothing and proudly display it.

Laws and Social Relations in Renaissance Italy," in *Disputes and Settlements: Law
and Human Relations in the West*, ed. John Bossy (Cambridge, UK, 1983).

[30] Sponsler, *Drama and Resistance: Bodies, Goods, and Theatricality in Late Medieval
England* (Minneapolis, 1997) p. 13. For a general discussion (and endorsement)
of this interpretation, see Van Uytven, "Showing off One's Rank," pp. 19–34.

[31] Cited in Welch, "New, Old, and Secondhand Clothing," p. 101.

However, even a superficial survey of a wide range of European legislation reveals that more than rank was at stake. For example, the laws from Florence described at the beginning of this chapter said nothing at all about rank, focusing instead simply on banning (and taxing) any use, by any woman at all, of certain kinds of materials or decorations, often in astonishingly misogynist rhetoric. The town council of Braunschweig expressed no such venom, but it too seemed indifferent to rank. Its 1343 law was addressed to all "women, single and married, citizens and residents"; the aldermen of Zittau directed themselves in 1353 to "rich and poor" alike; in 1356 Speyer targeted "all our citizens and residents, men and women."[32]

Even those laws that sought to equate dress with social place seemed unable to decide what groups needed regulation or even how many and what kind of groups made up society. Some regulations, such as the thirteenth-century French ordinance cited earlier, concentrated exclusively on the ranks of the aristocracy, meticulously separating mere knights from greater lords, or princes of the blood from ordinary noblemen. Other regulations, even those issued by princes, ignored the aristocracy and sought instead to organize urban society into neatly delineated ranks.[33] Still others seemed to make no sense at all. For example, the *Fürstlichen Bayrischen Landsordnung* of 1578 identified seven social groups, but each of the groups was made up of odd combinations of people, and the entire list hardly described a recognizable version of early modern Germanic society. The first of the seven groups consisted of peasants and miscellaneous residents of the countryside; the fourth was made up of the "patricians" from what were labeled the four "capitol cities" [*sic*]; the final group was composed of "servant girls."[34] The lawmakers also seemed unable to decide what the relationship between luxury and social place should be. Although more expensive or especially rare materials were always reserved for those at the top of whatever hierarchy the law established, if it was just the rarity or the cost of an

---

[32] See, for this evidence, Liselotte Constanze Eisenbart, *Kleiderordungen der deutschen Städte zwischen 1350 und 1700: Ein Beitrag zur Kulturgeschichte des deutschen Bürgertums* (Göttingen, 1962), pp. 55 and passim.

[33] For this pattern, see Baur, *Kleiderordnungen*.

[34] Another law of 1599 designated only three groups – peasants, urban citizens, and nobles – whereas a third from 1604 thought there were thirteen groups: in Baur, *Kleiderordnungen*, pp. 27–8.

item that made it appropriate for aristocrats alone, then the legislation would have targeted a lot more than clothing. Horses, armor, residences, servants, tapestries, books, coin hoards, hollowware – all these things and more would have been included in the list of reserved goods.[35] Clearly, there was something special about dress, something that made its ability to display status especially worrisome.

A comparison of laws from different places confirms the impression that among European governors there was no consensus about what or who needed to be controlled. For example, a 1417 law from the southern French city of Carpentras fulminated about women's dress and devoted five of its twelve articles to weddings and funerals, whereas legislation from nearby Avignon issued in 1462 said almost nothing about either issue, concentrating instead on rank.[36] The English evidence, taken as a whole, betrayed an inordinate concern with social hierarchy, attempting to construct what one scholar has called "a scheme of social groups and a related scheme of restricted fabrics," but in that realm women's attire rarely got attention until the sixteenth century.[37] In contrast, in Italian cities, worries about rank appeared late in the law books, whereas women's dress took center stage.[38] Even in a single place, the content

---

[35] As Harte, "State Control," points out, English legislators (king and parliament) did turn their attention to other kinds of imported goods (calicoes and wine, for example) in the later years of the period, but they did not do so in the context of sumptuary legislation but by means of import taxes and other formal restraints of trade. To judge from this evidence, the "economic" argument against dress was reduced to an argument against imported dress materials and incorporated into a larger, more general mercantilist concern that targeted all imports. In that context, dress lost the specific cultural valence given it by sumptuary legislation.

[36] For Carpentras, see H. Chobaut, "Le règlement somptuaire de Carpentras (avril 1417)," *Annales d'Avignon et du comtat venaissin* 2 (1913), pp. 155–64; for Avignon, see René de Maulde. "Anciens textes de droit français inédits ou rarissimes: Coutumes et règlements de la République d'Avignon au XII siècle," *Nouvelle revue historique de droit français et étranger* 1–2 (1877–8), in installments throughout Vols. 1 and 2.

[37] Harte, "State Control." p. 136.

[38] James Brundage argues explicitly that "statutory regulation of women's dress flourished most profusely in Mediterranean Europe": Brundage, "Sumptuary Laws," p. 346; also see Rainey, "Dressing down the Dressed-Up," and Killerby, "Problems." The latter argues, however, that although the majority of laws were

and tone of sumptuary legislation frequently changed over time.[39] The earliest Bavarian laws, for example, were directed at cities and featured a discourse about the need for thrift; later ordinances attacked social climbing and sought to create social hierarchies; still later, more generally moralizing language took precedence, and laws against dress came to be embedded in fulminations against drink, gambling, prostitution, and swearing. French royal legislation between 1485 and 1583 fought to defend nobility against commoners and to reinforce hierarchy within the nobility; in contrast, laws from 1601 to 1660 sought only to restrict luxury to the court.[40]

Legislators' apparent lack of agreement about how dress disturbed hierarchy and about the correct remedies for the disturbances suggests that the problem was not that dress upset a well-understood hierarchy. Their confusion reveals that legislators were uncertain about just what was the appropriate structure of society and, in fact, how rank itself was

directed against women's dress and ornamentation and although she found not a single prosecution of a man, misogyny as such was not the central concern of the authorities; it was, she suggests, luxury itself.

[39] For example, the English legislation, although always betraying acute anxiety about social order, shifted its focus from social group to social group and regularly redefined hierarchy itself. The legislation of 1363, for example, struggled mightily to relate urban groups and clerics to a traditional feudal and rural social order by setting income minimums. Merchants, citizens, burgesses, artificers, and handicraftsmen with incomes up to 500 pounds could, for example, dress in the manner of esquires and gentlemen with incomes of 100 pounds a year, whereas those with incomes of 1,000 pounds a year could dress as did esquires or gentlemen with income of 200 pounds per year; clerks with 200 marks per year could wear the same dress as knights with the same income. In contrast, the 1463 Act, although equally focused on the "rising" middle classes, presented a considerably more complex and almost incoherent social order, with many more categories; further, the act made almost no effort to relate one group to another by way of income. Just twenty years later, however, new legislation set forth another vision of social order, one that arranged aristocrats into a four-part hierarchy, lumped all male commoners into three ranked groups, making no distinction between rural and urban, and then finished with an odd category made up of "the wives and servants" of "artificers outside the city or borough." See Sponsler, "Narrating the Social Order," p. 279, for these details.

[40] For this argument, see Fogel, "Modèle d'état."

established.[41] Alan Hunt came to the same conclusion in his survey of sumptuary laws from the period; he argued that dress was incoherently being mobilized to figure out how to place people, in effect to create known identities in a society that had become unrecognizable.[42]

FASHION, COMMERCE, AND LAW

Dress could not solidify the identities of its wearers, however, because it was itself increasingly unstable. Clothing styles among Europe's elites had been changing rapidly since at least the twelfth century, exploding in variety and quantity as imported or European-made materials and styles became widely available. During the twelfth century, the male lay elite abandoned the short tunics and leggings that had for centuries been their usual dress, reverting to what historians of costume call the "long and draped" style. This style had been the aristocratic norm during the classical period, and it was already the standard garb of Europe's clergy, but only after about 1100 did it become the preferred dress of the lay aristocracy of both genders; once adopted, it would remain their formal dress for nearly two hundred years. Meanwhile, the short tunic and leggings would serve to identify ordinary men, whereas ordinary women would wear simple aprons and skirts that came to the calf.

The image here gives an idea of the long and draped style.

Some scholars consider this period, roughly the years between 1100 and 1300, the birthplace of European fashion, and if luxury and change

[41] It seems that the supposed link between dress and status became so confused that some artists reverted to the old styles in depicting aristocrats. Rather than adorning them in the latest fashions of the day as painters and sculptors typically did, even anachronistically picturing seventh- or eighth-century people in fifteenth-century garb, some artists dressed them in flowing, almost unisex robes, as though to recall the age when rank was unquestioned – and could be literally represented in clothing. See Margaret McEnchroe Williams, "Dressing the Part: Depictions of Noble Costume in Irish High Crosses," in *Encountering Medieval Textiles and Dress: Objects, Texts, Images*, eds. Désirée Koslin and Janet Snyder (New York, 2002), pp. 45–63, p. 46; and Susan L'Engle, "Addressing the Law: Costume and Signifier in Medieval Legal Minatures," in ibid. My thanks to Lauri Wilson for these references.

[42] Hunt, *Governance*, esp. Chapter 6. Also, Eisenbart, *Kleiderordnungen*, pp. 58–60.

Figure 14. *The Long and Draped Style.*
King Edward I Hearing a Lawsuit (late 13th century). London, British Library.
Photo Credit: HIP / Art Resource, NY.

alone are the measure of fashion, they are probably correct. It was
certainly then that miniatures like the one reproduced above began to
lavish detail on dress and that the clergy began to complain vociferously
about these "excesses."[43] However, most historians date the birth of
fashion to the fourteenth century, not to the twelfth, for it was then that
Europeans saw even more dramatic stylistic innovation.[44] It was then
that the "shaped and fitted" style emerged, and it was accompanied by an
even faster change of fads, ever more decorations, ever more fantasy – all
enabled by ever more skillful tailoring and the increasing availability
of luxury fabrics and ornamentations.[45] By the fifteenth century the
changes were unmistakable; by the sixteenth, they were out of control.

However, fashion is not just about style, although style is its
ephemeral essence. It is about change and originality, and in this respect
scholars who argue for a twelfth-century birth of fashion have a point.
Fashion is not simply a way of making or wearing clothes, but a way
of using clothing and fabrics that invites, indeed demands, constant

[43] For this argument, see Margaret Scott, *Medieval Dress and Fashion* (London,
2007), particularly Chapter 2.
[44] Francoise Piponnier, "Une révolution dans le costume masculin au XIVe
siècle," in *Le vêtement. Histoire, archéologie et symbolique vestimentaire au Moyen
Âge*, ed. Michel Pastoureau (Paris, 1989), pp. 225–41; Francoise Piponnier and
Perrine Mane, *Se vêtir au Moyen Âge* (Paris, 1995); Paul Post, "La naissance du
costume masculin moderne au XIVe siècle," in *Acts du Ier Congrès international
d'histoire du costume* (Milan, 1955), pp. 28–41; Francois Boucher, "Les conditions
de l'apparition de costume court en France vers le milieu du XIVe siècle," in
Recueil de travaux offerts à M. Clovis Brunel (Paris, 1955), pp. 183–92; Francois
Boucher, *20,000 Years of Fashion: The History of Costume and Personal Adornment*
(New York, 1967); Odile Blanc, "From Battlefield to Court: The Invention
of Fashion in the Fourteenth Century," in *Encountering Medieval Textiles*, eds.
Koslin and Snyder; Désirée G. Koslin, *Parades et Parures: L'invention du corps de
mode à la fin du Moyen Âge* (Paris, 1997); Anne Hollander, *Sex and Suits: The
Evolution of Modern Dress* (New York, 1994); and Sarah-Grace Heller, *Fashion in
Medieval France* (Rochester, NY, 2007). Also see Wilson, "La nouvelle manière."
[45] As Jones and Stallybrass explain, in early modern London tailors were thought
to construct, not just clothe, bodies and were maligned for their skill. For
example, the authors quote one critic who charged that tailors were "Idol-
makers" and "the diuels engineers" who "make the whole world with their new
inuentions." See Ann Rosalind Jones and Peter Stallybrass, *Renaissance Clothing
and the Materials of Memory* (New York, 2000), p. 85.

Figure 15. *The Shaped and Fitted Style, Fifteenth Century.*
Loyset or Louis Liedet (c. 1460–78), *Marriage of Renaud and Clarissa (Wedding Procession)*, from "Renaud de Montauban." Paris, Bibliotheque de l'Arsenal, Ms. 5073, fol. 117v. Photo Credit: Bridgeman-Giraudon / Art Resource, NY.

change, because "fashion" exists only as the new. "La mode, c'est ce qui démode," as Jean Cocteau is said to have put it.[46] It has no specific content; there are no precise fabrics, materials, cuts, shapes, lengths, or ornaments that constitute fashion and no particular arrangement among the elements of dress. Fashion is nothing but rearrangement, a kind of nervous play with those elements, an endless conversation with previous arrangements and with onlookers. Although rigorously conventional in that it always exists in reference to a norm and in that it always elicits compliance, fashion is also transgressive in that it compulsively tests the boundaries of the expected.[47]

[46] "Fashion is that which falls out of fashion."
[47] Christopher Breward, *The Culture of Fashion: A New History of Fashionable Dress* (Manchester, UK, 1994) describes in some detail the shifting styles of medieval

Figure 16. *The Shaped and Fitted Style, Sixteenth Century.*
Albrecht Duerer (1471–1528), *Amorous Couple.* Pen and brown ink, 25.8 ×
19.1 cm. Inv. 23918. Hamburg, Hamburger Kunsthalle. Photo: Christoph
Irrgang. Photo Credit: Bildarchiv Preussischer Kulturbesitz / Art Resource,
NY.

Countless laws from the period described fashion in exactly this way,
always condemning the new and insisting on the old. In 1357, the city
of Constance demanded that unmarried women crown their heads with
wreaths (*Kränze*) only in the "old style."[48] In 1420, the city of Ulm
mandated that the sleeves of women's dresses be no longer or wider
than those women "used to have or wear" and that their coats be lined
with silk only "in the original style." An ordinance from Basel in 1637

aristocratic dress from about 1350 forward, emphasizing the malleability of
fashion even in these early years of its history (pp. 13–19 in particular).
[48] Eisenbart, *Kleiderordnungen,* p. 79.

Figure 17. *Aged Bosoms.*
Quentin Metsys, *A Grotesque Old Woman* (c. 1525–30). Oil on oak, 64.1 ×
45.4 cm. Bequeathed by Miss Jenny Louise Roberta Blaker, 1947 (NG5769).
London, National Gallery. © National Gallery, London / Art Resource, NY.

forbade men the "recently arrived filthy long *alla mode* breeches."[49] In
1660, the city of Strasbourg prefaced a meticulous clothing ordinance by
condemning "the improper, luxurious, trifling, indecent things . . . new
in clothing from foreign, non-German nations."[50] Fashion thus sped
what was already in motion, making cloth and clothing an ever hotter
spot in an already heated economic culture precisely because it accelerated change, increased the circulation of dress materials and styles,

[49] Vincent, *Costume and Conduct*, pp. 56–7.
[50] Vincent, *Costume and Conduct*, pp. 68–9.

and inspired creativity in workshops where cloth was produced and costumes designed.[51]

The new clothing also created a dramatic gender dimorphism in a way that the old, loose draperies had not. The new fashions drew attention to the buttocks, chest, legs, and even the genitals of men and to the necks, shoulders, breasts, and bellies of women, inciting the attacks on "immodest" fashions that have already been described. For example, along with the Strasbourg ordinance about women's bosoms mentioned earlier, we have laws from Speyer banning décolletage and one from Florence telling women not to show their breasts.[52] And we have extraordinarily nasty pictures like the image reproduced here, which mocks an old woman who seems to think that breasts can substitute for youth and beauty.

There is no doubt that Europe's expanding commercial culture was both the precondition for fashion's emergence and the source of its dangers. Commerce brought new fabrics and materials to Europe, exposing Europeans to styles from Mediterranean and Eastern cultures and creating the institutions necessary for the easy circulation of goods, people, and modes of dress. It encouraged merchants and artisans in Flanders and elsewhere to invent new weaves and new dying techniques; it gave birth to skilled tailors who could cut a doublet, trim a sleeve, and transform a gown. It also produced new riches and a newly rich urban class of merchants who dressed themselves in their own wares, adorning themselves as once only landed aristocrats could have.

Still worse, with abundance and variety came choice, and with choice came anxieties about the quality of one's choice. As velvets, silks, furs, woolens, trimmings, and jeweled ornamentations multiplied in quantity and kind, individuals had to decide which velvet, which fur, which jewel to select. The choice was increasingly difficult – what colors spoke most clearly, what drape best flattered, what flourish was the most exotic, what decoration the loveliest? Thus was born the problem of

---

[51] This argument is made with particular force by Sponsler, "Narrating," pp. 265–83.

[52] For more examples of regulations concerning both men's and women's modesty in dress, see Baur, *Kleiderordnungen in Bayern*, pp. 3, 40–50, 65–6; Greenfield, *Sumptuary Law in Nürnberg*, p. 114; Roper, "Blood and Codpieces"; and Chabot, "La sponsa in nero," p. 86–2.

"taste," the cultural marker that distinguished those who knew how to use wealth from those who did not. As Pierre Bourdieu has pointed out, when culture can be bought and sold and made available to anyone, taste or the ability to choose "well" becomes an essential social skill.[53] Taste implies competition, differentiation, and rankings; it necessarily pits individuals and groups against one another in contests of aesthetic judgment.

However, there is more to ponder about the links between clothing and sumptuary legislation, for much of the legislation was not, in fact, focused on fashion but quite simply on clothing itself. Some laws from the thirteenth and early fourteenth century betray no concern with style or cut and no real sense that clothing is fashion. For the French crown issuing its thirteenth-century clothing ordinances, for example, the problem was the cost and color of *robes* and the opulence of banquets, just as it was for the English crown when it issued its first ordinances some fifty years later. How the clothing was cut, worn, or styled was not at issue. Even as we move later in time and sumptuary legislation more often takes up the question of style and cut, we still find the original concern with price, kind, and color. For example, a fourteenth-century ordinance from Nuremberg demanded that women citizens of any age

---

[53] Pierre Bourdieu, *La distinction: Critique sociale du jugement* (Paris, 1979) [in English: *Distinction: A Social Critique of the Judgement of Taste* (Cambridge, MA, 1984)]. It also is the justification for luxury spending, for taste would come to sanction the material desires of Europe's emergent bourgeoisie. Historians typically argue that the eighteenth century gave birth to the modern idea of taste as a signifier of class. It is no accident, they further argue, that this period also reworked the critique of luxury, coming to see the desire for luxuries as a source of social good, because it fueled commerce and promoted sociability. In that discourse, luxury was disruptive only when available to those unable to manage wealth well (i.e., the poor and the ordinary, those without "taste"). Bernard Mandeville's *Fable of the Bees* (London, 1714) is the seminal text; also see Berg and Eger, "The Rise and Fall of the Luxury Debates," Edward Hundert, "Mandeville, Rousseau and the Political Economy of Fantasy," and Dana Goodman, "Furnishing Discourses: Readings of a Writing Desk in Eighteenth-century France," all in *Luxury in the Eighteenth Century*, eds. Berg and Eger. Also see Christopher Berry, *The Idea of Luxury: A Conceptual and Historical Investigation* (Cambridge, UK, 1994).

or status not wear a veil or headdress that allowed the "ends in front
[to] lie upon the head," a reference to a new style of coif; at the same
time, however, the law forbade women to wear garments of silk, Roman
jackets, or garments trimmed with zendal (a kind of silk), gold, or silver,
thus repeating the kind of restrictions issued a century before.[54]

THE BODY POLITIC ON DISPLAY

Although it is clear that commerce set off the explosion of sumptuary legislation and motivated its obsession with dress, it is not
quite clear why it did. As we have seen, the issuers of such legislation offered an unstable mix of explanations, and historians have more
or less taken them at their word, giving special credit to the idea
that the new availability of luxurious clothing disrupted existing social
hierarchies. Questions remain, however. What cultural logic so tightly
linked dress not only to one's rank but also to one's person – to appropriate gender identity, to moral restraint, to economic prudence? Why
did governments think it was their job to preserve that logic? What
principle or principles of good government were they enacting?

In his 1918 study of Nuremberg's sumptuary laws, Kent Greenfield
sought to answer these questions by turning our attention from the
people who were under surveillance and looking instead at the issuers.
He concluded that sumptuary laws were an expression of new ideas
about government; as he put it, "the state was responsible not only for
the enforcement of thrift and industry, but as well for the economy and
the conformity of moral standards of family life of every person under
its care."[55] The preamble to an ordinance from Nuremberg expressed

---

[54] Greenfield, *Sumptuary Law in Nürnberg*, p. 108.

[55] Greenfield, *Sumptuary Law in Nürnberg*, p. 9. Greenfield's "paternalist" state
is often labeled the "police state," in the early modern sense of the term.
As Karl Bosl put it, "[Good policing] always implies the good ordering of
city, commune, etc. and includes safety and cleanliness, but also customs and
religion, that is policing includes and furthers the good of civil society, whatever
in city and land serves good order. Today one could almost otherwise formulate
policing as ordering": Karl Bosl, "Die Polizei: Ihre Entwicklung im modernen

the notion even more forcefully. The council, the document reported, was empowered by "the Almighty God . . . [to extricate] pride, folly and superfluous expenditure." According to Greenfield, the councilmen were consequently authorized to regulate "the manner and cost of weddings, funerals, christenings and clothes . . . because dress was an integral part of the moral order."[56] Maximilian I's *Landsordnung* of 1599 was more explicit still: "it is our most earnest duty to arrange each subject, servant, dependent and related persons in his proper station, without excess and disorder that dishonors, and to dress them as was the custom of the past in our realm."[57] The Germanic governments were not alone in positioning themselves as moral arbiters. Throughout this age, both local and regional governments defined themselves as custodians of the good society.

All these legislators agreed that the good society put in their care was one in which people dressed appropriately, but it is less obvious why they thought so. After all, no prince of earlier centuries would have considered it his job to regulate the dress of butchers or even to divide the entire aristocracy into ranks according to their costume, and he certainly would not have worried too much about his subjects' morals unless that meant their obedience to him. Implicitly following the lead of Greenfield, Neithard Bulst has given us the fullest response to this question by situating the legislation in the social and political history of the age, especially in the Germanic territories on which his research has been concentrated. He has argued that governments in this age of state building derived authority not so much from hereditary right or arms themselves (although they often claimed both), but from their ability to produce a good society. Over the some four hundred years of legislation that Bulst considered, however, the content of those

Staat und in der modernen Gesellschaft," in *Polizei in Bayern* 14 (1971), pp. 1–4, cited in Baur, *Kleiderordnungen in Bayern*, p. 159. On the early modern moralizing state, also see, for example, Marc Raef, *The Well-Ordered Police State: Social and Institutional Change through Law in the Germanies and Russia, 1600–1800* (New Haven, 1983); Gerhard Oestreich, *Neostoicism and the Early Modern State* (Cambridge, UK, 1982); and Greenfield, *Sumptuary Law in Nürnberg.*

[56] Greenfield, *Sumptuary Law in Nürnberg*, p. 109.

[57] Bauer, *Kleiderordnungen in Bayern*, pp. 27–8.

laws changed as the social and political landscape itself shifted. The first wave of sumptuary laws, which began after the Black Death in the middle of the fourteenth century, tended to be directed at the entire urban population and sought to establish moral and social order in the face of the demographic and physic devastations wrought by the plague. Dress was a key part of the moral order that required restitution, but the rules that cities sought to impose were generally unspecific. The legislation was laced with vague attacks on *Kosbarkeit, Hoffart, Übermut, Übermass, and Masslosigkeit*, (costliness, pride, arrogance, excess, self-indulgence), alongside appeals to the *gemeiner Nutzen* (common benefit). In contrast, during what Bulst considers the second and third phases, legislators made a concentrated effort to define rank by means of dress, in response to the growing fear that hierarchy itself was endangered. What particularly marked the third phase, which began in the sixteenth century, was the entrance of the territorial state into the picture and the relative decline of urban legislation. In effect, the central state replaced the city and in doing so claimed for itself the right not only to define rank (and collect the fines by prosecuting infractions of the laws) but also to "police" the society; that is, to produce a "good" society.

Although the chronological pattern Bulst described does not seem to fit Italy or England as neatly as it does the Germanic regions, much less areas like the Low Countries where the legislation seems to have been much sparser, his general point holds: sumptuary legislation was a form of what others have called "governmentality": a way public authorities constituted themselves. Dress was so obsessively targeted because when safely controlled, it seemed to guarantee the good society: not only to signal rank and thus secure social hierarchy but also to stabilize gender roles, assure appropriate sexuality, encourage fiscal restraint, and repress pride, medieval Europe's premier sin. Other scholars have offered similar arguments. For example, Diane Owen Hughes has proposed that the sumptuary laws of fourteenth-century Florence principally served to differentiate among, and hence to control, a mobile, unstable, and featureless mass of residents who jostled against one another in a single undifferentiated civic space.[58] In the same vein, Alan Hunt has claimed

---

[58] According to Hughes, it was only later, with the aristocratization of Italian urban societies, that concerns with rank in the English sense took center

that sumptuary laws of this period were an effort to make people "recognizable" to one another in cities dangerously crowded with transients, newcomers, and upstarts.[59]

The attacks on women that laced so much Italian legislation served a similar purpose, but not because women, qua women, were considered threats to social order. Rather, they served as the mark of that disorder. In the Florentine case, Hughes pointed out, women's clothes were said to have so increased the cost of marriage that men were driven "to sodomy and women into convents." She concluded that women were being scapegoated to atone for the spending on luxuries that seemed to violate moral codes, but was nevertheless indispensable in a city that lived from trade in such goods.[60] Carole Frick has argued that Florentine men used sumptuary legislation in much the same way. Although they dressed their wives and daughters in luxurious, even ostentatious, gowns for public display, they reserved for themselves the "old," more conservative (if nevertheless costly) dress for these rituals in order to evoke the republican traditions of the city. Simultaneously, however, they issued laws castigating women for vanity and greed, thus managing both to display their wealth and take the moral high ground by sequestering themselves from the charge of vanity, falseness, and extravagance.[61]

---

stage: Hughes, "Sumptuary Laws and Social Relations." Gerhard Jaritz makes a similar argument in "Kleidung und Prestige-Konkurrenz: Unterschiedliche Identitäten in der städitischen Gesellschaft unter Normierungszwangen," in *Zwischen Sein und Schein: Kleidung und Identität in der ständischen Gesellschaft*, eds. Neithard Bulst and Robert Jütte (Munich, 1993), pp. 8–32. He reasons that the object of sumptuary regulation was not simply to rank society, but to *differentiate* among members of an increasingly unsettled social order; rank was just one of many axes of differentiation, although one that perhaps best satisfied the cultural impulse to ensure stability.

[59] Hunt, *Governance* and his discussion of "recognizeability."

[60] Hughes, "Distinguishing Signs," pp. 3–59, pp. 37–38. Ronald Rainey noted that San Bernardino's charge that "thousands of young men . . . would take wives if it were not for the fact that they had to spend the entire dowry, and sometimes even more, in order to dress the women," provided lawmakers a convenient explanation for men's bankruptcies, for sodomy, and for the population decline that they attributed to male celibacy: San Bernardino, *La Prediche*, 1:246, cited in Rainey, "Dressing down the Dressed-Up," pp. 233–4.

[61] Frick, *Dressing*.

Sumptuary legislation's focus on public celebrations like weddings and funerals can be explained according to the same logic: the laws were efforts to define and empower the state by suppressing alternative or competing sites of public power. Elaborate funerals, christenings, or weddings, if organized by families as gatherings of the clan, were ritualized assertions of power, times when the lineage showed off its wealth and numbers. For the nascent states of the day, whether city-state or territorial court, that display was a threat because their own legitimacy derived in part from precisely the same kind of performances. This was the age of the "theater state," the period in western history when both princes and magistrates constituted themselves in large part with elaborate and stylized displays of themselves and their entourages.[62] Even the most powerful rulers of the day had no standing armies; they had no regular source of revenues except from their private domains and were heavily dependent on loans, extraordinary levies, and "voluntary" gifts from subordinates. Such rulers, even kings and dukes, and certainly the aldermen in cities who frequently had to compete with rich clans for control of urban space, had good reason to fear these gatherings. In effect, a splendid and costly "family" wedding was no private event: it was an implicit political challenge.[63] No wonder that the earliest wedding

---

[62] On the theater state, see in particular Peter Arnade, *Realms of Ritual: Burgundian Ceremony and Civic Life in Late Medieval Cities* (Ithaca, NY, 1996) and his "City, State, and Public Ritual in the Late-Medieval Burgundian Netherlands," *Comparative Studies in Society and History* 39, no. 2 (April 1997), pp. 300–18; also see David Nicholas, "In the Pit of the Burgundian Theater State: Urban Traditions and Princely Ambitions in Ghent, 1360–1420," *City and Spectacle in Medieval Europe*, in eds. Barbara A. Hanawalt and Katherine L. Reyerson (Minneapolis, 1994), pp. 271–95; Elodie Lecuppre-Desjardin, *La ville des cérémonies*; and D. Cannadine and S. Price, eds., *Rituals of Royalty: Power and Ceremonial in Traditional Societies* (Cambridge, UK 1987). Recent work on the gifts demanded from political subordinates in celebration of royal weddings and christenings illustrates another aspect of this history, for it shows the state's effort to monopolize such pageants, making them their own. See Werner Paravicini, "Introduction," in idem, ed., *Les invitations.*

On family clans and their threat to centralizing governments, see in general Jacques Heers, *Family Clans in the Middle Ages: A Study of Political and Social Structures in Urban Areas*, trans. Barry Herbert (Amsterdam, 1977).

[63] Peter Goodrich has made a similar argument. In his interpretation, in the early modern period sumptuary rules served nascent states as essential tools

regulations from Nuremberg forbade "open" weddings and that the city's compendious *Hochzeitsbüchlein* of 1485, although conceding some ground on the issue of a wedding's size, nevertheless limited the guest list to family and out-of-town friends.[64] It was not just the "expenses" of the wedding or the "ostentation" of the funeral alone that so concerned legislators, although that was the righteous rhetoric used to restrict the displays. Rather, it was the families' show of force, which rulers had good reason to see as considerably more than mere show.[65]

Given the importance of dress in any such public performance, it is no surprise that laws targeting these events regularly included regulations about dress.[66] From early modern Bavaria, for example, regulations about mourning dress, wedding clothes, and the apparel considered appropriate for christenings were systematically integrated into rules about the number of guests, the amount of food and wine, or the gifts exchanged at these events.[67] Similarly, seventeenth- and eighteenth-century Basel and Zurich carefully wrote dress restrictions into the

of public identity. "Custom and costume . . . governed the forms of professional and political community and depended upon a comparable manipulation of signs as the mechanism for instituting both the legitimacy and the love of law. . . . The history of sumptuary law is best understood as the narrative of a marginal jurisdiction that was rapidly incorporated into the sovereign and centralizing apparatus of early modern law": Peter Goodrich, "Signs Taken for Wonders: Community, Identity, and A History of Sumptuary Law," *Law and Social Inquiry* 23, no. 3 (1998), pp. 707–28, pp. 722–3.

[64] Greenfield, *Sumptuary Law in Nürnberg*, p. 38.

[65] In this regard it is surely significant that in Florence regulations against dress were *not* enforced during communal celebrations; in those instances the citizenry was enacting the commune, not their own political identity: For this evidence, see Frick, *Dressing*, pp. 170–80.

[66] Even the more general "police" laws, which so often included clothing ordinances, put dress at the top of their list – if not in the legislation itself, then in the energy with which infractions were prosecuted. For example, in 1681 in Bern, 133 of 289 cases brought before the *Chorgericht* concerned dress: Vincent, *Costume and Conduct*, p. 104. Bavarian legislation in particular embedded dress in laws generally intended to reform public morals. On this pattern, see Baur, *Kleiderordnungen in Bayern*, pp. 21 and passim.

[67] Baur, *Kleiderordnungen in Bayern*, pp. 69–76; the same combination appears regularly in Swiss ordinances from the period: Vincent, *Costume and Conduct*.

clauses of their so-called wedding laws.[68] A Florentine ordinance of 1349 attacked banquets, women's dress, and weddings, funerals, and christenings just as vigorously as it did counterfeiting, carrying weapons, and breaking the curfew.[69] The same city treated mourning dress as a central feature of funerals, in 1473 allowing only one adult woman from the family of the deceased to wear "deep mourning."[70]

Carole Frick has directly commented on the cultural logic that connected dress and such celebrations. She wrote, "Even in mourning and death, clothes were either designed to send or inadvertently sent a powerful message to the living. It was this power that the communal sumptuary laws sought to control and channel."[71] Implicitly making the same argument, the Florentine humanist Leon Battista Alberti specifically linked clothes with honor, the quintessential public "good" in this age: "It is thus necessary that virtue should be supplemented by the goods of fortune. Virtue ought to be dressed in those seemly ornaments . . . we want to have beautiful clothes . . . they do us honor."[72] For this reason, Frick concluded, rich Florentines invested as much as 40 percent of their assets in clothing and jewels worn exclusively for public performances, specifically for holidays, taking up or executing the duties of high office, and rites of passage such as weddings and funerals.[73]

---

[68] Vincent, *Costume and Conduct*, p. 156.

[69] In Rainey, "Dressing down the Dressed-Up," p. 222. As Catherine Killerby put it, there were "very few aspects of the private and public customs, habits and dress of their citizens with which Italian lawmakers did not concern themselves.": Killerby, "Problems," p. 99.

[70] Frick, *Dressing*, p. 90.

[71] Frick, *Dressing*, p. 86. Elsewhere, "riches made virtù visible and honor was the result. . . . Dress was controlled and manipulated by the males of the merchant elite to attain and retain power": Frick, *Dressing*, pp. 218 and 77–80. Sumptuary legislation rarely expressed interest in any clothing but that worn publicly, and even when banning possession rather than display itself, the laws attacked garments that were typically worn only in public. The few exceptions seem to attempt to set standards for modesty and targeted corsets, underskirts, and the like. On this point, also see Bulst, "Kleidung," pp. 32–3.

[72] Leon Battista Alberti, *I libri della famiglia*, eds. Ruggerio Romano and Alberto Tenenti (Turin, It., 1969), bk. 4, p. 268 (cited in Frick, *Dressing*, p. 78).

[73] Frick, *Dressing*, esp. pp. 80–6; in the Pucci's family estate (the Puccis belonged to the inner circle of the Medicis), clothing and jewels were worth 2,196

Figure 18. *A Wedding of State.*
Anonymous (French School), *Ball Given on September 24, 1581, at the Court of Henry III for the Marriage of the Duc de Joyeuse and Margaret of Lorrain.* Later 16th century. Oil on copper. Paris, Musee du Louvre. Photo: Daniel Arnaudet. Photo Credit: Réunion des Musées Nationaux / Art Resource, NY.

Figure 19. *A Bourgeois Wedding.*
Hieronymus Francken I, *The Wedding Dance* (c. 1600), Oil on oak wood, 49 × 66 cm. Antwerp, Museum Mayer van den Bergh. Photo Credit: Erich Lessing / Art Resource, NY.

Figure 20. *Ghent Undressed.*
The Amende Honorable of the Citizens of Ghent of 1493, from *Boek van de Priviligien van Gent en van Vlaanderen*. Vienna, Austrian National Library, ms. 2583, fol. 349v. © Austrian National Library Vienna, Picture Archive.

No wonder then that legislators considered a clan decked out in magnificent finery for a wedding or funeral a threat: this "family" celebration was a claim to public space that in their minds should be theirs.

Control of a population thus meant control of the population's dress. In a clear expression of this logic, after defeating revolts by cities like Ghent, the Burgundian dukes demanded the *"amende honorable,"* in which aldermen were required to appear *undressed*, in simple smocks, as they knelt in subjection before their lords.[74]

SIGNS OF THE SELF

The cultural logic that fundamentally drove sumptuary legislation was thus more than a simple equation between dress and rank. It was an assumption that dress – whether adorning an individual, a clan, the aldermen of cities like Ghent, or the members of a royal court – could create identity. As though accepting the literal meaning of the term "investiture" (from the Latin for "the putting on of clothes"), the laws seem to assume that a guildsman was someone who wore a corporation's livery, a servant was the "man" of the person whose colors and emblems made up his garments, a ruler was the person dressed most sumptuously, and the merchant a good businessman because he wore furs. In his famous customal of the late thirteenth century, Philippe Beaumanoir articulated this logic, explaining that if secular authorities arrested a man claiming

florins of a total 5,771 florins (counting immovables), p. 111. A single article of clothing in this age represented a huge expense. A fine woolen cloth from Brussels sold for the equivalent of 800 grams of gold, the price of one diamond, five rubies, and five emeralds. A scarlet woolen (the most expensive kind of luxury cloth made in the Low Countries) could easily cost 8 Flemish pounds; a dress of scarlet, lined in squirrel or ermine, would have sold for about 50 écus, each écu being the equivalent of 4.5 grams of gold. For these and other prices, see Raymond van Uytven, "Cloth in Medieval Literature of Western Europe," in ed. idem, *Production and Consumption in the Low Countries, 13th–16th Centuries* (Aldershot, UK, 2001). Dresses ornamented with jewels, fashioned from gold or silver-threaded brocades and cut velvets or satins, and lined in expensive furs – the kind worn by aristocrats for public performances – cost even more.

[74] For this evidence, see Arnade, *Realms of Ritual*; the ritual was widespread and lasted into subsequent centuries.

clerical status and wearing clerical vestments, it was their obligation to disprove his claim, not the accused's obligation to prove it.[75] San Bernardino evoked this understanding as well when, in a sermon given in 1427, he scolded widows who "are not as you used to be. I see a widow today . . . with her forehead bare and her cloak drawn back to show her cheek. And how she shapes it over the brow! That is a prostitute's gesture." In Diane Owen Hughes's words, the friar did not "attribute to signs a merely reflective power. He reminded his audiences that costume and gesture could actually create identity."[76]

Aaron Gurevich has argued that such examples expressed metaphysical predispositions typical of medieval society. People in this age, he said, had a "tendency to translate the spiritual into the concretely sensible and material."[77] The medical theory of humors exemplifies the code he described.[78] Magic can be considered another manifestation of the same concept; it "worked" because material substances were thought to be animated by spirit, because humans were thought to be immersed in a natural world that was indistinguishably spiritual and material, and because their bodies were available to spirit.[79]

According to this logic, clothing was considerably more than a producer of social status, more even than a *sign* of identity. It was constituent

[75] Philippe de Remi Beaumanoir, *The Coutumes de Beauvaisis of Philippe de Beaumanoir*, trans. F. R. P. Akenurst (Philadelphia, 1992), #354, Chapter 11. A lay judge who acted without such proof against a man later shown to have in fact been a cleric was subject to excommunication.

[76] Hughes, "Distinguishing Signs," p. 54. For the quote from San Bernardino, see San Bernardino da Siena, *La Prediche volgari di San Bernardino da Siena dette nella piazza del campo l'anno 1427*, ed. Luciano Banchi, Vol. II, p. 207; cited in Hughes, "Distinguishing Signs."

[77] Aaron Gurevich, *Medieval Popular Culture: Problems of Belief and Perception*, trans. J. A. Bak and P. A. Hollingsworth (Cambridge, UK, 1988).

[78] In the theory of humors, bodily fluids like bile and phlegm were considered essences of the person, not – as we might think – agents "causing" reactions in a physical body that was distinct both from the "self" and from the causative agent.

[79] As Charles Taylor put it, "the world of magic seems to entail a thralldom, an imprisoning of the self in uncanny external forces, even a ravishing or loss of self [in the modern sense]": Charles Taylor, *Sources of the Self: The Making of the Modern Identity* (Cambridge, MA, 1989), p. 192.

of identity. As one recent scholar has claimed, "public appearance and behavior [were] thought not to falsify personal identity but, on the contrary, to establish and maintain it."[80] In their recent *Renaissance Clothing and the Materials of Memory*, Anne Jones and Peter Stallybrass explained that clothes were then able to "inscribe themselves upon a person who comes into being through that inscription." Dresses and cloaks, tunics and capes were, they continue, "material memories" with "the power to constitute an essence"; they were "worn so deeply" that they constituted the self.[81] It wasthe same even for people low down on the social ladder. For example, Natalie Davis reported that a sixteenth-century Lyonnais peasant donated his tunic to the Corpus Christi confraternity in his village in order, he explained, "to be a participant in [their] prayers and services."[82] The issuers of sumptuary legislation who so randomly, almost comically, charged dress with the capacity to disrupt gender norms, unleash sexual lust, incite greed, feed pride, bring economic ruin, and confuse rank seem to have been struggling to stabilize their understanding of the relationship between the presentation of the person and the person. One way to understand this is that they were trying to preserve a "medieval" code in which the self was thought the equivalent of its external manifestation. I think, however, that it is not quite that simple. Rather than trying to preserve such a code, they were trying to decide what the code was – just how appearance was connected to reality, or the external to the internal. Understood in those terms, sumptuary legislation was a sign of a cultural crisis, the record of an historical moment when the relationship between the material and immaterial was being reformulated as a result of pressure on dress.[83]

---

[80] Susan Crane, *The Performance of Self: Ritual, Clothing, and Identity during the Hundred Years War* (Philadelphia, 2002), p. 4.

[81] Jones and Stallybrass, *Renaissance Clothing*, pp. 2–3. For a rich discussion of this issue, see in particular their entire introduction.

[82] Davis, *The Gift*: from Archives départementales du Rhône 3E1012 (1558).

[83] On enforcement (and its apparent futility) in England, see Hooper, "Tudor Sumptuary Laws"; Harte, "State Control," pp. 143–8; on Germany (Bavaria), see Baur, *Kleiderordnungen*, esp. pp. 81ff.; for Swiss cities, Vincent, *Costume and Conduct* and for Nuremberg, Greenfield, *Sumptuary Law in Nürnberg*. Some authors particularly focus on efforts to enforce these laws, arguing that the patterns of enforcement reveal intention. See in particular Killerby, "Problems."

In a larger sense, worries about the relationship between the material and immaterial were hardly new, and they were not confined to questions about dress. The best evidence we have of this cultural history comes from religious thought, for during most of the Middle Ages such debates took place in ecclesiastical chambers where scholars worried whether the apprehensible world of objects, images, and signs provided access to the divine. If so – that is, if the divine was manifested as real presence – the material world could reveal and even provide access to the divine. Brigitte Bedos-Rezak has recently explained that during the twelfth century, after centuries of uncertainty, a tentative resolution was reached. It was then decided that the eucharist was "in and of itself, what it represents" – an aspect of God's incarnation as Christ. By extension, material symbols had the "capacity to embody [the] . . . referent's ontological characteristics"; images could not just *represent* but also *embody* substance.[84] Bedos-Rezak also reasoned that the "turn to the material," as it might be called, had implications far beyond universities, monasteries, and ecclesiastical chambers, so that "the concepts of both social and personal identity came to be formulated in relation to such signs."[85]

---

[84] Brigitte Miriam Bedos-Rezak, "Medieval Identity: A Sign and a Concept," *American Historical Review* 105:5 (December 2000), pp. 1499 and 1503. Also see Brigitte Miriam Bedos-Rezak and Dominique Iogna-Prat, *L'individu au moyen âge: Individuation et individualization avant la modernité* (Paris, 2005).

Jeffrey Hamburger has made a similar point in an article about the work of the fourteenth-century mystic Seuse (the Latinized form of Suso). Hamburger comments that one finds in Seuse's work a counter to the "Platonic denigration of images. . . . The Christian emphasis on the Incarnation was the trump card." Quoting another scholar, Hamburger continues, "no matter what the reservations of theologians, just as the cross became the crucifix, so too, images increasingly were conflated with the bodies they represented. . . . For the invisible to be knowable or verifiable it had at some level to enter the realm of the visible": Hamburger, "Visible, yet Secret: Images as Signs of Friendship in Seuse," *Oxford German Studies* 36, no. 2 (2007), pp. 141–62, pp. 150–1, citing Jean-Claude Schmidt, *Le corps des images: essays sur la culture visuelle au Moyen Age* (Paris, 2002).

[85] She based her argument on a study of the wax seals that rulers had begun to attach to their written communications. They came to seem more than mere sign: they were a literal embodiment of the issuer's personal authority: Bedos-Rezak, "Medieval Identity."

A principle that has been labeled *imitatio* followed: the idea that individuals expressed and acquired identity by modeling their behavior and experience on externals, including, as Caroline Bynum has argued, on groups.[86]

However, to materialize the self in this manner was paradoxically to abstract and disembody the self in a way that potentially separated the individual from the image, sign, or symbol of his or her person. Bedos-Rezak mused, "It is as if absence were required for the question of identity even to become conceivable."[87] Dyan Elliott made a similar observation in an article examining men's efforts to control female dress during the twelfth and thirteenth centuries. To resist the standards men sought to impose, Elliott argued, women developed a more interiorized conception of the self, one free of or prior to the material world of fixed symbols, thereby spurring "a movement away from the twelfth-century paradigm of *imitatio*."[88] Thus was born what medievalists have often labeled the "medieval individual," in a sense a self-generating personality free from externals.[89]

Most Renaissance scholars would contest the notion that the "individual" emerged in medieval European culture, for it has long been taught that only during the fourteenth through sixteenth centuries and

[86] Caroline Bynum has argued that people in twelfth-century Europe tended to imagine that their interior selves could be formed by literally imitating the behavior of external models. Although aware of the possibility of hypocrisy – that one could simply masquerade as the model without internalization – "in general writers assumed that, in reform and moral improvement, exterior and interior will and should go together." It is for this reason, she continued, that we find so much emphasis on externality in medieval culture – on gestures, for example, or on radically ascetic practices: Caroline Walker Bynum, "Did the Twelfth Century Discover the Individual?" in *Jesus as Mother* (Berkeley, 1982), pp. 82–109.

[87] Bedos-Rezak, "Medieval Identity," p. 1532.

[88] Dyan Elliott, "Dress as Mediator between Inner and Outer Self: The Pious Matron of the High and Later Middle Ages," *Mediaeval Studies* 53 (1991), pp. 279–308, p. 307.

[89] Classic works include Charles Homer Haskins, *The Renaissance of the Twelfth Century* (Cambridge, MA, 1927); Colin Morris, *The Discovery of the Individual, 1050–1200* (New York, 1972); Walter Ullmann, *The Individual and Society in the Middle Ages* (Baltimore, 1966).

even later did people learn to separate their outer self from an interior in the way imagined by modern westerners. This interpretation was given its earliest and once dominant form by Jacob Burckhardt in his 1860 book *The Civilization of the Renaissance in Italy*. As he explained, the Renaissance was the time and Italy was the place that the individual was "discovered." Citizens in commercial cities uncovered their interior – their true – selves by consciously rejecting the external world that medieval people had thought the "real." In those benighted medieval centuries, he claimed,

Both sides of human consciousness – that which was within and that which was turned without – lay dreaming or half awake beneath a common veil.... In Italy this veil first melted into air; an *objective* treatment and consideration of the state and of all the things of this world became possible. The *subjective* side at the same time asserted itself with corresponding emphasis; man became a spiritual individual and recognized himself as such.[90]

The historiography that followed Burckhardt for more than a century eagerly pursued this line of reasoning, giving us a story of the Renaissance hero who triumphed over the hoary institutions of medievalism and that culture's infantile investment in things and outward appearance.[91] To quote a study written when the Burckhardtian model was ascendant, this "mighty and revolutionary generative idea" created

---

[90] Jacob Burckhardt, *The Civilization of the Renaissance in Italy*, trans. S. C. G. Middlemore (New York, 1990; orig. Basel 1860), p. 98.

[91] Johan Huizinga credited the Renaissance with the same discovery. He wrote that the period was the "great awakening," the instant when medieval culture exited the "illusion and dream" of a "beautiful and insecure play" where splendor and pomp were prized over the intangible. In his view, the famously elegant Burgundian court on which he concentrated was the epitome of medieval culture's overinvestment in appearances. It was marked, he said, by "an incredible superficiality and feebleness. [There] the complexity of things in general is ignored by it in a truly astounding manner. It [this culture's imagination] proceeds to generalizations unhesitatingly on the strength of a single instance. Its liability to wrong judgment is extreme.... All these defects are rooted in its fundamental formalism": Johan Huizinga, *The Waning of the Middle Ages* (New York, 1924) [orig. 1919], pp. 234–5 and 248.

a "dichotomy of all reality into *inner experience and outer world*, subject and object, private reality and public truth."[92]

Although scholars no longer accept Burckhardt's interpretation about the nature of the Renaissance or the discovery of the individual (however, his narrative is still very much alive in survey books and popular histories), most do agree that in this age it became possible to imagine a fully interiorized individual, one distinct from the material world of appearances.[93] What they reject is Burckhardt's claim that this was a "discovery."[94] Led by the New Historicists, critics now argue that the notion of an interior self was not found, but discursively created as people psychologically constructed an imagined barrier between their "real," interiorized self – Hamlet's "that within which passeth show" – and the person they showed to the world.[95] This was the inaugural

---

[92] Suzanne Langer, *Philosophy in a New Key: A Study in the Symbolism of Reason, Rite, and Art* (Cambridge, UK, 1942), quoted in Jonathan Dewald, *Aristocratic Experience and the Origins of Modern Culture, 1570–1715* (Berkeley, CA, 1993), p. 6.

[93] The current online *Dictionary of the History of Ideas* summarizes Burckhardt thus: "In Jacob Burckhardt's *Die Kultur der Renaissance in Italien* (1860)... 'individualism' combines the notion of the aggressive self-assertion of individuals freed from an externally-given framework of authority (as found in Louis Blanc) and that of the individual's withdrawal from society into a private existence (as in Tocqueville) with the idea, most clearly expressed by Humboldt, of the full and harmonious development of the individual personality, seen as representing humanity and pointing towards its highest cultural development.... The Italian of the Renaissance was for Burckhardt the firstborn of the sons of modern Europe in virtue of the autonomy of his morality, his cultivation of privacy, and the individuality of his character" (New York, 1992).

[94] As Charles Taylor has pointed out, the idea that individuals exist independently of the material or the external is "not a universal one.... Rather it is function of a historically limited mode of self-interpretation, one which has become dominant in the modern West": Taylor, *Sources of the Self*, p. 111.

[95] In the words of Stephen Greenblatt, the modern self is not "set off from linguistic convention, from social pressure, from the shaping force of religious and political power. Characters are not stable selves existing outside performances; rather people have 'always already experienced' themselves in fictional terms before inhabiting those selves." The sixteenth century was the moment of creation, the time when there was "an increased self-consciousness about the fashioning of human identity as a manipulable, artful process"; Stephen Greenblatt, *Renaissance Self-Fashioning: From More to Shakespeare* (Chicago, 1980),

moment of exit from the "self-imposed nonage" (*selbst verschuldeten Unmündigkeit*) that Kant considered the essence of Enlightenment, the time when Europeans are understood to have fashioned a new self.[96]

Whether a discovery or a process of psychological readjustment, this cultural transformation was not, however, the creation of a few advanced men of the Renaissance; it took centuries and unrolled in different intellectual, religious, and social venues, just as medievalists have long argued. However, most scholars agree that Descartes represents a kind of end point in this story. In Charles Taylor's summary, Descartes provided "the full realization of one's being as immaterial . . . [which]

pp. 120 and 237. That "artful" person was "fashioned" to protect and position the interior person who was confronted by a hostile world of competing, alien, and often brutalizing institutions of power, especially the church, the court, and Protestant interpretations of scripture. In addition, see Roy Porter, ed., *Rewriting the Self* (New York, 1997); Natalie Zemon Davis, "Boundaries and the Sense of Self in Sixteenth-Century France," in *Reconstructing Individualism: Autonomy, Individuality, and the Self in Western Thought*, eds. Thomas C. Heller et al. (Stanford, CA, 1986), pp. 53–63; John Martin, "Inventing Sincerity, Refashioning Prudence: The Discovery of the Individual in Renaissance Europe," *American Historical Review* 102, no. 5 (December 1997), pp. 1309–42; Michael Mascuch, *Origins of the Individualist Self: Autobiography and Self-Identity in England, 1591–1791* (Stanford, CA, 1996); Stephen Greenblatt and Giles Gunn, eds., *Redrawing the Boundaries: The Transformation of English and American Literary Studies* (New York, 1992).

Additional reading on the relationship between practice and performance on the one hand and identity on the other includes Charles S. Peirce, "The Fixation of Belief" and "How to Make Our Ideas Clearer" in *Peirce on Signs*, ed. J. Hooper (Chapel Hill, NC, 1991); Pierre Bourdieu, "Structures, *Habitus*, Practices" and "Belief and the Body," in *The Logic of Practice*, trans. Richard Nice (Cambridge, UK, 1990); Michel Foucault, "What is an Author?" in *Language, Counter-Memory, Practice*, trans. Donald F. Bouchard and Sherry Simon (Ithaca, NY, 1977); Michel de Certeau, *The Practice of Everyday Life* (Berkeley, CA, 2002). Also see Judith Butler, *Gender Trouble: Feminism and the Subversion of Identity* (New York, 1990), which focuses on gender and its constructions and makes a more complicated argument about identity and performance. Butler comments that "identity is performatively constituted by the very 'expressions' that are said to be its results" (p. 25).

[96] Immanuel Kant, "What is Enlightenment?" in ed. Peter Gay, *The Enlightenment: A Comprehensive Anthology* (New York, 1973), pp. 383–90, p. 384.

involves perceiving the ontological cleft between the soul and the material and this involves grasping the material world as mere extension."[97] In Weber's celebrated formulation, the post-Cartesian world was "disenchanted"; the self became the great moral project of modernity, as Kant instructed and as Foucault has most famously deconstructed; the individual as citizen was positioned outside of, indeed prior to, society, as political and social theorists like Locke and Hobbes insisted; and the individualist "rational" actor was presented as the neoclassical theorist's economic man.[98]

Whether we begin this story with Bedos-Rezak's medieval theologians and rulers, Burckhardt's Renaissance Italians, or the New Historicists' sixteenth-century Englishmen, the creation of the interiorized individual was not a smoothly linear process. Nor was the cultural process in which it was embedded – the conception of the material world "as mere extension." In fact, the period between 1300 and 1600 might be better depicted as a furious contest over the power of material objects rather than an epoch when the material was pacifically abandoned as a manifestation of the real. This was, after all, the age of witchcraft persecutions, when the corporeal was thought to be invaded by spirit. It was then that rioters throughout the continent went to the streets to smash sacred images.[99] Admittedly, Protestants would later come to agree that images were not the essence of the sacred, but rather "mere appearances . . . 'dark significations' or 'blind superstitions' that obstructed the eyes of the mind from directing their gaze upon a spiritual object," as a recent scholar said.[100] But the iconoclastic battles of the sixteenth century would not have been fought as they were had these early Reformers

---

[97] Taylor, *Sources of the Self*, p. 145.

[98] For Kant, see in particular Kant, "What is Enlightenment?" For Foucault, see "What is Enlightenment?" in *The Foucault Reader*, ed. Paul Rabinow (New York, 1984), pp. 32–50.

[99] Charles Taylor has explained the witchcraft persecutions in exactly these terms. He wrote that they lay "between a period in which people accepted without resistance their insertion in a universe of meaningful order and a period in which that universe of meaningful order was definitely shattered [and thus] could be a response to the fragility of the emerging identity as its was establishing itself": Taylor, *Sources of the Self*, p. 192.

[100] For the quotation, see Goodrich, "Signs Taken for Wonders," pp. 711–12.

actually believed that icons were inert. Natalie Davis's essay "Rites of Violence" makes the point elegantly, and more recent work by scholars such as Eamen Duffy shows the extent to which this materialist conception of the sacred pervaded early modern England, both among those who clung to the old faith and those who would reform it.[101] The same anxieties attended the so-called vestiarian controversy in Elizabethan England. In modern hindsight it appears to be a silly quarrel about what priests should wear; however, to contemporaries it was a struggle about the materialization of the sacred, one that passionately engaged both sides because Reformers and Catholics alike were staking a claim to what Jones and Stallybrass called the "animating and constitutive power of clothes."[102] For both sides dress mattered, and mattered desperately.

The fury that drove these battles on the streets or in courtrooms or churches, although evidence of how seriously contemporaries took the question about the relationship between appearance and reality, also reflects the equation's insecurity. The stories, poems, and plays from the age clearly voiced the uncertainty. For example, fairy tales like Cinderella or Puss in Boots not only simultaneously depended on but also played with the idea that dress equals personhood. The thirteenth-century's widely circulated *Romance of the Rose* worried about the equation's fragility, branding any fakery in dress as a moral transgression, equivalent to conscious deceit, thievery, or fraud.[103] Faux Semblant, a leading character in the story, brags that he is "very good at changing my clothes, at donning one outfit and discarding another. At one moment I am a knight, at another a prelate, now a canon, now a clerk, now a

---

[101] Natalie Davis, "The Rites of Violence," in *Society and Culture in Early Modern France* (Stanford, 1975); Eamon Duffy, *The Stripping of the Altars: Traditional Religion in England, C.1400–C.1580* (New Haven, CT, 1992); Duffy is particularly effective in detailing the visual aspects of worship and faith. Lyndal Roper concurs that the contrast between the two positions in the early centuries of the Reformation should not be overdrawn. This was a time of "theological instability.... For Catholics as for Protestants, the precise relationship between bodies, spirits and demons proved hard to define": Roper, "Exorcism and the Theology of the Body," in Roper, *Oedipus and the Devil* (London, 1994), pp. 171–99, p. 174. For more on the iconoclastic riots, see Arnade, *Beggars*.

[102] Jones and Stallybrass, *Renaissance Clothing*, p. 4.

[103] On the German fairy tales and other literary representations of the "Kleider machen Leute" theme, see Baur, *Kleiderordnungen*, pp. 8–15.

priest, now disciple, now master, now lord of the manor, now forester, in short I am of every calling. Again, I am prince one moment, page the next."[104] Royalty were not exempt from the worries dramatized by Faux Semblant. When finding herself surrounded by elegantly dressed bourgeoises on a visit to the Low Countries, the French queen, Jeanne of Navarre, is said to have complained, "I thought I was the only queen in Ghent and Bruges, [but] here I see hundreds of them."[105] Giovani Sercambi, an Italian writer of the fifteenth century, rudely mocked the equation with a tale about a furrier in Lucca who panicked when he undressed in the city's public baths, fearing "to lose his identity in the crowd." He thus put a straw crosier (*Strohkreuz*) on his right shoulder to identify himself. It fell, and a neighbor picked it up, shouting, "I am now you. Away! You are dead." The furrier, Sercambi tells us with some amusement, actually believed himself dead.[106]

Phillip Stubbes's sixteenth-century *Anatomie of Abuses* displayed an even deeper confusion. On the one hand, as Jones and Stallybrass emphasize, Stubbes reviled extravagant apparel as superfluous and economically damaging, precisely because, to quote them, the "superfluity" of apparel seemed to him to have "the power to constitute an essence." Quoting liberally from Stubbes's book, Jones and Stallybrass go on to argue the following:

Clothes . . . leave a "print or character" upon observer and wearer alike. And, when excessive, they visibly imprint "wickedness and sinne." Through its ability to "print or character" the wearer, exotic clothing "*transnatureth*" English gallants, "making them weake, tender and infirme." Clothes give a nature to what previously had no nature; they take an existing nature and transnature it, turning the virtuous into the vicious, the strong into the weak, the male into the female, the godly into the satanic [emphasis in original].[107]

On the other hand, the passages quoted from Stubbes betray a sense that there is, in fact, a self prior to clothing. Stubbes's fury is directed not simply at the power that dress has to *constitute* identity and not simply

[104] Cited by Heller, "Sumptuary Laws," p. 328.
[105] "Je croyais seule être reine à Gand et à Bruges, et j'en vois ici par les centaines." Baudrillart, *Historie du Luxe*, pp. 250–1.
[106] In Bulst, "Zum Problem," p. 37.
[107] Jones and Stallybrass, *Renaissance Clothing*, p. 4.

at its ability to disrupt the social order, but simultaneously at its ability to *disrupt* "nature," to make an individual what he or she was not – to "*transnatureth*" the person [emphasis added]. The gallant's own being, a place beyond rank and prior to his appearance, is apparently violated by the false apparel of extravagance.

One of the period's favorite stories, the tale of Griselda, can similarly be read to question the equation between dress and selfhood even as it deploys it. The plot is simple. An Italian nobleman chooses a peasant girl as his bride and dresses her in properly aristocratic garb, thus providing the dowry she did not have. With this act he claims her and her body as his own and transforms her identity from peasant to noble. He then cruelly tests her loyalty and reaffirms his ownership by systematically abusing her, most hideously by claiming to have murdered her daughter and son and then by demanding that she leave his house, stripped of her finery, so he can marry again, this time a woman just out of girlhood. Through it all, "patient Griselda" is stoic, obedient, unprotesting. In the end, the nobleman is convinced of her loyalty, takes her back, and presents her children to her, revealing that the girl who was to be his bride was in fact Griselda's daughter. And then, as most versions have it, he redresses Griselda in glorious celebration, reincorporating her into his household and into his station in life.

The many versions of this story that circulated throughout Europe played with these themes of clothes, bodies, men, women, identity, true nobility, the inner and outer person, all obsessing about the relationship between dress and self – some problematizing the equation, some accepting it. However, all the versions make this relationship the moral center of the play. All worry about whether one could perform on oneself the trick on which the Griselda story turns – become another person just by putting on new clothes. The story's popularity and its variant tellings bear witness to its power. It exposed, but disrupted, the equation between personhood and clothing. Griselda, whether naked, whether luxuriously or meagerly clothed, might still be Griselda.[108]

---

[108] Diane Owen Hughes has pointed to the way paintings, by playing with "distinguishing signs" (in this case earrings), could similarly force the turn inward. See her discussion of Bellini's *St. Francis in the Desert* in "Distinguishing Signs," p. 59.

But if there was a Griselda behind her dress, who was she? What "self" lay behind? This is the dark side of Burckhardt's "free" individual. As a recent commentator has put it, "His *auf sich selbst gestelllten Persönlichkeit* (so liberally translated as 'free personality') is the individual stripped bare of all traditional defenses, standing naked before the world."[109] Naked, we might note, just like Griselda.

Sumptuary legislation seems to express precisely the disquiet evidenced in stories like Griselda, in Stubbes's vitriolic sermon, or in simple tales like Cinderella. Another scholar made this argument about the *Romance of the Rose*, claiming that it "gives insight into the emotions and fears propelling the creation of sumptuary laws . . . [and] provides an elaborated picture of the vestimentary hypocrisy irritating many levels of later thirteenth-century society."[110] In a commentary on Alan Hunt's *Governance of the Consuming Passions*, Peter Goodrich similarly proposed that controversies about clerical garb were animated by the same fears that drove sumptuary legislation. "The law of images is pivotal to an understanding of sumptuary regulation," he explained. The "licit image of a person [targeted by sumptuary legislation] was linked indissolubly to the order of images and the role of symbols, of what Reformers called the 'visible word,' in public and private life." The attack on dress was an attack on idolatry, to be condemned as "the painted and plastic accoutrements of false or misdirected worship."[111] The laws seemed to say that there was a "real" person underneath the clothes, and governors were desperately trying to figure out how to link the two – or wondering if such a link could be made.

Based on such evidence, I would argue that stories and events like those mentioned earlier do not express the last gasp of a "medieval"

---

[109] Zachary Sayre Schiffman, "Dimensions of Individuality: Recent French Works on the Renaissance," *Renaissance Quarterly* 49 (1996), pp. 114–23.

[110] Heller, "Sumptuary Laws," p. 331.

[111] Further, "the regulation of apparel and appearance was always and crucially a matter of theological significance, a question of moral governance of the means or media through which an invisible and divine order was to be seen and honored in its manifest form": Goodrich, "Signs Taken for Wonders," pp. 711–12. Goodrich goes on to argue that women were targeted by sumptuary legislation because "the idol was in essence an erotic image, a confusion of the soul with sensuality" (p. 714).

culture in which people had had no viable sense of an independent self. Rather, they reveal that in this age it had become urgent to decide just how the material and immaterial were related. To be sure, as Natalie Davis has put it in describing the sixteenth-century French, for them "the boundary around the conceptual self and the bodily self was not always firm and closed."[112] That surely does not mean that they could not conceive of distinct individuality; rather, it means that they imagined the relationship between the conceptual self and the bodily self differently than we might – or differently than Burckhardt thought they should have. As Lyndal Roper has protested, to deny them that self-consciousness does little but provide us "with a written guarantee of the modernity of our own time"; it reduces early modern Europeans adorned in expensive furs, sumptuous velvets, and outrageously decorated sleeves to "dancing marionettes, tricked out in ruffs and codpieces, whose subjectivities can neither surprise nor unsettle [us]," because they seem expressions of an exotic primitiveness that has nothing to do with us.[113] Throughout those long centuries, dress and display were surely connected to subjectivity in ways that seem strange to us, but these attachments were not the expressions of "an incredible superficiality and feebleness," as Huizinga charged in his *Waning of the Middle Ages*; nor were these people trapped, as Burckhardt said, "beneath a common veil, dreaming or half awake."

I would argue instead that sumptuary legislation was the sign of a cultural crisis, a crisis born of commerce and given expression in dress. The crisis was born in the early days of the commercial revolution when the luxuries provided by commerce had seemed to clarify and heighten clothing's ability to mark status, express character, inspire awe, and even define both sexuality and gender. Shimmering silks from the East, elaborately brocaded satins and taffetas produced in high-priced workshops, European woolens so luxuriously fulled that they draped like velvet – all could make those so adorned seem utterly unlike the mass of ordinary onlookers. But the very abundance and variety that made such display possible simultaneously eroded its power. When Europeans began to experiment with style, cutting and shaping their clothes in

[112] Davis, "Boundaries and the Sense of Self in Sixteenth-Century France," p. 53.
[113] Roper, *Oedipus and the Devil*, p. 11.

extraordinary ways, dress seemed to lose all solidity – just what did a puffed sleeve, a gold trim, a fur lining, or a brocaded doublet actually mean? Dress became so excessive and overcharged that it became a fetish. When people of low birth acquired the means to buy these clothes, when artisans in Europe learned to make cheaper copies of imported silks or luxury draperies, and when tailors and dressmakers invented yet another new sleeve or cap or jacket, the game was up.

However, this did not mean that elites and aspiring elites would "give up" on clothes; instead, it meant that they would wonder and worry about them. Thus, storytellers played with, queried, or sometimes insisted on the link between clothes and the self – not just a self defined by rank, although that was part of their plots, but also a gendered, sexed, and moral self.[114] As though in response to the trouble signaled by such tales, legislators scrambled to write a code into law, creating volumes of statutes, none of them able to provide a convincing argument about the link between clothes and status, morality, gender, sex, economic well-being, or political order. But all desperately trying.

TOWARD THE MODERN CONSUMER

In the end the lawmakers lost the battle. Their inability to enforce their laws as they wished and their evident confusion even about the links to be forged did little more than expose the impossibility of their task.[115] Their failure left the self unclothed, adrift in a sea of choices and of taste, naked like Griselda. It then became urgent to create an

---

[114] For such practices, see Welch, "New, Old, and Secondhand Clothing," and Frick, *Dressing*.

[115] Most scholars have argued that the laws were impossible to enforce and that the issuers gained little from their promulgation. However, Neithard Bulst has provided good evidence showing that legislators did collect the fines and even that many issuers depended on these fines for a significant portion of their budget. He reasoned that fiscal interests thus combined with political needs. In particular, see his "Vom Luxusverbot zur Luxussteuer. Wirtschafts – und sozialgeschichtliche Aspekte von Luxus and Konsum in der Vormoderne," in *Der lange Weg in den Überfluss: Anfänge und Entwicklung der Konsumgesellschaft seit der Vormoderne*, ed. Michael Prinz (Aschendorff: Münster, 2003), pp. 47–60.

imagery in which, as Jones and Stallybrass have put it, "subjects are prior to objects, wearers to what is worn."[116] That process would take many forms and a lot of time, not ending until well into the early modern period and perhaps never really ending, although signs of change can be seen in the centuries before 1600. For example, some versions of the Griselda story gave her a secret interior self that was unavailable to her brutal husband – a place where she despaired, wept, raged, and protested; a place where, we might argue, the modern "self" took root, a self divorced from appearance, indeed from the material world itself.[117] It was then that essayists, poets, theologians, dramatists, and novelists took up the challenge of defining that self by crafting tools that allowed us to imagine, sketch, and perform Hamlet's "that within which passeth show." Their texts, like the versions of the Griselda story that gave her an interior self, are thus rightly recognized as important signposts in the history of European culture – markers of the moments when people "fashioned" themselves as modern. At the same time, in some court circles, the obsession with "power dressing" that had reached absurd heights in the court of Elizabeth I of England began to disintegrate. After her reign, a recent scholar has explained, English courtiers began to have themselves painted in costumes that self-consciously differed from the baroque constructions typical of her court; instead, they sought a more "natural" dress that was supposed to display their "true" selves.[118]

Clothes would by no means lose cultural significance in the centuries to come. Awash in the possibilities of fashion, faced with the infinity of choices produced by commerce, westerners would become voracious, endlessly desiring consumers of dress. However, they would do so self-consciously, strategically choosing how they would present themselves to the public, not imagining that they were creating or exposing the "real" self that made the choice. Instead, they would nervously, sometimes

---

[116] Jones and Stallybrass, *Renaissance Clothing*, p. 2.

[117] Petrarch's and Boccacio's versions both allow Griselda a small space of independent, separate identity. Chaucer's Clerk's Tale, in contrast, makes Griselda equivalent to her performance of herself. On this difference, see Crane, *The Performance of Self*, pp. 29–38.

[118] For this argument, see Breward, *Culture of Fashion*, pp. 41–74.

playfully, fiddle and experiment. This was and is a game, but it is a serious one. Clothes serve us in the creation of a self-image, a mirror into which we gaze as we fashion selfhood. In the world of sumptuary legislation, a time when stories about Cinderella, Griselda, and Faux Semblant were told and retold to adults and children alike, clothing was not supposed to be a costume that one put on and took off at will. When Faux Semblant boasted that he did just that, listeners understood that something was wrong – socially, morally, and psychically. When these people dressed, they were not yet "fashioning" themselves as he said he was doing or as someone today might say he or she was doing; they were wondering what it meant to be "fashioned."

Commerce made clothing fungible. As a commodity, an article of cloth-ing was potentially exchangeable for some other thing, almost anything, for price alone. As a material object always available to the market, it could also easily escape its original owner. The costume that had made the alderman's wife recognizable could be cut up to fashion the bodice for her daughter's dress; exotic materials such as finely cut velours or newly colored silks could easily be had from local merchants to trans-form her own gown. In secondhand markets where many such garments made their way, the sleeves of the woman's gown might be reattached to the dress of the butcher's wife and its overskirt refashioned for the butcher's daughter. No longer did the act of remaking a dress seem so innocent, so normal. Now and still worse, tailors could cut the fabric into new shapes, making even the same tissues utterly unrecognizable. Commodified in this way, clothing could no longer easily be imagined to constitute identity. It was this ambiguity that made the relationship between appearance and reality a question and contributed to the cul-tural crisis that marked the period: what was the relationship, after all, between the material and the immaterial?

Significantly, sumptuary legislation would not survive liberal theory of the eighteenth century. According to that paradigm, the govern-ment had no automatic right to control individual choices, especially choices of material goods. Instead, an informed and "free" citizenry whose members were able to decide for themselves about such acqui-sitions was considered the source of the state's own power. It was no accident that Adam Smith called sumptuary legislation "the highest impertinence and presumption . . . in kings and ministers."[119] To us, sumptuary legislation can indeed seem "impertinent and presumptive," nothing more than the futile efforts of muddleheaded legislators who were not yet in control of the states they sought to govern and still unclear about what good governance might be. But in fact that legislation was less the residue of a primitive past than one of the ways that Europeans became "modern." Although lawmakers' attacks may have failed to control dress, their laws allowed – indeed, implicitly drove – a new discourse about clothing and about the person inside the clothing. However archaic it may seem, however bizarre an artifact of a lost age, sumptuary legislation both created new meanings for clothing and helped give birth to the discourse of the modern self.

[119] Harte, "State Control," p. 134. In a wide-ranging survey and analysis of the western European sumptuary legislation of the age and the discourses in which it was embedded, Alan Hunt has extended this argument. In his reasoning, sumptuary legislation was not so much "policing" in the Germanic sense, but instead "an early form of the project that comes to target as the proper task of government the manifestations of citizenship understood in terms of the social and moral well being of an aggregated population." As such, it was a "significant step . . . in the passage to modernity." In his view, modern states have not dropped the burden of moral and social caretaking; they have simply shifted their target, from the external to the internal being – from dress to diet, from public order to public health: Hunt, *Governance*, pp. 7 and 9.

5 Rescuing Commerce

THE COMMERCIAL REVOLUTION GAVE NEW IMPETUS TO A
centuries-old discourse about the evils of surplus wealth. Merchants,
tradespeople of all kinds, and women were targets of the vitriolic attacks,
figured both as embodiments of the harm unleashed by commerce and as
the agents of those evils. It was said that merchants greedily accumulated
and hoarded riches, depriving the needy of basic subsistence and literally
stealing from hapless consumers. Artisans produced shoddy goods, made
up stories about their wares, and schemed to earn more for less work.
Women, who were imagined to be particularly susceptible to material
desires, readily abandoned spiritual pursuits for corporeal pleasures and
used their sexuality to obtain the luxuries they craved.

Yet even the most passionate critics of commerce knew that commerce
was necessary and that tradespeople performed essential services.
Europeans of the day thus did not seek to ban commerce or banish its
practitioners; rather, they sought to make trade honest, to render its
practitioners honorable, and to ensure that consumers bought wisely. This
chapter describes two avenues of such reform, one focusing on how to
cleanse trade and the other on how to manage consumption. Although
apparently unrelated developments, they combined to produce
unmistakable changes in cultural discourses and social practices during the
late medieval centuries. This period would by no means unreservedly
celebrate commerce, but by its end it was easier to grant merchants a role
in Europe's moral economy, to argue that an individual's energetic pursuit
of profits could serve the social whole, and to concede that consumption
could be virtuous.

Historians usually begin the story of Europe's commercial revolution around the turn of the millennium, when long-distance traders began to flood Europe with luxury goods. In most versions of this history, these traders were men of little account. In *Gold and Spices: The Rise of Commerce in the Middle Ages*, Jean Favier offers a standard version of that narrative. He explains that the commercial revolution began with the "dusty-footed peddler" of the Middle Ages who only later was transformed into the *homme d'affaires* (businessman) of early modernity (the original French edition carries the subtitle, *naissance de l'homme d'affaires au moyen âge*).[1] Specialists focusing on southern Europe have described another pattern, in which Genoese nobles learned to trade during their military exploits in the Mediterranean, where they encountered Muslim and Jewish merchants who had long been engaged in commerce.[2] Although the Europeans in these histories were male, trade did not grant them honorable masculinity. Favier's peddler was a marginal figure, hardly a "man" at all, and the Genoese nobles who proffered their wares (or plunder) were proud warriors of honorable lineage whose honor certainly did not derive from their mercantile activities.

During the late medieval centuries, however, commercial people were gradually, if unsteadily and incompletely, rescued from the margins of Europe's moral economy. Although suspicion would cling to merchants and their practices for centuries to come (and continues to do so today), by the end of the early modern period, commerce had in some places decidedly become the "business of states." Nowhere was this truer than in England and The Netherlands, where merchants were even figured as cultural heroes in certain settings, and everywhere in western Europe it was acknowledged that commerce could be useful, even good. Although scholars have not denied this shift, they have generally described commerce's cautious redemption as though it automatically followed from

---

[1] Favier, *Gold & Spices* (New York, 1998).

[2] For the early history of commerce in Europe see McCormick, *Origins of the European Economy*; for more on the commercial revolution, see Lopez, *The Commercial Revolution*, and Spufford, *Power and Profit* (New York, 2003). For recent studies of Mediterranean commerce in the early years of the revolution, Van Doosselaere, *Commercial Agreements and Social Dynamics*; Avner Greif, *Institutions and the Path to the Modern Economy: Lessons from Medieval Trade* (Cambridge, UK, 2006); and Lebecq, *Marchands et navigateurs* are useful.

the achievements of commercial people. They have argued that the riches brought by trade, the sophisticated technologies of merchants, and the energy unleashed by the commercialization of production made it impossible to ignore commerce's power and foolish to despise its practitioners.

Although the power of commerce to generate wealth was certainly the essential condition of its rehabilitation and eventual ascendance to full respectability, the story of how merchants became partners to princes, how market exchange came to seem not only natural but also normative, or how unbridled consumption came to be considered socially useful cannot be told within the confines of traditional economic history. As the episodes investigated in the last four chapters demonstrate, the commercialization of society was not just an economic history as we understand the term but a social, legal, and cultural story, and it is incomprehensible if told from the perspective of one of these modern conceptual categories alone. In fact, the social and cultural were the roots of the economic, not footnotes to it.[3] This final chapter, even more directly than the previous ones, takes such an approach by sketching how cultural discourses about market norms and gender roles helped make commerce morally acceptable. As we shall see, however, these discourses were not simply cultural texts; they articulated widely held social values and powerfully influenced social practice.

THE EVILS OF COMMERCE: GREED, DECEIT, LUST

From the earliest centuries of the Middle Ages, commerce had been embedded in a scathing discourse that flatly condemned the desire for material goods as a spiritual threat and a manifestation of temporal evils. In later centuries, as the commercial revolution took shape, moralists reworked this condemnation by putting trade, merchants, and city people at the center of the story about moral corruption: As Aquinas wrote,

If the citizens themselves devote their life to matters of trade, the way will be opened to many vices. Since the foremost tendency of tradesmen is to make money,

---

[3] In general, see Polanyi's *Great Transformation*. As he put it in a slightly different way, we should consider the social and cultural the "bed" of the economic.

greed is awakened in the hearts of the citizens through the pursuit of trade. The result is that everything in the city will become venal; good faith will be destroyed and the way opened to all kinds of trickery; each one will work only for his own profit, despising the public good; the cultivation of virtue will fail since honour, virtue's reward, will be bestowed upon the rich. Thus in such a city, civil life will necessarily be corrupted.[4]

Although Aquinas himself, along with many other commentators of the Middle Ages, recognized that merchants provided necessary goods and could thus benefit society and he often provided sophisticated analyses of market exchange, there is no doubt that the attacks on trade and tradespeople accelerated from the twelfth century forward.[5] Indeed, Aquinas was only one of a multitude of later medieval critics. Franciscan and Dominican friars regularly preached the same criticisms, usually with considerably more venom, and they were repeated in countless late medieval penitentials. As a recent scholar summarized the churchmen's complaint, commerce was

morally hazardous. No one becomes inflamed by greed like the merchant, whose very occupation is centered on wealth and on the daily opportunity to augment his property. . . . In order to make a profit, the merchant is tempted to cheat on weights and measures, to hide defects in his wares, to swear falsely about their qualities, etc.[6]

The church itself did not escape the attacks. Writing in the twelfth century, for example, John of Salisbury moaned that church officials

---

[4] *De regno*, II, 7 (ii, 3), cited in Odd Langholm, *Economics in the Medieval Schools: Wealth, Exchange, Value, Money and Usury According to the Paris Theological Tradition, 1200–1350* (Leiden, 1992), p. 222; for a fuller discussion of Aquinas on commerce, see Joel Kaye, "Changing Definitions of Money, Nature and Equality (c. 1140–1270) and Their Place within Thomas Aquinas' Question of Usury," in *Credito e usura fra teologia, deiritto e admministratione. Linguaggi a confronto (sec, XII–XVI)*, eds. D. Quaglioni, G. Todeschini, and G. M. Varanini (Rome, 2005), pp. 25–55.

[5] Lester Little's *Religious Poverty and the Profit Economy in Medieval Europe* (Ithaca, NY, 1978) conveniently summarizes the attack. Paul Freedman's *Out of the East* (New Haven, 2008), Chapter 6, describes how the "lust" for spices in the period evoked the same kinds of criticisms.

[6] Langholm, *Economics*, p. 573.

themselves had succumbed to commerce's poison: "They deliver justice not for the sake of truth but for a price. . . . The palaces of priests glitter and in their hands the Church of Christ is demeaned."[7]

The church's ban of usury, given new force by late medieval scholastics, compounded the opprobrium, making it, in Jacques Le Goff's words, "one of the huge problems of the thirteenth century."[8] As John Munro recently summarized it, "from at least the era of St. Thomas' own *Summa Theologiae* (1266–73), both theologians and jurists had come to consider any interest on any loan to be a sin against not just charity but commutative justice and natural law, and thus a truly mortal sin. It was even a mortal sin for the lender to hope for any such gain beyond the principal."[9] The theoretical basis of the attack on usury was both complex and unstable, but neither jurists nor theologians of that period,

---

[7] John of Salisbury, *Policraticus: Of the Frivolities of Courtiers and the Footprints of Philosophers*, ed. and trans. Cary J. Nederman (Cambridge, UK, 1990), p. 133; cited in Kaye, "Reflections of Money," p. 4.

[8] Le Goff, *La bourse et la vie* (Paris, 1986), p. 10. Although scholastics did allow many exceptions to the rule of "no interest," the ban nevertheless had a profound effect on the structure of debt instruments and on the way trade was conducted. For a discussion of these mechanisms, see John Munro, "The Late-Medieval Origins of the Modern Financial Revolution: Overcoming Impediments from Church and State," *International History Review* 25, no. 2 (June 2003), pp. 505–62.

[9] Munro, "Late-Medieval Origins," p. 510.

On the scholastic definitions, see in particular Langholm, *Economics*; idem, *The Merchant in the Confessional: Trade and Price in the Pre-Reformation Penitential Handbooks* (Leiden, 2003); idem, *The Aristotelian Analysis of Usury* (Bergen, Norway, 1984); Jacques Le Goff, "The Usurer and Purgatory," in *The Dawn of Modern Banking*, ed. Fredi Chiappelli (New Haven, 1979), pp. 25–52 and his *La bourse et la vie*; James A. Brundage, "Usury," in *Dictionary of the Middle Ages*, eds. Joseph R. Strayer et al., 13 vols. (New York, 1982–89), XII (1989), pp. 335–9; Raymond de Roover, "Scholastic Economics: Survival and Lasting Influence from the Sixteenth Century to Adam Smith," *Quarterly Journal of Economics* 69, no. 2 (1955), pp. 161–90, reprinted in ed. Julius Kirshner, *Business, Banking, and Economic Thought in Late Medieval and Early Modern Europe: Selected Studies of Raymond de Roover* (Chicago, 1974); also see his "Raymond de Roover on Scholastic Economic Thought," in the same volume, pp. 15–36; John T. Noonan, *The Scholastic Analysis of Usury* (Cambridge, MA, 1957); T. P. McLaughlin, "The Teaching of the Canonists on Usury (xii, xiii, and xiv Centuries)," *Medieval Studies* 1 (1939), pp. 8–147 and 2 (1940), pp. 1–22.

or of the next few centuries, deviated from their conviction that usury should be banned.[10]

To be sure, not all interest was considered usurious, and during the thirteenth century some guidelines had been formulated to separate licit from illicit interest. For example, it was fair to exact interest in compensation for damages or the loss of money's use during the term of the loan. More cautiously endorsed but nevertheless accepted were the ideas that interest could be charged to offset risk or to measure uncertainty of return. In principle, there was also a fifth, firm exemption based on the notion that one could be paid for work – creation or delivery of a material good. Nevertheless, as Le Goff commented, "[the term] usury designated a multiplicity of practices, which complicated the process of drawing a clear line between the licit and illicit in dealings involving interest."[11]

Despite church rules and sometimes even seeming to make mockery of them, borrowing and lending went on almost – almost – unabated. In fact, throughout the greater Low Countries, the so-called Lombards (Italian moneylenders) were regularly granted rights to manage "tables" where loans were arranged at as much as 62 percent annual rates of

---

[10] Some theorists proposed that money was sterile, unable to "fructify," and that interest charges were thus robbery; others suggested that interest charges were a price extracted for time and thus a theft from God, who alone "owned" time. Others reasoned that usury was a way of taking money without working for it. According to Lawrin Armstrong, the more serious objection derived from the Roman law definition of a *mutuum*, a loan of a fungible asset (something consumed in use according to that legal tradition). In that case, the debtor owned the thing loaned and could not legitimately be expected to return more than the value of the thing itself: Lawrin Armstrong, "Law, Ethics and Economy: Gerard of Siena and Giovanni d'Andrea on Usury," in *Money, Markets and Trade in Late Medieval Europe: Essays in Honor of John H. Munro*, eds. Lawrin Armstrong, Ivana Elbl, and Martin M. Elbl (Leiden, 2007), pp. 41–59.

Joel Kaye's "Changing Definitions of Money" argues that changes in the understanding of money, nature, and equality during the commercial revolution forced Aquinas to abandon many of the central arguments against usury of traditional scholastic thought. Aquinas essentially based his critique on the point that usury was charging for the use of money that has already been sold.

[11] Le Goff, *La bourse et la vie*, p. 19; for Le Goff's description of the exemptions for licit interest, see in particular pp. 94–5.

interest. Even ecclesiastics made use of these tables, and in this part of the world it was not until the sixteenth century that the tables were gradually replaced by *Monts de Piété* set up by the state.[12] Even though the gap between theory and practice was thus very large, there is no doubt that theory affected practice. Effectively excommunicated while they practiced their trade, "Lombard" bankers were obliged to renounce their businesses in order to gain salvation after death, and they were compelled to pay significant fines to obtain absolution.[13] It was common practice as well for merchants to assuage their guilt about "illegitimate" business practices with postmortem gifts to charity and the church.[14] As John Munro has argued, the rules about usury also directly affected the structure of financial instruments, including, as was explained in Chapter 1, the rents issued by cities in the north of Europe.[15]

The suspicions and even opprobrium that surrounded "usurers" were echoed in learned and popular texts. Scholars often remind us that Dante put usurers in the seventh circle of hell, just below blasphemers and sodomites.[16] A fourteenth-century language manual from Bruges,

---

[12] For a recent study, see Brian S. Pullan, "Catholics, Protestants, and the Poor in Early Modern Europe," *Journal of Interdisciplinary History* 35, no. e (2005), pp. 441–56; also see Boone, "Le crédit financier dans les villes de Flandre" and Greilsammer, *La roue de la fortune: Le destin d'une famille d'usuriers lombards dans les Pays-Bas à l'aube des Temps modernes* (Paris, 2009) and the sources they cite.

[13] For such examples, see Greilsammer, *La roue de la fortune.*

[14] See, for example, B. Nelson, "The Usurer and the Merchant Prince: Italian Businessmen and the Ecclesiastical Law of Restitution," *Journal of Economic History* 7 (Supplement) (1947), pp. 104–22; F. L. Galassi, "Buying a Passport to Heaven: Usury, Restitution and the Merchants of Medieval Genoa," *Religion* 22 (1992), pp. 313–26; Lawrin Armstrong, "Usury, Conscience, and Public Debt: Angelo Corbinelli's Testament of 1419," in *A Renaissance of Conflicts: Visions and Revisions of Law and Society in Italy and Spain*, eds. J. A. Marino and T. Kuehn (Toronto, 2004), pp. 173–240; de Roover, "Scholastic Economics," p. 187.

[15] For his argument, see Munro, "The Medieval Origins of the Financial Revolution."

[16] Attacks on usurers are leitmotifs of chronicle literature as well. In his *Chronica Maiora* of the mid-thirteenth century, for example, Matthew Paris lamented that "we might fall into the snares of the usurers": J. A. Giles, ed. and trans., *Matthew Paris's English History: From the Year 1235 to 1273*, Vol. 3 (London, 1852) p. 155; cited in Kaye, "Monetary and Market Consciousness in Thirteenth and Fourteenth Century Europe," in *Ancient and Medieval Economic Ideas and*

ostensibly intended for practical use by the citizenry, attributed the
usurer's extravagant lifestyle to his usury, implying that the luxury was
undeserved, the profits unfairly won[17]:

> Julliens, li usuriers,
> Est moult enrichis,
> Puis qu'il presta
> Premierement as usures;
> Il ha moult amassé
> De boins joyaus
> Et de belles mansions;
> Il preste sur boin gage
> Le livre pour iiii mites
>
> Julien, the usurer
> Has become very rich
> Because he lends
> First at usurious rates of interest;
> He has amassed so many
> Fine jewels
> And beautiful houses;
> He lends at favorable rates
> [earning] 4 miten the pound

Even without the illicit interest charged by usurers, money itself provided ample opportunities for shady profits, giving concrete meaning to
the term "filthy lucre." The fourteenth-century poem "*Le pelerinage de vie
humaine*" has Lady Usurer magically turn *livres tournois* into *livres parisis*:
this supernatural act represents both the confusions between the two

Concepts of Social Justice, eds. S. Todd Lowry and Barry Gordon (Leiden, 1998),
pp. 371–403, p. 8.

[17] Jan Gessler, *Het Brugsche Livre des Mestiers en zijn navolgingen, Livres des Mestiers*,
p. 35. The *mite* was worth 1/24 of a *groot*. The implied annual interest rate (4
mitten in the pound *mitten* of 240 *mitten*) is 20%, assuming monthly exactions
of interest (and no compounding); given that "official" rates could approach
62%, however, the 20% seems "reasonable." See Appendix I for a description
of the various Flemish pounds. A version of the passage is repeated in Caxton's
edition (*Right Good Lernyng*) and in the Flemish-French edition from Antwerp
(*Vocabulaer*), both also in *Het Brugsche Livre des Mestiers en zijn navolgingen*.

different monies of account and the illegitimacy of interest.[18] Geoffrey de Paris's *Chronique metrique* of the same century has Merlin predict that all *tournois* will become the more valuable *parisis*, another magical act that threatened to destroy the economy.[19] Outside the world of fiction, the chicanery continued. Princes regularly debased their coinage, especially during what Barbara Tuchman called the "calamitous" fourteenth century. By calling in circulating coinage and reissuing it at a lower weight or fineness, they not only collected fees and taxes from the reminting but they also gave themselves a way to repay their own debts in money containing less bullion. Employers were positioned to enjoy a similar windfall, for they could pay their workers in coin that now cost them less in real terms than had been implied when the wages were set, and the wages themselves, being "sticky upward," as a modern economist might say, did not immediately rise with the inflation that resulted from devalued coinage. The other losers in this game were creditors, whether the sophisticated financiers of cities and courts, ordinary people receiving annuities denominated in ever less valuable coin, or landlords whose rents had been commuted from in-kind payments to price.[20]

Moneylending and money itself were not the only source of commerce's dangers. To judge from the popular tales of the age, deceit was endemic to commerce.[21] As Lady Lucre explains in Wilson's *Three Ladies*

---

[18] Sharon L. Collingwood, *Market Pledge and Gender Bargain: Commercial Relations in French Farce, 1450–1550* (New York, 1997), pp. 17–18.

[19] "Dont mains en gesirent en chaume/Et on widerent le pays," in Collingwood, *Market*, pp. 18–19.

[20] For discussion of these dislocations, see, for example, John H. Munro, *Wool, Cloth, and Gold: The Struggle for Bullion in Anglo-Burgundian Trade, 1340–1478* (Toronto, 1972); Harry A. Miskimin, "The Enforcement of Gresham's Law," in *Credito, banche e investimenti, secoli XIII–XX*, ed. Anna Vannini Marx (Florence, 1985); and Peter Spufford, *Money and Its Uses in Medieval Europe* (Cambridge, UK, 1988).

[21] These themes are developed in an examination of early modern English drama in Derrick Higginbotham, "All the World's A Market: Economic Life on English Stages, c. 1400 – c. 1600" (Ph.D. diss., Columbia University, 2009). For a recent study of narratives of scarcity and exoticism in medieval trade, see Paul Freedman, "Spices and Late-Medieval European Ideas of Scarcity and Value,"

of London, merchants lie about the origins of their goods to escape import duties[22]:

> I know you Merchants haue many a sleight and subtill cast.
> So that you will by stealth bring ouer great store:
> And say it was in the Realme a long time before.
> For being so many of these trifles here as there are at this day,
> You may increase them at pleasure, when you send ouer sea.

Producers were just as bad. Bread might be made with spelt, not wheat, or sold at short weights. A silver coin might be clipped or debased with mere copper. A clever artisan might even fake a holy relic. Guildsmen masked shoddy workmanship, skimped on materials, used inferior ingredients to reduce costs. Cloth bearing the honored seal of Ghent or Ypres might, in fact, be a cheaper copy made in some unknown village with Spanish, not Cotswold, wool. As a thirteenth-century teacher of Latin grammar explained in a text depicting daily life in Paris, drapers were "driven by greed, [they] sell false white and black cloths, camelins and blues and imitation burnets, greens, imitation scarlets, striped cloths and stamforts . . . they defraud buyers by measuring the cloths badly with a short ell and a false thumb."[23]

The greed and deceit unleashed by commerce not only led to economic injustice, but they also brought moral and social collapse. For example, in Chaucer's well-known Shipman's Tale, a cleric's avarice leads him not only to break religious vows but also to feign, and then betray, kinship. The fifteenth-century English *Play of the Sacrament* has greed lure a Christian merchant into selling the host to a Jewish trader. Christopher Marlowe's sixteenth-century *Jew of Malta* presents the rapacious merchant Barabas, who dishonors even the sacred bond of friendship: he boasts, "And he from whom my most advantages comes shall be my friend."[24] In *Mélite* (1633), Pierre Corneille has Eraste describe "those

Speculum 80, no. 4 (October 2005), pp. 1209–28 and his more recent *Out of the East*.

[22] Lines 441–5: cited in Higginbotham, "All the World's A Market."

[23] Cited in Martha Carlin, "Shops and Shopping in the Thirteenth Century: Three Texts," in *Money, Markets and Trade in Late Medieval Europe*, pp. 491–537, p. 513.

[24] viii, lines 113–14; cited in Higgnbotham, "All the World's A Market."

Figure 21. *Greed Personified.*
Quentin Metsys, *The Money-Lenders*. Rome, Galleria Doria Pamphili. © ADP –
Management Fratelli Alinari. Photo Credit: Alinari / Art Resource, NY.

common souls" who, "having no stake in anyone's plans/ Their service
and faith belong to whoever gives the most/ When they are blinded
by that treacherous metal/ They no longer know right from wrong."[25]
Although such texts typically derived their power by ambiguously combining a celebration of the pleasures and excitement of commerce with
an exposé of its dangers, they never failed to deploy some mix of the
old canards in telling their stories – merchants are greedy liars, artisans
are lazy or incompetent cheaters, consumers are fools, and money is a
false god.

If the merchant himself did not betray, commerce did it for him.
Shakespeare's *Merchant of Venice* gives us Antonio and Bassanio, dabblers

[25] Cited in Jotham Parsons, "Money and Merit in French Renaissance Comedy,"
Renaissance Quarterly 60, no. 3 (2007), pp. 852–82, p. 856. Parsons notes that,
in a later edition of the text, that passage was replaced with the single line "Ces
ames du commun n'ont pour but que l'argent."

Figure 22. *Greed.*
Pieter van der Heyden (after Pieter Bruegel the Elder), *Greed* (*The Seven Deadly Sins: Avaritia*). Published by Hieronymus Cock (1558). London, The British Museum, AN62777001. © The Trustees of the British Museum.

in trade whose loyalty to one another marks them as men of "credit," and Shylock, the mercenary Jew who almost undoes them. However, it is not Shylock alone who threatens the social order. The story turns on storms, lost cargoes, uncollected debts – all the usual risks of commerce. Moral collapse follows; rings are passed from hand to misrecognized hand, disguises are donned, and lies are shamelessly told. Although Antonio and Bassanio are rescued in the end, it is not their character, business acumen, or generally good sense that saves them, but a clever woman, and Shylock himself is rendered fully human, if not entirely honorable. In fact, honor is in short supply in a story that illustrates how commerce confuses the social and moral order. The attacks did not subside even in places where commerce was not the corrosive intruder that Shakespeare described, but a normal way of life. In the southern Low Countries where commerce ruled, Bruegel regularly gave visual form to the usual critique with, for example, his memorable allegories of Avarice.[26]

In concert with Bruegel, storytellers in the region ridiculed and scolded merchants who betrayed the trust so necessary to the smooth functioning of commerce, in effect inverting the image of the idealized man of "credit" so honored in those societies. For example, *The Tale of the Grain Merchant*, a Dutch-language *fabliau* or *sproke*, describes how merchants secretly hoard grain in times of plenty in order to sell it dearly in times of dearth. The rhetoricians' dramas from the same region take up similar themes. In Cornelis Everaert's *The Wealth of Someone Else (Eens Anders Welvaren)*, Pracktijkeghe List and Suptyl Bedroch misrepresent their wares, and merchants sell their goods at the highest prices in certain markets while neglecting to supply other markets.[27] In his fourteenth-century *Der leken spieghel*, Jan van Boendale uses aristocratic values as a foil for criticism of the commercial world. In his story, a knight berates the city dweller for tricking the poor countryman: "Citizens engage themselves gladly with forestalling, deceitful business and many other unbelievable practices; playing games for money, . . . they always look out for profit like hungry dogs."[28]

Adding to the venom, critics often drew upon centuries-old moralist literature charging women with vanity and lust for material goods, thereby giving the critique of commerce a decidedly misogynist cast.

[26] On Bruegel, see Bret Rothstein, "The Problem with Looking at Pieter Bruegel's *Elck*," *Art History* 26, no. 2 (April 2003), pp. 143–73; Ethan Matt Kavaler, *Pieter Bruegel: Parables of Order and Enterprise* (Cambridge, UK, 1999). More generally on artists and commerce in the early modern Low Countries, see Keith P. F. Moxey, "The Criticism of Avarice in Sixteenth-century Nether-landish Painting," in *Netherlandish Mannerism: Papers Given at a Symposium in Nationalmuseum Stockholm September 21–22 1984*, ed. Görel Cavalli-Björkman (Stockholm, 1985), pp. 21–3; Elizabeth Alice Honig, *Painting and the Market in Early Modern Antwerp* (New Haven, 1998).

[27] His plays are published in Cornelis Everaert, *Spelen van Cornelis Everaert*, eds. J. W. Muller and L. Scharpé (Brill, 1920).

[28] In Jan Van Boendale, *Der Leken Spieghel: Leerdicht van den Jare 1330*, ed. M. De Vries (Leiden, 1848). On Van Boendale, see W. Van Anrooij, *Al t'Antwerpen in die stad: Jan van Boendale en de literaire cultuur van zijn tijd* (Amsterdam, 2002). Also see the more recent Jan Van Boendale, *Lekenspiegel*, eds. L. Jongen and M. Piters (Amsterdam, 2003).

Figure 23. *Woman as Vanitas.*
Albrecht Duerer (1471–1528), *Vanitas* (reverse side of the portrait of a young man). Limewood, 35 × 29 cm. Vienna, Kunsthistorisches Museum. Photo Credit: Erich Lessing / Art Resource, NY.

Women consumers even surpassed the perfidy of merchants and artisans by trading their bodies for the luxuries they craved. For example, the wives in the fifteenth-century *Quinze joies de marriage* exchange sex for finery, lie without shame, and spend their hours plotting how to accumulate jewels and clothing. In Chaucer's Shipman's Tale, the cleric wins both her husband's money and her body by satisfying a wife's lust

Figure 24. *Sex, Money, and Women.*
Lucas Cranach the Younger (1515–1586), *Three Lovers* (after 1537). Oil on beech
wood. Dresden, Gemaeldegalerie Alte Meister, Staatliche Kunstsammlungen,
Inventar-Nr.: Gal. Nr. 1936. Photo: Elke Estel / Hans-Peter Klut. Photo
Credit: Bildarchiv Preussischer Kulturbesitz / Art Resource, NY.

for elegant dress. As Chapter 4 described, issuers of Italian sumptuary
laws justified the legislation with similar rhetoric.

Giacomo della Marca, a Franciscan polemicist, drew on it as well,
begging husbands to "have another look when they [wives] leave the
house. They dress up in anticipation of their own pleasure, but when
they come home they take off their jewels and look like bakers' wives."[29]

Elites whose own social position was threatened by men of the
market – men who were simultaneously their creditors, suppliers, and
competitors for power – could distance themselves, ideologically at least,
from commerce by imagining that they inhabited a world "governed by
a different economic and social calculus," as Jonathan Dewald has put
it. Dewald further wrote that

the omnipresent threats to this ideal tended to be organized around the phenomena
of money, monetary exchanges and counterfeit: all forms of social interaction that

[29] S. Jacobus, *Sermones Dominicales*, Vol. 1, p. 112; cited in Diane Owen Hughes,
"Distinguishing Signs," pp. 3–59, p. 25.

replaced natural worth and identity, and settled social values like nobility, with external, arbitrary, and easily manipulated values.[30]

The kind of evidence presented in this chapter suggests that commercial people themselves shared the disquiet about the "monetary exchange" and "counterfeit" that Dewald attributed to elites. Merchants, artisans, and city people more generally seem also to have understood that commerce made people anonymous, creating "external, arbitrary, and easily manipulated values," and that it so sped the circulation of things that they lost social meaning. Unlike their social betters, however, these people had no readily available ideological retreat, at least not until they could buy their way into the *rentier* class and erase memory of their pasts. For them, it would thus not be enough simply to repeat the traditional justification for commerce – that it provided essential goods. They needed to make a stronger claim; in effect, they needed to stop apologizing for commerce and find a way to rid it of its dangers, to render consumption not just necessary but good, and perhaps above all, to redefine "value" in a world of constantly changing prices and fungible goods.

TRANSPARENCY

Even the most vitriolic critics of the later Middle Ages seemed to agree, because even as they attacked trade and the people who trafficked in it, they were beginning to seek a cure for commerce's evils. According to the redemptive narrative that gradually took shape, the problem with commerce was not so much the wealth it generated or even the social upset that came with new wealth and newly wealthy people. The problem was secrecy. Commerce too easily went underground, escaping the scrutiny that could prevent illegitimate gains and protect the populace from trickery and fraud. The cure, it followed, was to force trade into the open; if markets were made transparent, trade would automatically become socially beneficial and tradespeople themselves could be redeemed. Even churchmen took up the task of ensuring transparency.

---

[30] Jonathan Dewald, *The European Nobility, 1400–1800* (Cambridge, UK, 1996), p. 12, cited in Jonathan Parson, "Money and Merit," p. 854.

The mendicant friars, whose public sermons so often excoriated merchants, explained in their penitential handbooks that a merchant who contributed to charities and traded fairly could ultimately be saved. To merit salvation, he must do business in the open and bring supplies to market promptly, without any attempts to corner markets or create monopolies; he should sell at prices that had been negotiated publicly with knowledgeable buyers.[31]

Scholastics offered similar lessons about honesty and openness. The "just price," the fullest statement of their ideas about how markets worked or should work, made an explicit connection between open markets and social justice.[32] The just price itself was a purely normative concept, informed by what Aristotle had called "commutative justice," the equilibrium reached when individuals with different needs were able to satisfy themselves by means of fair trade. Although the price agreed upon in such a transaction would necessarily vary because individual needs were different and were differentially affected by supply conditions, it was "just" if it had been negotiated in an open market by people who were roughly equal and who had approximately equal access to information.[33] In the minds of scholastic theorists, this was the physical marketplace of face-to-face exchange, which Fernand Braudel

[31] For this discussion, see Langholm, *Merchant in the Confessional*, esp. Chapter 14, pp. 233–43.

[32] Joel Kaye has influentially exposed the link between commercial practices and their logics on the one hand and scholastic theory more generally on the other. See in particular *Economy and Nature in the Fourteenth Century: Money, Market Exchange, and the Emergence of Scientific Thought* (Cambridge, UK, 1998) and "Monetary and Market Consciousness." For scholastic theories of the just price, see Raymond De Roover, "The Concept of the Just Price: Theory and Economic Policy," *Journal of Economic History* 18 (December 1958), pp. 418–34; idem, "Scholastic Economics"; idem, *La pensée économique des scolastiques: Doctrines et méthodes* (Montreal, 1971); and, more recently, Langholm, *Merchant*, esp. Chapter 15, pp. 244–56.

There were differences of opinion about the precise definition of the just price, but the Aristotelian schematic was at the basis of all theory. On the just price, see De Roover, "Concept of the Just Price"; idem, *Doctrines économiques*; idem, *La pensée économique*; Langholm, *Economics*; idem, *The Legacy of Scholasticism in Economic Thought: Antecedents of Choice and Power* (Cambridge, UK, 1998); idem, *Merchant*; Kaye, *Economy and Nature*.

[33] For Aristotle, see *Nicomachean Ethics*, esp. Book V.

called the "normal" market of "economic life" where "the transactions necessary for everyday life . . . were exchanged for money or vice versa and the deal was resolved on the spot, the moment these things changed hands."[34] As Cardinal Cajetan, the authoritative sixteenth-century commentator on Aquinas's *Summa*, put it, the just price was "the one, which at a given time, can be gotten from the buyers, assuming common knowledge and in the absence of all fraud and coercion."[35]

Much like later neoclassical economic theorists, scholastics reasoned that prices would be just in what modern economists would describe as a "perfect market." However, their emphasis on market transparency was not the same as the "value-free" economic theory of modern social science. It was a moral statement, an insistence that markets can be just if they are transparent. Prices should be negotiated in open markets not because that process produces the lowest price (although scholastics seem to have understood and endorsed that argument) but because that price is most likely to satisfy both parties. Mutual satisfaction or equilibrium, not "efficiency" as modern economists understand it, was the measure of justice. However, these scholars knew that in many situations these conditions did not obtain, especially in an age of inefficient communication networks and uncertain supply. If a fairly negotiated price was impossible, governors were instructed to impose a price based on what was often called the "common" price, usually understood as the prevailing or average market price. Because the goal was not the best price, however, but the just price, scholars also argued that in some instances prices should be fixed in accord with another standard of justice, what Aristotle had called distributive justice. In that case, neither the common nor the negotiated price was the guideline; rather, the governing principle was the good of the community as a whole and maintenance of social order. For example, in times of famine, prices might be set or supplies commandeered so that the poor could eat.

Scholastic theorists were thus, as some have told it, ahead of their time. Indeed, Giacomo Todeschini has taught us that perhaps the most famous Spiritual Franciscan of the thirteenth century, Peter John Olivi,

---

[34] Braudel, *Wheels*, p. 455.

[35] Comments on the *Summa theologica*, II, ii, qu. 77, art. I (Leonine edition, VI, 149), cited in De Roover, "The Concept of the Just Price," p. 423.

developed a sophisticated analysis of markets, merchants, and prices that eerily presaged later fifteenth-century thought and even, in significant ways, modern economic theory. In this discourse, which circulated widely among thirteenth-century scholastics, the problem with commerce was not wealth, trade, or merchants as such but individual greed. That odious vice was embodied as the usurer who "accumulates not in order to invest and distribute but in order to accumulate more and more."[36] In contrast, the "merchant" (as opposed to the "usurer") circulated wealth fairly and by doing so aided society.[37] It was he who knew how to negotiate correctly in a world of relative values and mysterious monetary systems, he who could produce the "just" market situation. In Todeschini's words, "the image which Olivi gives of the merchant is, from all accounts, less that of a commercial actor [*commerçant*] than that of a connoisseur who is knowledgeable about the mysterious connections that exist between [real] values and the prices of goods that are useful for humankind."[38] By the fourteenth century, Franciscan scholars were even arguing that the market was the expression of civic values, the place where reasoned accord and equitable exchange could be realized. By the fifteenth century, the good merchant could even be figured as the good governor, someone who disciplined himself for the benefit of a disciplined community.

These ideas, precocious in their day, gradually permeated less learned cultural texts, and not just in the South where the early theorists were concentrated. Some northern literary texts of later centuries seemed almost to echo this theory by inverting the usual trope about the evils of commerce and arguing that open trade produced plenty, benefited the entire community, and redeemed the merchant. For example, the 1561 *Landjuweel* in Antwerp (the major competition among Brabant's most prominent chambers of rhetoric, guild-like organizations that produced plays, poetry, and the like) challenged competitors to explain "how

---

[36] Giacomo Todeschini, *Richesse franciscaine: De la pauvreté volontaire à la société de marché* (Paris, 2008), p. 31.

[37] In his study of twelfth- and thirteenth-century moral thought, Le Goff similarly distinguished usury from both trade and profit-seeking: "Usury entered the picture where there was neither production nor transformation of concrete goods": *La bourse et la vie*, p. 20.

[38] Todeschini, *Richesse franciscaine*, p. 161.

proper are the smart, talented merchants who conduct their business fairly?"[39] All the plays entered in the competition distinguished the good merchant from the bad in terms of his fair dealing, but they also praised his trade for enabling him to serve the common good. The play presented by the victorious chamber even made nobles the allies of merchants by having them join to persuade reluctant peasants of the social benefits brought by trade.[40] Given that the competitions were staged and financed by Antwerp's merchants, it is no wonder that trade was celebrated, but the terms of the praise are significant.[41] Merchants were not just to be tolerated; they were to be honored. They brought goods from afar, they protected against the uncertainties both of the harvest and of markets, they paid for defense, they set up schools, they

[39] For a detailed analysis of this competition and the themes on display in the various performances, see Alexandra Kirkman Onuf, "Local Terrains: The *Small Landscape* Prints and the Depiction of the Countryside in Early Modern Antwerp" (Ph.D. diss., Columbia University, 2005). Similar competitions were held throughout the southern Low Countries in this period. For studies of the chambers, known as *rederrijkers* in Dutch, see the work of Anne-Laure Van Bruaene, including "'A Wonderfull tryumfe, for the wynnyng of a pryse,' Gilds, Ritual, Theater and the Urban Network in the Southern Low Countries, ca. 1450–1650," *Renaissance Quarterly* 59, no. 2 (Summer 2006), pp. 374–406; idem, "Sociabiliteit en competitie: De sociaal-institutionele ontwikkeling van de rederijkerskamers in de Zuidelijke Nederlanden (1400–1650)," in *Conformisten en rebellen. Rederijkerscultuur in de Nederlanden, 1400–1650*, ed. B. Ramakers (Amsterdam, 2003); and idem, "De contouren van een nieuw cultuurmodel: Rederijkers in Vlaanderen en Brabant in de zeventiende eeuw," in *Handelingen der Koninklijke Zuid-Nederlandse Maatschappij voor Taal – en Letterkunde en Geschiedenis* 58 (2005), pp. 221–37; and Peter Arnade, *Realms of Ritual: Burgundian Ceremony and Civic Life in Late Medieval Ghent* (Ithaca, NY, 1996).

[40] *Spelen van sinne, vol scone moralisacien, uutleggingen ende bediedenissen op alle loeflijcke consten* (Antwerp, 1562). See Onuf, "Local Terrains," pp. 140–50 for a detailed analysis.

[41] The plays about merchants in Antwerp were not, as An Kint has pointed out, universally laudatory; instead they often functioned more as cautionary tales, stories about what made a merchant bad rather than tales of just how good a merchant was. See An Kint, "Theater, Trade and a City's Identity: The Rhetorical Plays in Sixteenth-Century Antwerp," in *La ville à la Renaissance: Espaces, representations, pouvoir*, ed. Gérald Chaix (Paris, 2008), pp. 327–36.

supported civic activities, they provided the means to support charities, and they made Antwerp prosperous.[42]

Sixteenth-century English texts made similar claims. In the 1525 play *Gentleness and Nobility*, for example, the character of the merchant simply assumes his "nobility," boasting that the work of merchants saves the country from "beggary," bringing wealth, profit, and pleasure.[43]

> [I]f our commodities be utteryed for nought
> In to straunge landis, and no ryches brought
> Hydry therefore, we shuld come to beggary,
> And all men dryffn to lyf in mysery.
> Then we noble marchauntis that in this reame be,
> What a grete wealth to thys land do we:
> We utter our wayrs and by their good chepe,
> And bring them hyder, that grete proffet
> And pleasure dayly commyth to this region
> Too all maner people that here do won

Herman Pleij has even argued that many of the plays, poems, and stories produced throughout the late medieval Low Countries (principally in the fifteenth century) celebrated not only commerce's potential for good but also the qualities that ensured success in trade: "Enterprise, the desire for profit, approval of individual cleverness, moderation and self-control [became] principles for living."[44]

Lawmakers of the day evidently agreed that "enterprise" and "desire for profit" were the cure for "beggary," but like many of the moralists and cultural commentators, including the Franciscan friars who had

---

[42] Even Chaucer's Shipmen's Tale, which is easily read as the usual send-up of commerce, does not condemn the merchant. In fact the story turns on the priest's deceit and the wife's fibs; the merchant is portrayed as generous and kind, if a bit dim.

[43] Lines 246–55: "Gentleness and Nobility," in *Three Rastell Plays: Four Elements, Calisto and Melebea, Gentleness and Nobility*, ed. Richard Axton (Cambridge, UK, 1979); cited in Derrick Higginbotham, "All the World's A Market," p. 12.

[44] Herman Pleij, "Restyling 'Wisdom,' Remodeling the Nobility, Caricaturing the Peasant: Urban Literature in the Late Medieval Low Countries," *Journal of Interdisciplinary History* 32, no. 4 (2002), pp. 515–48; also see idem, *Het Gilde van de Blauwe Schuit. Literatuur, volksfeest en burgermoraal in de late Middeleeuwen* (Amsterdam, 1983), esp. pp. 248–50.

earlier praised the "disciplined" merchant, they did not think this cure happened automatically. In their view, commerce was destructive unless markets were open, and unless they were closely supervised, they would not be open. The nineteenth-century editors of Paris's first critical edition of guild ordinances, the *Livre des métiers* of the thirteenth century, introduced their volume with precisely this point: late medieval people, they emphasized, were convinced that markets were dangerous unless carefully regulated[45]:

> No one then would have imagined that the public could defend itself against producers of shoddy goods or against dishonest merchants, whether by denouncing them or refusing to patronize them. This notion of individual responsibility or "self government" [English in the original], applied to the ordinary business of life, would have been considered an enormity. . . . [S]ociety was based, in effect, on an implicit delegation of individual rights to the collectivity.

To carry out this logic, lawmakers everywhere took it upon themselves to punish practices such as hoarding, engrossing, and forestalling, the very sins featured in so many contemporary literary texts, not just to ensure supplies but also in pursuit of a just price.[46] For example, in Paris residents' access to food supplies was protected by a rule that allowed citizens to take a portion of the goods traded between merchants in the marketplace at the price negotiated by the merchants themselves (*le droit de partage*). Inhabitants were thereby assured that they could acquire provisions at what lawmakers considered the just price – the price obtained by the most knowledgeable bargainers. Similar objectives informed rules concerning the grain markets in sixteenth-century Lille, where residents were permitted to buy first, followed next by bakers, and only after them were merchants of milled grain finally allowed to deal.[47] In this way, it was assumed, ordinary consumers bought when

---

[45] *Les métiers et corporations de la ville de Paris: XIII siècle; Le livre des métiers d'Étienne Boileau*, eds. René Lespinasse and Francois Bonnardot (Paris, 1879), p. xi.

[46] De Roover, "The Concept of the Just Price," pp. 428ff. Also see Hans Van Werveke, "Les villes belges: Histoire des institutions économiques et sociales," in *La ville*, Vol. 2: *Institutions économiques et sociales* (Brussels, 1955).

[47] Paul Delsalle, "Façons de vendre, façons d'acheter, sur les marchés au cœur de l'Europe (XVIe siècle e première moitié du XVIIe siècle)," in *Fiere e mercati*, ed. Cavaciocchi, pp. 335–59.

supplies were plentiful and the more powerful could not corner the market. In accord with the same norm, peasants living near cities were urged, and sometimes forced, to deliver their goods to urban markets and were often forbidden to use middlemen of any kind, all in an effort to ensure supplies and their affordability. As a 1305 ordinance of Philip the Fair expressed it, "all products must be delivered to and sold in open markets, and we absolutely prohibit anyone from buying or selling provisions or foodstuffs other than in open markets and from buying wheat or other grains for resell on the same market days."[48]

Exactly as scholastic theorists advised, however, they did not seek to suppress markets themselves, and they generally seemed to respect market logics. They set retail prices only when there seemed no other way to provision the community and then only for the most basic foodstuffs or fuels, as though in conscious accord with a theory of distributive justice. Franz Irsigler has recently argued that the same logic was responsible for authorities' willingness to give local producers preferential access to markets. Although such legislation did protect the artisans who endlessly clamored for this help, its main purpose was not to aid local craftspeople, but to guarantee supply to the urban community.[49] Indeed, governors were perfectly willing to abandon the organized crafts if that seemed the best way to ensure food supplies. In 1305, for example, a royal ordinance overrode the objections of Parisian bakers (and previous legislation) in an apparent effort to guarantee regular supply: "On every day of the week, anyone may bring bread and wheat to Paris, and all other foodstuffs for sale, in complete security."[50]

---

[48] The provision was intended to prevent regratters from buying up supplies and reselling at higher prices. Although the *Livre des Métiers* of ca. 1268, ostensibly an edition of the regulations adopted by the guilds of Paris themselves, had permitted regratters to sell bread, later ordinances either omitted mention of bread as one of the products they handled or explicitly prohibited the practice. For example, a letter from the Provost from 1367 stated that "nul ne soit si hardi de revendre ne regrater pain en laditte ville, sur paine de perdre ledit pain ou sa valeur" (eds. Lespinasse and Bonnardo, *Les métiers*, p. 200).

[49] Franz Irsigler, "La fonction des foires dans l'intégration des économies européenes (Moyen-âge)," in *Fiere e mercati*, ed. Cavachiocchi, pp. 49–71.

[50] The thirteenth-century *Livre des Métiers* issued by the crafts themselves had succeeded in reinstating a rule that denied foreigners access to Parisian markets except on Saturdays (market day), justifying itself on the grounds that "the

Consumer protection could never have been the exclusive goal of lawmakers, however, for too many competing interests were in play. Governors themselves wanted market fees and excise taxes just as much as they wanted a contented populace, and they needed busy marketplaces to produce those revenues. A regulation issued to the Parisian weavers by Jean II in 1362 made exactly this case. It forbade weavers to sell in "non-customary" private places (where they might be able to avoid excise taxes) because "our rights are thereby lost and reduced, and "the Halls" (presumably *les Halles*, Paris's central marketplace) will be deserted."[51]

Tensions also fractured the community of producers and distributors. For example, master craftsmen often found themselves in fights with journeymen who did not yet have their own shops when the masters sought to give family members privileged access to the trade. For their part, merchants were often at loggerheads with artisans, especially when the craftsmen were organizing for limited work hours or direct access to raw materials. When aldermen encouraged production monopolies in the interests of quality control, small producers called foul. Consumers took to the streets when merchants threatened to corner the markets for grain or other necessities.[52] Nevertheless, none of the disputes that

bakers of Paris have paid the *taille*, contributed to the watch, and paid the *hauban* and the "custom" [fees for market rights]" (*Les métiers et corporations*, Première Partie, Titre Ier (Talemeliers), no. LIII, p. 13. For the 1305 ruling that denied that protection, see *Les métiers et corporations, Deuxième Partie: métiers de l'alimentation (Boulangers)*, I (1305, 28 avril), no. 3, p. 198.

To a certain extent, as some other scholars have noted, authorities tended to be more protective of those local crafts that supplied foodstuffs to the community than they were of crafts producing for export, for they needed above all to ensure that the population was fed, and they thus needed to keep local producers in business. In particular, see de Roover's comments in "The Concept of the Just Price," p. 428 and the sources he cites. But as the example from 1305 Paris demonstrates, even those local suppliers of foodstuffs could be sacrificed to consumer interests. Also see James Davis, "Baking for the Common Good: A Reassessment of the Assize of Bread in Medieval England," *Economic History Review* 57, no. 3 (2004), pp. 465–502.

[51] *Les métiers et corporations*: Sixième Partie: Tissus, Étoffes, Vêtement, III (1362, juillet), Lettres patentes du roi Jean, no. 19, p. 147.

[52] On the principles of monopoly that informed guild organizations, see Gunner Mickwicz, *Die Kartellfunktionen der Zünfte und ihre Bedeutung bei der Entstehung*

arose as merchants confronted artisans, as masters challenged workers, or as consumers protested suggests that regulation itself was considered a problem. The quarrels were about who should be regulated and to what end, not whether there should be regulation. Everyone seemed sure that commerce could meet no one's needs if it were not under firm control.[53]

des Zunftwesens: Eine Studie in spätantiker und mittelalterlicher Wirtschaftsgeschichte (Amsterdam, 1968) [orig. Helsinki, 1936]. For a reassessment of the role of guilds in commercialized cities of Flanders, see Peter Stabel, "Guilds in Late Medieval Flanders: Myths and Realities of Guild Life in an Export-Oriented Environment," Journal of Medieval History 30 (2004), pp. 187–212.

The Parisian Livre des métiers seemed to express a classically "guild" equation between the workplace and the family in regulating the number of apprentices. Tradesmen were strictly forbidden to employ more than one apprentice unless they were family members, in which case almost no limits applied, and "family" was defined generously to include even nephews and cousins; for example, see Les métiers et corporations de la ville de Paris: XIII siècle: Le livre des métiers d'Étienne Boileau (1879), Métiers de Paris, Première Partie, Titre XI (Orfèvres), no. IV, p. 33. The same text generally banned work at night, on holy days, and during Lent in a clear effort not just to honor sacred times or to prevent shoddy work but also to control the workday and prevent exploitation of the labor force [Les métiers et corporations de la ville de Paris: XIII siècle: Le livre des métiers d'Étienne Boileau (1879), Métiers de Paris, Première Partie, Titre LXVI (Garnisseurs de gaaines, des feiseurs de viroles, de heus, de coispeaus de laiton, d'archal et de quoivre), Titre LXVI, no. IV, pp. 136–7. However, a 1322 letter from the Provost overturned these rules: "We order and desire for the common good ("le commun prouffit"), that one is permitted to work day and night, as he wishes and seems useful, and that one can have several apprentices, even if they are not the sons of masters or apprentices, and one can pay what one wants" [Les métiers et corporations de la ville de Paris: I. XIVe–XVIIIe siècle (1886), Première Partie, Ordonnances et édits sur les métiers en général, I (1322, 19 janvier), p. 1].

On tensions within the crafts themselves, see, for example, a text from the same Livre des métiers ordering that "no weavers or dyers or fullers [i.e., masters in these trades] should collude to fix prices, which would prevent members in the craft from taking small orders [presumably at higher prices] and would allow [other] members to sell as cheaply as they wanted" (Les métiers et corporations de la ville de Paris: XIII siècle: Le livre des métiers d'Étienne, Métiers de Paris, Première Partie, Titre L (Tisserands), no. XXXV, p. 98.

[53] For a recent discussion of this issue and a good guide to the literature, see Gervase Rosser, "Crafts, Guilds, and the Negotiation of Work in the Medieval

In short, commerce had to be supervised if it was going to be transparent. This apparently contradictory principle explains the rules governing the classic fixed marketplace of medieval Europe. From a modern point of view (and certainly from the point of view of seventeenth- and eighteenth-century reformers) these market squares might seem archaic residues of a medieval past, sites of restriction, privilege, and monopoly. Both in inspiration and function, however, they expressed a norm that neoclassical theory would assign to modern marketplaces such as the New York Stock Exchange in its pre-Internet days. Such "closed" markets facilitated the face-to-face contact between buyer and seller that in this period played so central a role in legitimating a transaction. In doing so, they also allowed consumers to compare offerings, compelled sellers to display their wares, and in general created a space where information about supply, quality, and price was available to all. The same logic inspired governors to confine markets, usually by type of good being traded (the fish market or the wool market, for example), sometimes by type of transaction (retail/wholesale), sometimes by identity of the traders (locals in one place, "foreigners" in another). Such

Town," *Past and Present* 154 (February 1997), pp. 3–31, and Catharina Lis and Hugo Soly, "Ambachtsgilden en vergelijkenheid perspectief: de Noordelijke en zuidelijke Nederlanden, 15de–18de euw," in *idem*, eds., *Werelden van Verschil: Ambachtsgilden in de Lage Landen* (Brussels, 1997), pp. 11–42. Also see Heather Swanson, "The Illusion of Economic Structure: Craft Guilds in Late Medieval English Towns," *Past and Present* 121 (November, 1988), pp. 29–48, who emphasizes the extent to which guilds were creatures of municipal governors.

As Jean-Pierre Sosson has recently reminded us, however, most of the records we have, even the judicial records that track disputes about enforcement of such laws, foreground the normative and tend to obscure actual practice: Jean-Pierre Sosson, "Les métiers: norme et réalité: L'exemple des anciens Pays-Bas méridionaux aux XIVe et XVe siècles," in *Le travail au Moyen Âge*, eds. J. Hamesse and C. Muraille (Louvain-la-Neuve, 1990). In particular, we know too little about the thousands of workers seldom touched by such regulations: women, children, and the hoards of other unorganized workers. On this general point see P. J. P. Goldberg, "Female Labour, Service and Marriage," *Northern History* xxii (1986), pp. 18–38; Martha C. Howell, "Women's Work in the New and Light Draperies of the Low Countries," in *The New Draperies in the Low Countries and England, 1300–1800*, ed. Negley Harte (Oxford, 1997); Swanson, "Illusion"; and Rosser, "Crafts."

restrictions "forced a market" precisely as a modern economist might define it.[54] Even the trade that did not take place in formally situated market squares was informed by this logic. Long-distance merchants made deals and settled accounts at fairs whose principal functions were to generate a market and to govern the trade therein. Formal market-places were the visible center and the controlling standard of commerce, and no one thought that commerce could function properly without such supervision.

Expressions of these principles can be found almost everywhere. For example, a 1407 ruling of the Parlement of Paris required that all cloth merchants who were not members of the official weavers' *conférie* sell only in the *halle d'en haut*, whether at wholesale or retail, or at an assigned corner of the wool hall (*au bout de la halle à lainne*) where cloth was customarily sold at retail.[55] And another confined foreign merchants to the *halles d'en haut*, specifically prohibiting sales "in rooms" (*en chambres*) or in other "secret places" (*lieux secrez*).[56] Such rules surely allowed easier supervision of quality, but quality was only one aspect of their com-mitment to open markets. Both publicity and supervision – publicity in order to facilitate supervision – were necessary to ensure fair prices and commutative justice. This was the logic of what Braudel alter-nately called "economic life," the "normal market," and "transparent" exchange. Legislators seems to have been certain that only vigorous application of this principle could harness commercial power for the individual and general good.

---

[54] For a fuller statement of how these principles were applied in sixteenth-century Lille, see Delsalle, "Façon de vendre," p. 338: "Mais, au délà de cas particuliers, et exceptionnels, l'access au marché est prèsque toujours libre, dès que la cloche a sonné, cependant pas pour tout le monde au meme moment." ("But, outside of these particular and exceptional cases, access to the market was almost always free once the clock sounded, but not, however, for everyone at the same moment.")

[55] *Les métiers et corporations de la ville de Paris III. XIVe–XVIIIe siècle* (1897): Sixième Partie: Tissus, Étoffes, Vêtement, III (Arrêt de Parlement), #7, p. 156.

[56] *Les métiers et corporations de la ville de Paris III. XIVe–XVIIIe siècle* (1897): Sixième Partie: Tissus, Étoffes, Vêtement, III (Arrêt de Parlement), #9, p. 157.

An ordinance of 1351 issued by Jean II for Parisian merchants expressed the norms almost perfectly[57]:

It is ordered that all foreign merchants who bring any kind of merchandise or provisions to the city of Paris in order to sell them must take them to *les Halles* and the customary public marketplaces and may not sell them elsewhere, at the risk of losing their goods and paying fines. And further, no merchants, whether from Brabant or elsewhere, who bring or are accustomed to bringing to Paris shoes, *houreaux* [high leather boots or chaps], hats of beaver or fur, saddles, bridles, boots, candles made of fat or other materials, *patins* [high-heeled slippers], spurs, canvases, arms and other goods for sale, or those who buy them for resale in Paris, may take them into their houses for resale, [and may sell nowhere] except in the said marketplaces or in public places, at the risk of the above mentioned punishments. And should anyone suspect that any of these goods are not authentic or well made [*loyalux et souffisant*], they must inform the Provost. . . . [A]nd if any Parisian merchant goes elsewhere to foreign places to buy merchandise, he may not bring it to, sell it in, or have it sold in any place except *les Halles* and the places above mentioned. . . . [A]nd the same applies to foreign merchants. . . . [B]ut, all merchants from other places who want to sell goods in Paris may do so securely and without any hesitation.

As this ordinance suggests, market transparency also extended to production, for goods had to be "loyally" and "sufficiently" made to meet the standard of transparency. Cloth, the principal industrial good

---

[57] *Les métiers et corporations de la ville de Paris* (1886), Première Partie, II. Ordonannces de Jean, 30 jan., 1351, Titre XIV.

What I have termed "the struggle for market transparency" would have a long legacy in French economic thought. As a recent series of studies has illuminated, historians of Old Regime economic thought are steadily eroding an old narrative that had resolutely traced the emergence of liberal thought (understood as free trade little fettered by regulation) from critics of mercantilism to the Physiocrats and then on to people like Jean-Baptiste Say. See Judith A. Miller, "Economic Ideologies, 1750–1800: The Creation of the Modern Political Economy?" *French Historical Studies* 23, no. 3 (Summer 2000), pp. 497–511 and Simone Meyssonier, *La balance et l'horloge: La genèse de la pensée libérale en France au XVIII siècle* (Paris, 1989). Instead, what Miller called "a distinctly French version of liberalism" emphasized the importance of law both as "stimulator and regulator of the market" in the interests of the common good.

of the commercial revolution, went through multiple inspections to ensure that it was worthy of bearing the city's seal, which certified its quality and provenance to buyers who had few other means for verifying its identity and who typically ordered it through factors who had themselves seen only samples. To be sure, the fees imposed along the way fed the governors' treasuries, but this purpose was inseparable from the more generalized objective of providing the information that would effectively "open" the market. This transparency was not only the condition of "good" commerce; it was also the condition of a smoothly functioning commercial economy. As Peter Stabel has recently argued in speaking of the Low Countries, "the overall concern of the authorities [aldermen and guildsmen alike] was to guarantee fair trade, market transparency, safety for the various parties, and provide the ideal conditions in which the parties could meet."[58]

VIRTUOUS CONSUMERS AND RESPONSIBLE PROVIDERS

Rescuing commerce required more, however, than cleansing market practices. No matter how fairly conducted, commerce awakened greed and lust, too easily turning people into ravenous consumers for whom material things, rather than spiritual experience, were the objects of desire. However, the cure could not be suppression of consumption, for the populace had to be fed, clothed, and housed; the rich had to have luxuries; and commercial people needed to survive. The task, then, was to make gathering and spending wealth ethical. That task was taken up, and to a significant extent accomplished, by turning women into virtuous consumers and men into responsible providers.

Although a story about gender, this was also a story about class, for it featured a single social group – prosperous commercial people in cities and the countryside. The leading actors came primarily from northwestern Europe, where this class was taking its clearest form, but also from the South, where the commercial revolution had begun. These

---

[58] Peter Stabel, "Markets in the Cities of the Late Medieval Low Countries: Retail, Commercial Exchange and Socio-cultural Display," in *Fiere e mercati*, ed. Cavaciocchi, pp. 797–818, p. 808.

people were not numerically dominant in Europe at the beginning of the period and not even at its end. Nor were they the most powerful, not in 1600 and not even in 1700, except in a few places like the Italian cities where commerce had turned merchants into urban princes or in the Dutch republic where such men had taken the reins of government. Throughout the rest of Europe, landholding aristocrats still ruled, and they would long claim cultural hegemony, only slowly and often reluctantly entering commerce themselves or allowing commercial people to join their ranks. But in the end commercial people triumphed, making the modern period of western history the age of the bourgeoisie.

At the center of this gender history was the emergence of a new, socially differentiated sexual division of labor. As described in Chapter 2, at the beginning of the long period constituting what we call the commercial revolution, ordinary women played a largely unchallenged role in market production, taking an essential, if clearly subordinate, part in the workshops and market stalls of their fathers and husbands and sometimes managing their own small businesses. However, by its end, the wives and daughters of more prosperous artisans and merchants were being gradually edged out of direct participation in the market. At the same time, marital property regimes that had once implicitly recognized women's ability to manage commercial property were being rewritten, a process also described in Chapter 2, to assign these women the relatively passive task of carrying property from fathers to husbands and then on to children. Although the wives and widows of small retailers and simple craftsmen, along with poor women, did not exit commerce at the same rate, if at all, the women married to merchants, rich shopkeepers, and master craftsmen in elite trades were taking another route toward the future. Quietly and ever more tentatively submerging any work for the market or any assets they brought to the marriage under the umbrella of their husbands' business, they were adjusting to a new role as manager of a domestic space ideologically separated from market production.[59]

---

[59] Although, as Davidoff and Hall have shown, they could play a key role in financing the household enterprise by means of their dowries and the connections to their own families, which could be direct and indirect sources of capital: Davidoff and Hall, *Family Fortunes*. Bourgeois women also continued to work actively in market production in some places beyond this period, as Bonnie Smith has documented (in the *Nord* in France); there too, however, they gradually retreated: Smith, *Ladies of the Leisure Class*. According to Steven Kaplan,

In fact, the space of the market was coming to be considered danger-ous for proper women, even in northern cities like Cologne or London where exclusively female guilds had existed, some of them populated by women from prosperous artisanal families. As Barbara Hanawalt has reminded us, the fifteenth-century English poem "What the Goodwife Taught Her Daughter" cautioned that a woman in any public space acquired "an yvel name"; to avoid scandal, the daughter was instructed to dress carefully, walk "modestly," and speak quietly when on the streets or in the marketplace.[60] As Joan Scott has eloquently argued, nineteenth-century French polemicists would make good use of these tropes in their own political vendettas, labeling the female wage worker (the *l'ouvrière*) *impie* and *sordide* and the laboring woman's availability to the market a sign that her sexuality, like her labor, was for sale.

It was in this context that women from prosperous commercial fam-ilies turned their energies to a newly privatized domestic space. There they were absorbing the lessons imparted by the conduct books and housekeeping manuals of the period, which taught that a woman's job was to manage consumption in her husband's interests, carefully choos-ing and wisely using the treasures he brought home. This monotonously repeated instruction did crucial ideological work. It not only defanged

Parisian married and widowed women also remained active in grain broker-age into the eighteenth century: Steven Kaplan, *Provisioning Paris* (Ithaca, NY, 1984), esp. p. 501. For an argument based on such evidence – that women's exit from market production and the associated social model of "separate spheres" were more an ideological construct than a social reality – see Amanda Vickery, "Golden Age to Separate Spheres? A Review of the Categories and Chronology of English Women's History," *Historical Journal* 36, no. 2 (1993), pp. 383–414. Be that as it may, this ideological construct had material bases and material con-sequences. Women may still have participated in market production – not just poor women or the wives of small shopkeepers, but richer women as well – but there is no doubt that the latter were in steady retreat from active participation. For an attempt to reconcile the apparently contradictory evidence that women were being driven from (or were voluntarily exiting) market production even while many continued to run shops, help in their husbands' businesses, and take part in household financial management, see Collins, "The Economic Role of Women."

[60] Barbara A. Hanawalt, "Medieval English Women in Rural and Urban Domestic Space," *Dumbarton Oaks Papers* 52 (1998), pp. 19–26, p. 22. The same lesson is imparted in the *Ménagier de Paris* of the same period.

consumption by domesticating it, but it also provided ideological justification for men's control of productive assets. Just as wise consumption
was woman's duty and the home her space, these books taught that wise
production was man's and the market his realm.

In 1580, the Italian moralist Torquato Tasso put it this way:

> It is well ordered that . . . the office of acquiring should be attributed to the man
> and that of preserving to the woman. The man struggles to acquire and carries out
> farming or operates in commerce in the city. . . . But the woman looks after that
> which been acquired and her virtues are employed inside the house, just as the
> man demonstrates his outside.[61]

Juan Luis Vives's 1523 *Institutio foeminae christianae* was the implicit
and often explicit model for such texts. Nowhere was its impact better
registered than in the Low Countries, where the cozy domestic interior
and the industrious housewife would serve as the antidote to what Simon
Schama has memorably called "the embarrassment of riches."[62] There,
moralists repeatedly issued *exempla* describing the good housewife as a
nurturer of family and domesticity, and painters set out to illustrate
Vives's instructions. Heemskerck's well-known print series of 1555,
Praise of the Virtuous Wife, was typical. Although one of the six prints
displays the wife selling the cloth she has woven and another has her
buying a piece of land, all her buying and selling are for her family;
her activities in the market represent her as the good consumer and
household manager, not as a player in commerce. Another three prints
have her spinning, dressing her family, serving their meals, and the last
one pictures her bestowing a crown on the husband she serves.[63]

[61] Torquato Tasso, *Discorso della virtú feminile e donnesca*, ed. Maria Luisa Doglio
(Palermo: Sellerio, 1997), pp. 56–7, quoted in Evelyn Welch, *Shopping in
the Renaissance: Consumer Cultures in Italy 1400–1600* (New Haven, 2005),
pp. 221–2 [her translation].

[62] Simon Schama, *The Embarrassment of Riches: An Interpretation of Dutch Culture in
the Golden Age* (London, 1987).

[63] These images are reproduced and described in Ilja M. Veldman, "Lessons for
Ladies: A Selection of Sixteteenth- and Seventeenth-Century Dutch Prints,"
Simiolus: Netherlands Quarterly for the History of Art 16, no. 2 (1986), pp. 113–
27.

Figure 25. *Provisioning the Household.*
Dirck Volkertsz Coornhert (after Maarten van Heemskerck), *The Woman Selling Her Wares to a Merchant*, from the series *Praise of the Virtuous Wife* (1555), engraving. Vienna, Albertina.

Such images and texts insisted that women had important work in the house, and although that did not preclude contact with the market economy, a wife's place was "inside," a husband's "outside." England was no different; there, for example, an early seventeenth-century text almost repeated the Italian language of a generation earlier:

The dutie of the Husband is to get goods; and of the Wife to gather them together, and save them. The dutie of the Husband is to travel abroad, to seeke [a] living; and the Wives dutie is to keep the house. The dutie of the Husband is to get money and provision; and of Wives, not vainly to spend it.[64]

[64] Robert Cleaver, *A Godlie Forme of Householde Government: For the Ordering of Private Families, According to the Direction of Gods Word* (London, 1612), pp. 167–8, quoted in Alexandra Shepard, "Manhood, Credit and Patriarchy in Early Modern England, c. 1580–1640," *Past and Present* 167 (2000),

It was the same in German-speaking cities. As Heidi Wunder has explained, patrician and upper middle-class women in these places "began to limit themselves to organizational tasks in the household and devoted more time to decorating the living spaces in a stately manner and enjoying a 'homey' life with their children and husbands." Although Wunder admits that the wives of middling artisans could not depend on servants as their richer neighbors could, she argues that even for them domesticity "began to determine their work roles. In the process, a woman's position as mistress of a household with authority over children and domestics became much more important."[65]

Scholars have rightly been cautious about taking conduct books as literal descriptions of practice. However, these tracts are useful evidence for historians, for they articulate a vision of womanhood that would serve to demarcate class, and it is perhaps that function that made them so attractive a model for behavior. These "good housewives" – a group that ideologically could include the shopkeeper's spouse as well as the alderman's wife – would never spend wastefully or wantonly; they would leave it to the aristocrats to dress fancifully and to the poor to try to copy that flamboyance with second- and thirdhand goods. Freed from the sins associated with commerce's wildness, these women were not the voracious, undisciplined – even sexually available – consumers depicted in sumptuary legislation or comic literature; nor were they the public

pp. 75–106. For the way these tropes were endlessly reproduced in drama, see Natasha Korda, *Shakespeare's Domestic Economies: Gender and Property in Early Modern England* (Philadelphia, 2002); and for an exploration of the relationship between male and female honor in this ideology, Faramerz Dabhoiwala, "The Construction of Honour, Reputation and Status in Late Seventeenth- and Early Eighteenth-Century England," *Transactions of the Royal Historical Society* 6th ser., 6 (1996), pp. 201–13.

[65] Wunder, *He is the Sun*, p. 81. For examples of German conduct books of the period, see Paul Münch, ed., *Ordnung, Fleiss, und Sparsamkeit: Texte und Dokumente zur Entstehung der 'bürgerlichen Tugenden'* (Munich, 1984); Helmut Puff, "Die Ehre der Ehe: Beobachtungen zum Konzept der Ehre in der Frühen Neuzeit an Johann Fischarts 'Philosophisch Ehzuchtbüchlein' (1578) und anderen Ehelehren des 16. Jahrhunderts," in *Ehrkonzepte in der Frühen Neuzeit: Identitäten und Abgrenzungen*, eds. Sibylle Backmann, Hans-Jörg Künast, Sabine Ullmann, and B. Ann Tlusty (Berlin, 1998), pp. 99–119; and Steven Ozment, *When Fathers Ruled: Family Life in Reformation Europe* (Cambridge, 1983).

women whose labor was for sale and whose bodies were on public display. They were the wise managers of tasteful consumption, the people who tamed it by being themselves tamed.

The narrative that excluded proper women from active participation in market production simultaneously gave men exclusive control of it. In truth, the man of the market might be an adventurer and cheater, and he might need his wife's money or require her labor as bookkeeper or shop assistant. However, the emergent discourse about the man of "credit" denied that possibility, making him both a trustworthy businessman and a responsible householder who was fully in control of his family and an active participant in governance of his community. As the rhetorician's play from Antwerp described earlier in this chapter put it and as fifteenth-century Italian theorists had earlier insisted, he was the source of money for defense, schools, and charities; the protector against uncertain markets and bad harvests; and the guarantor of urban prosperity. Like his wife, however, he disciplined commerce through self-discipline. She learned to consume wisely; he governed himself in order to govern both the economy and the polity.

To be sure, tricksters and liars still lurked on the borders of the image of the man of "credit," reminding everyone of just what perfidy was possible – just as the image of the vain and silly woman liable to whoredom threatened the industrious housewife, the tasteful consumer, and the conjugal household in which such women served. These tropes, used in such texts as the fifteenth-century *Play of the Sacrament* or the later *Jew of Malta*, *Merchant of Venice*, and the French comedy *La Trésorie*, would long circulate.[66] But alongside them circulated their antidote – conduct books, plays, stories, and poems that featured civic-minded merchants and honest tradesmen whose well-ordered households were graced by women who bought and sold – not to satisfy their vanity but to serve their families. These were fictions, but they did nonfiction work by marking the boundaries of honor and encouraging discipline.

No age of western history, including our own, has been free of anxieties about commerce's destructive capacity, and every period has struggled

---

[66] For a reading of *La Trésorie*, a relatively obscure Renaissance comedy that emphasizes the problem of money and commerce in sixteenth-century France, see Parsons, "Money and Merit."

to harness its power for individual and social good. But not every period has defined the dangers in the same way or sought identical remedies. During the late Middle Ages, when commerce was relentlessly escaping the enclaves where it had long been insecurely sequestered and was for the first time settling into broad regions of western Europe, no one imagined that unfettered commerce could benefit society as a whole. On the contrary: princes, moralists, theologians, even the very people who lived from trade knew commerce to be both a danger to society and a serious spiritual threat. Hence, when they endorsed and sought to establish open markets, they were not precociously anticipating liberal market theory; they were announcing that only transparent trade could be just. When they ideologically assigned consumption to the newly confined "virtuous housewife" of conduct literature, they were not celebrating its capacity to produce economic growth or encourage sociability as eighteenth-century commentators sought to do. They were relegating consumption to a place able to contain women's lust for things and were directing their labor toward supporting the male role in the marketplace, where public power lay.

But the commercial ideology of this age was not a continuation of the past.[67] During the earlier centuries of the Middle Ages, moralists had indeed tolerated material accumulation, but they had generally done so by arguing that riches were the source of the charity expected of Christians and the *largesse* and *liberalité* necessary for rule. When they argued that merchants should be accepted if not exactly honored, their claim was essentially that merchants provided necessary goods or that, as Olivi argued, they could deliver goods at a fair price because they knew how

---

[67] The literature on the broader debates about the social benefits of consumption, even greed, in the eighteenth century, when a way was unsteadily being found to celebrate consumption, is summarized in Berg and Eger, "The Rise and Fall of the Luxury Debates," pp. 7–28; also see Istn Hunt and Michael Ignatieff, eds. *Wealth and Virtue: The Shaping of Political Economy in the Scottish Enlightenment* (Cambridge, UK, 1983); Hirschman, *The Passions and the Interests*; and John Pocock, *Virtue, Commerce, and History: Essays on Political Thought and History, Chiefly in the Eighteenth Century* (Cambridge, UK, 1985). John Shovlin's more recent *The Political Economy of Virtue: Luxury, Patriotism, and the Origins of the French Revolution* (Ithaca, NY, 2006) provides a full account of these debates in eighteenth-century France.

to reckon material values. But these medieval commentators, no matter how cautiously appreciative of merchants, did not offer the discourses of market transparency, feminine virtue, and masculine responsibility of later centuries. The centuries that closed the Middle Ages and began the modern period thus gave commerce a wider terrain; no longer was it possible to flatly condemn the energetic pursuit of profit or to treat consumption as lust. Commerce was not only necessary and merchants capable of public service, but it also could be an active source of moral good – if, and only if, the purveyors, producers, and consumers of its products were under firm control.

Afterword

Few scholars would argue that the commercial economy of the three centuries before 1600 was capitalist if by that term we understand an early version of the modern western economy. Nevertheless, the story of how the modern western economy grew out of these centuries, or how it failed to do so as quickly as might be expected, dominates scholarly literature concerning this period's economic and social practices. Marxist scholars have taken this approach most forthrightly. Labeling the period "the transition to capitalism," they have searched, for example, for the first signs of modern class formations, for the moments when landlords began to treat their property as economic investments, or for the events that turned small producers into propertyless wage workers.[1] Even scholars less convinced about the inevitability of the transition and dubious about Marxist categories have concentrated on identifying the causal relations that linked the fourteenth or the sixteenth century with the eighteenth, nineteenth, or twentieth.

However instructive this scholarship has been, such a framework ineluctably gives us a naturalized model of the modern economy with "laws" and a logic so immutable that its only history can be the story of its discovery. Scholars working within such a framework have thus been led to search for the setting, the moment, or the set of circumstances that allowed "it" to emerge. The economic history of fourteenth-century commercial giants like Venice or Bruges thus easily becomes the story

[1] For a discussion of the role of commerce in capitalism's emergence in Marxist literature, see Sweezy et al., *The Transition from Feudalism to Capitalism*, especially pp. 31–68. For additional literature, see note 4, "Introduction."

of capitalism's birth. Such a frame evokes something like a biological narrative, as though "the market economy" of modernity was the harvest of a seed that contained, even in 1300, the DNA of the future. It also freezes the future, as though there was a moment in the modern centuries when "the market" or "capitalism" reached its predestined maturity and the perfected form written into its genetic code.[2]

This book has sought to rescue this period from such a historiography, in part because it risks making these three centuries little more than a way station between the medieval and modern. Although there is no doubt that modern capitalism took shape by building on sociocultural foundations that existed long before Europeans had a word for the concept, the structure in place in 1600 looked very little like the new construction to come. If we want to understand that original, we need to study it without the lens of the future. Otherwise, we will never be able to appreciate, for example, what merchants and artisans of cities like Ghent thought they were doing when they gave gifts that to us look like salaries or when they insisted that all property was freely alienable but then shielded a huge proportion of it from the market. We risk turning them into infantile – and not very bright – versions of ourselves.

---

[2] Many economic historians have warned of this risk, but it has proven very difficult to escape what John Munro called "a progress-oriented narrative." The title of James Murray's recent *Bruges: Cradle of Capitalism* unambiguously evokes the teleology, and its jacket calls Bruges "an early model of a great capitalist city." Jean Favier's *De l'or et des épices: naissance de l'homme d'affaires au moyen age* (literally translated as "From Gold and Spices: The Birth of the Businessman in the Middle Ages,"), although an admirable exposition of how the abstraction of wealth produced by financial techniques made "business" possible, tells an even more celebratory version of the same progressive story. Even studies that expose the stubborn nonlinearity of the story of capitalism's past do not escape the narrative of "becoming." A recent collection of essays called *Early Modern Capitalism: Economic and Social Change in Europe, 1400–1800*, for example, ruefully concludes its introduction lamenting that the essays yield no theory about capitalism's birth. Instead, they tell a meandering tale of stops and starts, of "fast-track regions and those traveling along more traditional routes at slower speeds . . . [when] over at least three centuries capitalism was struggling to emerge from a largely non-capitalist world.": Maarten Prak, ed., *Early Modern Capitalism: Economic and Social Change in Europe, 1400–1800* (London, 2001). p. 9.

As importantly, such a lens actually obscures rather than exposes important connections between this age and the next centuries. Had changes of the kinds described in the previous five chapters not occurred as they did, modern capitalist society would not have developed as it did. For example, it is obvious that had some version of the process by which Gentenaren learned to redefine property as capital not occurred in many other places of Europe, the market economy would have been frozen, isolated as one segment of an economy still dominated by subsistence production and nonmarket exchange. Similarly, had marriage not been reinforced by a new emphasis on conjugal love as described in my second case study, nuclear households might not have become the powerful accumulators of capital that they became. Had gifts not secured personal honor as I argued in Chapter 3, there could have been no men whose "credit" allowed them to assemble riches vast enough to finance kings, to purchase their own social mobility, and eventually to take the reins of government. Had the struggle to enforce sumptuary laws not compelled people to reconsider the relationship between material representations of identity and identity itself, it is hard to imagine how Westerners could have become the voracious consumers of modernity. Had moralists, lawmakers, and cultural commentators not found a way to allow trade, consumption, and commercial people into their moral economy, the so-called bourgeois revolutions of the modern centuries could not have taken place.

This groundwork is hidden from us, however, if we treat Ghent's fish market as an embryonic form of the mall. Even though such marketplaces institutionalized rules about transparency and access that are fundamental to modern economic life, they were hardly sites where "faceless buyers and sellers, households and firms . . . [met] . . . for an instant to exchange standardized goods at equilibrium prices," as Avner Greif put it (quoting Ben-Porath) in describing exchange in a modern capitalist market.[3] We would be guilty of the same kind of anachronism if we thought that when Elizabeth I chose her gowns she was playing today's fashion game. Although the extravagance of her dress may have so overloaded the cultural circuits that she helped produce the more skeptical, even ironic, attitude toward clothing typical of modern

---

[3] For the Greif quotation from Ben-Porath, see note 9, "Introduction."

Westerners, Elizabeth was by no means playing a game and she did not think of her costumes as "fashion." For her, dress was deadly serious politics, an unambiguous claim to monopolize power.

In regard to the relationship between then and now, however, my study does offer a direct lesson. If we can fully appreciate that the practices I have described surrounding, for example, inheritance or gift-giving reflected cultural assumptions about property and its role in establishing social bonds that were particular to late medieval society, we will be better able to see that the buying and selling, investing and disinvesting characteristic of modern western society are expressions of no less fundamental and just as particular understandings about property and social order.[4] Hence, although this book was begun as an effort to understand some puzzling or little examined features of economic and social practices in late medieval commercial centers like Ghent, its general claim that economic systems are historically specific sociocultural systems has implications for the contemporary global economy. Like the people in fifteenth-century Bruges or Antwerp, people in Delhi, Lagos, or Beijing today (or for that matter in Toledo, Ohio, or Houston, Texas) are confronting a world where property is changing form and place with astonishing and unprecedented speed. As it does, their sense of themselves and their relationship with others will change, but just how the changes occur, and what kind of changes they may be, will depend as much on how these people have traditionally used and understood material goods as on any logic inherent in economic "laws." Unless we understand those traditions, we cannot hope to predict the future. However, we can be sure that these places will experience no "transition" to the kind of capitalist market society that defines the modern West, for they belong to a world economy that looks very little like Europe of 1600.

---

[4] For a recent critique of modern economic theory that concentrates on its inability to take account of culture, see Odd Langholm, *The Legacy of Scholasticism in Economic Thought: Antecedents of Choice and Power* [Historical Perspectives on Modern Economics] (Cambridge, 1998).

Appendix I: Monies of Account Used in Contemporary Accounts and Conversion Ratios of Principal Currencies

Several systems of account were used during this period; in the fourteenth century the pound *payement* was typically used, to be replaced by the pound *groot* in the fifteenth. The pound *miten* and the pound *parisis*, sometimes more specifically labeled the pound *parisis monnie de Flandre* (in contradistinction to the old French pound *parisis*), were also employed in the region. The Flemish *groot* was the basis of all these systems so that

Pound *groot* (lb. gr. Vl.): 240 *groten*
= 6 "pounds of 40 *groten*," each with 40 *groten**
= 12 "pounds parisis monnaie de Flandre" (mdf), each with 20 groten
= 24 "pounds *mitten*," each with 10 *groten*
= 40 "pounds *payement*," each with 6 *groten*

After the unification of the coinages of the Burgundian Netherlands in 1433–5, the former moneys of the other principalities were tied in fixed relationships to the new Burgundian coinage, which was in effect a continuation of the money of Flanders. Thereafter the pound *groot* of Flanders equaled

1 lb., 10s. *groot* of Brabant
6 lbs. of Artois
6 pounds of Holland

* The pound of 40 *groten* was originally set to equal the gold *Rheingulden* of the Electors in the 1440s and thus referred to as the "gulden." That name was retained even as the value of the *Rheingulden* itself rose in the course of the century, reaching 42 Flemish *groten* in 1467 and 90 in 1488.

12 *livres tournois* of Hainault

12 *livres parisis* of Flanders (i.e., the pound *parisis*, m[monnaie] d[e]
f[landre])

The value of the Flemish *groot* declined in the course of the fourteenth and fifteenth centuries in relationship to the relatively stable gold
Florentine florin (and other comparably stable coins). The following figures suggest the slope of the decline (taken from MEMDB, Rutgers
University, Spufford Data Set):

In 1317, florin = ca. 13 gr.
In 1354, florin = ca. 20 gr.
In 1370s, florin = ca. 30 gr.
In 1399, florin = ca. 33 gr.
In 1410s, florin = ca. 40 gr.
In 1440s, florin = ca. 50 gr.
In 1470s, florin = ca. 50–60 gr.
In 1500, florin = ca 65–75 gr.

The French gold *écu* was commonly used in commerce throughout
this region. The *chaise à l'écu* was first struck in 1337 by Philip VI; in
1385 it was replaced by the *écu à la couronne* and then the *écu au soleil*.
Approximate equivalents in various monies of account of the region are
listed as follows (rates are taken from Douaisien archival sources and
MEMDB, Rutgers University, Spufford Data Set):

1337: *chaise à l'écu* = 20 *sous tournois* (ca. 20 *groten*)
1362: *écu* = 20 *groten*
1377: *écu* = 20 *groten*
Late 14th century: *écu (vieux)* = 29 *groten*,
1400: *écu à la couronne* – 37 *sous parisis mdf* (ca. 30 *groten*)
1421: *écu à la couronne* = 42 *groten*
1433: *écu à la couronne* = 50 *gros mdf* (50 *groten*)
1441: *écu* = 48 *sous mdf* (48 *groten*)
1495: *écu* = 48 *sous mdf* (48 *groten*)

The *franc*, originally a gold coin (the principal French coin between
1360 and 1380s), was also used as a money of account in the southern
Low Countries, where it was set at 33 *sous* in the *livres parisis mdf*

(or 33 *groten*; rates are taken from Douaisien archival sources and MEMDB, Rutgers University, Spufford Data Set).

1360: *franc* = 20 *sous livres tournois* (ca. 20 *groten*)
1374: *franc* = 36 *sous mdf* (36 *groten*)
1378: *franc du roy* = 36 *groten*
1388: *franc d'or de France* = 33 *sous mdf* (33 *groten*)
1390: *franc francais* = 33 *sous mdf* (33 *groten*)
1391: *franc d'or* = 33 *groten* (33 *groten*)

Appendix II: Daily Wage of a Master Mason in Bruges, in Flemish d. gr.*

1341–50: 5.0
1351–60: 5.6
1361–70: 7.4
1371–80: 8.4
1381–90: 9.8
1391–1400: 9.4
1401–10: 10.0
1411–20: 10.0
1421–30: 10.0
1431–40: 10.9
1441–50: 11.0
1451–1500: 11.0

For more detailed records of wages, see, for Bruges, Etienne Scholliers, "Lonen te Brugge en in het Brugse Vrije (XVe–XVIIe eeuw)," in C. Verlinden, *Dokumenten voor de geschiedenis van prijzen en lonen in Vlaanderen en Brabant* [Werken Rijksuniverseiteit Gent II] (Bruges, 1965), pp. 87–160; and, for Ghent, Walter Prevenier, "Prix et salaries dans les domains des abbayes gantoises (13e–14e siècles)," in C. Verlinden, *Dokumenten voor de geschiedenis van prijzen en lonen in Vlaanderen en Brabant* [Werken Rijksuniversiteit Gent IV] (Bruges, 1973), pp. 230–325.

* From: John H. Munro, "Changing Patterns of Colours and Values of Woollen Textiles in the Southern Low Countries, 1300–1550: The Anti-Red Shift – to the Dark Side," *Working Paper Archive of Department of Economics and Institute for Policy Analysis* (JEL Classification: F10, L11, L15, L67, M30, N63, N93, O52).

Bibliography

Primary Sources (Manuscript)

Archives Municipales de Douai (AMD)

Séries FF

Dossiers Referenced in their Entirety

FF 290
FF 291
FF 292
FF 609
FF 610
FF 616

Documents Referenced (Dates Modernized)

FF 448 (16 December 1438)
FF 594/780 (11 October 1389)
FF 600/1258 (29 May 1402).
FF 612/1934 (1433)
FF 613/2069 (1436)
FF 615/2208 (1439)
FF 616/2321 (23 April 1441)
FF 616/2366 (21 September 1442)
FF 616/2347 (26 November 1441)
FF 639/4288 (1 May 1495)
FF 655/5551 (5 March 1555)
FF 655/5564 (8 November 1558)

FF 655/5582 (1 February 1567)
FF 655/5584 (25 August 1570)
FF 861 (August 1270)
FF 861 (December 1303)
FF 862 (May 1327)
FF 862 (August 1328)
FF 862 (26 January 1355)
FF 869 (13 April 1402)
FF 869 (3 August 1402)
FF 869 (22 May 1403)
FF 869 (19 September 1403)
FF 869 (25 March 1405), FF 869 (4 June 1405)
FF 875 (28 April 1443)
FF 875 (15 July 1443)

Stadsarchief Gent (Document Referenced)

Gedele 330, #39, fols. 133–4 (13 April 1491).

Primary Sources (Published)

Alberti, Leon Battista. *Libri della famiglia*. Edited by Ruggiero Romano and Alberto Tenenti. Turin: Einaudi, 1969.

Aquinas, Thomas. *Opera omnia*. Edited by Leo XIII. 48 vols. Rome: Ex typographia Polyglotta, 1882–.

———. *De regno, ad regem Cypri*. Westport, CT: Hyperion Press, 1979.

Atkinson, J. A., and B. Flynn, eds. *Darlington Wills and Inventories, 1600–1625*, Newcastle upon Tyne: Athenaeum Press, 1993.

Bastian, Franz, ed. *Das Runtingerbuch 1383–1407 und verwandtes Material zum Regensburger-südostdeutschen Handel und Munzwesen*. 3 vols, Deutsche Handelsakten des Mittelalters und der Neuzeit, 6–7. Regensburg, Ger., 1935–44.

Beaumanoir, Philippe de Remi. *Coutumes de Beauvaisis*. Edited by Amédée Salmon. 2 vols. Paris: A. Picard, 1899. Reprint, Paris, 1972.

———. *The Coutumes de Beauvaisis of Philippe de Beaumanoir*. Translated by F. R. P. Akenurst. Philadelphia: University of Pennsylvania Press, 1992.

Boon, J., ed. *Regesten op de jaarregisters van de keure: Schepenjaar 1400–1401*. Ghent, Belg.: Stadsarchief te Gent, 1967–72.

————, ed. *Regesten op de jaarregisters van de schepenen van de Keure te Gent 1339–40, 1343–44, 1345–46, 1349–50*, Ghent, Belg.: Stadsarchief te Gent, 1968.

————, ed. *Regesten op de jaarregisters van de schepenen van de Keure te Gent 1353–54 en 1357–58*, Ghent, Belg.: Stadsarchief te Gent, 1969.

Bruni, Leonardo. *Oeconomicorum Aristotelis libelli: {in Latinum conversi} cum comentariis Leonardi Aretini*. Senis, It.: Symeonez Nicolai Nardi, 1508.

Bücher, Karl, and Benno Schmidt, eds. *Frankfurter Amts – und Zunfturkunden bis zum Jahre 1612*. Vol. 6, *Veröffentlichungen der historischen Kommission der Stadt*. Frankfurt a.M., VI. Frankfurt: W. Kramer, 1909.

"Cahier primitive de la coutume de Gand." In *Coutumes des pays et comté de Flandre: Coutumes de la ville de Gand*. Vol. I, edited by A. E. Gheldolf, 169–383. Brussels: Fr. Gobbaerts, 1868.

Cajetan, Tommaso de Vio Cardinal. *Comments on the Summa Theologica*. Edited by Leo XIII. Vol. VI. Rome: Ex typographia Polyglotta, 1882.

"The Canons of the Fourth Lateran Council, 1215." http://www.fordham.edu/halsall/basis/lateran4.html (accessed September 15, 2008).

Capellanus, Andreas. *The Art of Courtly Love*. Translated by John Jay Parry. New York: Columbia University Press, 1990.

Cleaver, Robert, and John Dod. *A Godlie Forme of Householde Government: For the Ordering of Private Families, According to the Direction of Gods Word*. London: Printed by Thomas Creede, for Thomas Man, 1612.

Corneille, Pierre. *Mélite: Pièce comique; Texte de la première édition (1633)*. Edited by Mario Roques and Marion Lièvre. Lille: Giard, 1950.

"Costumen gheusseert ende onderhauden binnen der stede von Ghendt in materie van successien ende verdeelen." In *Het Oost-Vlaamsch erfrecht*, edited by Eduard M. Meijers, 242 pp. Haarlem, Neth.: Tjeenk Willink, 1936.

"Coutume homologuée de la ville de Gand." In *Coutumes des pays et comté de Flandre: Coutumes de la ville de Gand*. Vol. I, edited by A. E. Gheldolf, 1–167. Brussels: Fr. Gobbaerts, 1868.

Daniel, Rogers. *Matrimoniall Honour*. London: Thomas Harper, 1650. Microform.

Defoe, Daniel. *An Essay upon Publick Credit; Being an Enquiry How the Publick Credit Comes to Depend upon the Change of the Ministry, or the Dissolutions of Parliaments; and Whether It Does So or No*. London: Printed and sold by the booksellers, 1710.

————. *Defoe's Review*. Edited by Arthur Wellesley Secord. 22 vols. New York: Published for the Facsimile Text Society by Columbia University Press, 1938.

Delamare, Nicolas. *Traité de la Police*. Paris: Jean & Pier, 1707–1738.

de Lannoy, Ghillebert. "Denkbeelden van een vliesridder de Instruction d'un juene prince van Guillebert van Lannoy." Edited by C. G. van Leeuwen. Amsterdam: Graduate Press, 1975.

"*Dictionnaires d'autrefois: French dictionaries of the 17th, 18th, 19th and 20th centuries*." University of Chicago Press. http://artfl-project.uchicago.edu/node/17 (accessed June 8, 2009).

Everaert, Cornelis. *Spelen van Cornelis Everaert . . . Met inleiding en aanteekeningen uitgegeven door Dr. J. W. Muller en Dr. L. Scharpé*. Edited by J. W. Muller and L. Scharpé. Leiden: Brill, 1920.

Fagniez, Gustave, ed. "Fragment d'un répertoire de jurisprudence parisienne au XVe siècle." *Mémoires de la Société de l'histoire de Paris et de l'Ile-de-France* XVII (1890).

Gessler, Jan, ed. *Het Brugsche Livre des Mestiers en zijn navolgingen*. Vol. 6. Bruges, Belg.: Publications of the Institute of French Studies, 1931.

Giles, J. A., ed. *Matthew Paris's English History: From the Year 1235 to 1273*. 3 vols. London: H. G. Bohn, 1852.

The Good Wife's Guide (Le ménagier de Paris): A Medieval Household Book. Translated and edited by Gina L. Greco and Christine M. Rose. Ithaca, NY: Cornell University Press, 2009.

"Grande Charte des Gantois." In *Coutumes des pays et comté de Flandre: Coutumes de la ville de Gand*, edited by A. E. Gheldolf, 426–95. Brussels: Fr. Gobbaerts, 1868.

Greve, Anke, Emilie Lebailly, and Werner Paravicini, eds. *Comptes de l'argentier de Charles le Téméraire, Duc de Bourgogne Année 1468*. 2 vols, Recueil des historiens de la France: Documents financiers et administratifs. Paris: Boccard, 2001.

———. *Comptes de l'argentier de Charles le Téméraire, Duc de Bourgogne Année 1469*. 2 vols. Vol. 2, Recueil des historiens de la France: Documents financiers et administratifs. Paris: Boccard, 2002.

Hiltmann, Torsten, and Werner Paravicini, eds. *Die Hofordnungen der Herzöge von Burgund*. Vol. 2, Herzog Karl der Kühne, 1468–1477. Paris: Deutsches Historisches Insitut, forthcoming.

Jacobus de Marchia, Saint. *Sermones dominicales*. Edited by Renato Lioi. 3 vols. Falconara M[arittima], It.: Biblioteca francescana, 1978.

John of Salisbury. *Policraticus: Of the Frivolities of Courtiers and the Footprints of Philosophers*. Translated by Cary J. Nederman, Cambridge Texts in the History of Political Thought. Cambridge, UK: Cambridge University Press, 1990.

Kant, Immanuel. "What is Enlightenment?" In *The Enlightenment: A Comprehensive Anthology*, edited by Peter Gay, 383–90. New York: Simon and Schuster, 1973.

Kruse, Holger, and Werner Paravicini, eds. *Die Hofordnung der Herzöge von Burgund*, Herzog Philipp der Gute, 1407–1467. Paris: Deutsches Historisches Institut, 2005.

Lang, Sheila, and Margaret McGregor, eds. *Tudor Wills Proved in Bristol, 1546–1603*. Bristol, UK: Bristol Record Society, 1993.

Lespinasse, René, and Francois Bonnardot, eds. *Les métiers et corporations de la ville de Paris: XIII siècle: Le livre des métiers d'Étienne Boileau.* Histoire Générale de Paris, Paris, 1879.

Luders, Alexander, John Raithby, and Great Britain Record Commission, eds. *The Statutes of the Realm: Printed by command of His Majesty King George the Third; In pursuance of an address of the House of Commons of Great Britain; From original records and authentic manuscripts.* 9 vols. London: George Eyre and Andrew Strahan, 1810–1828.

Mandeville, Bernard. *The Fable of the Bees: Or, Private Vices, Publick Benefits.* Oxford, UK: Clarendon Press, 1957.

Meijers, Eduard M., ed. *Het Oost-Vlaamsch erfrecht.* Het Ligurische erfrecht in de Nederlanden 7. Haarlem, Neth.: Tjeenk Willink, 1936.

Montaigne, Michel de. *Œuvres completes.* Edited by Albert Thibaudet and Maurice Rat. Paris: Gallimard, 1962.

Nicholas, David, and Walter Prevenier, eds. *Gentse stads – en baljuwsrekeningen (1365–1376)*, Brussels: Palais des Académies, 1999.

Pauw, N. de, and J. Vuylsteke, eds. *De rekeningen der stad Gent: Tijdvak van Jacob van Artevelde, 1336–1349.* 3 vols. Ghent, Belg.: Hoste, 1874–85.

Potter, Frans de, ed. *Petit cartulaire de Gand.* Ghent, Belg.: S. Leliaert & A. Siffer, 1885.

Prevenier, Walter. *De oorkonden der graven van Vlaanderen: 1191 – aanvang 1206.* 2nd ed. Brussels: Palais des Académies, 1964.

Rastell, John. *Three Rastell Plays: Four Elements, Calisto and Melebea, Gentleness and Nobility.* Edited by Richard Axton. Rochester, NY: D. S. Brewer, 1979.

Salisbury, Eve, ed. *The Trials and Joys of Marriage*, Kalamazoo, MI: Medieval Institute Publications, 2002.

San Bernardino da Siena. "Le prediche volgari di San Bernardino de Siena dette nella piazza del campo l'anno 1427." Edited by Luciano Banchi. Siena, It.: Tip. edit all'inseg, 1880–8.

Seuse, Heinrich. *Heinrich Seuse's Horologium Sapientiae*. Edited by Pius Künzle, Spicilegium Friburgense 23. Fribourg, Switzerland: Universitätsverlag, 1977.

Spelen van sinne vol scone moralisacien vvtleggingen ende bediedenissen op alle loeflijcke consten vvaer inne men claerlyck ghelyck in eenen spieghel... Op die Questic VVat den mensch aldermeest tot conste vervvect. Antwerp: s.n., 1562.

Tasso, Torquato. "Discorso della virtú feminile e donnesca." Edited by Maria Luisa Doglio. Palermo: Sellerio, 1997.

Van Boendale, Jan. *Lekenspiegel*. Edited by L. Jongen and M. Piters. Amsterdam: Athenaeum, Polak & Van Gennep, 2003.

———. *Der Leken Spieghel: Leerdicht van den Jare 1330*. Edited by M. de Vries. Leiden: Du Mortier, 1848.

Van Werveke, Alfons, ed. *Gentse stads – en baljuwsrekeningen (1351–1364)*, Brussels: Palais des Académies, 1970.

Vigneulles, Philippe de, ed. *Les cent nouvelles nouvelles*. Travaux d'humanisme et Renaissance 120. Geneva: Droz, 1972.

von Brandt, Ahasver, ed. *Mittelalterliche Bürgertestamente: Neuerschlosssene Quellen zur Geschichte der Materiellen und Geistigen Kultur.* Sitzenungsberichte der Heidelberger Akademie der Wissenschaften, philosophische-historische Klasse 1973 Abhang 3. Heidelberg: Carl Winter, 1973.

Woolgar, C. M., ed. *Household Accounts from Medieval England*. Records of Social and Economic History, 17–18. Oxford, UK: Oxford University Press, 1992.

Secondary Sources

Abraham-Thisse, Simonne. "La valeur des draps au moyen âge: De l'économique au symbolique." In *In But Not of the Market: Movable Goods in the Late Medieval and Early Modern Economy*, edited by Marc Boone and Martha Howell, 17–53. Brussels: Koninklijke Vlaamse Academie, 2007.

Agnew, Jean-Christophe. *Worlds Apart: The Market and the Theater in Anglo-American Thought, 1550–1750.* Cambridge: Cambridge University Press, 1986.

Algazi, Gadi. "Introduction: Doing Things with Gifts." In *Negotiating the Gift: Pre-Modern Figurations of Exchange*, edited by Gadi Algazi, Valentin Groebner, and Bernhard Jussen, 9–27. Göttingen: Vandenhoeck & Ruprecht, 2003.

Aliosio, Mark A. "A Test Case for Regional Market Integration? The Grain Trade between Malta and Sicily in the Late Middle Ages." In *Money,*

Markets and Trade in Late Medieval Europe: Essays in Honour of John H.A. Munro, edited by Lawrin D. Armstrong, Martin Elbl, Ivana Elbl, and John H. A. Munro, 297–309. Boston: Brill, 2007.

Amussen, Susan Dwyer. "'Being stirred to much unquietness': Violence and Domestic Violence in Early Modern England." *Journal of Women's History* 6 (1994): 70–89.

———. "Punishment, Discipline, and Power: The Social Meanings of Violence in Early Modern England." *Journal of British Studies* 34, no. 1 (1995): 1–34.

Anderson, Robert Ralph, Ulrich Goebel, and Oskar Reichmann. *Frühneuhochdeutsches Wörterbuch*. Berlin: W. de Gruyter, 1986.

Appadurai, Arjun. *The Social Life of Things: Commodities in Cultural Perspective*. 1st ed. Cambridge: Cambridge University Press, 1986.

Archer, Rowena. "Rich Old Ladies: The Problem of Late Medieval Dowagers." In *Property and Politics: Essays in Later Medieval English History*, edited by A. J. Pollard, 15–35. Gloucester, UK: A. Sutton, 1984.

Ariès, Philippe. Review of *The Family, Sex and Marriage in England, 1500–1800* by Lawrence Stone. *American Historical Review* 83, no. 5 (December 1978): 1221–4.

Armstrong, Lawrin. "Usury, Conscience, and Public Debt: Angelo Corbinelli's Testament of 1419." In *A Renaissance of Conflicts: Visions and Revisions of Law and Society in Italy and Spain*, edited by J. A. Marino and T. Kuehn, 173–240. Toronto: Center for Renaissance and Reformation Studies, 2004.

———. "Law, Ethics and Economy: Gerard of Siena and Giovanni d'Andrea on Usury." In *Money, Markets and Trade in Late Medieval Europe: Essays in Honour of John H. A. Munro*, edited by Lawrin Armstrong, Ivana Elbl, and Martin Elbl, 41–58. Leiden: Brill, 2007.

Arnade, Peter. *Realms of Ritual: Burgundian Ceremony and Civic Life in Late Medieval Ghent*. Ithaca, NY: Cornell University Press, 1996.

———. *Beggars, Iconoclasts, and Civic Patriots: The Political Culture of the Revolt of the Netherlands*. Ithaca, NY: Cornell University Press, 2008.

———. "City, State, and Public Ritual in the Late-Medieval Burgundian Netherlands." *Comparative Studies in Society and History* 39, no. 2 (April 1997): 300–18.

Arnould, Maurice-A. "L'origine historique des pots-de-vins." *Bulletin de la classe des lettres et des sciences morales et politques*. 5th series, LXII (1976): 216–67.

Ashley, Kathleen. "Material and Symbolic Gift-Giving: Clothes in England and French Wills." In *Medieval Fabrications: Dress, Textiles, Clothwork, and*

Other Cultural Imaginings, edited by E. Jane Burns, 137–46. New York: Palgrave Macmillan, 2004.

Aston, T. H., and C. H. E. Philpin, eds. *The Brenner Debate: Agrarian Class Structure and Economic Development in Pre-Industrial Europe*. Past and Present Publications. Cambridge: Cambridge University Press, 1985.

Auffroy, Henri. *Évolution du testament en France des origines au XIIIe siècle*. Paris: Arthur Rousseau, 1899.

Baker, John Hamilton. *An Introduction to English Legal History*. 3rd ed. London: Butterworths, 1990.

Baron, Hans. "Franciscan Poverty and Civic Wealth in Humanistic Thought." *Speculum* 13 (1938): 1–37.

Barrett, Michèle, and Mary McIntosh. *The Anti-Social Family*. London: NLB, 1982.

Bartier, John. *Légistes et gens de finances au XVe siècle: Les conseilliers des ducs de Bourgogne Philippe le Bon et Charles le Téméraire*. t 50, fasc 2. Brussels: s.n., 1955.

Baudrillard, Jean. *For a Critique of the Political Economy of the Sign*. St. Louis, MO: Telos Press, 1981.

Baudrillart, Henri. *Historie du luxe privé et public depuis l'antiquité jusqu'à nos jours*. Le Moyen âge et la Renaissance 3. Paris: Hachette, 1881.

Baur, Paul. *Testament und Bürgerschaft: Alltagsleben und Sachkultur im spätmittelalterlichen Konstanz*. Konstanzer Geschichts – und Rechtsquellen 31. Sigmaringen, Ger.: Thorbecke, 1989.

Baur, Veronika. *Kleiderordnungen in Bayern vom 14. bis zum 19. Jahrhundert*. Miscellanea Bavarica Monacensia 62. Munich: Stadtarchivs München, 1975.

Beaulieu, Michèle, and Jeanne Baylé. *Le costume en Bourgogne, de Philippe le Hardi á Charles le Téméraire (1364–1477)*. Paris: Presses Universitaires de France, 1956.

Bedos-Rezak, and Brigitte Miriam. "Medieval Identity: A Sign and a Concept." *American Historical Review* 105, no. 5 (December 2000): 1489–533.

Bedos-Rezak, Brigitte Miriam, and Dominique Iogna-Prat. *L'individu au moyen âge: Individuation et individualization avant la modernité*. Paris: Aubier, 2005.

Bellavitis, Anna. *Identité, mariage, mobilité sociale: Citoyennes et citoyens à Venise au XVIe siècle*. Collection de l'Ecole française de Rome 282. Rome: Ecole Française de Rome, 2001.

Ben-Porath, Y. "The F-Connection: Families, Friends and Firms and the Organization of Exchange." *Population and Development Review* 6 (1980): 1–30.

Bennett, Judith M. "Confronting Continuity." *Journal of Women's History* 9 (1997): 73–94.

———. *History Matters: Patriarchy and the Challenge of Feminism*. Philadelphia: University of Pennsylvania Press, 2006.

———. "Conviviality and Charity in Medieval and Early Modern England." *Past & Present* 134 (February 1992): 19–41.

Berg, Maxine, and Elizabeth Eger. "The Rise and Fall of the Luxury Debates." In *Luxury in the Eighteenth Century: Debates, Desires and Delectable Goods*, edited by Maxine Berg and Elizabeth Eger, 7–27. Basingstoke, UK: Palgrave Macmillan, 2003.

Berry, Christopher J. *The Idea of Luxury: A Conceptual and Historical Investigation*. Ideas in Context 30. Cambridge: Cambridge University Press, 1994.

Bestor, Jane Fair. "Marriage Transactions in Renaissance Italy and Mauss's Essay on the Gift." *Past & Present* 164 (August 1999): 6–46.

Bijsterveld, Arnoud-Jan A. "The Medieval Gift as Agent of Social Bonding and Political Power: A Comparative Approach." In *Medieval Transformations: Texts, Power, and Gifts in Context*, edited by Esther Cohen and Mayke De Jong, 123–56. Leiden: Brill, 2001.

———. *Do ut des: Gift Giving, Memoria and Conflict Management in the Medieval Low Countries*. Hilversum, Neth.: Verloren, 2007.

Bindman, David. *Hogarth and History Times: Serious Comedy*. Berkeley: University of California Press, 1997.

Blanc, Odile. "From Battlefield to Court: The Invention of Fashion in the Fourteenth Century." In *Encountering Medieval Textiles and Dress: Objects, Texts, Images*, edited by Désirée G. Koslin and Janet Ellen Snyder. New York: Palgrave Macmillan, 2002.

Bloch, Howard R. *Medieval Misogyny and the Invention of Western Romantic Love*. Chicago: University of Chicago Press, 1991.

Bloch, Marc. *Feudal Society*. Translated by L. A. Manyon. Chicago: University of Chicago Press, 1961.

Blockmans, Willem Pieter. "Corruptie, patronage, makelaardij en venaliteit als symptomen van een ontluikende staatsvorming in de Bourgondisch-habsburgse Nederlanden." *Tijdschrift voor sociale Geschiedenis* 11, no. 3 (1985): 231–47.

———. "Patronage, Brokerage and Corruption as Symptoms of Incipient State Formation in the Burgundian – Habsburg Netherlands [translation of Corruptie, patronage, makelaardij]." In *Klientelsysteme im Europa der Frühen Neuzeit*, edited by Antoni Maczak, 117–26. Munich: Oldenbourg Wissenschaftsverlag, 1988.

————. "Vete, partijstrijd en staatsmacht." In *Bloedwraak, partijstrijd en pacificatie in laat-middeleeuws Holland*, edited by J. W. Marsilje, 9–33. Hilversum, Neth.: Verloren, 1990.

Blockmans, Willem Pieter, and Maurice-A Arnould. *Le privilège général et les privilèges régionaux de Marie de Bourgogne pour les Pays-Bas*. Standen en Landen LXXX: Kortnjk-Heule, 1985.

Blockmans, Willem Pieter, and Walter Prevenier. *The Promised Lands: The Low Countries under Burgundian Rule, 1369–1530*. Philadelphia: University of Pennsylvania Press, 1999.

Blondé, Bruno. "Botsende consumptiemodellen? De symbolische betekenis van goederenbezit en verbruik bij de Antwerpse adel (ca. 1780)." In *Adel en macht: Politiek, cultuur, economie*, edited by Guido Marnef and René Vermeir, 123–39. Maastricht: Shaker Publishing, 2004.

Bonfield, Lloyd. *Marriage Settlements, 1601–1740: The Adoption of the Strict Settlement*. Cambridge Studies in English Legal History. Cambridge: Cambridge University Press, 1983.

Boone, Marc. "Dons et pots-de-vin, aspects de la sociabilité urbaine au bas Moyen Âge: Le cas Gantois pendant la période bourguignonne." *Revue du Nord* LXX (1988): 471–87.

————. *Geld en macht: De Gentse stadsfinanciën en de Bourgondische staatsvorming (1384–1453)*. Ghent: Maatschappij voor Geschiedenis en Oudheidkunde te Gent, 1990.

————. "'Plus dueil que joie' Les ventes de rentes par la ville de Gand pendant la période bourguignonne: Entre interêts privés et finances publiques." *Bulletin Trimestriel du Crédit Communal de Belgique* 176 (1991–2): 3–25.

————. "Le crédit financier dans les villes de Flandre, XIVe–XVe siècles: Typologie des crédirentiers, des créditeurs et des techniques de financement." *Barcelona Quaderns d'Història* 13 (2007): 59–78.

Bos-Rop, Yvonne. "The Power of Money: Financial Officers in Holland in the Late 15th and Early 16th Century." In *Powerbrokers in the Late Middle Ages: The Burgundian Low Countries in a European Context*, edited by Robert Stein, 47–66. Turnhout, Belg.: Brepols, 2001.

Bosl, Karl. "Die Polizei: Ihre Entwicklung im modernen Staat und in der modernen Gesellschaft." *Polizei in Bayern* 14 (1971): 1–4.

Bossy, John. *Disputes and Settlements: Law and Human Relations in the West*. Cambridge: Cambridge University Press, 2003.

Boucher, François. "Les conditions de l'apparition de costume court en France vers le milieu du XIVe siècle." In *Recueil des travaux offerts à*

M. Clovis Brunel par ses amis, collègues et élèves, 183–92. Paris: Société de l'École des Chartes, 1955.

————. *20,000 Years of Fashion: The History of Costume and Personal Adornment*. New York: H. N. Abrams, 1967.

Bourdieu, Pierre. *Outline of a Theory of Practice*. Translated by Richard Nice. Cambridge: Cambridge University Press, 1977.

————. *La distinction: Critique sociale du jugement*. Paris: Éditions de Minuit, 1979.

————. *Distinction: A Social Critique of the Judgement of Taste*. Cambridge, MA: Harvard University Press, 1984.

————. *The Logic of Practice*. Translated by Richard Nice. Cambridge: Polity Press in Association with Basil Blackwell, 1990.

————. "The Work of Time." In *The Gift: An Interdisciplinary Perspective*, edited by Aafke E. Komter, 135–47. Amsterdam: Amsterdam University Press, 1996.

Bourin, Monique. "Introduction." http://lamop.univ-paris1.fr/W3/Treilles/introduction.html (accessed September 19, 2008).

Brand, Hanno. "Twistende Leidenaars: Verkenningen naar het voorkomen van clan en kerngezin, partij en factie aan de hand van drie oproeren in een Hollandse stad in de 15e eeuw." In *Bloedwraak, partijstrijd en pacificatie in laat-middeleeuws Holland*, edited by J. W. Marsilje, 82–105. Hilversum, Neth.: Verloren, 1990.

Braudel, Fernand. *Capitalism and Material Life: 1400–1800*. Vol. 1. London: Weidenfeld & Nicolson, 1973.

————. *Afterthoughts on Material Civilization and Capitalism*. Translated by Patricia Ranum. Baltimore: Johns Hopkins University Press, 1977.

————. *The Wheels of Commerce*. Translated by Siân Reynolds. Vol. 2, *Civilization and Capitalism*. London: Collins, 1982. Reprint, Les jeux de l'échange, Paris, 1979.

Breward, Christopher. *The Culture of Fashion: A New History of Fashionable Dress*. Studies in Design and Material Culture. Manchester, UK: Manchester University Press, 1995.

Brewer, D. S. "Love and Marriage in Chaucer's Poetry." *MLR* 49 (1954): 461–4.

Briggs, Chris. "Credit and the Freehold Land Market in England, c.1200 – c.1350: Possibilities and Problems for Research." In *Credit and the Rural Economy in Europe, c. 1100–1850, Comparative Rural History of the North Sea Area*, edited by T. Lambrecht and P. R. Schofield. Turnhout, Belg.: Brepols, forthcoming.

Brissaud, Jean. *A History of French Private Law*. Translated by Rapelje Howell. The Continental Legal History Series 9. Boston: Little, Brown and Company, 1912.

Britnell, R. H. *The Commercialisation of English Society, 1000–1500*. Cambridge: Cambridge University Press, 1993.

———. "Markets, Shops, Inns, Taverns and Private Houses in Medieval English Trade." In *Buyers & Sellers: Retail Circuits and Practices in Medieval and Early Modern Europe*, edited by Bruno Blondé, Peter Stabel, Jon Stobart, and Ilja Van Damme, 109–25. Turnhout, Belg.: Brepols, 2006.

Brooke, Christopher Nugent Lawrence. *The Medieval Idea of Marriage*. Oxford: Oxford University Press, 1989.

Brucker, Gene. *The Society of Renaissance Florence: A Documentary Study*. New York: Harper & Row, 1971.

Brundage, James A. *Law, Sex, and Christian Society in Medieval Europe*. Chicago: University of Chicago Press, 1987.

———. "Sumptuary Laws and Prostitution in Late Medieval Italy." *Journal of Medieval History* 13 (1987): 343–55.

———. "Usury." In *Dictionary of the Middle Ages*, edited by Joseph R. Strayer et al., 335–9. New York: Charles Scribner's Sons-MacMillan, 1989.

Brunel, Ghislain. "Le marché de la terre en France septentrionale et en Belgique: Esquisse historiographique." In *Le marché de la terre au Moyen Âge*, edited by Laurent Feller and Chris Wickham, 99–111. Rome: École française de Rome, 2005.

Buettner, Brigitte. "Past Presents: New Year's Gifts at the Valois Courts, ca 1400." *Art Bulletin* 83, no. 4 (December 2001): 598–625.

Bulst, Neithard. "Zum Problem städtischer und territorialer Kleider-, Aufwands – und Luxusgesetzgebung in Deutschland (13.–Mitte 16. Jahrhundert)." In *Renaissance du pouvoir législatif et genèse de l'état*, edited by André Gouron and Albert Rigaudière. Montpellier, Fr.: Socapress, 1988.

———. "Kleidung als sozialer Konfliktstoff: Problem kleidergesetzlicher Normierung im sozialen Gefüge." *Saeculum* 44 (1993): 32–47.

———. "Les ordonnances somptuaires en Allemagne: Expression de l'ordre social urbaine (XIVe–XVe siècles)." *Comptes-rendus des séances de l'Académie des inscriptions et belles-lettres* 137, no. 3 (1993): 771–81.

———. "Vom Luxusverbot zur Luxussteuer: Wirtschafts – und sozialgeschichtliche Aspekte von Luxus and Konsum in der Vormoderne." In

Der lange Weg in den Überfluss: Anfänge und Entwicklung der Konsumgesellschaft seit der Vormoderne, edited by Michael Prinz, 47–60. Münster: Aschendorff, 2003.

Burckhardt, Jakob. *The Civilization of the Renaissance in Italy*. Translated by S. G. C. Middlemore. New York: Penguin Classics, 1990.

Burguière, André, Christiane Klapisch-Zuber, Martine Segalen, and François Zonabend. *Histoire de la famille: Mondes lointains, mondes anciens*, Vol. 1. Paris: A. Colin, 1986.

———. *Histoire de la famille: Le choc des modernités*, Vol. 2. Paris: A. Colin, 1986.

Burns, E. Jane. "Courtly Love: Who Needs It? Recent Feminist Work in the Medieval French Tradition." *Signs: The Journal of Women in Culture and Society* 27, no. 1 (2002): 23–57.

———. "Courtly Love." In *Women and Gender in Medieval Europe: An Encyclopedia*, edited by Margaret Schaus, Thomas M. Izbicki, and Susan Mosher Stuard, 173–7. New York: Routledge, 2006.

Butler, Judith. *Gender Trouble: Feminism and the Subversion of Identity*. Thinking Gender. New York: Routledge, 1990.

Bynum, Caroline Walker. "Did the Twelfth Century Discover the Individual?" In *Jesus as Mother*, 82–109. Berkeley: University of California Press, 1982.

Camille, Michael. *The Medieval Art of Love: Objects and Subjects of Desire*. New York: Abrams, 1998.

Campbell, Lorne. *The Fifteenth-Century Netherlandish School*. London: National Gallery in association with Yale University Press, 1998.

———. "Quentin Massys, Desiderius Erasmus, Pieter Gillis, and Thomas More." *Burlington Magazine* CXX, no. 908 (November 1978): 716–24.

Cannadine, David, and Simon Price, eds. *Rituals of Royalty: Power and Ceremonial in Traditional Societies*, Cambridge: Cambridge University Press, 1987.

Carlier, Myriam. *Kinderen van de minne? Bastaarden in het vijftiende-eeuwse Vlaanderen*. Verhandelingen van de Koninklijke Vlaamse Academie van België voor Wetenschappen en Kunsten 3 [New Series]. Brussels: Paleis der Academiën, 2001.

Carlier, Myriam, and Tim Soens. *The Household in Late Medieval Cities: Italy and Northwestern Europe Compared; Proceedings of the International Conference, Gent, 21st–22nd January 2000*. Leuven: Garant, 2001.

Carlin, Martha. "Shops and Shopping in the Thirteenth Century: Three Texts." In *Money, Markets and Trade in Late Medieval Europe: Essays in Honour of John H.A. Munro*, edited by Lawrin D. Armstrong, Martin Elbl, Ivana Elbl, and John H. A. Munro, 297–309. Boston: Brill, 2007.

Carlson, Eric Josef. *Marriage and the English Reformation*. Family, Sexuality and Social Relations in Past Times. Oxford, UK: Blackwell, 1994.

Caron, Marie-Thérèse. "Les choix de consummation d'un jeune prince à la cour de Philippe le Bon." In *La vie matérielle au Moyen Âge: l'apport des sources littéraires, normatives et de la pratique. Actes du Colloque international de Louvain-la-Neuve, 3–5 octobre 1996*, edited by Emmanuelle Rassart-Eeckhout, 49–65. Louvain-la-Neuve, Belg.: Université catholique de Louvain Institut d'études médiévales, 1997.

Carrier, James G. *Gifts and Commodities: Exchange and Western Capitalism since 1700*. London: Routledge, 1994.

Carroll, Margaret D. "In the Name of God and Profit: Jan van Eyck's Arnolfini Portrait." *Representations* 44 (1993): 96–132.

Cartlidge, Neil. *Medieval Marriage: Literary Approaches, 1100–1300*. Woodbridge, UK: D. S. Brewer, 1997.

Castaldo, André. "Beaumanoir, les cateux et les meubles par anticipation." *Tijdschrift voor rechtsgeschiedenis* 68, no. 1 (2000): 1–46.

Cavallo, Sandra, and Lyndan Warner. *Widowhood in Medieval and Early Modern Europe*. Women and Men in History. Harlow, UK: Longman, 1999.

Certeau, Michel de. *The Practice of Everyday Life*. Berkeley: University of California Press, 1984.

Chabot, Isabelle. "La loi du lignage: Notes sur le système successoral florentin (XIVe/XVe–XVIIe siècle)." *Clio* 7 (1998): 51–72.

————. "'La sponsa in nero': La ritualizzazione del lutto delle vedove fioretine (secoli XIV–XV)." *Quaderni storici* 86, no. 2 (August 1994): 421–62.

Charbonnier, Pierre. "Les noces de sang: Le mariage dans les lettres de rémission de la fin du XVe siècle." In *Le mariage au Moyen Âge (XIe–XVe siècle)*, edited by Josiane Teyssot, 133–54. Clermont-Ferrand, Fr.: Université Clermont-Ferrand, Fr. II, 1997.

Chattaway, Carol M. "Looking a Medieval Gift Horse in the Mouth: The Role of Giving of Gift Objects in the Definition and Maintenance of Power Networks of Philip the Bold." *Bijdragen en medelingen betreffende de geschiedenis der Nederlanden* 4 (1999): 1–15.

————. *The Order of the Golden Tree: The Gift-Giving Objectives of Duke Philip the Bold of Burgundy*. Burgundica 12. Turnhout, Belg.: Brepols, 2006.

Chaytor, Miranda. "Household and Kinship: Ryton in the Late 16th and Early 17th Centuries." *History Workshop* 10 (1980): 25–60.

Chevrier, Georges. "Sur quelques caractères de l'histoire du régime matrimonial dans la Bourgogne ducale aux diverse phases de son développement." In *Les droits des gens mariés*, 257–85. Dijon, Fr.: Faculté de Droit des Science Économiques de Dijon, 1966.

Chiffoleau, Jacques. *La comptabilité de l'au-delà: Les hommes, la mort et la religion dans la région d'Avignon à la fin du Moyen Âge (vers 1320–vers 1480)*. Collection de l'École française de Rome 9. Rome: École française de Rome, 1980.

Chobaut, H., ed. "Le règlement somptuaire de Carpentras (avril 1417)." *Annales d'Avignon et du comtat venaissin* 2 (1913): 155–64.

Chojnacka, Monica. *Working Women of Early Modern Venice*. Baltimore: Johns Hopkins University Press, 2001.

Chojnacki, Stanley. "The Power of Love: Wives and Husbands in Late Medieval Venice." In *Women and Power in the Middle Ages*, edited by Mary Carpenter Erler and Maryanne Kowaleski, 126–48. Athens: University of Georgia Press, 1988.

Cipolla, Carlo M. *Before the Industrial Revolution: European Society and Economy, 1000–1700*. 1st ed. New York: Norton, 1976.

Clancy, M. T. *From Memory to Written Record, England 1066–1307*. 2nd ed. Oxford, UK: Blackwell, 1993.

Cohen, Esther. *Gift, Payment and the Sacred in Medieval Popular Religiosity*. Uhlenbeck Lecture 9. Wassenaar: Netherlands Institute for Advanced Study in the Humanities and Social Sciences, 1991.

Cohn, Samuel Kline. *Death and Property in Siena, 1205–1800: Strategies for the Afterlife*. Johns Hopkins University Studies in Historical and Political Science. Baltimore: Johns Hopkins University Press, 1988.

————. *The Cult of Remembrance and the Black Death: Six Renaissance Cities in Central Italy*. Baltimore: Johns Hopkins University Press, 1992.

Coleman, Peter Everard, and Michael J. Langford. *Christian Attitudes to Marriage: From Ancient Times to the Third Millennium*. London: SCM Press, 2004.

Collingwood, Sharon L. *Market Pledge and Gender Bargain: Commercial Relations in French Farce, 1450–1550*. Studies in the Humanities. New York: Peter Lang, 1997.

Collins, James. "The Economic Role of Women in Seventeenth-Century France." *French Historical Studies* 16 (1989): 436–70.

Cowley, Robert L. S. *Marriage a-la-mode: A Review of Hogarth's Narrative Art*. Manchester, UK: Manchester University Press, 1982.

Crane, Susan. *The Performance of Self: Ritual, Clothing, and Identity during the Hundred Years War*. Philadelphia: University of Pennsylvania Press, 2002.

Crawford, Patricia, and Laura Gowring, eds. *Women's Worlds in Seventeenth-Century England: A Sourcebook*. London: Routledge, 2000.

Crosby, Alfred W. *The Measure of Reality: Quantification and Western Society, 1250–1600*. Cambridge: Cambridge University Press, 1997.

Crouzet, Denis. "Recherches sur la crise de l'aristocratie en France au XVIe siècle." *Annales: Économies, sociétés, civilisations* 1 (1982): 7–50.

Curta, Florin. "Merovingian and Carolingian Gift Giving." *Speculum* 81 (July 2006): 671–700.

Cust, R. "Honor and Politics in Early Stuart England." *Past & Present* 27, no. 149 (1995): 57–94.

Dabhoiwala, Faramerz. "The Construction of Honour, Reputation and Status in Late Seventeenth – and Early Eighteenth-Century England." *Transactions of the Royal Historical Society*, 6th series, no. 6 (1996): 201–13.

Dallapiazza, Michael. *Minne, hûsêre und das ehlich leben: Zur Konstitution bürgerlicher Lebenmuster in spätmittelalterlichen und frühhumanistischen Didaktiken*. Frankfurt a.M: Lang, 1981.

Dambruyne, Johan. *Corporatieve middengroepen: Aspiraties, relaties en transformaties in de 16e-eeuwse Gentse ambachtswereld*. Gent: Academia Press, 2002.

Damen, Mario. "Gift Exchange at the Court of Charles the Bold." In *In but Not of the Market: Movable Goods in the Late Medieval and Early Modern Economy*, edited by Marc Boone and Martha C. Howell, 81–99. Brussels: Académie Royale de Belgique, 2007.

Danneel, Marianne. *Weduwen en wezen in het laat-middeleeuwse Gent*. Studies in Urban Social, Economic and Political History of the Medieval and Modern Low Countries, Vol. 3. Leuven: Garant, 1995.

Davidoff, Leonore, and Catherine Hall. *Family Fortunes: Men and Women of the English Middle Class, 1780–1850*. Chicago: University of Chicago Press, 1987.

Davis, James. "Baking for the Common Good: A Reassessment of the Assize of Bread in Medieval England." *Economic History Review* 57, no. 3 (2004): 465–502.

Davis, Natalie Zemon. "The Rites of Violence: Religious Riot in Sixteenth-Century France." *Past & Present* 59, no. 1 (1973): 51–91.

————. "Women on Top: Symbolic Sexual Inversion and Political Disorder in Early Modern Europe." In *The Reversible World: Symbolic Inversion in Art and Society*, edited by Barbara A. Babcock, 147–90. Ithaca, NY: Cornell University Press, 1978.

————. "Boundaries and the Sense of Self in Sixteenth-Century France." In *Reconstructing Individualism*, edited by Thomas C. Heller, 53–63. Stanford: Stanford University Press, 1986.

————. *Fiction in the Archives: Pardon Tales and Their Tellers in Sixteenth-Century France*. The Harry Camp Lectures at Stanford University. Stanford: Stanford University Press, 1987.

————. *The Gift in Sixteenth-Century France*. The Curti Lectures. Madison, WI: University of Wisconsin Press, 2000.

Day, Gerald W. *Genoa's Response to Byzantium, 1155–1204: Commercial Expansion and Factionalism in a Medieval City*. Urbana: University of Illinois Press, 1988.

Day, John. *The Medieval Market Economy*. Oxford, UK: Blackwell, 1987.

Delsalle, Paul. "Façons de vendre, façons d'acheter, sur les marchés au coeur de l'Europe (XVIe siècle et première moitié du XVIIe siècle)." In *Fiere e mercati nella integrazione delle economie europee, secc. XIII-XVIII: atti della "trentaduesima settimana di studi," 8–12 maggio 2000*, edited by Simonetta Cavaciocchi, 335–59. Florence: Le Monnier, 2001.

de Malestroit, M. "Memoires sur le faict des monnoyes." In *Paradoxes inédits du seigneur de Malestroit touchant les monnoyes avec le response du président de la Tourette*, edited by Luigi Einaudi. Turin, It.: Giulio Einaudi, 1937.

de Maulde, René. "Anciens textes de droit français inédits ou rarissimes: Coutumes et règlements de la République d'Avignon au XIIIe siècle." *Nouvelle revue historique de droit français et étranger* 1–2 (1877–8): Vol. I: 47–98; 179–238; 325–43; 465–88; 557–604; Vol. II: 367–85; 581–607.

De Moor, Tine, and Jan Luiten van Zanden. *Vrouwen en de geboorte van het kapitalisme in West-Europa*. Amsterdam: Boom, 2006.

De Moor, Tine, and Jan Luiten van Zanden. "Girlpower: The European Marriage Pattern (EMP) and Labour Markets in the North Sea Region in the Late Medieval and Early Modern Period." www.iisg.nl/hpw/papers/demoor-vanzanden.pdf (accessed September 19, 2008).

De Roover, Raymond. *La pensée économique des scolastiques: Doctrines et méthodes*. Conférence Albert-le-Grand 1970. Montreal: *Inst. d'Études Médiévales*, 1971.

————. "The Concept of the Just Price: Theory and Economic Policy." *Journal of Economic History* 18, no. 4 (December 1958): 418–34.

————. "Scholastic Economics: Survival and Lasting Influence from the Sixteenth Century to Adam Smith." *Quarterly Journal of Economics* 69, no. 2 (May 1955): 161–90.

Derville, Alain. "Les pots-de-vin dans le derniers tiers du XVe siècle (d'après les comptes de Lille et de St. Omer)." In *Le privilège général et les privilèges régionaux de Marie de Bourgogne pour les Pays-Bas, 1477*, edited by Willem Pieter Blockmans, 449–71. Kortrijk-Heule, Belg.: UGS, 1985.

————. "Pots-de-vin, cadeaux, racket, patronage: Essai sur les mécanismes de décision dans l'Etat bourguignon." *Revue du Nord* 56, no. 222 (July–September 1974): 341–64.

Despy, Georges, and Adriaan Verhulst. *La fortune historiographique des thèses d'Henri Pirenne*. Brussels: Archives et Bibliothèques de Belgique, 1986.

de Vries, Jan. *The Industrious Revolution: Consumer Behavior and the Household Economy, 1650 to the Present*. Cambridge: Cambridge University Press, 2008.

————. "The Industrial Revolution and the Industrious Revolution." *Journal of Economic History* 54, no. 2 (June 1994): 249–70.

Dewald, Jonathan. *Pont-St-Pierre, 1398–1789: Lordship, Community, and Capitalism in Early Modern France*. Studies on the History of Society and Culture. Berkeley: University of California Press, 1987.

————. "The Ruling Class in the Marketplace: Nobles and Money in Early Modern France." In *The Culture of the Market: Historical Essays*, edited by Thomas L. Haskell and Richard F. Teichgraeber, 43–66. Cambridge: Cambridge University Press, 1993.

————. *Aristocratic Experience and the Origins of Modern Culture, 1570–1715*. Berkeley: University of California Press, 1993.

————. *The European Nobility, 1400–1800*. New Approaches to European History. New York: Cambridge University Press, 1996.

Diefendorf, Barbara. *Paris City Councillors in the Sixteenth Century: The Politics of Patrimony*. Princeton: Princeton University Press, 1983.

Dinges, Martin. "Die Ehre als Thema der Stadtgeschichte: Eine Semantik im Übergang vom Ancien Régime zur Moderne." *Zeitschrift für Historische Forschung* 16 (1989): 409–40.

————. "Die Ehre als Thema der Historischen Anthropologie: Bemerkungen zur Wissenschaftsgeschichte und der Konzeptualisierung." In *Verletzte Ehre: Ehrkonflikte in Gesellschaften des Mittelalters unter der frühen Neuzeit*, edited by Klaus Schreiner and Gerd Schwerhoff, 29–63. Cologne: Böhlau, 1995.

_____. "Ehre und Geschlecht in der Frühen Neuzeit." In *Ehrkonzepte in der Frühen Neuzeit: Identitäten und Abgrenzungen*, edited by Sibylle Backmann, Hans-Jörg Künast, Sabine Ullmann, and B. Ann Tlusty, 123–48. Berlin: Akademie Verlag, 1998.

Dixon, Laurinda S., ed. *In Detail: New Studies of Northern Renaissance Art in Honor of Walter S. Gibson*, Turnhout, Belg.: Brepols, 1998.

Dobb, Maurice. *Studies in the Development of Capitalism*. New York: International Publishers, 1947.

Donahue, Charles J. "'Clandestine' Marriage in the Later Middle Ages: A Reply." *Law and History Review* 10 (1992): 315–22.

_____. "The Canon Law and Ecclesiastical Jurisdiction from 597 to the 1640s." Review of R. H. Helmholz. *Law and History Review* 25, no. 1 (2004).

Donzelot, Jacques. *The Policing of Families*. 1st American ed. New York: Pantheon Books, 1979.

Duby, Georges. "Prendre, donner, consacrer." In *Guerriers et paysans, VII–XIIe siècle; premier essor de l'économie européenne*, edited by Georges Duby, 60–9. Paris: Gallimard, 1973.

Duffy, Eamon. *The Stripping of the Altars: Traditional Religion in England, 1400–1580*. New Haven, CT: Yale University Press, 1992.

Dumolyn, Jan. *Staatsvorming en vorstelijke ambtenaren in het graafschap Vlaanderen: (1419–1477)*. Antwerp-Apeldorn, Bel.: Garant, 2003.

DuPlessis, Robert S. *Lille and the Dutch Revolt: Urban Stability in an Era of Revolution, 1500–1582*. Cambridge Studies in Early Modern History. Cambridge: Cambridge University Press, 1991.

_____. *Transitions to Capitalism in Early Modern Europe*. New Approaches to European History 10. Cambridge: Cambridge University Press, 1997.

_____. "Capital Formations." In *The Culture of Capital: Property, Cities, and Knowledge in Early Modern England*, edited by Henry S. Turner, 27–49. New York: Routledge, 2002.

Durand, Yves. "Clientèles et fidélités dans le temps et dans l'espace." In *Hommage à Roland Mousnier: clientèles et fidélités en Europe à l'époque moderne*, edited by Yves Durand. Paris: Presses Universitaires de France, 1981.

Durkheim, Émil. *Leçons de sociologie: physique des moeurs et du droit*. Paris: Presses Universitaires de France, 1969.

Dutour, Thierry. "Le mariage, institution, enjeu et ideal dans la société urbaine: Le cas de Dijon à la fin du moyen âge." In *Le mariage au Moyen Âge (XIe–XVe siècle)*, edited by Josiane Teyssot, 29–54. Clermont-Ferrand, Fr.: Université Clermont-Ferrand, Fr. II, 1997.

Dyer, Christopher. "Do Household Accounts Provide an Accurate Picture of Late Medieval Diet and Food Culture?" In *La vie matérielle au Moyen Âge: l'apport des sources litteraires, normatives et de la pratique. Actes du Colloque international de Louvain-la Neuve, 3–5 octobre 1996*, edited by Emmanuelle Rassart-Eeckhout, 109–27. Louvain-la-Neuve, Belg.: Université catholique de Louvain Institut d'études médiévales, 1997.

———. "The Peasant Land Market in Medieval England." In *Le marché de la terre au Moyen Âge*, edited by Laurent Feller and Chris Wickham, 65–76. Rome: École française de Rome, 2005.

Edwards, Robert, and Stephen Spector, eds. *The Olde Daunce: Love, Friendship, Sex, and Marriage in the Medieval World*. SUNY Series in Medieval Studies. Albany, NY: State University of New York Press, 1991.

Eisenbart, Liselotte Constanze. *Kleiderordnungen der deutschen Städte zwischen 1350 und 1700: Ein Beitrag zur Kulturgeschichte des deutschen Bürgertums*. Göttinger Bausteine zur Geschichtswissenschaft 32. Göttingen: Duehrkohp & Radicke, 1962.

Elliott, Dyan. "Dress as Mediator between Inner and Outer Self: The Pious Matron of the High and Later Middle Ages." *Medieval Studies* 53 (1991): 279–308.

Ellrodt, Robert, and Université de Paris III. *Genèse de la conscience moderne: Études sur le développement de la conscience de soi dans les littératures du monde occidental*. Publications de la Sorbonne: "Littératures II" 14. Paris: Presses universitaires de France, 1983.

Engelen, Theo. "The Hajnal Hypothesis and Transition Theory." In *Marriage and the Family in Eurasia: Perspectives on the Hajnal Hypothesis*, edited by Theo Engelen and Arthur P. Wolf, 51–71. Amsterdam: Aksant, 2005.

Epstein, Steven. *Wills and Wealth in Medieval Genoa, 1150–1250*. Harvard Historical Studies 103. Cambridge, MA: Harvard University Press, 1984.

Erickson, Amy Louise. *Women and Property in Early Modern England*. London: Routledge, 1993.

Ertzdorff, Xenja von, and Marianne Wynn, eds. *Liebe, Ehe, Ehebruch in der Literatur des Mittelalters*. Vol. 58, Beiträge zur deutschen Philologie. Giessen, Ger.: W. Schmitz, 1984.

Esmein, A. *Études sur l'histoire du droit canonique privé: Le mariage en droit canonique*. Paris: s.n., 1891.

Fairchilds, Cissie. "The Production and Marketing of Populuxe Goods in Eighteenth-Century Paris," in *Consumption and the World of Goods* edited by John Brewer and Roy Porter, 228–49. London: Routledge, 1994.

Favier, Jean. *Gold and Spices: The Rise of Commerce in the Middle Ages.* Translated by Caroline Higgitt. New York: Holmes & Meier, 1998.

Fédou, René. *Les hommes de loi lyonnais à la fin du moyen âge.* Paris: Belles Lettres, 1964.

Feller, Laurent. "Enrichissement, accumulation et circulation des biens: Quelques problèmes liés au marché de la terre." In *Le marché de la terre au Moyen Âge*, edited by Laurent Feller and Chris Wickham, 3–28. Rome: École française de Rome, 2005.

Feller, Laurent, and Chris Wickham. *Le marché de la terre au Moyen Âge.* Rome: École française de Rome, 2005.

Ferguson, Margaret W., A. R. Buck, and Nancy E. Wright. *Women, Property, and the Letters of the Law in Early Modern England.* Toronto: University of Toronto Press, 2004.

Ferrante, Joan M. *Woman as Image in Medieval Literature, from the Twelfth Century to Dante.* New York: Columbia University Press, 1975.

Filhol, René. "Propriété absolue et démembrement de la propriété dans l'ancien droit français." *Travaux et recherches de l'Institut de droit comparé de l'université de Paris* 22 (1963).

Flandrin, Jean-Louis. *Families in Former Times: Kinship, Household and Sexuality.* Cambridge: Cambridge University Press, 1979.

Fleming, Peter. *Family and Household in Medieval England.* Social History in Perspective. New York: Palgrave Macmillan, 2001.

Fliegel, Stephen N., Sophie Jugie, and Virginie Barthélémy. *Art from the Court of Burgundy: The Patronage of Philip the Bold and John the Fearless 1364–1419.* Cleveland: Cleveland Museum of Art, 2004.

Fogel, Michèle. "Modèle d'état et modèle social de dépense: Les lois somptuaires en France de 1485 à 1660." In *Genèse de l'état moderne: Prélèvement et redistribution*, edited by J.-Ph. Genet and M. Le Mené, 227–35. Paris: Éditions du CNRS, 1987.

Forster, Robert. *Merchants, Landlords, Magistrates: The Depont Family in Eighteenth-Century France.* Baltimore: Johns Hopkins University Press, 1980.

Fossier, Robert. *La Terre et les hommes en Picardie jusqu'à la fin du XIIIe siècle.* Paris: B. Nauwelaerts, 1968.

———. *Peasant Life in the Medieval West.* New York: Blackwell, 1988.

Foucault, Michel. "What is an Author?" In *Language, Counter-Memory, Practice: Selected Essays and Interviews*, edited by Donald F. Bouchard, 124–42. Ithaca, NY: Cornell University Press, 1977.

———. "What is Enlightenment?" In *The Foucault Reader*, edited by Paul Rabinow, 32–50. New York: Pantheon Books, 1984.

Freedman, Paul H. *Out of the East: Spices and the Medieval Imagination*. New Haven: Yale University Press, 2008.

————. "North American Historiography of the Peasant Land Market." http://lamop.univ-paris1.fr/W3/Treilles/freedman.html (accessed 2008).

————. "Spices and Late-Medieval Ideas of Scarcity and Value." *Speculum* 80, no. 4 (October 2005): 1209–28.

Fréjaville, Marcel. *Des meubles par anticipation: Questions juridiques et fiscales relatives aux cessions de droits d'extractions, aux ventes de matériaux de démolition, d'immeubles par destination, de coupes de bois, récoltes sur pied, etc.* Paris: E. de Boccard, 1927.

Frick, Carole Collier. *Dressing Renaissance Florence: Families, Fortunes, and Fine Clothing*. Johns Hopkins University Studies in Historical and Political Science. Baltimore: Johns Hopkins University Press, 2002.

Friedländer, Max J. *Lucas van Leyden: Meister der Graphik*. Leipzig: Klinkhardt & Biermann, 1924.

————. *Early Netherlandish Painting from Van Eyck to Bruegel*. 1st English ed. London: Phaidon, 1956.

Frye, Roland M. "The Teachings of Classical Puritanism on Conjugal Love." *Studies in the Renaissance* 2 (1955): 148–59.

Galassi, F. L. "Buying a Passport to Heaven: Usury, Restitution and the Merchants of Medieval Genoa." *Religion* 22 (1992): 313–26.

Gazzetti, Linda. *Venezianische Vermächtnisse: Die soziale und wirtschaftliche Situation von Frauen im Spiegel spätmittelalterlicher Testamente*. Ergebnisse der Frauenforschung, Bd. 50. Stuttgart: Verlg J. B. Metzler, 1998.

Geary, Patrick J. "Gift Exchange and Social Science Modeling: The Limitations of a Construct." In *Negotiating the Gift: Pre-Modern Figurations of Exchange*, edited by Gadi Algazi, Valentin Groebner, and Bernhard Jussen, 129–40. Göttingen: Vandenhoeck & Ruprecht, 2003.

Gelderblom, Oscar. "The Governance of Early Modern Trade: The Case of Hans Thijs, 1556–1611." *Enterprise and Society* 4, no. 4 (2003): 606–39.

Génicot, L. "Aspects de la vie rurale aux environs de Gand dans la première moitié du XIIIe siècle." *Etudes rurales* 21 (April-June 1966): 122–4.

Giesey, Ralph E. "Rules of Inheritance and Strategies of Mobility in Prerevolutionary France." *American Historical Review* 82, no. 2 (April 1977): 271–89.

Gilissen, John. "Le statut de la femme dans l'ancien droit belge." In *Recueils de la Société Jean Bodin*, 255–321. Brussels: Editions de la Librarie Encyclopédique, 1962.

Gillis, John R. "Affective Individualism and the English Poor." Review of *The Family, Sex and Marriage in England, 1500–1800* by Lawrence Stone. *Journal of Interdisciplinary History* 10, no. 1 (Summer 1979): 121–8.

Godbout, Jacques, Alain Caillé, and Donald Winkler, eds. *The World of the Gift*. Montreal: McGill-Queen's University Press, 1998.

Godding, Philippe. "Dans quelle mesure pouvait-on disposer de ses biens par testament dans les anciens Pays-Bas méridionaux?" *Tijdschrift voor rechtsgeschiedenis* 50 (1982): 279–96.

———. *Le droit privé dans les Pays-Bas méridionaux du 12e au 18e siècle*. Mémoires de la Classe des Lettres series 2, 14/1. Brussels: Académie Royale de Belgique, 1987.

———. "La pratique testamentaire en Flandre au 13e siècle." *Legal History Review* 58, no. 3 (1990): 281–300.

———. "Le droit au service du patrimoine familial: Les Pays Bas méridionaux (12e–18e siècles)." In *Marriage, Property, and Succession*, edited by Lloyd Bonfield, 15–36. Berlin: Duncker & Humbolt, 1992.

Godefroy, Frédéric. *Dictionnaire de l'ancienne langue française et de tous ses dialectes du IXe au XVe siècle composé d'après le dépouillement de tous les plus importants documents manuscrits ou imprimés qui se trouvent dans les grandes bibliothèques de la France et de l'Europe et dans les principales archives départementales, municipales, hospitalières ou privées*. 10 vols. Vol. 7. Paris: Émile Bouillon, 1892.

Goldberg, P. J. P. "Female Labour, Service and Marriage." *Northern History* 22 (1986): 18–38.

Gonthier, N. "Les rapports du couple d'après les sources judiciaries à la fin du Moyen Âge." In *Le mariage au Moyen Âge (XIe–XVe siècle)*, edited by Josiane Teyssot, 155–65. Clermont-Ferrand, Fr.: Université Clermont-Ferrand, Fr. II, 1997.

Goodman, Dena. "Furnishing Discourses: Readings of a Writing Desk in Eighteenth-Century France." In *Luxury in the Eighteenth Century: Debates, Desires and Delectable Goods*, edited by Maxine Berg and Elizabeth Eger, 71–88. Basingstoke, UK: Palgrave Macmillan, 2003.

Goodrich, Peter. "Signs Taken for Wonders: Community, Identity, and a History of Sumptuary Law." *Law and Social Inquiry* 23, no. 3 (1998): 707–28.

Goody, Jack. *Production and Reproduction: A Comparative Study of the Domestic Domain*. Cambridge: Cambridge University Press, 1976.

———. *The Development of the Family and Marriage in Europe*. Past and Present Publications. Cambridge: Cambridge University Press, 1983.

Goody, Jack, and Ian Watt. "The Consequences of Literacy." In *Literacy in Traditional Societies*, edited by Jack Goody, 347 pp. Cambridge: Cambridge University Press, 1968.

Gottlieb, Beatrice. "Getting Married in Pre-Reformation Europe: The Doctrine of Clandestine Marriage and Court Cases in Fifteenth-Century Champagne." Ph.D. diss., Columbia University, 1974.

Gowing, L. "Gender and the Language of Insult in Early Modern London." *History Workshop* 35 (Spring 1993): 1–21.

Grabar, Oleg. "The Shared Culture of Objects." In *Byzantine Court Culture from 829 to 1204*, edited by Henry Maguire. Washington, DC: Dumbarton Oaks Research Library and Collection, 1997.

Greaves, Margaret. *The Blazon of Honour: A Study in Renaissance Magnanimity*. London: Methuen, 1964.

Green, D. H. "Orality and Reading: The State of Research in Medieval Studies." *Speculum* 65, no. 2 (April 1990): 267–80.

Greenblatt, Stephen. *Renaissance Self-fashioning: From More to Shakespeare*. Chicago: University of Chicago Press, 1980.

Greenblatt, Stephen, and Giles Gunn, eds. *Redrawing the Boundaries: The Transformation of English and American Literary Studies*. New York: Modern Language Association, 1992.

Greenfield, Kent Roberts. *Sumptuary Law in Nürnberg: A Study in Paternal Government*. Johns Hopkins University Studies in Historical and Political Science. Baltimore: Johns Hopkins University Press, 1918.

Gregory, C. A. *Gifts and Commodities*. London: Academic Press, 1982.

Greif, Avner. "On the Interrelations and Economic Implications of Economic, Social, Political, and Normative Factors: Reflections from Two Late Medieval Societies." In *The Frontiers of the New Institutional Economics*, edited by John N. Drobak and John V. C. Nye, 57–94. San Diego: Academic Press, 1997.

———. *Institutions and the Path to the Modern Economy: Lessons from Medieval Trade*. Political Economy of Institutions and Decisions. Cambridge: Cambridge University Press, 2006.

———. "The Fundamental Problem of Exchange: A Research Agenda in Historical Institutional Analysis." *European Review of Economic History* 4 (December 2000): 251–84.

Greilsammer, Myriam. *La roue de la fortune: Le destin d'une famille d'usuriers lombards dans les Pays-Bas à l'aube des Temps modernes*. Paris: Éditions de l'École des hautes études en sciences sociales, 2009.

———. *L'envers du tableau: Mariage et maternité en Flandre médiévale*. Paris: Colin, 1990.

Grierson, Philip. "Commerce in the Dark Ages: A Critique of the Evidence." *Transactions of the Royal Historical Society* 5th series, no. 9 (1959): 123–40.

Grimm, Jacob, and Wilhelm Grimm. *Deutsches Wörterbuch*. Edited by Moriz Heyne. Munich: Deutscher Taschenbuch Verlag, 1984.

Groebner, Valentin. "Accountancies and Arcana: Registering the Gift in Late Medieval Cities." In *Medieval Transformations: Texts, Power, and Gifts in Context*, edited by Esther Cohen and Mayke De Jong, 219–44. Leiden: Brill, 2001.

———. *Liquid Assets, Dangerous Gifts: Presents and Politics at the End of the Middle Ages*. Philadelphia: University of Pennsylvania Press, 2002.

Guéry, Alain. "Le roi dépensier: Le don, le contrainte, et l'origine du système financier de la monarchie française d'Ancien Régime." *Annales: Économies, sociétés, civilisations* 34 (1984): 1241–64.

Gurevich, Aron I. Akovlevich. *Medieval Popular Culture: Problems of Belief and Perception*. Cambridge Studies in Oral and Literate Culture 14. Cambridge: Cambridge University Press, 1988.

Habakkuk, H. J. "Marriage Settlements in the Eighteenth Century." *Transactions of the Royal Historical Society* 4th series, no. 32 (1950): 15–30.

Haferland, Harold. *Höfische Interaktion: Interpretationen zur höfischen Epik und Didatik um 1200*. Munich: Fink, 1989.

Hagstrum, Jean H. *Esteem Enlivened by Desire: The Couple from Homer to Shakespeare*. Chicago: University of Chicago Press, 1992.

Hajnal, John. "European Marriage Patterns in Perspective." In *Population in History*, edited by D. V. Glass and D. E. C. Eversley, 101–46. London: Edward Arnold, 1965.

Hakluyt, Richard. *Voyages and Discoveries: The Principal Navigations, Voyages, Traffiques and Discoveries of the English Nation*. Edited by Jack Beeching. Hammondsworth, UK: Penguin Books, 1972.

Hall, Edwin. *The Arnolfini Betrothal: Medieval Marriage and the Enigma of Van Eyck's Double Portrait*. Berkeley: University of California Press, 1994.

Hamburger, Jeffrey F. "Visible, yet Secret: Images as Signs of Friendship in Seuse." *Oxford German Studies* 36, no. 2 (2007): 141–62.

Hanawalt, Barbara. *Women and Work in Preindustrial Europe*. Bloomington: Indiana University Press, 1986.

———. *The Ties That Bound: Peasant Families in Medieval England*. New York: Oxford University Press, 1986.

———. *The Wealth of Wives: Women, Law, and Economy in Late Medieval London*. Oxford: Oxford University Press, 2007.

_____. "Women and the Household Economy in the Preindustrial Period: An Assessment of Women, Work, and Family." *Journal of Women's History* 11, no. 3 (Autumn 1999): 10–16.

Hanley, Sarah. "The Jurisprudence of the Arrêts: Marital Union, Civil Society, and State Formation in France, 11550–1650." *Law and History Review* 21, no. 1 (Spring 2003): 1–41.

Harbison, Craig. "Sexuality and Social Standing in Jan van Eyck's Arnolfini Double Portrait." *Renaissance Quarterly* 43 (1990): 249–91.

Harding, Vanessa. "Shops, Markets and Retailers in London's Cheapside, c. 1500–1700." In *Buyers & Sellers: Retail Circuits and Practices in Medieval and Early Modern Europe*, edited by Bruno Blondé, Peter Stabel, Jon Stobart, and Ilja Van Damme, 155–70. Turnhout, Belg.: Brepols, 2006.

Harte, N. B. "State Control of Dress and Social Change in Pre-industrial England." In *Trade, Government and Economy in Pre-industrial England: Essays Presented to F. J. Fisher*, edited by Donald Cuthbert Coleman and A. H. John, 132–65. London: Weidenfeld & Nicolson, 1976.

Hartman, Mary S. *The Household and the Making of History: A Subversive View of the Western Past*. Cambridge: Cambridge University Press, 2004.

Harvey, P. D. A. *The Peasant Land Market in Medieval England*. Oxford: Oxford University Press, 1984.

_____. "Medieval Society and the Manor Court." In *The Peasant Land Market in Medieval England – and beyond*, edited by Zvi Razi and Richard Michael Smith, 392–407. Oxford: Oxford University Press, 1996.

Haskell, Thomas L., and Richard F. Teichgraeber. "Introduction." In *The Culture of the Market: Historical Essays*, edited by Thomas L. Haskell and Richard F. Teichgraeber, 1–42. Cambridge: Cambridge University Press, 1993.

Haskins, Charles Homer. *The Renaissance of the Twelfth Century*. Cambridge, MA: Harvard University Press, 1927.

Hatcher, John, and Mark Bailey. *Modelling the Middle Ages: The History and Theory of England's Economic Development*. New York: Oxford University Press, 2001.

Heers, Jacques. *Family Clans in the Middle Ages: A Study of Political and Social Structures in Urban Areas*. Translated by Barry Herbert. Amsterdam: North-Holland Publisher, 1977.

Heijden, Manon Van Der. "Women as Victims of Sexual and Domestic Violence in 17th century Holland: Criminal Cases of Rape, Incest, and Maltreatment in Rotterdam and Delft." *Journal of Social History* 33 (2000): 623–44.

Heirbaut, Dirk. *Over lenen en families: Een studie over de vroegste geschiedenis van het zakelijk leenrecht in het graafschap Vlaanderen ca. 1000–1305.* Vol. 2, *Verhandelingen van de Koninklijke Vlaamse Academie van België voor Wetenschappen en Kunsten. nieuwe reeks.* Brussels: Palais der Academiën, 2000.

Heller, Sarah-Grace. "Anxiety, Hierarchy, and Appearance in Thirteenth-Century Sumptuary Laws and the Romance de la Rose." *French Historical Studies* 27, no. 2 (Spring 2004): 311–48.

Helmholz, R. H. *Marriage Litigation in Medieval England.* Cambridge Studies in English Legal History. Cambridge: Cambridge University Press, 1974.

Henwood, Philippe. "Administration et vie des collections d'orfèverie royale sous le règne de Charles VI (1380–1422)." *Bibliothèque de l'Ecole des Chartes* 138 (1980): 179–215.

Herlihy, David. "Family." *American Historical Review* 96, no. 1 (February 1991): 1–16.

Herlihy, David, and Christiane Klapisch-Zuber. *Les Toscans et leurs familles: Une étude du "catasto" florentin de 1427.* Paris: Presses de la Fondation des Sciences Politiques, 1978.

Herzog, Dagmar. *Intimacy and Exclusion: Religious Politics in Pre-Revolutionary Baden.* Princeton Studies in Culture/Power/History. Princeton: Princeton University Press, 1996.

Higginbotham, Derrick. "All the World's a Market: Economic Life on English Stages, c. 1400–c. 1600." Ph.D. diss., Columbia University, 2009.

Hilaire, Jean. *Le régime des biens entre époux dans la région de Montpellier du début du XIII siècle à la fin du XVI siècle.* Paris: Éd. Montehrestien, 1957.

Hill, Christopher. "Sex, Marriage, and the Family in England." Review of *The Family, Sex and Marriage in England, 1500–1800* by Lawrence Stone. *Economic History Review* 31, no. 3 [New Series] (August 1978): 450–63.

Hirsch, Jennifer S., and Holly Wardlow, eds. *Modern Loves: The Anthropology of Romantic Courtship and Companionate Marriage.* Ann Arbor: University of Michigan Press, 2006.

Hirschbiegel, Jan. *Étrennes: Untersuchungen zum höfischen Geschenkverkehr im spätmittelalterlichen Frankreich der Zeit König Karls VI. (1380–1422).* Pariser historische Studien 60. Munich: Oldenbourg, 2003.

Hirschman, Albert O. *The Passions and the Interests: Political Arguments for Capitalism before its Triumph.* Princeton: Princeton University Press, 1977.

Hoecke, Willy van, and Andries Welkenhuysen. *Love and Marriage in the Twelfth Century.* Leuven: Leuven University Press, 1981.

Hoffman, Philip T. *Growth in a Traditional Society: The French Countryside, 1450–1815.* Princeton: Princeton University Press, 1996.

Hoffman, Philip T., Gilles Postel-Vinay, and Jean-Laurent Rosenthal. *Priceless Markets: The Political Economy of Credit in Paris, 1660–1870.* Chicago: University of Chicago Press, 2000.

Hollander, Anne. *Sex and Suits.* New York: Knopf, 1994.

Honig, Elizabeth Alice. *Painting and the Market in Early Modern Antwerp.* New Haven: Yale University Press, 1998.

Hooper, Wilfrid. "The Tudor Sumptuary Laws." *English Historical Review* 30, no. 119 (July 1915): 433–49.

Houlbrooke, Ralph A. *The English Family, 1450–1700.* Themes in British Social History. London: Longman, 1984.

Howell, Martha C. *Women, Production, and Patriarchy in Late Medieval Cities.* Women in Culture and Society. Chicago: University of Chicago Press, 1986.

———. "Women's Work in the New and Light Draperies of the Low Countries." In *The New Draperies in the Low Countries and England, 1300–1800,* edited by Negley Harte, 197–216. Oxford: Oxford University Press, 1997.

———. *The Marriage Exchange: Property, Social Place, and Gender in Cities of the Low Countries, 1300–1550.* Women in Culture and Society. Chicago: University of Chicago Press, 1998.

———. "Fixing Movables: Gifts by Testament in Late Medieval Douai." *Past & Present* 150 (February 1996): 3–45.

———. "The Gender of Commerce, 1200–1700." *Gender & History* 20:3 [special issue: Gender and Change: Agency, Chronology and Periodisation, eds. Alexandra Shepard and Garthine Walker] (2008).

Hoyle, R. W. "The Land and Family Bond in England." *Past & Present* 146 (1995): 151–73.

Hughes, Diane Owen. "Urban Growth and Family Structure in Medieval Genoa." *Past & Present* 66, no. 1 (1975): 3–28.

———. "Kinsmen and Neighbors in Medieval Genoa." In *The Medieval City,* edited by Harry A. Miskimin, David Herlihy, Abraham L. Udovitch, and Robert Sabatino Lopez, 3–28. New Haven: Yale University Press, 1977.

———. "Sumptuary Laws and Social Relations in Renaissance Italy." In *Disputes and Settlements: Law and Human Relations in the West,* edited by John Bossy, 69–100. Cambridge: Cambridge University Press, 1983.

———. "Distinguishing Signs: Ear-Rings, Jews and Franciscan Rhetoric in the Italian Renaissance City." *Past & Present* 112, no. 1 (1986): 3–59.

Huizinga, Johan. *The Waning of the Middle Ages: A Study of the Forms of Life, Thought and Art in France and the Netherlands in the xivth and xvth Centuries.* New York: St. Martin's Press, 1924.

Hull, Isabel V. *Sexuality, State, and Civil Society in Germany, 1700–1815.* Ithaca, NY: Cornell University Press, 1996.

Hundert, Edward. "Mandeville, Rousseau and the Political Economy of Fantasy." In *Luxury in the Eighteenth Century: Debates, Desires and Delectable Goods,* edited by Maxine Berg and Elizabeth Eger, 28–40. Basingstoke, UK: Palgrave Macmillan, 2003.

Hunt, Alan. *Governance of the Consuming Passions: A History of Sumptuary Law.* Language, Discourse, Society. New York: St. Martin's Press, 1996.

———. "The Governance of Consumption: Sumptuary Laws and Shifting Forms of Regulation." *Economy and Society* 25, no. 3 (1996): 410–28.

Hunt, Istvan, and Michael Ignatieff. *Wealth and Virtue: The Shaping of Political Economy in the Scottish Enlightenment.* Cambridge: Cambridge University Press, 1983.

Hunt, Margaret. "Wife Beating, Domesticity and Women's Independence in Eighteenth-Century London." *Gender & History* 5, no. 1 (1992): 10–33.

Huppert, George. *Les Bourgeois Gentilshommes: An Essay on the Definition of Elites in Renaissance France.* Chicago: University of Chicago Press, 1977.

Hutton, Shennan. "'On Herself and All Her Property': Women's Economic Activities in Late Medieval Ghent." *Continuity and Change* 20, no. 3 (2005): 325–49.

Hyam, P. "The Origins of a Peasant Land Market in England." *Economic History Review* 23, no. 1 (1970): 18–31.

Innes, Matthew. "Memory, Orality and Literacy in an Early Medieval Society." *Past & Present* 158 (February 1998): 3–36.

Irsigler, Franz. "La fonction des foires dans l'intégration des économies européenes (Moyen-âge)." In *Fiere e mercati nella integrazione delle economie europee, secc. XIII-XVIII: atti della "trentaduesima settimana di studi," 8–12 maggio 2000,* edited by Simonetta Cavaciocchi, 49–71. Florence: Le Monnier, 2001.

Jacob, Robert. "Les structures patrimoniales de la conjugalité au moyen âge dans la France du Nord. Essai d'histoire comparée des époux nobles et roturiers dans les pays du groupe de coutumes 'picard – wallon.'" Ph.D. diss., Université de Droit, d'Economie et de Science sociales de Paris, 1984.

―――――. *Les époux, le seigneur et la cité: Coutume et pratiques matrimoniales des bourgeois et paysans de France du Nord au Moyen Âge.* Brussels: Publications des Facultés Universitaires Saint-Louis, 1990.

Jaeger, C. Stephen. *Ennobling Love: In Search of a Lost Sensibility.* Philadelphia: University of Pennsylvania Press, 1999.

James, M. E. "English Politics and the Concept of Honor 1485–1642." *Past and Present Supplement* iii. Oxford: Oxford University Press, 1978.

Jaritz, Gerhard. "Kleidung und Prestige-Konkurrenz: Unterschiedliche Identitäten in der städitischen Gesellschaft under Normierungszwangen." In *Zwischen Sein und Schein: Kleidung und Identität in der ständischen Gesellschaft,* edited by Neithard Bulst and Robert Jütte, 8–32. Munich: Alber, 1993.

Jean, Marcel, and Árpád Mezei. *Genèse de la pensée moderne dans la littérature française: Essai.* Le chemin de la vie. Paris: Corrêa, 1950.

Jeannin, P. "*Der Livre des Métiers*: Das älteste vielsprachige Kaufmannslexikon." In *Brügge-Colloquium des hansischen Geschichtsvereins 26.-29. Mai 1988: Referate und Diskussionen,* edited by Klaus Friedland, 121–30. Cologne: Böhlau, 1990.

Jobert, Philippe. *La notion de donation: Convergences, 630–750.* Publications de l'Université de Dijon 49. Paris: Les Belles Lettres, 1977.

Jones, Ann Rosalind, and Peter Stallybrass. *Renaissance Clothing and the Materials of Memory.* Cambridge Studies in Renaissance Literature and Culture 38. New York: Cambridge University Press, 2000.

Kaminisky, Howard. "Estate, Nobility, and the Exhibition of Estate in the Later Middle Ages." *Speculum* 68, no. 3 (July 1993): 684–709.

Kaplan, Steven L. *Provisioning Paris: Merchants and Millers in the Grain and Flour Trade during the Eighteenth Century.* Ithaca, NY: Cornell University Press, 1984.

Karras, Ruth Mazo. *From Boys to Men: Formations of Masculinity in Late Medieval Europe.* Philadelphia: University of Pennsylvania Press, 2003.

Kavaler, Ethan Matt. *Pieter Bruegel: Parables of Order and Enterprise.* Cambridge: Cambridge University Press, 1999.

Kaye, Joel. "Money and Market Consciousness in Thirteenth and Fourteenth Century Europe." In *Ancient and Medieval Economic Ideas and Concepts of Social Justice,* edited by S. Todd Lowry and Barry Gordon, 371–403. Leiden: Brill, 1998.

―――――. *Economy and Nature in the Fourteenth Century: Money, Market Exchange, and the Emergence of Scientific Thought.* Cambridge Studies in Medieval Life and Thought. New York: Cambridge University Press, 1998.

————. "Changing Definitions of Money, Nature and Equality (c. 1140–1270) and Their Place within Thomas Aquinas' Question of Usury." In *Credito e usura fra teologia, deiritto e admministratione: Linguaggi a confronto (sec, XII–XVI)*, edited by D. Quaglioni, G. Todeschini, and G. M. Varanini, 25–55. Rome: École Française de Rome, 2005.

Keene, Derek. "Sites of Desire: Shops, Selds and Wardrobes in London and Other English Cities, 1100–1550." In *Buyers & Sellers: Retail Circuits and Practices in Medieval and Early Modern Europe*, edited by Bruno Blondé, Peter Stabel, Jon Stobart, and Ilja Van Damme, 125–53. Turnhout, Belg.: Brepols, 2006.

Kelly, Henry Ansgar. "Clandestine Marriage and Chaucer's Troilus." *Viator* 4 (1973): 413–501.

————. *Love and Marriage in the Age of Chaucer*. Ithaca, NY: Cornell University Press, 1975.

Kermode, J. "Money and Credit in the Fifteenth-Century." *Business History Review* 65 (1991): 475–501.

Kettering, Sharon. "Patronage and Kinship in Early Modern France." *French Historical Studies* 16, no. 2 (1989): 408–35.

Killerby, Catherine Kovesi. "Practical Problems in the Enforcement of Italian Sumptuary Law, 1200–1500." In *Crime, Society and the Law in Renaissance Italy*, edited by Trevor Dean and K. J. P. Lowe, 99–120. Cambridge: Cambridge University Press, 1994.

Kint, An. "Theater, Trade and a City's Identity: The Rhetorical Plays in Sixteenth-Century Antwerp." In *La ville à la Renaissance: Espaces, représentation, pouvoirs; Actes XXXIXe colloque international d'études humanistes, 1996*, edited by Gérard Chaix, Marie-Luce Demonet, and Robert Sauzet, 327–36. Paris: Champion, 2008.

Kirshner, Julius. "Raymond de Roover on Scholastic Economic Thought." In *Business, Banking, and Economic Thought in Late Medieval and Early Modern Europe: Selected Studies of Raymond de Roover*, edited by Julius Kirshner, 15–36. Chicago: University of Chicago Press, 1974.

————. "Wives' Claims against Insolvent Husbands in Late Medieval Italy." In *Women of the Medieval World: Essays in Honor of John H. Mundy*, edited by Julius Kirshner and Suzanne Fonay Wemple, 256–303. Oxford, UK: Blackwell, 1985.

Klapisch-Zuber, Christiane. *Women, Family, and Ritual in Renaissance Italy*. Chicago: University of Chicago Press, 1985.

Kloek, W. Th, Willy Halsema-Kubes, and R. J. Baarsen. *Art before the Iconoclasm: Northern Netherlandish Art, 1525–1580*. 2 vols, De Eeuw van de beeldenstorm. The Hague: Staatsuitgeverij, 1986.

Koenigsberger, Helmut. "Patronage, Clientage and Elites in the Politics of Philip II, Cardinal Granvelle and William of Orange." In *Klientelsysteme im Europa der Frühen Neuzeit*, edited by Antoni Maczak, 127–48. Munich: Oldenbourg Wissenschaftsverlag, 1988.

Komter, Aafke E., ed. *The Gift: An Interdisciplinary Perspective*. Amsterdam: Amsterdam University Press, 1996.

Korda, Natasha. *Shakespeare's Domestic Economies: Gender and Property in Early Modern England*. Philadelphia: University of Pennsylvania Press, 2002.

Koslin, Désirée G. *Parades et Parures: L'invention du corps de mode à la fin du Moyen Âge*. Paris: Gallimard, 1997.

Kosto, Adam. "Laymen, Clerics, and Documentary Practices in the Early Middle Ages: The Example of Catalonia." *Speculum* 80, no. 1 (2005): 44–74.

Kowaleski, Maryanne. "A Consumer Economy." In *A Social History of England, 1200–1500*, edited by Rosemary Horrox and W. M. Ormrod, 238–59; 493–4. Cambridge: Cambridge University Press, 2006.

Kriedte, Peter. *Peasants, Landlords, and Merchant Capitalists: Europe and the World Economy, 1500–1800*. Cambridge: Cambridge University Press, 1983.

Kriedte, Peter, Hans Medick, and Jürgen Schlumbohm. *Industrialization before Industrialization: Rural Industry in the Genesis of Capitalism*. Cambridge: Cambridge University Press, 1981.

Kuehn, Thomas. *Law, Family & Women: Toward a Legal Anthropology of Renaissance Italy*. Chicago: University of Chicago Press, 1991.

L'Engle, Susan. "Addressing the Law: Costume and Signifier in Medieval Legal Minatures." In *Encountering Medieval Textiles and Dress: Objects, Texts, Images*, edited by Désirée G. Koslin and Janet Snyder, 137–72. New York: Palgrave Macmillan, 2002.

Langer, Suzanne. *Philosophy in a New Key: A Study in the Symbolism of Reason, Rite, and Art*. Cambridge: Cambridge University Press, 1942.

Langholm, Odd. *The Aristotelian Analysis of Usury*. Bergen, Norway: Universitetsforlaget, 1984.

———. *Economics in the Medieval Schools: Wealth, Exchange, Value, Money, and Usury According to the Paris Theological Tradition, 1200–1350*. Studien und Texte zur Geistesgeschichte des Mittelalters. Leiden: Brill, 1992.

———. *The Legacy of Scholasticism in Economic Thought: Antecedents of Choice and Power*. Historical Perspectives in Modern Economics. Cambridge: Cambridge University Press, 1998.

————. *The Merchant in the Confessional: Trade and Price in the Pre-Reformation Penitential Handbooks.* Studies in Medieval and Reformation Thought. Leiden: Brill, 2003.

Lardinois, Philippe. "Diplomatische studie van de akten van vrijwillige rechtspraak te Gent van de XIIIe tot de XVe eeuw." Licentiate thesis, University of Ghent, 1975–6.

Lasch, Christopher. *Haven in a Heartless World: The Family Besieged.* New York: Basic Books, 1977.

Laslett, Peter. "Family, Kinship and Collectivity as Systems of Support in Pre-industrial Europe: A Consideration of the 'Nuclear-Hardship' Hypothesis." *Continuity and Change* 3 (1988): 153–75.

Laslett, Peter, and Richard Wall, eds. *Household and Family in Past Time.* Cambridge: Cambridge University Press, 1972.

Lavalleye, Jacques. *Pieter Bruegel the Elder and Lucas Van Leyden: The Complete Engravings, Etchings, and Woodcuts.* London: Thames and Hudson, 1967.

Le Goff, Jacques. "The Usurer and Purgatory." In *The Dawn of Modern Banking*, edited by Fredi Chiappelli, 25–52. New Haven: Yale University Press, 1979.

————. *La bourse et la vie: Économie et religion au Moyen Âge.* Paris: Hachette, 1986.

Lebecq, Stéphane. *Marchands et navigateurs frisons du haut Moyen Âge.* 2 vols. Lille: Presses Universitaires de Lille, 1983.

Lecuppre-Desjardin, Elodie. *La ville des cérémonies: Essai sur la communication politique dans les anciens Pays-Bas bourguignons.* Studies in European Urban History (1100–1800) 4. Turnhout, Belg.: Brepols, 2004.

Lefebvre, Charles. *Les fortunes anciennes au point de vue juridique: leçons d'ouverture, cours de 1911–1912.* Paris: Sirey, 1912.

Leites, Edmund. "The Duty to Desire: Love, Friendship, and Sexuality in Some Puritan Theories of Marriage." *Journal of Social History* 15 (1982): 383–408.

Lemire, Beverly. *The Business of Everyday Life: Gender, Practice and Social Politics in England, c. 1600–1900.* Manchester, UK: Manchester University Press, 2005.

Lévi-Strauss, Claude. *The Elementary Structures of Kinship.* Rev. ed. Boston: Beacon Press, 1969.

Lis, Catharina, and Hugo Soly. "Ambachtsgilden en vergelijkenheid perspectief: de noordelijke en zuidelijke Nederlanden, 15de–18de euw." In *Werelden van Verschil: Ambachtsgilden in de Lage Landen*, edited by Catharina Lis and Hugo Soly, 11–42. Brussels, 1997.

Little, Lester K. *Religious Poverty and the Profit Economy in Medieval Europe.* Ithaca, NY: Cornell University Press, 1978.

Loengard, J. Senderowitz "'Of the gift of her husband': English Dower and Its Consequences in the Year 1200." In *Women of the Medieval World: Essays in Honor of John H. Mundy,* edited by Julius Kirshner and Suzanne Fonay Wemple, 215–55. Oxford, UK: Blackwell, 1985.

Lopez, Robert Sabatino. *The Commercial Revolution of the Middle Ages, 950–1350.* Englewood Cliffs, NJ: Prentice-Hall, 1971.

Lorcin, Marie-Thérèse, "Le sot, la fille et le prêtre: Le mariage dans les contes à rire." In *Le mariage au Moyen Âge (XIe–XVe siècle),* edited by Josiane Teyssot, 125–32. Clermont-Ferrand, Fr.: Université Clermont-Ferrand, Fr. II, 1997.

Macfarlane, Alan. "Review of *The Family, Sex and Marriage in England, 1500–1800* by Lawrence Stone." *History and Theory* 18 (1979): 103–26.

————. *Marriage and Love in England: Modes of Reproduction, 1300–1840.* Oxford, UK: Blackwell, 1986.

Macpherson, C. B. *The Political Theory of Possessive Individualism: Hobbes to Locke.* London: Oxford University Press, 1962.

Maczak, Antoni. *Klientelsysteme im Europa der Frühen Neuzeit.* Schriften des Historischen Kollegs 9. Munich: Oldenbourg Wissenschaftsverlag, 1988.

————. "Patronage im Herzen des frühneuzeitlichen Europa." In *Klientelsysteme im Europa der Frühen Neuzeit,* edited by Antoni Maczak, 83–9. Munich: Oldenbourg Wissenschaftsverlag, 1988.

Maes, Marleen. "Kledij als teken van marginaliteit in de late middeleeuwen." In *Sociale structuren en topografie van armoede en rijkdom in de 14e en 15e eeuw,* edited by Walter Prevenier and R. van Uytven, 135–56. Ghent: Uit de Seminaries voor Geschiedenis van de Rijksuniversiteit te Gent, 1985.

Malinowski, Bronislaw. *Argonauts of the Western Pacific: An Account of Native Enterprise and Adventure in the Archipelagoes of Melanesian New Guinea.* 3rd ed. New York: E.P. Dutton, 1950 [original edition 1922].

————. "The Principle of Give and Take." In *The Gift: An Interdisciplinary Perspective,* edited by Aafke E. Komter, 15–18. Amsterdam: Amsterdam University Press, 1996.

Martin, John. "Inventing Sincerity, Refashioning Prudence: The Discovery of the Individual in Renaissance Europe." *American Historical Review* 102, no. 5 (December 1997): 1309–42.

Marx, Karl. *Capital: A Critique of Political Economy.* Translated by Ben Fowkes. 3 vols. Vol. 1. New York: Penguin Books in association with New Left Review, 1976.

Mascuch, Michael. *Origins of the Individualist Self: Autobiography and Self-Identity in England, 1591–1791.* Stanford: Stanford University Press, 1996.

Masschaele, James. "The Public Space of the Marketplace in Medieval England." *Speculum* 77 (2002): 383–421.

Mathias, Peter. "Risk, Credit and Kinship in Early Modern Enterprise." In *The Early Modern Atlantic Economy,* edited by John J. McCusker and Kenneth Morgan, 15–36. Cambridge: Cambridge University Press, 2000.

Mauss, Marcel. "Essai sur le don: Forme et raison de l'échange dans les sociétés archaiques (1923–1924)." *Sociologie et Anthropologie* 9, no. 1 (1950): 143–279.

———. *The Gift: The Form and Reason for Exchange in Archaic Societies.* Translated by W. D. Hall. New York: Routledge, 1990.

McCormick, Michael. *Origins of the European Economy: Communications and Commerce, A.D. 300–900.* Cambridge: Cambridge University Press, 2001.

McIntosh, Marjorie Keniston. "The Benefits and Drawbacks of Femme Sole Status in England, 1300–1630." *Journal of British Studies* 44, no. 3 (2005): 410–38.

McKitterick, Rosamond. *The Carolingians and the Written Word.* Cambridge: Cambridge University Press, 1989.

McLaughlin, T. P. "The Teaching of the Canonists on Usury (XII, XIII and XIV Centuries)." *Medieval Studies* 1–2 (1939–1940): 81–147; 1–22.

McSheffrey, Shannon. "Place, Space, and Situation: Public and Private in the Making of Marriage in Late-Medieval London." *Speculum* 79 (2004): 960–90.

———. *Marriage, Sex, and Civic Culture in Late Medieval London.* Philadelphia: University of Pennsylvania Press, 2006.

Medick, Hans. "Zur strukturellen Funktion von Haushalt und Familie im Übergang von der traditionellen Agrargesellschaft zum industriellen Kapitalismus: die proto – industrielle Familienwirtschaft." In *Sozialgeschichte der Familie in der Neuzeit Europas: Neue Forschungen,* edited by Werner Conze, 254–82. Stuttgart: Klett, 1976.

Mestayer, Monique. "Testaments douaisiens antérieurs à 1270." *Nos Patois du Nord* 7 (1962): 64–77.

Meyssonier, Simone. *La balance et l'horloge: La genèse de la pensée libérale en France au XVIII siècle.* Paris: Editions de la Passion, 1989.

Mickwicz, Gunner. *Die Kartellfunktionen der Zünfte und ihre Bedeutung bei der Entstehung des Zunftwesens: Eine Studie in spätantiker und mittelalterlicher Wirtschaftsgeschichte.* Amsterdam: A. M. Hakkert, 1968.

Miller, Judith. "Economic Ideologies, 1750–1800: The Creation of the Modern Political Economy?" *French Historical Studies* 23, no. 3 (2000): 497–511.

Miskimin, Harry A. *The Economy of Early Renaissance Europe, 1300–1460.* Cambridge: Cambridge University Press, 1975.

———. *The Economy of Later Renaissance Europe, 1460–1600.* Cambridge: Cambridge University Press, 1977.

———. "The Enforcement of Gresham's Law." In *Credito, banche e investimenti, secoli XIII–XX,* edited by Anna Vannini Marx, 347 [1] folded leaf of plates. Florence: F. Le Monnier, 1985.

Mitchell, L. E. "The Lady is a Lord: Noble Widows and Land in Thirteenth-Century Britain." *Historical Reflections* 18 (1992): 71–87.

Mitterauer, Michael, and Reinhard Sieder. *The European Family: Patriarchy to Partnership from the Middle Ages to the Present.* Oxford, UK: Blackwell, 1982.

Mollat, Michel. *Jacques Cœur ou l'esprit d'entreprise au XVe siècle.* Collection historique. Paris: Aubier, 1988.

Moranville, Henri. "Remonstrances de l'Université et de le Ville de Paris à Charles VI sur le gouvernement du royaume." *Bibliothèque de l'École des Chartes* 51 (1890): 420–42.

Morgan, Edmund Sears. *The Puritan Family: Essays on Religion and Domestic Relations in Seventeenth-Century New England.* Boston: Trustees of the Public Library, 1944.

Morris, Colin. *The Discovery of the Individual, 1050–1200.* New York: Harper & Row, 1972.

Mousnier, Roland. *La venalité des offices sous Henri IV et Louis XIII.* 2nd ed. Paris: Presses Universitaires de France, 1971.

Moxey, Keith. "The Criticism of Avarice in Sixteenth-Century Netherlandish Painting." In *Netherlandish Mannerism: Papers Given at a Symposium in Nationalmuseum Stockholm, September 21–22 1984,* edited by Görel Cavalli-Björkman, 21–3. Stockholm: Nationalmuseum, 1985.

———. *Peasants, Warriors, and Wives: Popular Imagery in the Reformation.* Chicago: University of Chicago Press, 1989.

Mukerji, Chandra. *From Graven Images: Patterns of Modern Materialism.* New York: Columbia University Press, 1983.

Muldrew, Craig. *The Economy of Obligation: The Culture of Credit and Social Relations in Early Modern England*. New York: St. Martin's Press, 1998.

Münch, Paul, ed. *Ordnung, Fleiss, und Sparsamkeit: Texte und Dokumente zur Entstehung der 'bürgerlichen Tugenden'*. Munich: Deutscher Taschenbuch Verlag, 1984.

Munro, John H. *Wool, Cloth, and Gold: The Struggle for Bullion in Anglo-Burgundian Trade, 1340–1478*. Toronto: University of Toronto Press, 1972.

————. "Money, Wages, and Real Income in the Age of Erasmus: The Purchasing Power of Coins and of Building Craftsmen's Wages in England and the Low Countries, 1500–1540." In *The Correspondence of Erasmus*, edited by R. A. B. Mynors, D. F. S. Thomson, Wallace Klippert Ferguson, James McConica, and Peter G. Bietenholz, 311–48. Toronto: University of Toronto Press, 1974.

————. "The 'New Institutional Economics' and the Changing Fortunes of Fairs in Medieval and Early Modern Europe: The Textile Trades, Warfare, and Transaction Costs." *Vierteljahrsschrift für Sozial – und Wirtschaftsgeschichte* 88, no. 1 (2001): 1–47.

————. "Money, Wages, and Real Incomes in the Age of Erasmus: The Purchasing Power of Coins and of Building Craftmen's Wages in England and the Low Countries from 1500 to 1540." In *Erasmus: Letters 1668 to 1801 (January 1526–March 1527)*, edited by Charles G. Nauert Jr., 551–702. Toronto, 2003.

————. "Money and Coinage: Western Europe." In *Europe 1450 to 1789: Encyclopedia of the Early Modern World*, edited by Jonathan Dewald, 174–84. New York: Charles Scribner's Sons, 2004.

————. "The Economic History of Later-Medieval and Early-Modern Europe: Lecture Topic No. 3." http://www.economics.utoronto.ca/munro5/03MONEY.pdf (accessed May 29, 2009).

————. "Money and Coinage in Late-Medieval and Early Modern Europe." *História e Economia: Revista Interdisciplinar* 4, no. 1 (2008): 13–71.

————. "Warfare, Liquidity Crises, and Coinage Debasements in Burgundian Flanders, 1384–1482: Monetary or Fiscal Remedies?" University of Toronto Department of Economics Working Paper 335. http://repec.economics.utoronto.ca/files/tecipa-355.pdf (accessed June 9, 2009).

————. "The Late-Medieval Origins of the Modern Financial Revolution: Overcoming Impediments from Church and State." *International History Review* 25, no. 2 (June 2003): 505–62.

_____. "The Medieval Origins of the Financial Revolution: Usury, Rentes, and Negotiability." *International History Review* 25, no. 3 (September 2003): 505–62.

Murray, James M. *Bruges, Cradle of Capitalism, 1280–1390.* Cambridge: Cambridge University Press, 2005.

Nelson, Benjamin. "The Usurer and the Merchant Prince: Italian Businessmen and the Ecclesiastical Law of Restitution." *Journal of Economic History* supplement 7 (1947): 104–22.

_____. *The Idea of Usury: From Tribal Brotherhood to Universal Otherhood,* Princeton: Princeton University Press, 1949.

Nevola, Fabrizio. "'Piu honorati et suntuosi ala Republica': Botteghe and Luxury Retail along Siena's Strada Romana." In *Buyers & Sellers: Retail Circuits and Practices in Medieval and Early Modern Europe,* edited by Bruno Blondé, Peter Stabel, Jon Stobart, and Ilja Van Damme, 65–78. Turnhout, Belg.: Brepols, 2006.

Nicholas, David. *The Domestic Life of a Medieval City: Women, Children, and the Family in 14th-Century Ghent.* Lincoln: University of Nebraska Press, 1985.

_____. "In the Pit of the Burgundian Theater State: Urban Traditions and Princely Ambitions in Ghent, 1360–1420." In *City and Spectacle in Medieval Europe,* edited by Barbara Hanawalt and Katherine L. Reyerson, 271–95. Minneapolis: University of Minnesota Press, 1994.

_____. "Commercial Credit and Central Place Function in Thirteenth-Century Ypres." In *Money, Markets and Trade in Late Medieval Europe: Essays in Honour of John H. A. Munro,* edited by Lawrin D. Armstrong, Martin Elbl, Ivana Elbl, and John H. A. Munro, 310–48. Boston: Brill, 2007.

Nightengale, P. "Montary Circulation and Mercantile Credit in Later Medieval England." *Economic History Review* 43 (1990): 560–75.

Noonan, John Thomas. *The Scholastic Analysis of Usury.* Cambridge, MA: Harvard University Press, 1957.

_____. "Marriage in the Middle Ages." *Viator* 4 (1973): 419–34.

Oestreich, Gerhard. *Neostoicism and the Early Modern State.* Cambridge: Cambridge University Press, 1982.

Olivier-Martin, François. *Histoire de la coutume de la prévôté et vicomté de Paris.* Paris: E. Leroux, 1922.

Onuf, Kirkman. "Local Terrains: The Small Landscape Prints and the Depiction of the Countryside in Early Modern Antwerp." Ph.D. diss., Columbia University, 2005.

Osteen, Mark. *The Question of the Gift: Essays across Disciplines.* Routledge Studies in Anthropology 2. London: Routledge, 2002.

Otis-Cour, Leah. *Lust und Liebe: Geschichte der Paarbeziehungen im Mittelalter.* Frankfurt a.M.: Fischer, 2000.

Ourliac, Paul, and Jean-Louis Gazzaniga. *Histoire du droit privé français de l'an mil au Code civil.* Evolution de l'humanité. Paris: A. Michel, 1985.

Ourliac, Paul, and Jehan de Malafosse. *Histoire du droit privé: Le droit familial.* Paris: Presses Universitaires de France, 1968.

Outhwaite, R. B. *Clandestine Marriage in England, 1500–1850.* London: Hambledon, 1995.

Oxford English Dictionary, 2nd ed., OED Online. Oxford: Oxford University Press, 1989.

Ozment, Steven. *When Fathers Ruled: Family Life in Reformation Europe.* Cambridge, MA: Harvard University Press, 1983.

Palazzi, Maura. "Female Solitude and Patrilineage: Unmarried Women and Widows during the Eighteenth and Nineteenth Centuries." *Journal of Family History* 15 (1990): 443–59.

Panofsky, Erwin. "Jan van Eyck's 'Arnolfini Portrait.'" *Burlington Magazine* 64 (1934): 117–27.

————. *Early Netherlandish Painting: Its Origins and Character.* Charles Eliot Norton Lectures 1947/48. Cambridge, MA: Harvard University Press, 1953.

Paravicini, Werner, ed. *Les invitations au mariage: Pratique sociale, abus de pouvoir, intérêt de l'Etat à la cour des ducs de Bourgogne 1399–1489.* Instrumenta 6. Stuttgart: Thorbecke, 2001.

————. "Introduction." In *Les invitations au mariage: Pratique sociale, abus de pouvoir, intérêt de l'Etat à la cour des ducs de Bourgogne 1399–1489,* edited by Werner Paravicini. Stuttgart: Thorbecke, 2001.

Parker, William Nelson, and E. L. Jones. *European Peasants and Their Markets: Essays in Agrarian Economic History.* Princeton: Princeton University Press, 1975.

Parry, Jonathan P. "On the Moral Perils of Exchange." In *Money and the Morality of Exchange,* edited by Jonathan P. Parry and Maurice Bloch, 64–93. Cambridge: Cambridge University Press, 1989.

Parry, Jonathan P., and Maurice Bloch. *Money and the Morality of Exchange.* Cambridge: Cambridge University Press, 1989.

————. "Introduction: Money and Morality of Exchange " In *Money and the Morality of Exchange,* edited by Jonathan P. Parry and Maurice Bloch, 1–32. Cambridge: Cambridge University Press, 1989.

Parsons, Jotham. "Money and Merit in French Renaissance Comedy." *Renaissance Quarterly* 60, no. 3 (2007): 852–82.

Patault, Anne-Marie. *Introduction historique au droit des biens*. Paris: Presses Universitaires de France, 1989.

Peirce, Charles Sanders. "The Fixation of Belief." In *Peirce on Signs*, edited by James Hooper, 144–59. Chapel Hill: University of North Carolina Press, 1991.

———. "How to Make Our Ideas Clearer." In *Peirce on Signs*, edited by James Hooper, 160–79. Chapel Hill: University of North Carolina Press, 1991.

Perol, Céline. "Le mariage et les lois somptuaires en Toscane au XIVe siècle." In *Le mariage au Moyen Âge (XIe–XVe siècle)*, edited by Josiane Teyssot, 133–54. Clermont-Ferrand, Fr.: Université Clermont-Ferrand, Fr. II, 1997.

Philippot, Paul. *La peinture dans les anciens Pays-Bas: XVe–XVIe siècles*. Idées et recherches. Paris: Flammarion, 1994.

Piponnier, Françoise. *Costume et vie sociale: La cour d'Anjou XIVe–XVe siècle*. Civilisations et sociétés 21. Paris: Mouton & Co, 1970.

———. "Une révolution dans le costume masculine au XIVe siècle." In *Le vêtement: Histoire, archéologie et symbolique vestimentaire au Moyen Âge*, edited by Michel Pastoureau, 225–42. Paris: Le Léopard d'Or, 1989.

Piponnier, Françoise, and Perrine Mane. *Se vêtir au Moyen Âge*. Paris: A. Biro, 1995.

Pirenne, Henri. *Medieval Cities: Their Origins and the Revival of Trade*. Translated by Frank D. Halsey. Princeton: Princeton University Press, 1939.

———. *Mohammed and Charlemagne*. New York: Norton, 1939.

———. *Histoire économique de l'Occident médiéval*. Bruges: Desclée de Brouwer, 1951.

Pitt-Rivers, Julian. "Honor and Social Status." In *Honour and Shame: The Values of Mediterranean Society*, edited by J. G. Peristiany. Chicago: University of Chicago Press, 1966.

———. "Honor." In *International Encyclopedia of the Social Sciences*, edited by David Sills, 6: 503–11. New York: Macmillan Co., 1968.

———. "The Anthropology of Honour." In *The Fate of Shechem, or, the Politics of Sex: Essays in the Anthropology of the Mediterranean*, edited by Julian Pitt-Rivers, 1–17. Cambridge: Cambridge University Press, 1977.

Pitti, Buonaccorso, and Gregorio Dati. *Two Memoirs of Renaissance Florence: The Diaries of Buonaccorso Pitti and Gregorio Dati*. Edited by Gene Brucker. Prospect Heights, Illinois: Waveland Press, 1991.

Pleij, Herman. *Het Gilde van de blauwe schuit: Literatuur, volksfeest en burger-moraal in de late middeleeuwen, met een nabeschouwing van de auteur.* 2nd ed. Amsterdam: Meulenhoff, 1983.

———. "Restyling 'Wisdom,' Remodeling the Nobility, and Caricaturing the Peasant: Urban Literature in the Late Medieval Low Countries." *Journal of Interdisciplinary History* 32, no. 4 (2002): 689–704.

Pocock, J. G. A. *The Machiavellian Moment: Florentine Political Thought and the Atlantic Republican Tradition.* Princeton: Princeton University Press, 1975.

———. *Virtue, Commerce, and History: Essays on Political Thought and History, Chiefly in the Eighteenth Century.* Ideas in Context. Cambridge: Cambridge University Press, 1985.

Polanyi, Karl. *The Great Transformation.* Boston: Beacon Press, 1957.

Poos, L. R., and Lloyd Bonfield. "Law and Individualism in Medieval England." *Social History* 11, no. 3 (October 1986): 287–301.

Porter, Roy, ed. *Rewriting the Self: Histories from the Renaissance to the Present,* London: Routledge, 1997.

Post, Paul. "La naissance du costume masculine moderne au XIVe siècle." In *Acts du 1er Congrès international d'histoire du costume,* 28–41. Milan: Centro Internazionale delle Arti e del Costume, 1955.

Postan, M. M., E. E. Miller, and C. Postan, eds. *Cambridge Economic History of Europe.* Vol. 2, *Trade and Industry in the Middle Ages.* Cambridge: Cambridge University Press, 1987.

Postan, M. M., E. E. Rich, and E. E. Miller, eds. *Cambridge Economic History of Europe.* Vol. 3, *Economic Organization and Policies in the Middle Ages.* Cambridge: Cambridge University Press, 1965.

Postan, M. M., E. E. Rich, C. H. Wilson, D. C. Coleman, and P. Mathias. *The Economic Organization of Early Modern Europe.* 1st ed. Vol. 5, *The Cambridge Economic History of Europe.* Cambridge: Cambridge University Press, 1977.

Prak, Maarten. "Introduction." In *Early Modern Capitalism: Economic and Social Change in Europe 1400–1800,* edited by Maarten Roy Prak, 7–8. London: Routledge, 2000.

Prevenier, Walter. "Officials in Town and Countryside in the Low Countries: Social and Professional Developments from the Fourteenth to the Sixteenth Century." *Acta Historiae Neerlandicae* 7 (1977): 1–17.

———. "Violence against Women in a Medieval Metropolis: Paris around 1400." In *Law, Custom, and the Social Fabric in Medieval Europe: Essays in Honor of Bryce Lyon,* edited by B. S. Bachrach and D. Nicholas, 262–84. Kalamazoo: Western Michigan University, 1990.

_____. "La stratégie et le discours politique des ducs de Bourgogne concernant les rapts et les enlèvements de femmes parmi les élites des Pays-Bas au XVe siècle." In *Das Frauenzimmer: Die Frau bei Hofe in Spätmittelalter und früher Neuzeit. 6. Symposium der Residenzen-Kommission der Akademie der Wissenschaften in Göttingen, Dresden 26. bis 29. September 1998*, edited by J. Hirschbiegel and Werner Paravicini, 429–37. Stuttgart: Thorbecke, 2000.

_____. "Les multiples vérités dans les discours sur les offenses criminelles envers les femmes dans les Pays-Bas méridionaux (XIVe et XVe siècles)." In *Retour aux sources: Textes, études et documents d'histoire médiévale offerts à Michel Parisse*, edited by Sylvain Gouguenheim and Michel Parisse, 955–64. Paris: Picard, 2004.

Prevenier, Walter, and Willem Pieter Blockmans. *The Burgundian Netherlands*. Cambridge: Cambridge University Press, 1986.

Prevenier, Walter, and Thérèse de Hemptinne. "Ehe im Recht und Ehe in der Gesellschaft des Mittelalters." In *Lexikon des Mittelalters III*, 1635–40. Munich: Artemis, 1986.

Prevenier, Walter, Thérèse de Hemptinne, and Marc Boone. "Gender and Early Emancipation in the Low Countries in the Late Middle Ages and Early Modern Period." In *Gender, Power and Privilege in Early Modern Europe*, edited by Jessica Munns and Penny Richards, 21–39; 176–80. London: Harlow, 2003.

Pullan, Brian S. "Catholics, Protestants, and the Poor in Early Modern Europe. *Journal of Interdisciplinary History* 35, no. 3 (2005): 441–56.

Puff, Helmut. "Die Ehre der Ehe: Beobachtungen zum Konzept der Ehre in der Frühen Neuzeit an Johann Fischarts 'Philosophisch Ehzuchtbüchlein' (1578) und anderen Ehelehren des 16. Jahrhunderts." In *Ehrkonzepte in der Frühen Neuzeit: Identitäten und Abgrenzungen*, edited by Sibylle Backmann, Hans-Jörg Künast, Sabine Ullmann, and B. Ann Tlusty, 99–119. Berlin: Akademie Verlag, 1998.

Puyvelde, Leo van. "Un portrait de marchand par Quentin Metsys et les percepteurs d'impôts par Marin van Reymerswael." *Revue belge d'Archéologie et d'Histoire de l'Art* 26 (1957): 3–23.

Raef, Marc. *The Well-Ordered Police State: Social and Institutional Change through Law in the Germanies and Russian, 1600–1800*. New Haven: Yale University Press, 1983.

Rainey, Ronald. "Sumptuary Legislation in Renaissance Florence." Ph.D. diss., Columbia University, 1985.

_____. "Dressing down the Dressed-Up: Reproving Feminine Attire in Renaissance Florence." In *Renaissance Culture and Society*, edited by John

Monfasani and Ronald G. Musto, 217–37. New York: Italica Press, 1991.

Redondo, Manuel Santos. "The Moneychanger and His Wife: From Scholastics to Accounting." Revised version of a paper presented in the 8th World Congress of Accounting Historians, Madrid, July 2000. http://www.ucm.es/BUCM/cee/doc/00–23/0023.htm (accessed September 8, 2008).

Reid, Charles J. *Power over the Body, Equality in the Family: Rights and Domestic Relations in Medieval Canon Law*. Emory University Studies in Law and Religion. Grand Rapids, MI: Eerdmans, 2004.

Resnick, Irven M. "Marriage in Medieval Culture: Consent Theory and the Case of Joseph and Mary." *Church History* 69, no. 2 (June 2000): 350–71.

Reynolds, Philip Lyndon, and John Witte. *To Have and to Hold: Marrying and Its Documentation in Western Christendom, 400–1600*. Cambridge: Cambridge University Press, 2007.

Richet, Denis. "Les liens de clientèle: L'exemple de la 'robe' en France aux XVI et XVII siècles." In *Klientelsysteme im Europa der Frühen Neuzeit*, edited by Antoni Maczak and Elisabeth Müller-Luckner, 147–52. Munich: R. Oldenbourg, 1988.

Rigaudière, Albert. *L'assiette de l'impôt direct à la fin du XIVe siècle*. Paris: Presses Universitaires de France, 1977.

———. "Connaissance, composition et estimation du 'moble' à travers quelque livres d'estimes du Midi français (XIVe–XVe siècles)." In *Gouverner la ville au Moyen Âge*. Paris: Anthropos, 1993.

Roper, Lyndal. "Blood and Codpieces: Masculinity in the Early Modern German Town." In *Oedipus and the Devil: Witchcraft, Sexuality, and Religion in Early Modern Europe*, 107–25. London: Routledge, 1994.

———. "Exorcism and the Theology of the Body." In *Oedipus and the Devil: Witchcraft, Sexuality, and Religion in Early Modern Europe*, 171–99. London: Routledge, 1994.

Rosenwein, Barbara H. *Rhinoceros Bound: Cluny in the Tenth Century*. The Middle Ages. Philadelphia: University of Pennsylvania Press, 1982.

———. *To Be the Neighbor of Saint Peter: The Social Meaning of Cluny's Property, 909–1049*. Ithaca: Cornell University Press, 1989.

Rosser, Gervase. "Crafts, Guilds and the Negotiation of Work in the Medieval Town." *Past & Present* 154 (February 1997): 3–31.

Rothenberg, Winifred Barr. *From Market-Places to a Market Economy: The Transformation of Rural Massachusetts, 1750–1850*. Chicago: University of Chicago Press, 1992.

Rothstein, Bret. "The Problem with Looking at Pieter Bruegel's Elck." *Art History* 26, no. 2 (April 2003): 143–73.

Ryan, Mary P. *Cradle of the Middle Class: The Family in Oneida County, New York, 1790–1865.* Interdisciplinary Perspectives on Modern History. Cambridge: Cambridge University Press, 1981.

Ryckbosch, Wouter. *Tussen Gavere en Cadzand: De Gentse stadsfinanciën op het einde van de middeleeuwen (1460–1495).* Ghent: Verhandelingen der Maatschappij voor Geschiedenis en Oudheidkunde te Gent, 2007.

Safley, Thomas Max. "Bankruptcy: Family and Misfortune in Early Modern Augsburg." *Journal of European Economic History* 1 (2000): 53–73.

————. *Bankruptcy: Economics and Ethics in a Capitalistic Age.* Forthcoming.

Sahlins, Marshall David. *Stone Age Economics.* New York: Aldine, 1972.

Scattergood, John. "Fashion and Morality in the Late Middle Ages." In *England in the Fifteenth Century: Proceedings of the 1986 Harlaxton Symposium,* edited by Daniel Williams, 255–72. Woodbridge, UK: Boydell Press, 1987.

Schama, Simon. *The Embarrassment of Riches: An Interpretation of Dutch Culture in the Golden Age.* New York: Knopf, 1987.

Schiffman, Zachary Sayre. "Dimensions of Individuality: Recent French Works on the Renaissance." *Renaissance Quarterly* 49 (1996): 114–23.

Schmidt, Ariadne. *Overleven na de dood: Weduwen in Leiden in de Gouden Eeuw.* Amsterdam: Bert Bakker, 2001.

————. "Touching Inheritance: Mannen, vrouwen en de overdracht van bezit in de zeventiende eeuw." *Historisch Tijdschrift Holland* 33, no. 4 (2002): 175–89.

Schmidt, Jean-Clau. *Le corps des images: Essais sur la culture visuelle au Moyen Âge.* Paris: Gallimard, 2002.

Schnapper, Bernard. *Les rentes au XVIe siècle.* Paris: SEVPEN, 1957.

Schnell, Rüdiger. "The Discourse on Marriage in the Middle Ages." *Speculum* 73, no. 73 (1998): 771–86.

Schofield, Phillipp R. "Manorial Courts and the Land Market in Eastern England." In *Le marché de la terre au Moyen Âge,* edited by Laurent Feller and Chris Wickham, 237–71. Rome: École française de Rome, 2005.

Schulz, Knut. "Die Norm der Ehrelichkeit im Zunft-und Bürgerrecht im spätmittelalterliche Städte." In *Illegitimität im Spätmittelalter,* edited by Ludwig Schmugge and Béatrice Wiggenhauser, 67–84. Munich: Oldenbourg, 1994.

Schulz, Ulrike-Marianne. *Liebe, Ehe und Sexualität im vorreformatorischen Meistersang.* Göppingen: Kümmerle, 1995.

Schwoerer, Lois. "Seventeenth-Century English Women Engraved in Stone?" Review of *The Family, Sex and Marriage in England, 1500–1800* by Lawrence Stone. *Albion* 16, no. 4 (1984): 389–403.

Scott, Joan "'L'ouvrière! Mot impie, sordide . . .' Women Workers in the Discourse of French Political Economy, 1840–1860." *Gender and the Politics of History*, 139–67. New York: Columbia University Press, 1999.

Scott, Margaret. *Medieval Dress and Fashion*. London: British Library, 2007.

Sebek, Barbara. "Good Turns and the Art of Merchandising: Conceptualizing Exchange in Early Modern England." http://emc.eserver.org/1–2/Sebek.html (accessed September 23, 2008).

Seidel, Linda. "Jan van Eyck's 'Arnolfini Portrait': Business as Usual?" *Critical Inquiry* 16 (1989): 54–86.

Sekora, John. *Luxury: The Concept in Western Thought, Eden to Smollett*. Baltimore: Johns Hopkins University Press, 1977.

Sharpe, J. A. *Defamation and Sexual Slander in Early Modern England: The Church Courts at York*. Borthwick papers no. 58. York, UK: University of York, 1980.

Sheehan, Michael M., and James K. Farge. *Marriage, Family and Law in Medieval Europe: Collected Studies*. Toronto: University of Toronto Press, 1996.

Shepard, Alexandra. "Manhood, Credit, and Patriarchy in Early Modern England, c. 1580–1640." *Past & Present* 167 (2000): 75–106.

Sherman, Sandra. "Promises, Promises: Credit as Contested Metaphor in Early Capitalist Discourse." *Modern Philology* 94, no. 3 (February 1997): 327–49.

Shorter, Edward. *The Making of the Modern Family*. New York: Basic Books, 1975.

Shovlin, John. *The Political Economy of Virtue: Luxury, Patriotism, and the Origins of the French Revolution*. Ithaca, NY: Cornell University Press, 2006.

Signoria, Gabriela. "Family Traditions: Moral Economy and Memorial 'Gift Exchange' in the Urban World of the Late Fifteenth Century." In *Negotiating the Gift: Pre-Modern Figurations of Exchange*, edited by Gadi Algazi, Valentin Groebner, and Bernhard Jussen, 285–318. Göttingen: Vandenhoeck & Ruprecht, 2003.

Silver, Larry. "Love and Marriage in the Art of Lucas van Leyden." In *In Detail: New Studies of Northern Renaissance Art in Honor of Walter S. Gibson*, edited by Laurinda S. Dixon, 97–111. Turnhout, Belg.: Brepols, 1998.

Smith, Bonnie G. *Ladies of the Leisure Class: The Bourgeoises of Northern France in the Nineteenth Century*. Princeton: Princeton University Press, 1981.

Smith, D. Vance. *Arts of Possession: The Middle English Household Imaginary.* Vol. 33, *Medieval cultures.* Minneapolis: University of Minnesota Press, 2003.

Smith, Elise Lawton. *The Paintings of Lucas van Leyden: A New Appraisal, with Catalogue Raisonné.* Columbia: University of Missouri Press, 1992.

Smith, Richard Michael. "Some Reflections on the Evidence for the Origins of the 'European Marriage Pattern' in England." In *The Sociology of the Family: New Directions for Britain,* edited by Chris Harris and Michael Anderson, 74–112. Keele, UK: University of Keele, 1979.

Sokol, B. J., and Mary Sokol. *Shakespeare, Law, and Marriage.* Cambridge: Cambridge University Press, 2003.

Sosson, Jean-Pierre. *Les Travaux publics de la ville de Bruges, XIVe–XVe siècles: Les Materiaux, les hommes.* Collection Histoire Pro Civitaté. Brussels: Crédit Communal de Belgique, 1977.

———. "Les métiers: Norme et réalité: L'exemple des anciens Pays-Bas méridionaux aux XIVe et XVe siècles." In *Le travail au Moyen Âge: Une approche interdisciplinaire; Actes du Colloque international de Louvain-la-Neuve, 21–23 mai 1987,* edited by J. Hamesse and C. Muraille. Louvain-la-Neuve, Fr.: Université Catholique de Louvain, 1990.

Sperling, Jutta. "Marriage at the Time of the Council of Trent (1560–70): Clandestine Marriages, Kinship Prohibitions, and Dowry Exchange in European Comparison." *Journal of Early Modern History* 8, no. 1–2 (May 2004): 67–108.

Sponsler, Claire. "Narrating the Social Order: Medieval Clothing Laws." *CLIO* 21 (1992): 265–83.

———. *Drama and Resistance: Bodies, Goods, and Theatricality in Late Medieval England.* Medieval cultures 10. Minneapolis: University of Minnesota Press, 1997.

Spufford, Peter. "Appendix II: Money of Account." In *Money and Its Uses in Medieval Europe,* 411–14. Cambridge: Cambridge University Press, 1988.

———. *Money and Its Uses in Medieval Europe.* Cambridge: Cambridge University Press, 1988.

———. *Power and Profit: The Merchant in Medieval Europe.* New York: Thames & Hudson, 2003.

Sreenivasan, Govind P. *The Peasants of Ottobeuren, 1487–1726: A Rural Society in Early Modern Europe.* Cambridge: Cambridge University Press, 2004.

Stabel, Peter. "Markets in the Cities of the Late Medieval Low Countries: Retail, Commercial Exchange and Sociocultural Display." In *Fiere e mercati nella integrazione delle economie europee, secc. XIII-XVIII: atti della "trentaduesima settimana di studi," 8–12 maggio 2000*, edited by Simonetta Cavaciocchi, 797–817. Florence: Le Monnier, 2001.

————. "Guilds in Late Medieval Flanders: Myths and Realities of Guild Life in an Export-Oriented Environment." *Journal of Medieval History* 30 (2004): 187–212.

————. "From the Market to the Shop: Retail and Urban Space in Late Medieval Bruges." In *Buyers & Sellers: Retail Circuits and Practices in Medieval and Early Modern Europe*, edited by Bruno Blondé, Peter Stabel, Jon Stobart, and Ilja Van Damme, 79–109. Turnhout, Belg.: Brepols, 2006.

Stiglitz, Joseph, and Andrew Weiss. "Credit Rationing in Markets with Imperfect Information." *American Economic Review* 71 (1981): 393–410.

Stock, Brian. *Implications of Literacy: Written Language and Models of Interpretation in the 11th and 12th Centuries*. Princeton: Princeton University Press, 1987.

Stone, Lawrence. *The Family, Sex and Marriage in England, 1500–1800*. New York: Harper & Row, 1977.

Strathern, Marilyn. *The Gender of the Gift: Problems with Women and Problems with Society in Melanesia*. Berkeley: University of California Press, 1988.

Street, Brian V. *Literacy in Theory and Practice*. Cambridge Studies in Oral and Literate Culture 9. Cambridge: Cambridge University Press, 1984.

Styles, John. "Product Innovation in Early Modern London." *Past & Present* 168 (2000): 124–69.

Swanson, Heather. *Medieval Artisans: An Urban Class in Late Medieval England*. Oxford, UK: Blackwell, 1989.

————. "The Illusion of Economic Structure: Craft Guilds in Late Medieval English Towns." *Past & Present* 121 (November 1988): 29–48.

Sweezy, Paul M. *The Transition from Feudalism to Capitalism*. Verso ed. London: Verso, 1978.

Taylor, Charles. *Sources of the Self: The Making of the Modern Identity*. Cambridge, MA: Harvard University Press, 1989.

Terry, Reta A. "'Vows to the Blackest Devil': Hamlet and the Evolving Code of Honor in Early Modern England." *Renaissance Quarterly* 52, no. 4 (Winter 1999): 1070–86.

Testart, Alain. "Les trois modes de transfert." *Gradhiva* 21 (1997): 39–58.

————. "Échange marchand, échange non marchand." *Revue Française de Sociologie* 42, no. 4 (2001): 719–48.

Thirsk, Joan. *Economic Policy and Projects: The Development of a Consumer Society in Early Modern England*. Oxford, UK: Clarendon Press, 1978.

Thomas, Keith. "Numeracy in Early Modern England." *Transactions of the Royal Historical Society* 37 (1987): 103–32.

Thompson, Edward P. "Folklore, Anthropology and Social History." *Indian Historical Review* 3 (1977): 252–72.

Thrupp, Sylvia. *The Merchant Class of Medieval London, 1300–1500*. Chicago: University of Chicago Press, 1948.

Tits-Dieuaide, Marie-Jeanne. *La formation des prix céréaliers en Brabant et en Flandre au XVe siècle*. Brussels: Éditions de l'Université de Bruxelles, 1975.

Todeschini, Giacomo. *Richesse franciscaine: De la pauvreté volontaire à la société de marché*. Paris: Verdier, 2008.

Tracy, James D. *A Financial Revolution in the Habsburg Netherlands: Renten and Renteniers in the County of Holland, 1515–1565*. Berkeley: University of California Press, 1985.

————. "On the Dual Origin of Long-Term Urban Debt in Medieval Europe." In *Urban Public Debts: Urban Governments and the Market for Annuities in Western Europe (14th–18th Centuries)*, edited by Marc Boone, C. A. Davids, and Paul Janssens, 13–24. Turnhout, Belg.: Brepols, 2003.

Traer, James F. *Marriage and the Family in French Law and Social Thought*. Ithaca: Cornell University Press, 1980.

Trexler, Richard. *Public Life in Renaissance Florence*. Ithaca, NY: Cornell University Press, 1980.

Tulchin, Allan. "Same-Sex Couples Creating Households in Old Regime France: The Uses of the Affrèrement." *Journal of Modern History* 79 (September 2007): 613–47.

Turlan, Juliette M. "Recherches sur le mariage dans la pratique coutumière (XIIe–XIVe s.)." *Revue d'histoire de droit français et étranger* 35 (1957): 477–528.

Ullmann, Walter. *The Individual and Society in the Middle Ages*. Baltimore: Johns Hopkins University Press, 1966.

Unger, W. "Thresholds for Market Integration in the Low Countries and England in the Fifteenth Century." In *Money, Markets and Trade in Late Medieval Europe: Essays in Honour of John H.A. Munro*, edited by Lawrin D. Armstrong, Martin Elbl, Ivana Elbl, and John H. A. Munro, 349–80. Boston: Brill, 2007.

Vanderlinden, J., ed. *Actes à cause de mort/Acts of Last Will*. 4 vols, Recueils de la société de Jean Bodin pour l'histoire comparative des institutions lix-lxii. Brussels: DeBoeck-Wesmael, 1992–1994.

Van Anrooij, Wim. *Al t`Antwerpen in die stad: Jan van Boendale en de literaire cultuur van zijn tijd*. Amsterdam: Prometheus, 2002.

van Bavel, B. J. P. "The Organization and Rise of Land and Lease Markets in Northwestern Europe and Italy, c. 1000–1800." *Continuity and Change* 23, no. 1 (2008): 13–54.

————. "Agrarian Change and Economic Development in the Late Medieval Netherlands." In *Agrarian Change and Economic Development in Europe before the Industrial Revolution*, edited by R. Brenner, J. de Vries, and E. Thoen, forthcoming.

van Bavel, B. J. P., and Tine de Moor, eds. *Continuity and Change*. Vol. 23:1, Special Issue on the Institutional Organization of Land Markets, 2008.

Van Bruaene, Anne-Laure. "Sociabiliteit en competitie: De sociaal-institutionele ontwikkeling van de rederijkerskamers in de Zuidelijke Nederlanden (1400–1650)." In *Conformisten en rebellen: Rederijkerscultuur in de Nederlanden (1400–1650)*, edited by B. A. M. Ramakers, 45–63. Amsterdam: Amsterdam University Press, 2003.

————. "De contouren van een nieuw cultuurmodel: Rederijkers in Vlaanderen en Brabant in de zeventiende eeuw." *Handelingen der Koninklijke Zuid-Nederlandse Maatschappij voor Taal-en Letterkunde en Geschiedenis* 58 (2005): 221–37.

————. "'A Wonderfull tryumfe, for the wynnyng of a pryse,' Gilds, Ritual, Theater and the Urban Network in the Southern Low Countries, ca. 1450–1650." *Renaissance Quarterly* 59, no. 2 (Summer 2006): 374–406.

Van der Velden, Hugo. *The Donor's Image: Gerard Loyet and the Votive Portraits of Charles the Bold*. Turnhout, Belg.: Brepols, 2000.

Van der Wee, Herman. *The Growth of the Antwerp Market and the European Economy (Fourteenth – Sixteenth Centuries)*. 3 vols. The Hague: Martinus Nijhoff, 1963.

————. "Monetary Credit and Banking Systems." In *The Economic Organization of Early Modern Europe*, edited by E. E. Rich and Charles Wilson. Cambridge: Cambridge University Press, 1977.

Van Doosselaere, Quentin. *Commercial Agreements and Social Dynamics in Medieval Genoa*. Cambridge: Cambridge University Press, 2009.

van Gent, M. J. "De Hoekse factie in Leiden circa 1445–1490: Het verhaal van verliezers." In *Bloedwraak, partijstrijd en pacificatie in laat-middeleeuws Holland*, edited by J. W. Marsilje, 122–40. Hilversum, Neth.: Verloren, 1990.

Van Nieuwenhuysen, A. *Les finances du duc de Bourgogne Philippe le Hardi, 1384–1404*. Brussels: Editions de l'Universite de Bruxelles, 1984.

Van Uytven, Raymond. "De datering van het Brugse Livre des Mestiers." *Archief – en bibliotheekwezen in België* 48 (1977): 649–53.

————. *De zinnelijke Middeleeuwen.* Leuven: Davidsfonds, 1998.

————. "Showing off One's Rank in the Middle Ages." In *Showing Status: Representation of Social Positions in the Late Middle Ages,* edited by Willem Pieter Blockmans and Antheun Janse, 19–35. Turnhout, Belg.: Brepols, 1999.

————. "Splendour or Wealth? Art and Economy in the Burgundian Netherlands." In *Production and Consumption in the Low Countries, 13th–16th Centuries,* edited by Raymond Van Uytven, XIII, 346 S. [getr. Zählung]. Aldershot, UK: Ashgate, 2001.

————. "Cloth in Medieval Literature of Western Europe." In *Production and Consumption in the Low Countries, 13th–16th Centuries,* edited by Raymond Van Uytven, 151–83. Aldershot, UK: Ashgate Variorum, 2001.

Van Werveke, Hans. "Le mort-gage et son role économique en Flandre et en Lotharingie (aux XIIe et XIIIes.)." *Revue belge philogie et histoire* 8 (1929): 53–91.

————. "Les villes belges: Histoire des institutions économiques et sociales." In *La ville* vol. 2: *Institutions économiques et sociales,* 551–76. Paris: Societé Jean Bodin, 1955.

Vaughan, Richard. *Philip the Bold: The Formation of the Burgundian State.* London: Longman, 1962.

Veldman, Ilja M. "Lessons for Ladies: A Selection of Sixteteenth and Seventeenth-Century Dutch Prints." *Simiolus: Netherlands Quarterly for the History of Art* 16, no. 2 (1986): 113–27.

Vercauteren, F. "Note sur l'origine et l'évolution du contrat de mort-gage en Lotharingie du XIe au XIIe siècle." In *Miscellanea L. Van der Essen,* 217–27. Brussels: Pro Civitate, 1948.

Verhulst, Adriaan. "La genèse du regime domanial classique en France au haut moyen âge." *Agricoltura e mondo rurale in Occidente mell' alto medioevo Settimano* 13 (1966): 135–60.

————. "Der Handel im Mereowingerreich: Gesamtdarstelling nach schriftlichen Quellen." *Early Medieval Studies* 2 (Antikvariskt Arkiv 39), (1970): 2–54.

Vermeylen, Filip. *Painting for the Market: Commercialization of Art in Antwerp's Golden Age.* Vol. 2, Studies in European Urban History (1100–1800). Turnhout, Belg.: Brepols, 2003.

Verwijs, Eelco, and Jacob Verdam. *Middelnederlandsch woordenboek*. The Hague: M. Nijhoff, 1885.

Vickery, Amanda. "Golden Age to Separate Spheres? A Review of the Categories and Chronology of English Women's History." *Historical Journal* 36, no. 2 (1993): 383–414.

Vincent, John Martin. *Costume and Conduct in the Laws of Basel, Bern, and Zurich, 1370–1800*. Baltimore: Johns Hopkins University Press, 1935.

Wagner-Hasel, Beate. "Egoistic Exchange and Altruistic Gift: On the Roots of Marcel Mauss's Theory of the Gift." In *Negotiating the Gift: Pre-Modern Figurations of Exchange*, edited by Gadi Algazi, Valentin Groebner, and Bernhard Jussen, 141–71. Göttingen: Vandenhoeck & Ruprecht, 2003.

Walker, Garthine. "Expanding the Boundaries of Female Honour in Early Modern England." *Transactions of the Royal Historical Society* 6th series, no. 6 (1996): 235–45.

Wallerstein, Immanuel M. *The Modern World-System*. 2 vols. Studies in Social Discontinuity. New York: Academic Press, 1974.

Watt, Jeffrey R. *The Making of Modern Marriage: Matrimonial Control and the Rise of Sentiment in Neuchâtel, 1550–1800*. Ithaca, NY: Cornell University Press, 1992.

Weiner, Annette B. *Inalienable Possessions: The Paradox of Keeping-While-Giving*. Berkeley: University of California Press, 1992.

Welch, Evelyn. "New, Old, and Second-Hand Culture: The Case of the Renaissance Sleeve." In *Revaluing Renaissance Art*, edited by Gabriele Neher and Rupert Shepherd, 101–19. Aldershot, UK: Ashgate, 2000.

———. *Shopping in the Renaissance: Consumer Cultures in Italy 1400–1600*. New Haven: Yale University Press, 2005.

———. "The Fairs of Early Modern Italy." In *Buyers & Sellers: Retail Circuits and Practices in Medieval and Early Modern Europe*, edited by Bruno Blondé, Peter Stabel, Jon Stobart, and Ilja Van Damme. Turnhout, Belg.: Brepols, 2006.

Wensinger, Arthur S., and William B. Coley. *Hogarth on High Life: The 'Marriage a la mode' Series from G. C. Lichtenberg's Commentaries*. Middletown, CT: Wesleyan University Press, 1970.

Wensky, Margret. *Die Stellung der Frau in der stadtkölnischen Wirtschaft im Spätmittelalter*. Cologne: Böhlau, 1980.

White, Stephen D. *Custom, Kinship, and Gifts to Saints: The Laudatio Parentum in Western France, 1050–1150*. Studies in Legal History. Chapel Hill: University of North Carolina Press, 1988.

Whitney, Marian Parker. "Queen of Mediaeval Virtues: Largessse." In *Vassar Mediaeval Studies*, edited by Christabel Forsyth Fiske, 183–215. New Haven: Yale University Press, 1923.

Wiesner, Merry E. *Working Women in Renaissance Germany*. New Brunswick, NJ: Rutgers University Press, 1986.

————. "Wandervogels and Women: Journeymen's Concepts of Masculinity in Early Modern Germany." *Journal of Social History* 24, no. 4 (Summer 1991): 767–82.

Williams, Maggie McEnchroe. "Dressing the Part: Depictions of Noble Costume in Irish High Crosses." In *Encountering Medieval Textiles and Dress: Objects, Texts, Images*, edited by Désirée G. Koslin and Janet Snyder, 45–63. New York: Palgrave Macmillan, 2002.

Williams, Raymond. *Keywords: A Vocabulary of Culture and Society*. New York: Oxford University Press, 1976.

Wilson, Jean C. *Painting in Bruges at the Close of the Middle Ages: Studies in Society and Visual Culture*. University Park: Pennsylvania State University Press, 1998.

Wilson, Laural. "La nouvelle manière: The Birth of Fashion in the Fourteenth Century." Ph.D. thesis, Fordham University, in process.

Witte, John. *From Sacrament to Contract: Marriage, Religion, and Law in the Western Tradition*. Louisville, KY: Westminster John Knox Press, 1997.

————. *Law and Protestantism: The Legal Teachings of the Lutheran Reformation*. Cambridge: Cambridge University Press, 2002.

————. "The Reformation of Marriage Law in Martin Luther's Germany: Its Significance Then and Now." *Journal of Law and Religion* 4, no. 2 (1986): 293–351.

Wolff, Philippe. *Commerce et marchands de Toulouse (vers 1350–1450)*. Paris: Plon, 1954.

Wood, Diana. *Medieval Economic Thought*. Cambridge: Cambridge University Press, 2002.

Wunder, Heide. *He is the Sun, She is the Moon: Women in Early Modern Germany*. Translated by Thomas Dunlop. Cambridge, MA: Harvard University Press, 1998.

Zaretsky, Eli. *Capitalism, the Family and Personal Life*. London: Pluto Press, 1976.

Zink, Anne. *L'héritier de la maison: Géographie coutumière du Sud-Ouest de la France sous l'Ancien Régime*. Civilisations et sociétés 87. Paris: Éditions de l'École des Hautes Études en Sciences Sociales, 1993.

Zuijderduijn, Jaco. "Assessing a Late Medieval Capital Market: The Capacity of the Market for Renten in Edam and De Zeevang (1462–1563)." *Jaarboek voor middeleeuwse Geschiedenis* 11 (2008): 138–65.

Zunkel, Friedrich. "Ehre." In *Geschichtliche Grundbegriffe: Historisches Lexikon zur politisch-sozialen Sprache in Deutschland*, edited by Werner Conze, Otto Brunner, and Reinhard Koselleck, 1–63. Stuttgart: E. Klett, 1972–1997.

Index